Substance Abuse and Counseling

Amos Sales, Editor

PO Box 26171
Greensboro, NC 27402-6171

ISBN 1-56109-088-3

This publication was funded in part by the US Department of Education, Office of Educational Research and Improvement, Contract no. ED-99-CO-0014. Opinions expressed in this publication do not necessarily reflect the positions of the US Department of Education, OERI, or ERIC/CASS.

Foreword

Counselors and other helping specialists are frequently called upon to offer assistance to clients in areas where they have neither had specialized training or have access to an updated basic resource. Such is true of the situation in substance abuse. Many, if not the majority, of counselors and other helping specialists have not had formalized training in assisting clients with substance abuse problems; and there has not been an adequate resource available to which they could turn.

This new monograph by Dr. Amos Sales admirably fills the void. It can be equally useful whether the user is experienced in responding to substance abuse problems or entirely new to the area. In short, it has much to offer to almost anyone. In addition, it has unique features which distinguish it from other resources dealing with substance abuse.

Among its unique features are: (1) its orientation as a *practical* resource for specialists responding to substance abuse; (2) a counseling perspective with emphasis on the counseling relationship as a key factor in treatment; (3) an emphasis on both knowledge acquisition and skill building on the part of the reader; (4) a sequential delivery of the contents so the user may either start at the beginning and go through the entire volume or selectively choose where there is a need; (5) chapters written by individuals and teams who are acknowledged experts in the areas they are writing on as well as committed to offering creative and innovative approaches to responding to vexing substance abuse problems; and (6) the availability of a separate *Facilitators Manual* which features a matching chapter for each chapter in the monograph with creative ideas and activities for assisting both instructors and students to apply and utilize the ideas and interventions offered in each of the monograph's chapters

In all, it is a wonderful monograph—highly substantive, rewarding and interesting to read and offering what every substance abuse counselor and helping specialist can profit from learning about and using.

Garry R. Walz
Director
ERIC/CASS

Preface

The focus of *Substance Abuse and Counseling* is on the identification of practical knowledge and skill needed for counseling with individuals with substance abuse problems. The text is written as a resource to assist practitioners, students, and faculty in school counseling, rehabilitation counseling, mental health counseling, school psychology, or social work in recognizing, preventing, and treating individual substance abuse problems. It is designed to facilitate development of knowledge and skill needed to empower individual clients with substance abuse problems. The quality of the counseling relationship is the key factor related to treatment outcome. This holds true across all clients with addiction problems and all client populations and settings, no matter what the age of clients or whether treatment is individual or group based.

This edited text is organized in what is believed to be a sequential delivery of the knowledge needed to learn about counseling with individuals with substance abuse problems. In Chapter l, I provide a brief overview of the scope of substance abuse as a problem in our society and define the term as utilized in the text. A brief discussion of causation is provided and the prevalence is discussed. Counseling perspectives related to the process with individuals who have substance abuse problems are provided.

Chapter 2, Drug Addiction by Smith and Miller, provides an overview of models or theories of addiction, a description of the substances or drugs abused in our society, a discussion of the physiological functions and psychological characteristics of the user, and an outline of drug classification and regulation in our society.

Chapter 3, by Buck and Sales, discusses Related Addictive Behaviors, referred to in some literature as process addictions. The authors suggest these addictive behaviors, including eating, gambling, and exercise disorders as well as relationship disorders such as love or sexual addiction, should be considered by beginning counselors as within their broad definition of addiction or substance abuse.

In Chapter 4, Moore discusses the definition, models, and purpose of prevention and provides information on why and how counselors should be involved in various school, rehabilitation, and mental health settings in developing prevention programs.

Mullis, in Chapter 5, Assessment, Diagnosis, and Treatment

Planning, emphasizes the importance of comprehensive assessment. The assessment process utilizes a clinical interview to identify an appropriate diagnosis which is required for effective treatment planning. In this chapter, Mullis, while placing emphasis on assessment of adolescents, provides process information that can apply to any age group and setting.

Treating Addictive Behaviors in individual counseling is addressed by Varhely in Chapter 6 through a review of research supporting the importance of the counselor as a person and his/her abilities to establish a therapeutic relationship. Counseling of individuals with substance abuse problems is dependent on the individual committing to a counseling relationship. The importance of motivating clients for change and various research-supported treatment interventions are discussed.

McAllan, Freidman, and Spears in Chapter 7 address Change Through Group Work by discussing the therapeutic aspects of types, history and nature of groups. Research support for and ethical considerations within groups are examined. The importance of this chapter is highlighted by the fact that a combination of treatment groups and self-help groups represents the predominant treatment strategy for individuals with substance abuse problems in our society.

In Chapter 8, Working with Families, English discusses substance abuse and family systems. Key definitions, cultural influences, and codependence are presented. Stages related to and six types of family counseling are outlined within a chapter that recognizes the singular importance of the family in successful treatment of individuals with substance abuse problems.

Multicultural Issues related to and individual problems of substance abuse are presented in Chapter 9 by Reid and Kampfe. Cultural influences on individual abuse of substances and on the processes of prevention, assessment, and treatment are identified. Gay and lesbian considerations similarly are addressed.

Sales provides an overview of Substance Abuse and Disability in Chapter 10. This chapter is of importance because of both the prevalence, both known and unknown, of individuals with disabilities on caseloads within schools, rehabilitation, and mental health settings and the magnitude of the substance abuse problems they face.

In Chapter 11, Preventing Adolescent Relapse: Concepts, Theories and Techniques, Mishra and Ressler discuss determinants of relapse and related models and strategies of relapse-prevention that can be applied to youth and adults. Specific emphasis is provided on adolescents, who as a group are the least likely to receive treatment and if treated have the highest relapse rates. However, the discussions, models, and strategies presented in this chapter apply across all age groups.

Rapp, in Chapter 12, Program Planning and Evaluation, provides a very concrete model and process for the beginning practitioner to implement effective program planning and evaluation. Specific strategies for the beginning practitioner to implement in support of the counselor-client relationships are provided.

Sales in Chapter 13, Substance Abuse and Counseling: Prologue, provides a summary of the text, discusses current topics and issues, and concludes with some perspectives on the future.

Editor intent is to create an introductory overview of knowledge needed to counsel with individuals with substance abuse problems. Thus, the chapter components address major knowledge areas and, in a practical way, identify counselor skills needed to counsel with this population. The selection of authors is based on their recognized expertise in their content area and their sensitivity and experience in working with clients with substance abuse. Their selection also is based on editor interest in having professionals with backgrounds in school counseling, rehabilitation counseling, school psychology, rehabilitation psychology, mental health counseling, mental health psychology and social work contribute to a text designed for these professions. Readers can verify from the "About the Authors" section that these criteria were met. Readers will be exposed to and treated to the varied viewpoints of these authors who are some of the most creative in their fields.

Amos Sales

Acknowledgments

I gratefully acknowledge each and every one of the authors who contributed chapters to this text. Without their sharing their expertise and being understanding in response to editing and deadlines, this text would not exist. My gratitude also is offered to Garry Walz (ERIC/CASS) who believed in the concept of this edited text and supported me on the journey toward its development. Finally, a special thanks to Cathy Sales, my wife and dearest friend, who painstakingly read every word of this text in support of my editing efforts. To Chris and Clint: Enjoy.

Contributors

Tina Buck, MA, CRC, CPC

Tina Buck has worked in the dual-diagnosis and addictions treatment field since 1991. She has worked in residential treatment settings in Arizona and Hawaii, as well as provided outpatient counseling services in rural Arizona settings with children, adolescents, and adults. Tina earned her bachelor of science and master of arts degrees from the University of Arizona in Tucson, AZ. She is currently a doctoral student and graduate associate in rehabilitation education at the University of Arizona. Her interest is the application of integrated medicine to the field of rehabilitation.

William English, Ph.D.

Dr. R. William (Bill) English received the doctoral degree in Counseling and Behavioral Studies from the University of Wisconsin, Madison. Dr. English's postdoctoral positions have been at Syracuse University, the University of Oregon, and The Florida State University (FSU). Currently, he is a Professor of Rehabilitation Counseling and Counseling Psychology at FSU. Administratively, he is the Coordinator of the FSU Rehabilitation Services undergraduate degree program and Chair of the Department of Human Services and Studies, College of Education.

Dr. English is a recipient of the Research Achievement Award from the American Rehabilitation Counseling Association, for a nationwide, state-of-the-art study of rehabilitation supervision in state vocational rehabilitation agencies. He has produced 65 publications and made over 250 professional presentations on topics concentrated in five content areas: (1) psychological-social aspects of adjustment; (2) supervisory management; (3) leadership development; (4) family involvement in rehabilitation; and (5) service delivery practices in counseling and rehabilitation.

Dr. English has done an extensive amount of continuing education, in addition to teaching over 20 different university courses, and providing research or clinical supervision to numerous students. Bill English is married to a counselor (Norma) and has two grown children (Becca and Robb), both of whom are professionals in human services.

Amy Friedman

Amy Friedman is a graduate of the University of Wisconsin-Madison. She is currently a doctoral student at the University of Arizona in Rehabilitation. She is also the Program Manager for a local vocational rehabilitation agency.

Charlene Kampfe, Ph.D.

Dr. Charlene M. Kampfe has a Ph.D. in rehabilitation counseling from the University of Arizona. She has a CRC and an NCC and is presently an Associate Professor of the Department of Special Education, Rehabilitation, and School Psychology; with a secondary appointment in Gerontological Studies at the University of Arizona, Tucson. Dr. Kampfe has been on the Governing Council of the American Counseling Association (ACA), has served as president of the Association for Adult Development and Aging (AADA), and is presently serving on the Board of the American Rehabilitation Counseling Association (ARCA). She has over 40 publications, has many more than 50 presentations, and has received the Outstanding Research Award from Chi Sigma Iota/ERIC-CASS. She has received the distinguished Service Award and the Mentor Award from AADA. She has received two state awards for outstanding service and teaching. She has received two outstanding faculty awards from the University of Arizona.

Leslie C. McAllan, Ph.D., CRC

Dr. McAllan received his B.S. Degree in Psychology and his MS Degree in Rehabilitation Counseling from the University of Wisconsin-Milwaukee in 1973 and 1975 respectively. Since that time, he has had extensive individual and group clinical experience as a rehabilitation counselor and licensed psychologist in private and public settings. As an Assistant Professor at the University of Arizona for the past eight years, Dr. McAllan has had primary responsibility for coordinating the delivery of undergraduate and graduate degree programs utilizing work-study and distance learning models. He is Past-President of the Arizona Rehabilitation Association and President of the US/Mexico Disability Resource Consortium. Dr. McAllan's research interests include studying the effectiveness of different models of degree delivery, spirituality and disability, and psychosocial responses to disability.

Eva Miller, Ph.D.

Dr. Eva Miller has extensive experience working with adults aged 18 through old age with multiple psychiatric disorders, cognitive impairments, physical and developmental disabilities, and coexisting substance abuse problems. She has taught a number of courses at the University of Arizona at the graduate and undergraduate level, including Rehabilitation Counseling Practicum I and II, Rehabilitation Service Delivery, Strategies of Vocational Development and Supported Employment, Rehabilitation of the Aged, and Interviewing and Client Services. For the past two years, Dr. Miller has been responsible for developing, coordinating, and facilitating ongoing educational opportunities and statewide training for community rehabilitation programs in accordance with a federally funded grant. Prior to obtaining her doctorate degree at the University of Arizona in 1999, Dr. Miller worked for the Arizona Department of Economic Security, Division of Developmental Disabilities for 13 years as a training specialist, case manager, and most recently as the coordinator of residential services.

Shitala Mishra, Ph.D.

Shitala P. Mishra is Professor of School Psychology in the Department of Special Education, Rehabilitation, and School Psychology at the University of Arizona. His research spans a broad array of methodological and substantive concerns related to the delivery of school psychological services to school-age children and youth. He has published widely in the areas of clinical and cognitive assessment, applied psychometrics, and nondiscriminatory assessment. He is currently serving as an Associate Editor of *Journal Adolescent Research.* He also serves as a member on the editorial boards of several journals in education and psychology fields.

Susan Fordney Moore, Ph.D.

Susan Fordney Moore is a faculty member in the Department of Special Education, Rehabilitation, and School Psychology at the University of Arizona. A licensed psychologist and certified rehabilitation counselor, Dr. Moore has extensive experience in prevention, education, and treatment of addiction. As the former Director of the Smith Project for Substance Abuse Prevention/Education, she oversaw the development of a pre-service prevention curriculum for teacher preparation which has been used on a national basis. She teaches coursework in Prevention of Addictions, Problems of Drug Abuse, and Rehabilitation of the Public Offender.

Thomas Mullis, Ph.D.

Dr. Mullis holds a Ph.D. in counseling from the University of Utah. He is a Professor of Psychology in the counseling center at Radford University in Radford, Virginia. He is a licensed professional counselor in Virginia, He teaches graduate courses in counseling psychology and adolescent psychology. He has worked in private practice for over twenty years. Recently, he published a text on *State Licensure Requirements for Professional Counselors.*

Robert E. Rapp, Ph.D.

Robert E. Rapp, Ph.D. is a Professor of Counseling at Western New Mexico University in Silver City. He is a National Certified Counselor (NCC), a National Certified School Counselor (NCSC), and a Licensed Professional Clinical Mental Health Counselor (LPCC) in New Mexico. He is certified in Reality Therapy and is a Faculty member of The William Glasser Institute. He is also a Professional Associate of The Center For Quality Education. In addition, he currently serves as a consultant and therapist for at-risk students.

During his career, Dr. Rapp has developed and directed numerous innovative human service programs for children, adolescents and adults. He specializes in working with at-risk and delinquent children and adolescents. Most recently, he has concentrated upon developing substance abuse, violence and gang prevention and intervention programs.

Charrles Reid, Ph.D., CRC

Chuck Reid, Ph.D., CRC, is an Assistant Professor at the University of Texas-Pan American. He earned a doctorate in Special Education and Rehabilitation from The University of Arizona. His research interests include second language acquisition, non-captive cocaine users, cultural compatibility, and mental health issues.

Robert A. Ressler

Robert A. Ressler is a graduate student at the University of Arizona. He is pursuing a graduate degree program in School psychology. He has wide ranging experiences in working with school-age children and youth from Native American and Hispanic cultures.

Amos Sales, Ed.D., CRC

Dr. Sales, Professor, and Director, Rehabilitation Programs, University of Arizona, has devoted his academic, research, and service efforts over the past 34 years to human resource development within education and rehabilitation. Since 1985, Dr. Sales' research, program development, and service have been devoted to the field of prevention of substance abuse and the application of prevention concepts and practices to professional preparation and development. Dr. Sales formulated the original proposal for the University of Arizona Smith Project, which assumed a leadership position nationally in teacher education and substance abuse prevention. His work has resulted in publications and model demonstration programs of national impact.

Dr. Sales, through successful competition, has received yearly funding under grants and contacts to administer research, model service delivery, and personnel preparation programs. He has been awarded over forty grants and/or contracts totaling just over $17,000,000. Dr. Sales has developed and taught coursework in all content and experiential areas in rehabilitation at the undergraduate and graduate levels.

Dr. Sales' significant professional contributions have been recognized at the local, state, and national levels through the receipt of over thirty (30) citations, certificates or awards. He is unique in having received the highest awards provided by the National Rehabilitation Association at the state, regional, and national levels for distinction in professional contributions to the fields of education and rehabilitation. He has served as President of the National Rehabilitation Association and recently received the National Council on Rehabilitation Education's "Distinguished Career Award." Dr. Sales has published over forty (40) refereed articles, chapters, or monographs. Since 1988, he has published eight (8) articles and co-edited one (1) book specifically *Preparing Tomorrow's Teachers in Substance Abuse Prevention.* Dr. Sales is an Arizona Licensed Psychologist and a Certified Rehabilitation Counselor.

Mae Smith, Ph.D.

Dr. Mae Smith has been a member of the Rehabilitation Counseling faculty at the University of Arizona for 23 years. She has taught substance abuse courses at the University of Arizona, the University of Wisconsin - LaCrosse and the University of Wisconsin - Stout. Dr. Smith has extensive experience working with clients from junior high school age through old age (mid 90's) who sought assistance for substance abuse problems. Prior to joining the faculty at the University of Arizona, Dr. Smith directed a closed therapeutic community in Florida for female felons who resided in the program 24 hours a day for up to 18 months and whose substance abuse histories and criminal histories were so severe that they qualified for no other available treatment program. In addition Dr. Smith developed a treatment program for persons with narcotics addictions assigned to the Departments of Corrections and Parole in Florida; conducted Ala Teen groups in Wisconsin; has conducted individual, group and couples counseling related to substance abuse issues for young , middle aged and older adults; and provided psychological evaluations related to substance abuse in both hospital and non-hospital settings for persons with a wide-range of disabilities. In addition to publishing in the area of substance abuse, Dr. Smith was the Founding Editor of the *Journal of Offender Counseling* which has been renamed the *Journal of Correctional Counseling and Addictions*.

Evans Spears

Evans Spears is a doctoral student at the University of Arizona majoring in Rehabilitation Education and minoring in Special Education. Evans received his BA in Psychology at Coe College in Cedar Rapids, IA and his MA in Rehabilitation Counseling from the University of Iowa. He is a certified Rehabilitation Counselor and has worked in a variety of state, nonprofit, and for-profit settings. His major area of expertise is working with persons with HIV/AIDS, especially children with AIDS in educational settings. Evans has done extensive work with groups, again specializing in working with persons with HIV/AIDS.

Susan Varhely, Ph.D.

Susan Varhely, Ph.D. received her doctoral degree in counselor education from the University of North Texas in 1984. Since that time, she has held counselor education positions, maintained a private practice, and provided consultation to a variety of social service agencies, with emphasis in the substance specialty. While an Assistant Professor at Drake University, she created a master's program in Addictive Disorders and worked in close partnership with inpatient treatment facilities in Des Moines. Dr. Varhely is currently an Associate Professor in the Department of Counseling at Adams State College, Alamosa, Colorado and teaches the addictions component of the CACREP program.

TABLE OF CONTENTS

Chapter 1

Substance Abuse and Counseling

Amos Sales

Introduction

Substance abuse is a critical problem in the United States across all segments of the population. Inaba, Cohen, & Holstein (1997) provide data in support of the conclusion that substance abuse is the most prevalent mind disorder, the number one continuing health problem, and the number one prison problem in the United States. Substance abuse has received much attention in the popular as well as professional literature in recent years. The difficulties of public figures with various illicit substances receive almost weekly attention in the media. Given this visibility, the high incidence of substance abuse in our society, the economic costs, and the price in human suffering, it is imperative that counseling professionals are educated about substance abuse as a disability. Unfortunately, there is a lack of sufficiently educated counselors with skills to counsel individuals who have substance abuse problems.

A gap exists between the understanding and skills demanded of practitioners and the existence of graduate preparation programs offering this component as part of their curriculum. The need to establish a means in both preservice and inservice settings for practitioners to gain knowledge and expertise in substance abuse is easily documented.

All counselors, no matter what their professional specialty or setting, will encounter clients with presenting or related problems of substance abuse. Research shows that from one third to one half of clients on social service caseloads have an undiagnosed substance abuse problem. (DiNitto and Swab, 1991; Ohlmer, 1992). Thus, it is critical that all counselors in practice or in counselor preparation programs understand the process of substance abuse and addiction and related prevention and treatment strategies (Benshoff, 1990; Greer, Roberts, May & Jenkins, 1985).

Substance Abuse Defined

Professionals and the public face a multitude of terms used to identify individual abuse of substances. Addiction, alcoholism, alcohol abuse, drug abuse, and chemical dependency are representative. Most professionals and treatment programs now adhere to the related terms and criteria as identified in the *Diagnostic and Statistical Manual IV* (*DSM IV*) (American Psychiatric Association, 1994). In the *DSM IV*, previous terms are replaced by categories for the term "Substance-Related Disorders," which relates to the active use and dependency, or both on any mood-altering chemical, and "Substance-Induced Disorders," which are due to ingestion or exposure to a substance. Subcategories of "Substance-Related Disorders" are "substance dependence" and "substance abuse." The Substance-Induced Disorders include "substance intoxication" and "substance withdrawal." Substance dependence is the more severe diagnosis than substance abuse and is identified as the dysfunctional use of chemicals upon which the individual has become dependent. This dependence is equivalent to alcohol and drug addiction. Full diagnostic criteria from the *DSM IV* are provided in Chapter 2.

Substance abuse per the *DSM IV* refers specifically to the temporary abuse of a substance due to transient stresses. Within this text, we predominantly have used the term "substance abuse" interchangeably with the broad *DSM IV* term and criteria for "Substance-Related Disorders." The authors utilize the term "substance" to define alcohol, sedatives, amphetamine, cannabis, cocaine, hallucinogens, inhalants, opiods, caffeine, nicotine, and prescription drugs, as well as legal drugs. The legal nature of some drugs presents different issues related to their use and abuse than those related to illegal drugs.

While the above definition is provided for understanding in further references in this text, the beginning practitioner must understand that individuals with substance abuse cannot be categorized and defined by their substance abuse problem. An individual with a substance abuse problem is unique in his/her history, pattern of use or abuse, and treatment needs.

An individual's involvement with substances or substance use is often described as being on a continuum from non-use to dependence.

The first involvement is experimental use based on curiosity. It is sporadic, episodic, and relates to a desire to experience or "tryout" the drug by testing its physical, social, or both activity effects. This use may be influenced by modeling of peer-groups or parents. Next is recreational use, which is occasional and situationally controlled. It is associated with social or recreational activities in which the user would take part whether or not drugs were present. Enjoying the total experience is characteristic of this involvement wherein little or no effort is devoted to seeking out the drugs.

Next in the sequence is early dependence wherein the individual begins to believe the substance, person, or activity will improve his/her life and is sought out for such improvement. Negative features of involvement are not acknowledged. At the end point of the continuum is dysfunctional use. At this point, the individual begins to need a person, substance, or activity to feel normal. Friendships, work, and health begin to suffer because of the abuse. Denial, anxiety, and depression begin to occur. The individual feels miserable and uncomfortable when involved with the substance, person, or activity but is not willing to stop involvement. He/she must have "it" to survive. An awareness of this continuum leads to the obvious conclusion that there are varying degrees of involvement with substances and varying degrees of substance abuse. Some users are very conventional in every aspect of their lives except for their drug abuse while others are deeply involved in dysfunctional drug use and criminal activity to support it.

Until recently, the emphasis in treatment and prevention has been on the substance, i.e., "the demon rum," as if it were inherently alive and evil in itself (Brill, 1981). Fortunately, the current view is that substance abuse is a function of the person involved rather than the substance itself. Heavy dependence on drugs depends on the person not the drug. Given all the potential physical, cultural, and social influences, it is the personality of the user that determines how important substance use becomes "...whether it will dominate his or her life, become a recreational activity, or be dropped entirely" (Brill, 1981, p. 27.) Thus, it is the person who must be targeted in prevention and treatment of problems of substance abuse.

Causation

As is documented in an overview section on Etiology of Substance Abuse in Chapter 2, the individual use of drugs has been existent throughout recorded history to enhance a person's pleasure, alter one's state of consciousness, or decrease pain. The excessive use and abuse of substances by individuals has been viewed from differing cultural perspectives across time.

To date, no clear etiology or causation has been identified for substance abuse. Many models or theories of causation for substance abuse or addiction have been proposed. In the moral model of causation, substance abuse is viewed as a result of individual conscious choice of overindulgence and moral degradation. A cure could be obtained through willpower and a desire to abstain. The biological-disease model identifies substance abuse as biologically inherited and medically defined and caused by some biomedical reason to be vulnerable to a given substance. Avoidance of the "carcinogen" is the cure. Behavioral models view substance abuse as a result of faulty learning patterns and related ineffective attempts at stress reduction. Behavioral interventions are emphasized for treatment. Cultural models identify substance abuse as being fostered by cultural factors, social pressures, and environmental conditions. Treatment relates to developing social skills. The majority of practitioners and researchers currently support a biopsychosocial model which holds that substance abuse is developed as a result of a complex interaction of factors identified in all of the above models. This model identifies substance misuse, abuse, and addiction as multifaceted problems that vary across individuals, their cultures, and their families. In this model, multiple strategies of counseling from the other models are proposed as appropriate to treatment.

Research in support of any of these models is inconclusive. There is no clear consensus as to why people engage in substance abuse, and why some people become addicted (Erickson, 1998). Despite this, it is important for the beginning counselor to develop a conceptual position through a review of various models that attempt to explain substance abuse and related addictive disorders. From this review, the counselor can develop a position upon which he/she can make consistent therapeutic assumptions and decisions to guide counseling practice.

Prevalence

As is the case of problems with identifying specific terminology related to substance abuse, the difficulty of identifying specific incidence and prevalence data exists. Surveys and self-reports are replete with validity problems. Individuals who abuse one drug often abuse another and their individual reporting of use compounds the survey data. Thus, estimates of the prevalence of substance abuse problems in the population at large range from a low of 2% to a high estimate of 60%.

For the past five years, substance use has been viewed by the general population as the primary problem facing our society. Data from the 1996 National Household Survey on Drug Abuse (NHSDA) show that alcohol and cigarettes are the substances most frequently used. A majority of the respondents aged 12 and older reported that they had used alcohol (51%) at least once in the month prior to the survey. The next highest reported use was cigarettes (29%), followed by marijuana (5%), and smokeless tobacco (3%). Use of all other drugs was reported by 1% or less of the respondents. National statistics (National Institute on Drug Abuse [NIDA], 1993) indicate an increase in drug usage of various substances across all age groups.

It is difficult in reviewing the literature to estimate with any degree of accuracy the number of individuals who chronically abuse substances. Available statistics are usually cited for specific substances such as alcohol, cocaine, marijuana, or prescription medications. As was indicated earlier, references in the literature point to the fact that many individuals abusing one substance tend to abuse others, which makes it all the more difficult to determine the true extent of this problem.

Illicit Drugs

The National Institute of Drug Abuse (NIDA) Household Survey (1993) indicated that 5.6% of adults surveyed met the criteria for drug use and dependence. It is estimated that more than 2% of the population, about 5.5 million people, need treatment for drug abuse (Gerstein & Harwood, 1990). One in 35 Americans older than 12 abuses illicit drugs (NIDA, 1996). Thirty-seven percent of the population over the age of 12 indicate they have used illegal drugs. Twelve percent are current users. Additionally, over twenty million Americans use marijuana regularly, approximately eight million are regular cocaine users, and two million are heroin addicts.

Alcohol

In 1992, approximately 13.8 million United States citizens had problems with drinking, including 8.1 million who are alcoholic (National Institute of Alcohol Abuse and Alcoholism, 1994). Greer (1985) cites estimates of "heavy drinking" in the United States as 12 % and the prevalence of problem drinking among American males is considered to be as high as 20%. More than 500,000 Americans are treated yearly in more than 8,000 inpatient and outpatient alcohol treatment programs.

Prescriptions

Approximately 1.5 billion prescriptions are written each year in the United States. Over the past 25 years, the average annual number of prescriptions per person has increased from 2.4 to 7.5 (Stall, 1996). Investigators estimate that 13% of the men and 29 percent of the women in the United States use some form of psychotropic drug. The abuse of prescribed drugs in the United States may be as high as 20 percent of the general population (Hazelden, 1996).

Nicotine

One in four, or approximately 56 million, are addicted to nicotine (Inaba and Cohen, 1991). Fifty million smoke cigarettes and 6.1 million are current users of smokeless tobacco (Substance Abuse and Mental Health Services Administration, 1994).

Of obvious concern related to abuse of substances in our society is the early initiation to drugs. One in 3 teenagers by age 16 indicates he/she has been approached to buy or use drugs, and at least 4 of 10 school children say drugs are being sold in their schools (Gallup Poll, 1989). One in 10 high school students has used cocaine at least once and more than 1 in 5 teens have used illegal drugs (National Institute of Drug Abuse, 1991).

Prevalence figures indicate there is a major problem of substance abuse among individuals within our society. The estimates indicate approximately 6% of our population abuse illegal drugs, 12% have problems with drinking, 25% are addicted to nicotine, and conservatively 10% are addicted to prescription medications. Cumulatively, these percentages reflect a significant number of the United States population having a substance abuse problem. Substance abuse impacts in some way all members of our society at all ages.

Counseling Perspectives

A major perspective of this text is that counselors must avoid earlier thinking which stereotyped all individuals with substance abuse problems as "substance abusers" who have uniform characteristics treatable by one treatment approach. There is as great a diversity in substance abuse as there are individuals who abuse substances. While the abuse of substances across individuals has some similarities, the individual and his/her substance abuse problem is unique. Effective prevention and treatment strategies must target the individual with a substance abuse problem not the substance abuse problem.

Conclusions regarding effective counseling strategies for counseling individuals with substance abuse are limited in that this counseling specialty area has been driven more by experience and clinical intuition than by research. As a result, most traditional substance abuse treatment programs (e.g., Alcoholics Anonymous, alcoholism education, half-way house and therapeutic communities utilizing confrontation, group therapy, individual counseling, and use of medication) have not demonstrated their efficacy. Some successful treatment outcome has been linked to short-term interventions, aversion therapy, stress management, solution-focused brief therapy, and social skills training, yet seldom are these methods utilized in traditional substance abuse treatment programs in the United States. Given this, conclusions regarding counseling and substance abuse have to come from general counseling research data.

Counselors, regardless of their settings, impact as change agents within the context of therapeutic relationships with individuals. Successful relationships are facilitated by a skilled counselor who helps the client become more invested in the process and who utilizes therapeutic techniques appropriate to the client. A thorough review of *Counseling Outcome Research* (Sexton, Whiston, Bleur, and Walz, 1997 pp. 58-62, pp. 87-93) concludes the following:

1) Counseling is a process beneficial to most clients of skilled counselors. However, it is not always so. A significant number of clients get worse;
2) Counseling models (e.g. cognitive, experiential, behavioral, dynamic) are effective and when compared seem equivalent in their effect on counseling outcome.
3) Successful counseling has common factors which are consistently related to success and evident across various counseling models. These factors include "support" factors leading to the establishing of an open, trusting, collaborative relationship with the client, "learning" factors such as advice, corrective emotional experiencing, and feedback, and "action" factors including behavior regulation, cognitive mastery, and successful experiences.
4) Successful counseling outcome is dependent on counselor therapeutic skills such as focusing conversations on life problems, addressing presenting problems directly, and providing structure for counselor-client intervention, and
5) Successful counseling progresses through various process stages wherein different types of counselor-client interaction are reflected by different counseling techniques.

The above research conclusions support the following perspective regarding counseling with clients with substance abuse problems.

Counselors, to be effective, first must have the ability to develop an open, collaborative relationship with clients wherein clients perceive trust and commitment. Carl Rogers identifies, and research supports, this ability as related to the counselor's skill in conveying, in interaction with clients, unconditional positive regard and empathic understanding (Austin, 1999). Within this relationship, the counselor must provide focus for the process by addressing the client's presenting problems directly and identifying client need for change. Counselors of clients with substance abuse problems often find this process difficult because of the chronic nature of interrelated destructive attitudes and coexisting disorders these clients often bring to counseling. Once problem identification and client need for change are identified, the counselor must be able to articulate and implement counseling intervention strategies perceived by both the counselor and the client as appropriate to the client's need to change.

These process considerations in counseling clients with substance abuse problems hold to be true for specialists in this area and for counselors working in school, rehabilitation, mental health, and social work settings. The counselor emphasis is on the person not the substance abuse problem. Additional knowledge and skill on the part of the counselor relates to being able to assess the extent and impact of a client's substance abuse problem and the client's need to change. Familiarity with and ability to utilize standardized assessment instruments specific to substance abuse will help the counselor in this assessment process. Familial and social environment assessment also is required to identify the extent of and to utilize the client's support systems. The counselor's ability to identify, and the quality of, counseling and related treatment intervention strategies obviously is linked to his/her assessment and diagnostic skills.

Counselors should be thoroughly familiar with the facilities and services in his/her community to insure proper referral for clients with substance abuse problems. Referral options are determined by client need and collaboratively agreed upon as appropriate by the counselor and client. These include short-term, inpatient care lasting three to seven days for withdrawal from substance abuse, or intensive, outpatient programs lasting eight to twelve weeks wherein clients maintain vocational and family responsibilities while participating in treatment. Another option, the half-way house, provides moderately structured and supportive residential treatment lasting for three to six months, wherein successful living within the environment becomes part of the treatment plan. Other options include therapeutic communities, structured, highly intensive, residential treatment program such as Synanon, where clients may remain up to two years, and out-patient alcoholism treatment programs of two kinds, drug-free clinics with services lasting four to six months, and methadone or opiate clinics that a client may attend by medical referral for two to five years. Within these settings, group treatment is the predominant mode of therapy with individual counseling viewed as an adjunct.

In addition to these process and case management skills, there are other counseling considerations that are particularly appropriate for counselors working with clients with substance abuse problems. Corey (1996) has identified these as a list of 18 goals counselors in any setting should strive for to become models of awareness and growth for their clients.

1. Effective counselors have an identity. These are people who are not just doing what they think other people want from them. They are people with a solid sense of self, values, life direction, and principles that they live by. They can set goals and achieve them. They possess a certain sense of their own individuation and separateness but are also willing to evaluate their ideas.
2. Effective counselors respect and appreciate themselves. These people have good self-esteem and consider themselves to be good people. They can give and receive love, care and feel a connectedness to others.
3. Effective counselors are able to recognize and accept their own power. A counselor has power over his or her client by the nature of the relationship. A good counselor is aware of this power and uses it to help his or her client and does not abuse it. This is not to suggest a position of superiority, but to acknowledge that there is potential for abuse. It is not used to diminish others.
4. Effective counselors are open to change. There is a sense of flexibility and openness to other possibilities and growth. There is the ability to risk new behaviors for the potential of learning or experiencing something new that could make them a better person.
5. Effective counselors are expanding their awareness of self and others. These people are aware that they are limited in their experiences and move toward growth and development in themselves and learning about others' experiences.

6. Effective counselors are willing and able to tolerate ambiguity. Black-and-white, polarized thinking is prevalent in clients with chemical dependency and people who have lived with them. The ability to tolerate ambiguity means becoming comfortable with not knowing as well as exploring the gray areas of life. It is more comforting to stick with absolutes and unbending rules. It takes courage to risk the process of life and to trust that intuitions and novel ideas can produce self-growth and growth in others.
7. Effective counselors are developing their own counseling style. This process comes with experience and being open to learning. Counselors who try to exactly imitate another counselor or apply a counseling theory without modification will be less successful than if they are able to pull from many sources, including self-knowledge, to develop their own unique theories.
8. Effective counselors can experience and know the world of the client, yet their empathy is nonpossessive. This is the ability of counselors to know themselves in a way that allows them to put their own needs aside long enough to truly understand the worlds of their clients. They, however, do not lose themselves in this process. They can clearly distinguish between the clients' issues and theirs.
9. Effective counselors feel alive, and their choices are life oriented. These are people who take an active stance in life. They are not passive but are proactive.
10. Effective counselors are authentic, sincere, and honest. These are people who have demonstrated congruence between what they think, feel, and do. They do not play roles or hide behind masks.Their communication is straightforward and nondefensive.
11. Effective counselors have a sense of humor. These are people who use their sense of humor to put life in perspective. They can laugh at themselves and their mistakes. This is extremely important in treating substance abusing individuals and their families who have often forgotten, or never knew, how to laugh and play with one another. This is also the best antidote for burnout.

12. Effective counselors make mistakes and are willing to admit them. In a field where attempts at perfectionism abound, being able to admit and learn from mistakes is important to the chemical dependency counselor. They also become excellent role models for clients who hide their mistakes because of extreme guilt.
13. Effective counselors generally live in the present. Counselors who can live in the present are more available to their clients. Although the past may be interesting and useful in understanding their clients, they do not dwell on their own past or worry about the future.
14. Effective counselors appreciate the influence of culture. Counselors need to be aware of how their own cultures have affected them, and how they have integrated their cultures into themselves. They should also be aware of how culture, race, and gender create different experiences for others. They need to respect the differences of others.
15. Effective counselors are able to reinvent themselves. These are people who are always in the process of self-growth and can change themselves for the better. They have clear ideas of the person they would like to be, and they move in that direction.
16. Effective counselors are making choices that shape their lives. These people do not allow previous mistakes or incorrect decisions to make them victims. They learn from mistakes and make good choices based on continual self-evaluation.
17. Effective counselors have a sincere interest in the welfare of others. Their work is based on a genuine respect and desire to help others. They can respect and care for those they are helping.
18. Effective counselors become deeply involved in their work and derive meaning from it. These counselors enjoy the process of helping others and look forward to going to work. They recognize the ego needs that are met by helping others, yet they know how to balance their lives and are not workaholics. (In Lawson, Lawson, & Rivers, 1996, pp. 4-6.)**WWho**

Who Counsels?

The question of what personal and professional qualifications a counselor needs continues to be debated. Those in "treatment camps" with the perspective of treating the problem are committed to the belief that an effective counselor must be a recovering substance abuser who has experienced the disability, treatment, and "cure". Others, more oriented to counseling individuals, advocate training and clinical experience with clients who have substance abuse problems leading to a master's degree in counseling. In relation to the major debate in the substance abuse counselor field as to whether or not recovering or nonrecovering counselors are better able to treat individuals who have substance abuse problems, a survey of administrators of substance abuse programs believe the two groups do not differ in effectiveness (Anderson & Weimer, 1992). Counselor "effectiveness" across both groups relates more to the counselor person-related qualities and abilities identified throughout this text.

Counselors–Experience Based: Substance abuse counselors, since the birth of *Alcoholics Anonymous* in 1935, have "come from the ranks." They predominantly have been individuals who have overcome a drug or alcohol problem and have a commitment to helping others do the same. Thus, many substance abuse counselors entered the field and were credentialed based on their own recovery experiences. The predominant view in substance abuse counseling for at least four decades was that personal experience, not professional training, was the prerequisite to practicing as a counselor.

National Public Policy changes in 1970 began to impact this counseling view. In that year, the Hughes Act (Public Law 91-616) established the National Institute for Alcohol Abuse and Alcoholism (NIAA) to fund alcoholism research, and addiction treatment began to be reimbursed by insurance companies (O'Dwyer, 1993). The Hughes Act also funded states to establish alcohol units or divisions which funded treatment programs for federal employees (Fisher and Harrison, 1997). With these changes, states began in the 1980s to create licensing bodies to ensure the quality of counseling to substance abusers (O'Dwyer, 1993). Being a recovering addict no longer meant immediate access to employment as a substance abuse counselor. Instead, documentation of a combination of credentials regarding both counseling experience and training was required by states to practice.

The predominant number of substance abuse counselors in the United States identify with either the National Association of

Alcoholism and Drug Abuse Counselors (NAADC) or the American Academy of Health Care Providers in Addictive Disorders (AAHCPAD) through which they receive certification. The NAADC code of ethics is specific to practice with individuals who are substance abusers. NAADC has different levels of counselor certification depending on training and experience and requires a written examination at each level. AAHCPAD provides the Certified Addiction Specialist (CAS) credential to degreed persons with two years experience or to non-degreed persons with five years experience. No written examination is required. Few, if any, insurance companies will pay reimbursement for service unless it is provided by a certified mental health professional.

Counselors–Master's Level: Over the years, the word counselor has simply meant any "professional who practices counseling" (Chaplin, 1975, p. 120). More frequently because of legal and certification issues, individuals who refer to themselves as counselors will have master's degrees in counseling. While there are many different professional identities of counselors, all have shared common coursework in their master's degree programs of study, i.e., professional orientation, the individual and group counseling relationship, ethics, supervised practice in counseling, career development, appraisal, and social and cultural foundations. In addition to these, students will generally take specialty coursework linked to roles and functions related to knowledge and skills required within a specific work setting.

Delivery of a common core of knowledge and skill within a master's in counseling sequence of study dates back to early 1940's Veterans Administration guidelines for a two-year sequence of study leading to a designation of "psychological counselor." Evolving from this model was rehabilitation counseling, the specialty emphasizing counseling with individuals with disabilities. It was the first counseling specialty to develop a national accrediting body, the Council on Rehabilitation Education (CORE) and the first to develop a national certification process, the Commission on Rehabilitation Counseling Certification (CRCC) with the designation of Certified Rehabilitation Counselor (CRC). Utilizing this accreditation model, school counseling was the next counseling specialty to develop an accreditation and certification process. Accreditation as developed was through the Council for the Accreditation of Counseling and Related Educational Programs (CACREP). Certification was implemented under the National Board for Certified Counselors (NBCC) as National Certified Counselors (NCC). CACREP has evolved to recognize a variety of counseling specialties: community counseling, school counseling, marriage and family counseling, and mental health counseling.

Today, every state in the country has as a requirement by national law that counselors in state and federal vocational rehabilitation agencies have a master's degree and hold the CRC. Additionally, 43 states and the District of Columbia have adopted licensing laws that require a master's degree in counseling to practice as a Licensed Professional Counselor (LPC). In those states, NCC's and CRC's may be certified as LPC's.

While keeping in mind that a person obtaining a master's degree in counseling is first a counselor and second a "specialty" counselor, the following are some of the more prevalent counseling specialty areas. In all cases, the academic emphasis is on developing skills in counseling that are then applied to the specialty area. None of the following specialties have required coursework in substance abuse as a prerequisite for graduation from master's degree programs of study.

Rehabilitation Counselor: The Rehabilitation Counselor has a master's degree and works in state vocational rehabilitation agencies, unemployment agencies, or private rehabilitation agencies and counsels working age individuals who are physically or mentally disabled. Specialty knowledge and skill relates to this population. While there is no requirement by CORE for accredited master's degree programs in rehabilitation to have expertise in substance abuse as a requirement of graduation, CRCC did recognize in 1993-94 a growing specialty in rehabilitation counseling and substance abuse. It developed an additional and new certification procedure for Certified Rehabilitation Counselor: Substance Abuse Counselor (CRC-SAC). This certification requires an additional 12 semester hours of coursework specific to substance abuse counseling, a minimum of one year of supervised acceptable work experience and documentation of supervision by a CRC or related professional. Rehabilitation counselors identify with and join the professional organizations of the National Rehabilitation Counseling Association (NRCA) a professional division of the National Rehabilitation Association (NRA) or the American Rehabilitation Counseling Association (ARCA), a professional division of the American Counseling Association (ACA).

School Counselors: Historically, the counselor in the school setting has been called the guidance counselor. Recently, many educators and practitioners have tried to replace that term with school counselor in an attempt, of varying success, to de-emphasize the guidance activities of the school counselor. Credentialing by some state departments of education is on elementary, middle, and secondary levels and, in others, credentialing covers kindergarten through the twelfth grade. Some states, but not all, require that school counselors have teaching experience.

CACREP does not identify the delivery of substance abuse content as a requirement for accreditation master's degree programs in school counseling, although it does recommend that counselor education programs address prevention and treatment in this area. The school counselor's usual professional association of choice is the American School Counselor Association (ASCA), which is a professional division of the American Counseling Association (ACA).

Mental Health Counselor/Agency Counselor/Community Counselor: These counseling specialties require the master's degree and specialty preparation in their designated area. Although CACREP differentiates community counseling from mental health counseling, which requires more extensive training, individuals with these degrees work in similar settings, public agencies, or private practice. These counselors usually become LPC's if their state has a licensing procedure.

As is the case in school counseling, knowledge and skill specific to substance abuse is not required but recommended for CACEP accreditation in these specialties. The NBCC established in 1995 an addiction certification specialty for mental health counselors. In 1997, NBCC developed the Master's in Addiction Counseling (MAC) certification wherein counselors certified as addiction counselors by CRCC, NBCC, and NAADC could qualify. The usual choice of these counselors of a professional organization is the American Mental Health Counselor's Association (AMHCA), a professional division of ACA.

Social Workers: The term, social worker, can apply to graduates of either an undergraduate or graduate degree program in social work. Usually, the social worker has completed a master's degree in social work (MSW). While many differences exist in philosophy and theory between the master's degree in social work and the master's in counseling, the two have more similarities in curriculum than differences. Substance abuse knowledge and skill is not a requirement within MSW programs. MSW's can become nationally certified by the Academy of Certified Social Workers (ACSW), and most states have specific requirements for licensure as a Licensed Clinical Social Worker (LCSW). The National Association of Social Workers (NASW) is the professional association of choice for social workers.

The professional associations linked to the above professions have evolved as a means to protect the rights of their members and their clients and to enhance professional practice in the specialty area. These associations monitor professional practice through requiring member adherence to ethical standards and practice. They also provide access to continuing education through national, regional, and state conferences and workshops, impact national legislation through education and lobbying efforts, and provide a wide variety of member benefits such as insurance, job banks, and interest networks. It is beyond the scope of this publication to discuss associations in detail. It is important, however, to emphasize that individual counseling practice is governed by codes of ethics and standards of practice which should be well understood and followed no matter what the specialty area of counseling practice.

As is noted in the above discussions, counselor education programs appear to be deficient in their response to the major problem of substance abuse within our society. Most currently do not require knowledge or skill of graduates in this critical area. Counselor education programs must become more progressive and aggressive in insuring that their graduates have counseling knowledge and skill related to counseling individuals with substance abuse problems. Accreditation bodies, as well as professional organizations, could and should provide leadership for needed improvement in this area.

Summary

Individuals with substance abuse problems present a critical problem in the United States. Outside the social and economic losses presented by these problems, personal devastation is severe and usually ongoing. Many individuals with substance abuse problems are unable to, or do not, access treatment and of those who do, treatment success rates are low. Thus, there is a need to insure that counselors are available and competent to provide service within all counseling settings. Counselor preparation should insure graduates are effective in counseling individuals with substance abuse problems.

Effective counseling is proposed as holistic, individual based, and a person centered process. It emphasizes empowering the client, not treating the substance abuse problem. Counseling professions are identified, discussed, and found in most cases to be deficient in relation to developing counseling skills with individuals presenting substance abuse problems. Counselors, counselor education programs, and their related associations and accrediting bodies must begin to insure this expertise exists for us to be able to address the critical problem of substance abuse within our society.

References

American Psychiatric Association: (1994). *Diagnostic and statistical manual of mental disorders, (4th ed.)*. Washington, DC: Author.

Anderson, S. & Weimer, L. (1992). Administrators' beliefs about the relative competence of recovering and nonrecovering chemical dependency counselors. *Families in Society: The Journal of Contemporary Human Services, 73* (10), 596-603.

Austin, L. (1999). *The counseling premier.* Philadelphia, PA: Accelerated Development.

Benshoff, J. J. (1990). Substance Abuse: Challenges for the rehabilitation counseling profession. Editorial. *Journal of Applied Rehabilitation Counseling, 21* (3), 3.

Boy, A. & Pine, J. (1990). *A person-centered foundation for counseling and psychotherapy.* Springfield, IL: Charles C. Thomas Publishing.

Brill, L. (1981). *The clinical treatment of substance abuse.* New York: Free Press Macmillian.

Chaplin, J. P. (1975). *Dictionary of psychology (2nd ed.).* New York: Dell.

Corey, G. (1996). *Theory and practice of counseling and psychotherapy (5th ed.).* New York: Brooks/Cole Publishing Company.

Davis, S. & Meier, S. (1997). *Elements of Counseling (3rd ed.)* New York: Brooks/Cole Publishing Company.

DiNitto, D. M., & Schwab, A. V. (1991). *Substance abuse factors which interfere with entry or reentry into employment.* Austin: University of Texas, School of Social Work.

Erickson, S. (1998). Ethological theories of substance abuse. In Stevens-Smith, P., & Smith, R. R. *Substance abuse counseling* (pp. 25-64). Columbus, Ohio: Prentice Hall.

Fisher, S. L., & Harrison, T. C. (1997). *Substance abuse: Information for school counselors, social workers, therapists, and counselors.* Boston: Allyn and Bacon.

Gallup Poll (1989, August 4). pp. 10,16.

Gerstein, D. R., & Harwood, H. J. (1990). *Treating drug problems.* Vol. 1, Washington, D.C.: National Academic Press.

Greer, B. G., Roberts, R., May, G., & Jenkins, W. M. (1985). Identification of substance abuse in a vocational evaluation setting. *Journal of Rehabilitation, 54* (3), 42-45.

Hazelden Corporation. (1996). *Alcoholism and drug abuse: A growing problem with the elderly.* On the World Wide Web, 1-2.

Helwig, A. A. & Holicky, R. (1994). Substance abuse in persons with disabilities: Treatment considerations. *Journal of Counseling and Development, 72* (31), 227-233.

Inaba, D. S., Cohen, W. E., & Holstein, M. E. (1997). *Uppers, downers and all arounders: Physical and mental effects of drugs of abuse.* Ashland: CNS Publications.

Lawson, G. W., Lawson, A. W. & Rivers, P. C. (1996). *Essentials of chemical dependency* (2nd ed.). Gathersburg, MD: Apen Publishers, Inc.

National Institute of Alcohol Abuse and Alcoholism. (1994). *Alcohol Health and Research World, 18* (3), 243, 245.

National Institute of Drug Abuse. (1991). *An economical approach to addressing the drug problem in America.* Rockville, MD: Author.

National Institute of Drug Abuse (1993). *National household survey on drug abuse and population estimates 1990.* Rockville, MD: Author.

National Institute of Drug Abuse. (1996). *Preliminary results of the 1996 national household survey on drug abuse.* Rockville, MD: Author.

O'Dwyer, P. (1993) Alcohol treatment facilities. In S. L. A. Straussner (Ed.), *Clinical work with substance abusing clients* (pp. 119-134). New York: Guilford.

Ohlmer, V. L. (1992). *Undetected substance abuse among vocational rehabilitation clients.* Dissertation. University of Arizona.

Pines, M. (1998). *Circular reflections: Selected papers on group analysis and psychoanalysis.* Philadelphia, PA: Jessica Kingsley Publishers.

Sapp, M. (1997). *Counseling and psychotherapy: Theories, associated research, and issues.* New York: University Press of America, Inc.

Stall, R. S. (1996). Drug abuse in the elderly: Major issues. On the World Wide Web, 1-3.

Yalom, I. (1995). *The theory and practice of group psychotherapy* (4th ed.). New York: Basic Books, Inc.

Chapter 2

Drugs and Addictions

S. Mae Smith & Eva Miller

Characteristics of Drugs

The word "drug" in American society is no longer a neutral term. While many drugs are of great benefit to mankind, the word "drugs" is often used to refer only to drugs of abuse, illegal substances, or chemical compounds which are associated with high addiction potential. Drugs, such as vaccines, antibiotics, psychopharmaceuticals, oral contraceptives, and medications which assist to restore normal bodily functioning, used correctly greatly enrich quantity, quality of life or both. The great number of psychological, physical, and social problems associated with drugs arise from the illegal use, misuse and abuse, or both of substances rather than from the mere existence of these substances.

When substances themselves are blamed for drug-related problems, the tendency exists to focus on elimination of the drug itself rather than on addressing the factors that lead to the abuse of the drug. Effects of a drug will depend not only upon the drug itself but upon individual interactions of characteristics of the substance, the physiological and psychological states of the user, and the environment in which the drug is used (Blum, 1984). However, history indicates that some drugs have most commonly been used not just for their therapeutic effects but also for recreational purposes. Likewise, some drugs have been more commonly overused, abused, or misused than others. Knowledge of some common effects of the most frequently abused substances may assist the counselor in understanding and communicating about client behavior.

The purpose of this chapter is to introduce counselors to common characteristics of frequently abused substances. It is hoped that such information will increase the ability of counselors to: (1) understand certain drugs, their effects and client behavior; and (2) explain to clients and other publics the common effects of certain drugs.

General Considerations

Drugs affect the human body in many different ways. Individual variations occur with any drug. In analysis of how any drug affects the body, knowledge of several processes are important. As described by Leung (1976, p. 34), such processes include:

1. Administration, or how does the drug enter the body?
2. Absorption, or how does the drug get from the site of administration into the physiological system of the body?
3. Distribution, or how is the drug distributed to the parts of the body?
4. Action, or how and where does the drug produce its effects?
5. Physiological Fate, or how is the drug inactivated, metabolized and/or eliminated from the body?

The aforementioned factors are affected by many variables, including individual differences in body functioning; disease; presence of other drugs, foods or liquid; exercise and activity level; amount of substance placed in the body within a certain time frame; energy and endurance levels, including amount of sleep; and body weight (Seixas, 1975). Differences in when effects reported (subjective) and when actual (physiological/functional) effects ceased are typical of some substances (Levinthal, 1996). Also of importance is that "street drugs" often are not what they are claimed to be in purity, chemical composition, or quantity (Ray & Ksir, 1996). The actual concentrations, frequency, and duration of exposure over a lifetime to a particular substance or a similar substance may alter effects of a particular drug on a particular individual (Levinthal, 1996).

Studies of the effects of drugs are most commonly conducted on healthy adult males under age 35. In many drug studies, information is not available on the effects of substances upon older individuals or upon individuals whose physical systems have been compromised by disability or chronic illness. Often, drug studies focus on short-term effects to the exclusion of long-term effects.

Alcohol

Alcohol is the most abused drug in American society (Parsons, 1996). "Drug dependence of the alcohol type may be said to exist when the consumption of alcohol by an individual exceeds the limits that are accepted by his [sic] culture" (Leung, 1976, p. 45). Indications exist that alcohol was used in Egypt over 6,000 years ago. Because of the frequent resistance in American society to acknowledge that alcohol is a psychoactive drug, the phrase "drugs and alcohol" is commonly used, inaccurately implying that alcohol is not a drug (Levinthal, 1996). Wine, "dessert wines," wine-like variations such as hard cider or sake, beers (draft or lager beer, ale, and malt liquor), and distilled spirits or liquor all are alcoholic substances which contain alcohol but vary in percent of alcohol content (Becker, Roe, & Scott, 1979). Dependence, addiction or both may occur related to any of the above alcohol-containing substances.

Since alcohol is moderately soluble in fat and highly soluble in water and is a small molecule, it is easily absorbed by the gastrointestinal tract without the need for digestion (Levinthal, 1996). The solubility of alcohol facilitates its distribution to all bodily tissues. The solubility of alcohol in fat allows almost 90% of alcohol in the blood to reach the brain almost immediately.

Alcohol has a progressive, depressant effect upon the central nervous system [CNS] (Seixas, 1975; Levinthal, 1996). The CNS depressant effect of alcohol is often misinterpreted initially as a stimulant effect as the substance reduces functioning of an area of the brain that normally inhibits behaviors. Depressing the inhibitory effects of certain brain centers may result in increases in activity level, in increases in aggression or sexual behaviors, and in reduction of social inhibitions. Computerized brain tomography of chronic alcoholics has shown cortical shrinkage, ventricular dilation, or both (O'Donnell & O'Callaghan, 1997). Neuropsychological functioning associated with intermediate stages of alcoholism include mild to moderate impairment on tests measuring memory and learning, abstracting and problem-solving, perceptual-spatial abilities, information-processing speed, and perceptual-motor speed (Parsons, 1996). Verbal abilities of alcoholics usually remain intact.

"Alcoholism continues to be one of the leading public health problems in the western world" (O'Donnell & O'Callaghan, 1997, p. 272). The decrease in general physical health has been attributed to multiple aspects of alcoholism, including general life style, use of other drugs, inadequate hygiene, injury due to accidents, stress, and nutritional deficiencies. A number of immediate physiological effects may be produced by alcohol. One acute effect of alcohol may be toxic reactions which result in gastric irritation resulting in vomiting, unconsciousness, or both; or lethal effects which result from rapid ingestion (Levinthal, 1996). Contradictory to myths of alcohol warming-up the body, alcohol actually is a peripheral dilator which may increase bodily heat loss. Alcohol modifies reabsorption and elimination of water from the body and these modifications may be a serious concern, especially if considerable exercise has occurred immediately prior to ingestion. Alcohol alters functioning of the cardiovascular system, adversely affects sleep patterns, interacts with many other drugs, and may produce hangovers. Emergency signs of acute alcohol intoxication include stupor or unconsciousness; cool or damp skin; weak, rapid pulse; shallow and irregular breathing; and pale or bluish skin (Levinthal, 1996; Payne & Hahn, 1992; and Victor, 1976).

Chronic overuse of alcohol has been associated with three forms of liver disease (fatty liver, alcoholic hepatitis, alcoholic cirrhosis); cardiovascular problems; increased risk of several types of cancers; and cognitive impairments (e.g., alcoholic dementia, Wernicke-Korsakoff syndrome, and Korsakoff's psychosis). Chronic abuse of alcohol also is associated with increased physical injury resultant of accidents or violence, and is the direct cause of birth defects resulting from fetal alcohol syndrome (Serdula, Williamson, Kendrick, Anda, & Byers, 1991).

Chronic effects of alcohol results in tolerance and alcohol-dependence resulting in withdrawal (Levinthal, 1996; Parsons, 1996). One type of withdrawal, alcohol withdrawal syndrome, is associated with tremor, nausea and vomiting, sweating, agitation, anxiety, increased heart rate, increased blood pressure, and, in some cases, tonic-clonic seizures. A second type of withdrawal results in a cluster of symptoms referred to as delirium tremens [DTs]. During DTs, the possibility of life-threatening events such as heart failure, dehydration, or suicide may occur. Thus, hospitalization and medication are often recommended. Other symptoms which typically are associated with DTs include disorientation and confusion, fever, nightmares, profuse sweating, and hallucinations.

Dependence on alcohol is associated with tremendous economic burden; with a tremendous amount of human suffering for the individual and family members; with decline in work productivity, accidents on the job, and unemployment; with increased criminal behavior and violence; with motor vehicle accidents and other accidents associated with significant property damage and injury to others; and with physical, emotional, and cognitive difficulties for which societal supports may be required for many years (Leung, 1976; O'Donnell & O'Callaghan, 1997; Sher, 1991).

Inhalants

Since recorded history, mind-altering effects of inhaled substances have been known (Levinthal, 1996). Inhalation of fumes or burning substances has been linked to medical and religious ceremonies or rites as early as 3000 B.C. (Flournoy, 1974). Substances used as inhalants in present times are widely available and include such products as aerosol sprays, solvents, glues and other adhesives, typewriter correction fluid, permanent felt marker ink, gasoline, cleaning compounds and disinfectants, paints and paint thinners, fingernail polishes and polish removers, dry-cleaning products, a wide variety of other petroleum products, amyl nitrite, butyl nitrite, and nitrous oxide (Haverkos & Dougherty, 1988; Newell, Spitz, & Wilson, 1988; Sharp, Beauvais, & Spence, 1992; Siegel & Wason, 1992).

Inhalant abuse is rooted in psychological dependence rather than in physiological dependency (Oetting, Edwards, & Beauvais, 1988). Symptoms that have been associated with inhalant abuse include sneezing and sniffling; coughing and bad breath; nausea, vomiting, diarrhea and loss of appetite; headaches and dizziness; light sensitivity and irritated eyes; rash around the mouth; double vision; ringing in the ears; chest pains and cardiac arrhythmia; muscle and joint aches; slurred speech; muscle incoordination; hallucinations; euphoria, giddiness, and exhilaration (Flournoy, 1974; Fox & Forbing, 1992; Levinthal, 1996; Schuckit, 1989).

Toxic effects of inhalants vary considerably depending not only upon the inhalant drug but also upon accompanying compounds (which may not appear on the product label) (Levinthal, 1996; Maickel, 1988). Typically, inhalants act as CNS depressants (Flournoy, 1974). Inhalation of propane and butane have been linked to cardiac arrhythmia and death (Levinthal). Commonly, serious side-effects are linked to lack of oxygen or to hypoxia and asphyxiation. Freon has the unique effect of being so cold that it may actually freeze the larynx and throat upon contact. Prolonged use of inhalants has been linked to damage of the respiratory tract; cancer-related disorders (such as leukemia and Kaposi's sarcoma); peripheral nerve damage leading to muscular weakness and muscle atrophy; anemia; dysfunction of the cerebellum resulting in difficulties in movement and coordination; alterations in cardiovascular functioning and blood cell abnormalities; glaucoma; and cognitive damage resulting in confusion, disorientation, impaired judgment, inaccurate perceptions, and memory loss (Levinthal; Maickel). Some inhalants, specifically nitrous oxide, are believed to be associated with birth defects (Brodsky, 1985; Maickel).

Marijuana

Chinese writings five thousand years ago refer to marijuana (Levinthal, 1996). In the United States, marijuana was contained in medicines during the 1880s and became popular in the 1920s. Marijuana is composed of cured leaves, small stems, and flower clusters of the Cannabis sativa plant. The strength of marijuana is related to the type of plant as well as the conditions in which it is grown and the sex of the plant. Drying, curing, storage, and handling procedures also impact the potency of the final product (Gurley, Aranow, & Katz, 1998). The primary psychoactive ingredient in marijuana is delta-9-tetrahydrocannibinol or ∂-9-THC. Potency typically ranges from approximately 4-7% ∂-9-THC levels although some sinsemilla types of marijuana have ∂-9-THC levels that are as high as 14% (Gurley et al., 1998).

Acute effects of marijuana include reddening of eyes, cardiac acceleration, giddiness, feelings of euphoria, increased hunger, heightened sexual desire, perception of time elongation, impairments of attention and memory, and diminished ability to perform complex visual-motor skills. Marijuana can be administered in a number of ways, including eating it in foods (such as brownies and cookies), mixing it with clarified butter for use in foods, extracting it in teas, creating an alcohol-based tincture, and smoking it. Ingested marijuana tends to have a slower onset of action and a longer duration of effect than the smoked variety (Gurley et al., 1998).

Chronic use of marijuana does not produce physical dependence in moderate dosages (Levinthal, 1996), but physical dependence has been demonstrated with large doses (Jones & Benowitz, 1976). Only mild psychological dependence occurs for most users but a small number of marijuana users do become dependent upon daily use (Ray & Ksir, 1996). Marijuana smoking is thought to have carcinogenic effects similar to those resultant of tobacco smoking (Howlett, 1990). Although marijuana use has been commonly believed to result in amotivational syndrome (Fox & Forbing, 1992; McGothlin & West, 1968) and to serve as a gateway to the use of other drugs (Johnston, O'Malley, & Bachman, 1994), neither of these beliefs have been supported by research (Sommer, 1988). Medically, marijuana has been used with success to treat effects of glaucoma (Cohen, 1980); to reduce the effects of asthma, to control seizures, and for treatment of migraines (Gurley et al., 1998); and as an antiemetic agent (to reduce nausea) for persons undergoing chemotherapy or for individuals who have AIDS (Doblin & Kleiman, 1991; Grinspoon & Bakalar, 1993).

LSD and other Hallucinogens

Drugs referred to as hallucinogenics are most accurately described as resulting in states of altered awareness or perceptions rather than as being associated with hallucinations in the classic sense (Ray, 1996). Approximately four (Ray) or five (Levinthal, 1996) different types of hallucinogens exist, with each type having its own set of effects and specific neurotransmitters that it acts upon. Common subjective effects of hallucinogens include altered perceptions and an intermingling of senses or synesthesia, (e.g., colors are heard and sound waves are seen), visual distortions and perceptions of multilevel reality (e.g., seeing a chair and the molecules composing it), different and exaggerated appearances of objects or experiences such as an object melting or cutting an orange being experienced as tearing apart an animal, color enhancement, mental imagery, change in mood, disintegration in self boundaries, and the experience of altered time (Brown, 1972; Goode, 1989; Levinthal; Snyder, 1986). Considerable variation exists in the response to hallucinogens, both between individuals and in the same individual (Abraham, Aldridge, & Gogia, 1998).

Hallucinogens have no withdrawal effects (Abraham et al., 1998). Major risks of abuse of hallucinogens include "bad trips" (characterized by an adverse experience which may be associated with panic reaction and loss of emotional control) and flashbacks (in which the person reexperiences a bad trip when not using the substance). Unlike other hallucinogens, one, MDMA ("ecstasy") which is an amphetamine derivative that is related both to amphetamines and hallucinogens, has been associated with brain damage (Levinthal, 1996; Ray & Ksir, 1996). MMDA was patented in 1914 and returned as a designer drug in the late 1980s and early 1990s (Elk, 1996). MDMA is a white powder which is most commonly administered orally as a pill or capsule but it can also be administered intravenously or subcutaneously, by snorting, by smoking, and less frequently, as a suppository. Some of the psychoactive properties of MDMA (e.g., increased energy, euphoria, feelings of closeness to others, empathy and enhanced communication, and a need for intimacy) made it appealing as a potential therapeutic aid in psychotherapy. The hallucinogenic effects of MDMA are not as intense as those of other hallucinogens (e.g., LSD or mescaline), with hallucinations reported by users only 20% of the time.

LSD, lysergic acid diethylamide, is the best known hallucinogenic drug. LSD is synthetically derived from a fungus, ergot, that is present in molded rye and some other grains (Levinthal, 1996). Ergotism ("St. Anthony's fire") is believed to have occurred periodically during the Middle Ages when, due to famine, people baked bread from infected grain. One episode of ergotism in 944 A.D. is estimated to have resulted in 40,000 deaths (Mann, 1992). LSD affects brain receptors sensitive to serotonin. Although LSD is thought to be one of the most powerful psychoactive drugs known, it is believed not to produce either psychological or physical dependence (Goode, 1989; Levinthal). Although the possibility exists that birth defects may occur if ingested during pregnancy, LSD, contrary to some popular beliefs, does not cause panic or psychosis in otherwise mentally healthy individuals, does not increase creativity, does not damage chromosomes, and has not been scientifically linked to violent behavior. Flashbacks have been associated with LSD.

Caffeine

Western societies are so accepting of caffeine that it is used on a daily basis by more people than any other psychoactive drug (Kendler & Prescott, 1999; Ray, 1996). Caffeine is a member of a family of stimulant drugs called xanthines and is found in coffee, tea, chocolate, cola drinks, and several medications (Levinthal, 1996). Caffeine ingestion results in dilation of peripheral blood vessels and constriction of cerebral blood vessels, slight elevation in heart rate, and a bronchodilating effect. Caffeine excites neuronal activity in the brain, resulting in a feeling of mental alertness and lack of fatigue. While caffeine increases attentiveness and vigilance to low stimulus tasks, it has no effect or a deleterious effect on performance of complex tasks. With caffeine ingestion, a decrease in quality of sleep or difficulty in falling asleep may occur but these effects are lessened in chronically heavy caffeine users.

Data is inconclusive about the relationship between caffeine ingestion and cardiovascular functioning (Jick et al., 1973). Caffeine consumption has been associated with osteoporosis and bone fractures in elderly persons (Kiel, Felson, Hannan, Anderson, & Wilson, 1990), with infertility and with miscarriages, and with the onset of panic attacks in persons diagnosed with panic disorder.

Amphetamines and other Stimulants

Amphetamines are a group of psychoactive stimulants (Levinthal, 1996; Murray, 1998; Ray & Ksir, 1996) whose reasons for use and problems of abuse are very similar to those for cocaine. The origination of amphetamines has been traced to a Chinese medicinal herb that 5,000 years ago was used to treat asthma and respiratory problems. The first synthetic form was developed in 1927 for use in non-prescription inhalers. Abuse has occurred through oral use, by injection, and by inhalation.

Acute effects of amphetamines include increased sympathetic autonomic activity, decreased feelings of fatigue, feelings of euphoria, decreased sleepiness, increased confidence, decrease in depressive symptomology, decreased reaction time, and an increased threshold for pain perception (Levinthal, 1996; Ray & Ksir, 1996). Side effects may include restlessness, irritability, dry mouth, heart palpitations, increased speed of speech, muscle tremor, headaches, and nausea. Substantial evidence does not exist to substantiate the belief that brain damage occurs in humans associated with amphetamine abuse (Marek, 1990).

Amphetamines have been used successfully to treat narcolepsy and hyperactivity in children and for short-term weight reduction (Leung, 1976; Levinthal, 1996; Murray, 1998; Ray & Ksir, 1996). During World War II, amphetamines were used to increase efficiency of soldiers by Germany, in experiments on efficiency of soldiers by the United States, and to increase productivity of workers on the homefront by Japan (Benzedrine Alert, 1944; Hemmi, 1969; Kato, 1983; Ray & Ksir). However, research has indicated that while performance on some simple tasks may be improved by limited use of "smart pills" (amphetamines), performance on complex, difficult or both tasks is decreased (Ray & Ksir). Withdrawal from amphetamine use may include a physical and emotional "crash" resulting in prolonged sleep, depression, agitation, anxiety, inactivity, nightmares, headaches, cramps, tremors, and irritability.

Effects of chronic use of amphetamines include behavioral

fixations in which actions are repeated continually, elevated mood, feelings of power, tendencies toward violence, and amphetamine psychosis. Amphetamine psychosis is similar to paranoid schizophrenia and is characterized by paranoia, mood swings, impulsive behavior, hypersensitivity, delusions, and hallucinations persisting for weeks after the drug has been withdrawn (Ellinwood, 1971; Goode, 1989). Various behaviors of Hitler toward the end of World War II have been described as resultant of a disintegrating personality associated with heavy amphetamine abuse (Maser, 1971).

Tobacco

Tobacco was an essential ceremonial thread in North America's indigenous populations for centuries. "The compulsive use of tobacco has been observed in nearly every culture to which tobacco has been introduced" (Benowitz, 1998, p. 283). It was not until its introduction to Europe some 500 years ago that tobacco became considered unhealthy or socially undesirable, having lost its ceremonial purpose (Hartman, Caskey, Olmstead, & Jarvik, 1998). Only within the past 50 years have researchers begun to seriously investigate the deleterious effects of tobacco, including its highly addictive properties.

Nicotine is the primary reinforcing ingredient in tobacco and "is well established as one of the most toxic drugs known" (Ray & Ksir, 1996, p. 284). In addition to nicotine, cigarette smokers consume tar and carbon monoxide. Acute effects of smoking nicotine include an increase in metabolic rate, a slight increase in blood sugar level, deadening of taste buds, constriction of blood vessels of the skin, decrease in skin temperature, increase in blood pressure, decrease in oxygen-carrying ability of the blood, decrease in emotions and improved performance for a few minutes in sustaining attention to a task that required rapid processing of information from a computer screen (Gilbert, 1988; Wesnes, 1988). Cigarette smoking is linked to increased risk of heart disease, lung and other cancers, emphysema, chronic bronchitis, and stroke (Schlaadt, 1992). Pregnant women who smoke increase risks for obstetrical complications; for premature labor and delivery; for miscarriage and stillbirth, for growth retardation, low birth weight and neurological damage to the infant (Cook, Peterson, & Moore, 1990; Levinthal, 1996).

Dangers of secondary smoke indicate that nonsmokers are at risk (American Cancer Society, 1987). Nonsmoking wives of husbands who smoke have a 30% increased chance of having lung cancer in comparison of wives of nonsmokers. If the husband is a heavy smoker, the risk is two to three times greater. Children of a parent who smokes have increased chances of having chronic coughs and ear infections, of developing colds, and of acquiring asthma or bronchitis in comparison with children of non-smokers. Smokeless tobacco, including chewing tobacco and snuff, have been associated with increased risk of cancer of the oral cavity, pharynx, and esophagus; with gum disease; and with destruction of teeth enamel (NIH, 1986).

Barbiturates and Non-barbiturate Sedatives

Sedatives are drugs used to calm, to tranquilize, or to relax while hypnotics are drugs which are used to induce sleep (Levinthal, 1996; Ray & Ksir, 1996). Barbiturates represent a family of depressants which result in a sedative-hypnotic effect (Julien, 1995). Barbiturates were discovered by Adolf von Baeyer who also developed Bayer aspirin (Levinthal, 1996). Many different barbiturate drugs have been developed but all are almost tasteless and odorless and will induce sleep if the dosage is sufficient (Henningfield & Ator, 1986; Julien). Barbiturates have been used in the treatment of epilepsy since they slow down CNS activity. The length of time the depressant effect lasts is the primary basis for the classification of barbiturates as long-acting (six or more hours, e.g., phenobarbital or Luminal), intermediate (four to six hours, e.g., amobarbital or Amytal, Butabarbital or Butisol), or short-acting (less than four hours, e.g., Pentobarbital or Nembutal).

Tolerance and both physical and psychological dependence can develop with chronic use (Jacobs & Fehr, 1987); thus, barbiturates should be treated as highly addictive substances. A major consideration with barbiturate abuse is the potential of overdose, particularly if use is potentiated by combination with other depressants or alcohol (Jacobs & Fehr; Kauffman, Shaffer, & Burglass, 1985). Overdose of these depressant substances can result in inhibiting respiration to the point of death (Ray & Ksir, 1996), and the combination of barbiturates and alcohol have been used in many attempts to commit suicide (Palfai & Jankiewicz, 1991). Withdrawal from barbiturates needs careful management as withdrawal effects and symptoms can be severe and can result in death (Fraser, 1953; Sellers, 1988).

In the 1950s, drugs other than barbiturates, the benzodiazepines (which were referred to then as minor tranquilizers), began to become available for the treatment of anxiety (Palfai & Jankiewicz, 1991). Some benzodiazepines have been popular for the treatment of anxiety (e.g.,

Xanax, Librium, Valium, Ativan, Serax) and others for the treatment of sleep disorders (Restoril, Halcion). The most severe problem of misuse of benzodiazepines is their sedative hypnotic effects, including anterograde amnesia when given forcefully to someone as a "chemical knock out" in the preliminaries of intolerable or criminal behavior (Brinkmann, Kaplan, & Kauert, 1997). The benzodiazepines have proved to be less addictive than barbiturates and withdrawal symptoms are rarely as severe with benzodiazepines.

The benzodiazepines also are cross-tolerant with alcohol and other depressants. A newer type of antianxiety drug, Buspirone, shows less side-effects and no cross tolerance with alcohol or other depressants and no withdrawal symptoms (Lickey & Gordon, 1991). However, Buspirone has a long delay (several weeks) before relief from anxiety is experienced.

Opiates

The history of opioid use can be traced across major civilizations for approximately 8000 years (Uddo, Malow, & Sutker, 1993). The opiate drugs also are referred to as narcotics, whose Greek root means numbness. Opiates include a group of psychoactive drugs medically used for their analgesic (pain-reducing) effects. Opiates in general produce nausea and vomiting unless the user is accustomed to the drug. If heroin is injected, an immediate feeling of warmness in the lower abdomen and a feeling of intense euphoria, a "rush" results (Abel, 1985; Hofman, 1983). Next, a state of tranquil drowsiness ensues and is often referred to as being "on the nod." Other physiological changes which occur include a sudden release of histamine in the bloodstream resulting in red eyes and itching throughout the body, pupillary constriction, depression in breathing and blood pressure, and slowing down of the gastrointestional track, resulting in constipation. Effects of other opiates will vary in degree depending upon the specific drug, the amount and the method of administration, and the person's level of tolerance. Opiates produce physiological and psychological effects equivalent to those resultant of the body's own release of endorphins (Dum & Herz, 1984; Levinthal, 1988; Olsen, Olsen, Vaccarino, & Kastin, 1998).

Narcotics are used medically to relieve pain, for the treatment of acute diarrhea, and to suppress coughing (Hofman, 1983). Physical and psychological addiction as well as tolerance develops from chronic use. Opioid use also has been associated with antisocial lifestyle, enduring dysphoric mood states, and pathological mental and physical conditions (Uddo et al., 1993). Illness and death may be associated with street-purchased narcotics due to impurities, to the inability of effectively judging purity of the substance, and AIDS/HIV transmission associated with opioid injection.

Cocaine

Cocaine is an alkaloid derived from the leaves of the Erythroxylum plant found predominantly at high altitudes in Peru, Colombia, and Bolivia (Uddo et al., 1993). The Incas used coca to measure time and distance, describing a journey in terms of the mouthfuls of coca leaves that a person would need to chew to make the trip (Flynn, 1991). Cocaine is classified as a stimulant that is capable of inducing euphoric excitement and hallucinatory experiences (Leung, 1976). Upon initial use it produces an elevation in the sympathetic autonomic nervous system and a burst of energy. In the United States, several medicines and beverages were sold that contained cocaine, the most notable was the original formulation for Coca Cola (Uddo et al.). Routes of administration are intravenous injection, smoking, and intranasal. In some parts of South America, coca chewing is still prevalent among certain groups. In the mid 1980s as much as 90 percent of the male Peruvian population of the Andean highlands regularly chewed coca leaves (Jaffe, 1985). Smoking provides the most rapid delivery of cocaine to the brain.

Physical signs that accompany cocaine abuse include enlarged pupils, increased heart rate; increased irritability; insomnia; fatigue; decreased appetite, significant weight loss, and malnutrition; sexual dysfunction; and snorting, sneezing, and nose irritation (Levinthal, 1996; Uddo et al., 1993). Health risks include myocardial infarction, stroke, seizures, and psychotic episodes (Robinson, Heaton, & O'Malley, 1999). In addition, paranoia, depression, apathy, loss of interest in personal hygiene, participation in dangerous and unlawful behavior, and financial ruin have been associated with cocaine abuse (Uddo et al.). Cognitive impairments of memory, attention, or language abilities also have been documented with chronic cocaine abuse (Gillen et al., 1998). Although these impairments persist well beyond the period of acute withdrawal, the cognitive deficits associated with cocaine abuse appear to be relatively mild and more restricted than those reported for alcoholics.

Use of crack cocaine emerged in the 1980s. Crack cocaine is a smokable form of cocaine which exceeds the effects of cocaine which is snorted (Flynn, 1991). The effects of crack cocaine that is smoked are fast and powerful, resulting in, according to one author, "uncontrollable psychological dependence" (Levinthal, 1996, p. 97). Deep depression may accompany long-term cocaine use and excessive cocaine use can result in a paranoid psychotic state (Gawin, 1991). "Postcocaine anguish" has been described as a powerful motivator for people to continue abuse (Nuckols, 1989; Weiss & Mirin, 1987). An interactive effect between cocaine and alcohol (ethanol) produces a new drug, cocaethylene, which is more toxic than either substance alone (Randall, 1992).

Prescription Drug Abuse

Medicinal drugs may require prescriptions or may be sold over-the-counter [OTC] without prescription. Abuse of prescription medication is common, often including taking medication differently than prescribed, taking medication for different purposes than prescribed, and taking medications prescribed for other persons. Various substances mentioned earlier such as barbiturates, the benzodiazepines, amphetamines, and some narcotics may be obtained through prescription (Chabal, Erjavec, Jacobson, Mariano, & Chaney, 1997) but will not be rediscussed here. One type of medication which is of concern for abuse but has not been mentioned earlier is anabolic steroids.

Anabolic steroids have been listed as a Schedule III controlled substance, requiring more record-keeping and limiting prescription refills because of their potentials for abuse and for physical damage (Levinthal, 1996). Synthetic anabolics have been shown to have significant muscle-developing ability and thus have been sought by athletes. However, users risk liver damage and changes in blood lipids which may lead to atherosclerosis, high blood pressure, and heart disease. In addition, steroids may effect growth plates in the long bones thus limiting adult height of adolescent or child users.

Non-prescription Drug Abuse

Over-the-counter drugs are approved by the Federal Drug Administration for use when taken in recommended dosages. One common form of abuse involves taking these medications with other than the recommended dosages, for other than the described reasons, or in some manner that is not consistent with directions. Misuse of OTC analgesic drugs can present significant health risks (Conlan, 1992). Analgesic drugs include formulations with aspirin, ibuprofen, or acetaminophen. Misuse of aspirin may result in delayed clotting, gastrointestinal bleeding, an increase in the number of viruses present in cold sufferers, Reye's syndrome, or overdose poisonings. Acetaminophen has been associated with kidney and liver damage and ibuprofen with gastrointestinal problems. Sleep aids which contain either diphenhydramine or doxylamine succinate serve as CNS depressants and their effects may be potentiated by use of alcohol or other depressant drugs (Julien, 1995).

Cold and allergy products are commonly misused (Conlan, 1992). In particular, abuse of cough suppressants containing dextromethorphan, result in auditory and visual hallucinations, itching, nausea, and in some cases may be associated with seizures. OTC stimulants contain caffeine. OTC weight-control products contain phenylpropanolamine [PPA] and are prevented by the FDA from containing caffeine as the effects of ingestion of both PPA and caffeine have not been thoroughly studied. Concern is expressed about the stimulant effects of PPA upon persons with elevated blood pressure or cardiovascular disorders. Laxatives also are often abused and often persons with problems of constipation are cautioned against laxative abuse.

Models of Causation of Substance Abuse

A number of theories have been posited to explain the phenomenon of substance abuse; however, no single theoretical model fully explains why substance abuse occurs. The most widely known models of causation of substance abuse include the moral model, the medical model, the genetic model, the systems model, the behavioral model, the sociocultural model, and the biopsychosocial model. These seven models overlap in varying degrees in their attempts to clarify the etiology of substance abuse yet they are different in many ways. An overview of the therapeutic assumptions upon which each model is based is fundamental to understanding beliefs regarding the etiology of substance abuse.

The Moral Model

The moral model views substance abuse as the result of willful overindulgence and moral degradation (Erickson, 1998). Willpower and the desire to abstain are essential elements to overcoming substance abuse under the auspice of the moral model. Punishment is considered over treatment because a "cure" is considered unlikely. The moral model gained impetus during the Civil War when concern regarding heavy drinking arose in the United States. Figures of the church and conservative community members advocated that alcohol use was sinful, amoral, and intoloerable. Individuals with alcoholism and other substance abuse problems were essentially treated as social outcasts.

The Medical Model

The shift away from the moral was accompanied by the development of Alcoholics Anonymous (AA) in 1935 (Erickson, 1998). Although the philosophy of AA retained some elements of the moral model, including the belief that a "Higher Power" is needed to achieve sobriety, supporters of AA believed that individuals who engaged in alcohol abuse were not responsible for having the "disease" of alcoholism. In the 1950s, Jellinek defined alcoholism as a disease and developed the theory that alcoholism is caused by a physiological deficit in an individual that makes him/her unable to tolerate alcohol. Two key elements associated with the disease model are loss of control over the use of a substance and progression of the disease which ultimately results in death. According to the medical model, all individuals with substance abuse problems have the same disease and treatment is essentially the same for all who abuse alcohol and other drugs, regardless of the factors which precipitated the substance abuse. Supporters of the disease or medical model believe that abstinence is the only effective form of treatment for substance abuse and that individuals with substance abuse problems are responsible for seeking treatment. In addition, alcoholism and other substance abuses are treated in the same manner, without recognition for the complex factors which accompany polydrug use.

The Genetic Model

Proponents of the genetic model maintain that hereditary traits predispose certain individuals to substance abuse (Erickson, 1998). Intergenerational studies, twin studies, and adoption studies have been used to show that relatives of alcoholics have a substantially greater risk for alcoholism than nonalcoholics. Researchers have attempted to identify specific biochemical genetic markers that could indicate physiological differences between individuals who abuse alcohol and those who do not, including differing chemical breakdowns in the metabolism of ethanol. From the genetic perspective, alcoholism is considered a condition that arises from an imbalance in the brain's production of neurotransmitters responsible for metabolism of ethanol. Genetic predispositions to these imbalances make some people susceptible to developing alcohol abuse and addiction. Although children of alcoholic parents run a higher risk of developing alcoholism than children in the general population, genetic components of other types of substance abuse and addiction are less clear and, to date, research in this area is limited.

The Systems Model

Systems theorists look toward the family structure and family dynamics across generations to seek causative factors associated with substance abuse patterns (Erickson, 1998). The family systems theory views each family member in a synergistic manner, with each family member contributing to the family as a whole. Families of origin and the current family structure form a framework for perceptions of the roles one must play, one's place in the world, and the proper way to interact (Erickson, 1998). According to the systems model, viewing individuals who abuse substances in isolation of their family and the environment disregards the influences that others have on one's behavior. Achieving homeostasis within the family and making adjustments to maintain or restore equilibrium whenever it is threatened is a primary goal of the systems model. Individuals who abuse substances are described as being part of a family constellation in which substance abuse is a central theme around which the family is organized. Family changes occur when the substance is introduced into the family unit. Once the family assimilates the changes associated with the substance, these changes actually support the addiction or substance abuse.

The Behavioral Model

The behavioral model is imbedded in social learning theory (Erickson, 1998). Addictions are perceived as socially acquired, learned behaviors with multiple causes and effects. According to the behavioral model, substance abuse is seen as being influenced by past learning, reinforcement contingencies, biological make up, and cognitive processes. Although most behaviorists maintain that learning and contingencies are key elements relating to substance abuse and addiction, they do not discount the role of etiological factors such as genetics, sociocultural influences, and physiological conditions on predisposing a person to substance abuse. Supporters of the behavioral model posit that substance abuse occurs when an individual's coping abilities become overwhelmed. Thus, the abuse of substances is employed as a coping mechanism to counteract stressful situations yet the consequences of substance abuse in itself becomes increasingly stressful and leads to further substance abuse. Antecedents, including cognitive and emotional states, the time of day, the place in which drinking occurs, and association with certain people are considered to be important factors which can influence substance abuse. Addictive behavior is maintained by the rewarding aspects of drug consumption and the social setting. That is, the more pleasurable the experience of drug consumption and the greater the frequency of obtaining pleasurable experiences through drug consumption, the more likely that drugs will be consumed.

The Sociocultural Model

Sociocultural theorists emphasize social forces and cultural attitudes that influence substance abuse. Environmental support is considered to be an important factor contributing to substance abuse. Accordingly, the magnitude of social pressure in the development of substance abuse, particularly among adolescents is widely recognized (Erickson, 1998). Attitudes, tradition, and family values toward alcohol and other drugs varies across cultures and are viewed as largely impacting the amount and context in which consumption occurs. According to the sociocultural model, disruptive use of alcohol and other drugs tends to occur almost exclusively in social settings. Environmental factors which have been associated with increased substance abuse include single-parent households, urban ghettos, low socioeconomic status, limited educational opportunities, child abuse and neglect, and criminal activity. Societal trends also are considered to be important influences on substance use and abuse, with patterns and popularity of certain drugs changing over time. For example, throughout the 1960s and 1970s, marijuana, opiates, and psychedelic drugs were the drugs of choice. Cocaine was commonly used throughout the 1980s and crack cocaine has become a commonly used drug in the 1990s.

The Biopsychosocial Model

The biopsychosocial model views substance abuse as a complex, progressive behavior pattern that is influenced by biological, psychological, and social components (Erickson, 1998). This integrative model focuses on genetic factors which may predispose a person to substance abuse as well as a variety of mitigating sociocultural influences which can lead to the development of alcoholism and drug addiction. Psychological factors that may interact with genetic predispositions and sociocultural influences include personality traits, learned behaviors, and cognitive deficiencies that can influence substance abuse. Thus, all contributing factors in the development of substance abuse are considered within the biopsychosocial model.

Characteristics of the Individual and Society

Physiological Functioning of the User

Efforts to study physiological bases of substance abuse have been greatly hampered by the possible alterations in physiology as a result of chronic abuse of substances and unknown chemicals which may have been mixed with them; and as a result of lifestyles which may be composed of poor nutrition, poor exercise habits, poor sleeping habits, stress, general neglect, and sometimes violence and prostitution. To determine if altered physiology of the abuser is the result of pre-drug physiology or changes as a result of substance abuse itself is often impossible.

Using the Substance Abuse Subtle Screening Inventory (SASSI), Baker and Dooley (1998) concluded that college students with disabilities who took prescription medications on a regular basis were more likely to be identified as having substance abuse problems than were students with disabilities who were not regularly taking medications. They concluded that 50% of the college students with disabilities in their study had substance abuse problems.

Various authors have studied family history of drug disorders and have concluded that having a family member with a substance abuse problem constitutes a strong risk factor for developing a substance abuse disorder (Merikangas, Stolar, Stevens, Goulet, & Preisig, 1998). In a study of 3,516 twins from male-male pairs, the authors concluded that genetic factors played a major role in the development of alcoholism among males and that environmental factors in common for family members had little influence on whether males became alcoholic (Prescott & Kendler, 1999).

Another recently published study including 392 twin pairs, male and female, concluded that genetic influences were stronger for males than for females but existed for females and that genetic factors were linked to substance abuse,dependence or both, but not to substance use (van den Bree, Johnson, Neale, & Pickens, 1998). Some studies have also noted a correlation between alcoholism and neuropsychological impairment (Keenan, O'Donnell, Sinanan, & O'Callaghan, 1997).

Psychological Characteristics of the User

A purpose of a number of studies on substance abuse was to determine the foundation of the "addictive personality" that caused the person to continue to abuse a substance. Such research has lead to the conclusion that there is no one central personality characteristic that leads a person to addiction (Cox, 1986). Such studies have lead to the conclusion that personality may make some contribution to addiction but that it is not the sole cause of any addictive behavior to any particular substance.

A tendency has existed to demonize drugs and to attribute substance abuse to the drugs themselves. However, "Reinforcement is increasingly accepted as the real driving force behind drug addiction, (Ray & Ksir, 1996, p. 42) rather than the drugs, themselves. Some researchers have drawn conclusions about drugs that serve as "gateways" to abuse; drugs which are one of the first drugs used by an abuser. However, studies involving gateway drugs have typically used abusers only as subjects and failed to study subjects who used the "gateway" drug who did not proceed to abuse other drugs (Johnson, Gollub, & Fagan, 1995).

Many attempts have been made to study psychological characteristics of persons with substance abuse problems (Patalano, 1998). Such attempts are often complicated by studying persons after abuse occurs. If determination of pre-abuse psychological functioning is not made, then deciding what psychological characteristics laid a foundation for abuse and what psychological characteristics may be resultant of abuse is impossible.

Sociocultural Environment

Most of the information about drug use comes from large national surveys conducted in high schools or house-to-house (Ray & Ksir, 1996) or from DAWN, the Drug Abuse Warning Network. DAWN collects data from hospital emergency rooms and from medical examiners on drug-related crises and deaths.

Certain factors appear to be strong indicators for drug-taking behavior for youth (Goode, 1989; Newcomb, Maddahian, Skager, & Bentler, 1987). The strongest indicators for adolescents using drugs appear to reflect a tendency toward nonconformity with society. The more of the following characteristics that the young individual possesses, the more at risk for substance abuse that person may be

(a) attending school irregularly (not due to illness),
(b) having poor relationships with parents,
(c) getting into trouble,
(d) an early history of alcohol intoxication beginning at age 12 or earlier,
(e) the number of adults the youth knows that have drug problems,
(f) the degree to which peers approve of getting high on drugs, and
(g) generally low educational aspirations.

Parental abuse and economic hardship do not appear to correlate with substance abuse among adolescents (Fawzy, Coombs, Simon, & Bowman-Terrell, 1987) although some authors still indicate concerns about these as risk factors (Hanson & Carta, 1995). While other factors may affect beginning use of drugs, for persons who become addicted to a substance, increasingly the person's experience with the drug becomes central. Thus, the drug and its effects upon that individual become more important to continuing use than do social, cultural, or practical influences.

Drug-Classification

Depending upon needs, the conceptual basis for classification of drugs may vary. Thus, a variety of systems have been used for classifying drugs. Some common bases for classification have included: chemical structure, used frequently by biochemists; origin or source, often used by anthropologists, biologists and chemists; site or mechanism of action, as a means of determining or predicting physiological change; on the basis of their effects, yielding information for psychologists and human service providers interested in human behavior; and potential for abuse yielding significant information for treatment-oriented clinicians as well as for school, legal, justice, and law enforcement personnel and for parents and communities.

Under the Comprehensive Drug Abuse Prevention and Control Act of 1970, a classification system was legally adopted which attempted to organize drugs into five categories, referred to as schedules, based upon their potential for abuse (Levinthal, 1996). Schedule I included substances with a high potential for abuse and no acceptable medical use (e.g., heroin, LSD, marijuana, and mescaline) (*Physician's Desk Reference,* 1994). Schedule II contains substances with a high potential for abuse and some accepted medical use (e.g., codeine, morphine, cocaine, amphetamines, and short-acting barbiturates). Schedule III includes drugs with some potential for abuse and an accepted medical use (e.g., long-acting barbiturates and narcotic solutions such as paregoric or mixtures such as 1.8% codeine). Schedule IV contains drugs with a low potential for abuse and an accepted medical use (e.g., antianxiety drugs and sedativehypnotics such as Valium and Miltown). Schedule V contains drugs with minimal abuse potential and widespread medical use (e.g., laxatives and cough medications not containing codeine). Progressively more restrictions are placed upon drugs in moving up the classification system from Schedule V to Schedule I.

Not only have drugs and their effects been classified into categories, but the behaviors of individuals whose substance use is generally regarded as falling outside the range of appropriate, normal or both, also has been classified in the *Diagnostic and Statistical Manual of Mental Disorders, fourth edition (DSM-IV)* published by the American Psychiatric Association (1994). Substance-Related Disorders listed in the *DSM-IV* include disorders which are related to taking a drug of abuse, to the side effects of medication, and to toxin exposure. Substance-Related Disorders are divided into two groups, substance-use disorders and substance-induced disorders. Substances in the *DSM-IV* are grouped into 11 classes. The diagnostic categories related to substances in the *DSM-IV* are listed and discussed individually in Chapter 5 of this book.

Drug Regulation

Prior to the 1900s, the attitude toward drug addiction in the United States was one of laissez-faire, to allow people to do as they pleased (Brecher, 1972). Addiction of adults or children was not viewed with concern or scorn. Thus, regulation of drugs and drug use was not a concern. The two exceptions were movements to ban alcohol consumption and a strong opposition to the practice among some Chinese immigrants of smoking opium. Prior to the 1900s, cocaine was contained in coca-cola and in other beverages and medicines; opium prescriptions with multiple renewals were common; patent medicines contained large amounts of alcohol, opiates, and cocaine; morphine was readily available; and heroin was used to treat morphine addiction.

In 1906, the Pure Food and Drug Act was passed and required that food and drug manufactures list on the label the amounts of alcohol or habit-forming drugs contained in their products. The Harrison Act of 1914 was an attempt to regulate opiates and cocaine. It required that physicians, dentists, and veterinarians prescribe such drugs "in the course of their professional practice only." In 1920 The Eighteenth Amendment to the U.S. Constitution took effect, beginning the era of Prohibition which lasted for the next 13 years (Aaron & Musto, 1981). The Marijuana Tax Act of 1937 taxed growers, sellers, and buyers of marijuana (Brecher, 1972) . At that time, federal law did not make possession of marijuana illegal but state laws began to. Another notable law was the Comprehensive Drug Abuse and Prevention and Control Act of 1970 which was an attempt, as mentioned previously, to control and regulate drugs according to a ranking system based upon medical use and addiction potential (Levinthal, 1996). The 1970 Act also moved the Administration of Drug Enforcement from the Treasury Department to the Justice Department, ending efforts to regulate drug-taking through taxation.

Summary

Although the term, "drug" carries negative connotations, drugs, used correctly, have significant benefits to mankind. However, the misuse, abuse, overuse and illegal use of drugs results in a number of psychological, physical, and social problems. Information about drugs and their effects and about substance abuse may assist counselors in understanding and working with clients.

Drugs affect the human body in many different ways and

individual variations occur with any drugs. Healthy adult males under age 35 typically comprise the samples for which the effects of drugs are examined. Drugs have been used across the world for thousands of years; however, scientific exploration of the deleterious effects of drugs was not widely pursued until the past century. The effects of drug abuse and dependence vary, depending on the type of drug, polydrug use, and characteristics of the user. The influence of genetic, neurochemical, neurophysiological, psychological, sociocultural, and economic factors suggest that the etiology of substance abuse and dependence is multiply determined.

The Drug Abuse and Prevention Control Act was passed in 1970. The Act included the development of a drug classification system which was used to organize drugs based on their potentials for abuse. Because of the increased concern about social problems associated with substance abuse across America, beginning in the early 1900s, a number of laws designed to regulate and control drugs have been passed. Models explaining the causation of substance abuse have arisen and various classification systems for drugs, their effects and the behavior of persons abusing drugs have been developed.

An overview of characteristics of drugs commonly abused and their effects was presented in this chapter. Drugs included were: alcohol, inhalents, marijuana, LSD and other hallucinogens, caffeine, amphetamines and other stimulants, tobacco, barbiturates and non-barbiturate sedatives, opiates, cocaine, prescription drug abuse, and abuse of over-the-counter medications.

Information about drugs and about important aspects of substance abuse included in this chapter provides counselors with valuable perspectives that they can use to increase the effectiveness of their communications with clients and with others who work with or care about consumers and their families.

References

Aaron, P., & Musto, D. (1981). Temperance and prohibition in America: A historical overview. In M. H. Moore & D. R. Gerstein (Eds.), *Alcohol and public policy.* Washington, DC: National Academy Press.

Abel, E. L. (1985). *Psychoactive drugs and sex.* New York: Plenum Press.

Abraham, H. D., Aldridge, A. M., & Gogia, P. (1998). The pharmacology of hallucinogens. *Neuropsychopharmacology, 14,* 285-298.

American Cancer Society. (1987). *The smoke around you. The risks of involuntary smoking.* Author.

American Psychiatric Association. (1994). *Diagnostic and statistical manual of mental disorders* (4th ed.) (DSM-IV). Washington, D.C.: Author.

Baker, D. A., & Dooley, K. M. (1998). The relationship between the use of prescription medication and substance abuse in college students with disabilities. *Journal of Applied Rehabilitation Counseling, 29,* 18-21.

Becker, C. E., Roe, R. L., & Scott, R. A. (1979). *Alcohol as a drug: A curriculum on pharmacology, neurology, and toxicology.* Huntington, NY: Robert Krieger Publishing.

Benowitz, N. L. (1998). Pharmacology of nicotine. In R. E. Tarter, & R. T. Amerman (Eds.), *Handbook of substance abuse: Neurobehavioral pharmacology* (pp. 283-297). New York: Plenum Press.

Benzedrine Alert. (1944). *Air Surgeon's Bulletin, 1,* 19-21.

Blum, K. (1984). *Handbook of abusable drugs.* New York: Garden Press.

Brecher, E. M. and the editors of Consumer Reports. (1972). *Licit and illicit drugs.* Mount Bernon, NY: Consumers Union.

Brinkmann, R., Kaplan, C. D., & Kauert, G. (1997). Use, misuse, and abuse of benzodiazepines among polydrug addicts - therapeutic and health care implications. *Psychiatria Danubina, 9,* 153-158

Brodsky, J. B. (1985). Toxicity of nitrous oxide. In E.L. Eger, (Ed.), *Nitrous Oxide/N2O* (pp.259-280). New York: Elsevier.

Brown, F. C. (1972). *Hallucinogenic drugs.* Springfield, IO: Thomas, C.C.

Chabal, C., Erjavec, M. K., Jacobson, L., Mariano, A., & Chaney, E. (1997). Prescription opiate abuse in chronic pain patients: Clinical criteria, incidence, and predictors. *The Clinical Journal of Pain, 13,* 150-155.

Cohen, S. (1980). Therapeutic aspects. In R. C. Petersen (Ed.), *Marijuana research findings: 1980* (NIDA Research Monograph 31, pp. 199-221). Rockville, MD: National Institute on Drug Abuse.

Conlan, M. F. (1992). FDA can't keep track of OTCs, GAO charges in report. *Drug Topics,* March 23, 1992, pp. 58-60.

Cook, P. S., Petersen, R. C., & Moore, D. T. (1990). *Alcohol, tobacco, and other drugs may harm the unborn* (DHHS Publication No. [ADM] 90-1711). Washington DC: Office of Substance Abuse Prevention.

Cox, W. M. (1986). *The addictive personality.* New York: Chelsea House.

Doblin, R. E., & Kleiman, M. A. R. (1991). Marijuana as medicine: A survey of oncologists. In A. S. Trebach & K. B. Zeese, (Eds.), *New frontiers in drug policy* (pp. 242-245). Washington, DC: Drug Policy Foundation.

Dum, J., & Herz, A. (1984). Endorphinergic modulation of neural reward systems indicated by behavioral changes. *Pharmacology, Biochemistry, and Behavior, 21,* 259-266.

Elk, C. E. (1996). MDMA (Ecstacy): Useful information for health professionals involved in drug education programs. *Journal of Drug Education, 26,* 349-356.

Ellinwood, E. H. (1971). Assault and homicide associated with amphetamine abuse. *American Journal of Psychiatry, 127,* 90.

Erickson, S. (1998). Etiological theories of substance abuse. In P. Stevens-Smith & R. L. Smith (Eds.), *Substance abuse counseling: Theory and practice* (pp. 25-64). Columbus, OH: Prentice-Hall, Inc.

Fawny, F. L., Coombs, R. H., Simon, J. M., & Bowman-Terrell, M. (1987). Family composition, socioeconomic status, and adolescent substance use. *Addictive Behaviors, 12,* 79-83.

Flournoy, R. L. (1974). Some observations on solvent inhalation as a form of drug abuse. *Introspect, 4,* 1-2.

Flynn, J. C. (1991). *Cocaine: An in-depth look at the facts, science, history, and future of the world's most addictive drug.* New York: Birch Lane/Carol Publishing.

Fox, C. L., & Forbing, S. E. (1992). *Creating drug-free schools and communities: A comprehensive approach.* New York: Harper Collins.

Fraser, H. F. (1953). Death due to withdrawal of barbituates. *Annals of Internal Medicine, 38,* 1319-1325.

Gawin, F. H. (1991). Cocaine addiction: Psychology and neurophysiology. *Science, 251,* 1580.

Gilbert, O. G. (1988). Paradoxical tranquilizing and emotion reducing effects of nicotine. *Psychological Bulletin, 86,* 643-662.

Gillen, R. W., Kranzler, H.R., Bauer, L. O., Burleson, J. A., Samarel, D., & Morrison, D. J. (1998). Neuropsychologic findings in cocaine-dependent outpatients. *Progress in Neuro-Psychopharmacology & Biological Psychiatry, 22,* 1061-1076.

Goode, E. (1989). *Drugs in American society* (3rd ed.). New York: McGraw-Hill.

Grinspoon, L., & Bakalar, J. B. (1993). *Marijuana, the forbidden medicine.* New Haven, CT: Yale University Press.

Gurley, R. J., Aranow, R., & Katz, M. (1998). Medicinal marijuana: A comprehensive review. *Journal of Psychoactive Drugs, 30,* 137-147.

Hanson, M. J., & Carta, J. J. (1995). Addressing the challenges of families with multiple risks. *Exceptional Children, 62,* 210-212.

Hartman, N., Caskey, N. H., Olmstead, R. E., & Jarvik, M. E. (1998). Nicotine cravings and psychiatric diagnosis: Past, present, and future. *Psychiatric Annals, 28,* 547-551.

Haverkos, H. W., & Dougherty, J. S. (Eds.) (1988). *Health hazards of nitrite inhalants* (NIDA Research Monograph 83). Rockville, MD: National Institute on Drug Abuse.

Hemmi, T. (1969). How we have handled the problem of drug abuse in Japan. In F. Sjoqvist & M. Tottie (Eds.). *Abuse of central stimulants.* New York: Raven Press.

Henningfield, J. E., & Ator, N. A. (1986). *Barbiturates: Sleeping potion or intoxicant?* New York: Chelsea House.

Hofman, F. G. (1983). *A handbook of drug and alcohol abuse: The biomedical aspects.* New York: Oxford University Press.

Howlett, A. C. (1990). The cannabinoid receptor: Biochemical, anatomical and behavioral characterization. *Trends in Neuroscience, 13,* 420-423.

Jacobs, M. R., & Fehr, K. O. (1987). *Drugs and drug abuse: A reference text* (2nd ed.). Toronto: Addiction Research Foundation.

Jaffe, J. (1985). Drug addiction and drug abuse. In L. S. Goodman and A. Gilman (Eds.), *The pharmacological basis of therapeutics* (7th ed., pp. 552-555). New York: Macmillan.

Jick, H., Miettinen, O. S., Neff, R. K., Shapiro, S., Heinonen, O., & Slone, D. (1973). Coffee and myocardial infarction. *New England Journal of Medicine, 289,* 63-67.

Johnson, B. D., Golub, A., & Fagan, J. (1995). Careers in crack, drug use, drug distribution, and nondrug criminality. *Crime & Delinquency, 41,* 275-295.

Johnston, L. D., O'Malley, P. M., & Bachman, J. G. (1994). *National survey results on drug use from the monitoring the future study, 1985-1993,* (Vol. 1). Rockville, MD: National Institute on Drug Abuse.

Jones, R. T., & Benowitz, N. (1976). The 30-day trip-clinical studies of cannabis tolerance and dependence. In M. C. Braude & S. Szara (Eds.) (pp. 627-742). *Pharmacology of marijuana.* New York: Raven Press.

Julien, R. M. (1995). *A primer of drug action* (7th ed.). New York: Freeman.

Kato, M. (1983). A bird's eye view of the present state of drug abuse in Japan. *Drug and Alcohol Dependency 11,* 55-56.

Kauffman, J. F., Shaffer, H., & Burglass, M. E. (1985). The biological basics: Drugs and their effects. In T. E. Bratter & G. G. Forrest (Eds.), *Alcoholism and substance abuse: Strategies for clinical intervention* (pp. 107-136). New York: Free Press.

Keenan, E., O'Donnell, C., Sinanan, K., & O'Callaghan, E. (1997). Severity of alcohol dependence and its relationship to neurological soft signs, neuropsychological impairment and family history. *Acta Psychiatrica Scandinavica, 95,* 272-276.

Kendler, K. S., & Prescott, C. A. (1999). Caffeine intake, tolerance, and withdrawal in women: A population-based twin study. *American Journal of Psychiatry, 156,* 223-228.

Kiel, D. P., Felson, D. T., Hannan, M. T., Anderson, J. J., & Wilson, P. W. F. (1990). Caffeine and the risk of his fracture: The Framingham study. *American Journal of Epidemiology, 132,* 675-684.

Leung, P. (1976). *Problems of drug abuse.* Tucson, AZ: University of Arizona Division of Continuing Education.

Levinthal, C. F. (1988). *Messengers of paradise: Opiates and the brain.* New York: Doubleday.

Levinthal, C. F. (1996). *Drugs, behavior, and modern society.* Needham Heights, MA: Allyn & Bacon.

Lickey, M. E., & Gordon, B. (1991). *Medicine and mental illness.* New York: Freeman.

Maickel, R. P. (1988). The fate and toxicity of butyl nitrites. In H.W. Haverkos & J. A. Dougherty (Eds.). *Health hazards of nitrite inhalants.* (NIDA Research Monograph 83, pp. 16-20). Rockville, MD: National Institute on Drug Abuse.

Mann, J. (1992). *Murder, magic, and medicine,* New York: Oxford University Press.

Marek, G. J. (1990). Dopamine uptake inhibitors block long-term neurotoxic effects of methamphetamine upon dopaminergic neurons, *Brain Research, 513,* 274.

Maser, W. (1971). *Adolf Hitler: Legend, myth, and reality.* New York: Harper and Row.

McGothlin, W. H., & West, L. J. (1968). The marijuana problem: An overview. *American Journal of Psychiatry, 125,* 372.

Merikangas, K. R., Stolar, M., Stevens, D. E., Goulet, J., Preisig, M. A., Fenton, B., Zhang, H., O'Malley, S. S., & Rounsaville, B. J. (1998). Familial transmission of substance use disorders. *Archives of General Psychiatry, 5,* 973-979.

Murray, J. B. (1998). Psychophysiological aspects of Amphetamine-Methamphetamine abuse. *Journal of Psychology, 132,* 227-237.

Newcomb, M. D., Maddahian, E., Skager, R., & Bentler, P. M. (1987). Substance abuse and psychological risk factors among teenagers: Associations with sex, age, ethnicity, and type of school. *American Journal of Drug and Alcohol Abuse, 13,* 413-433.

Newell, G. R., Spitz, M. R., & Wilson, M. B. (1988). Nitrite inhalants: Historical perspective. In H. W. Haverkos & J. A. Dougherty (Eds.). *Health hazards of nitrite inhalants,* (NIDA Research Monograph 83). Rockville, MD: National Institute on Drug Abuse.

National Institute of Health. (1986). The health consequences of using smokeless tobacco: A report of the advisory committee to the Surgeon General, NIH Pub No 86-2874. Washington DC: U. S. Government Printing Office.

Nuckols, C. C. (1989). *Cocaine: From dependency to recovery* (2nd ed.). Blue Ridge Summit, PA: Tab Books.

O'Donnell, E. K., & O'Callaghan, K. S. (1997). Severity of alcohol dependence and its relationship to neurological soft signs, neurological impairments, and family history. *Acta Psychiatry Scandinavia, 95,* 272-276.

Oetting, E. R., Edwards, R. W., & Beauvais, F. (1988). Social and psychological factors underlying inhalant abuse. In R. A. Crider & B. A. Rouse (Eds.), *Epidemiology of inhalant abuse: An update* (NIDA Research Monograph 85, pp. 172-203). Rockville, MD: National Institute on Drug Abuse.

Olsen, G. A., Olsen, R. D., Vaccarino, A. L. & Kastin, A. J. (1998). *Endogenous opiates: 1997. Peptides, 19,* 1791-1843.

Palfai, T., & Jankiewicz, H. (1991). *Drugs and human behavior.* Dubuque, IA: W. C. Brown.

Parsons, O. A. (1996). Alcohol abuse and alcoholism. In R. L. Adams, & O. A. Parsons (Eds.). *Neuropsychology for Clinical Practice: Etiology, Assessment, and treatment of Common Neurological Disorders.*

Patalano, F. (1998). Cross-cultural similarities in the personality dimensions of heroine users. *The Journal of Psychology, 132,* 671-673.

Payne, W. A., & Hahn, D. B. (1992). *Understanding your health* (3rd ed.). St Louis: Times Mirror Mosby.

Physician's Desk Reference. (1994). Oradell, N.J.: Medical Economics Company.

Prescott, C. A., & Kendler, K. S. (1999). Genetic and environmental contributions to alcohol abuse and dependence in a population based sample of twins. *American Journal of Psychiatry, 156,* 34-40.

Randall, T. (1992). Cocaine, alcohol mix in body to form even longer lasting, more lethal drug. *Journal of the American Medical Association, 267,* 1043.

Ray, O., & Ksir, C. (1996). *Drugs, society, & human behavior* (7th ed.). St. Louis: Mosby.

Robinson, J. E., Heaton, R. K., & O'Malley, S. S. (1999). Neuropsychological functioning in cocaine abusers with and without alcohol dependence. *Journal of International Neuropsychological Society, 6,* 10-19.

Schlaadt, R. G. (1992). *Tobacco and health.* Guilford, CT: Dushkin Publishing.

Schuckit, M. S. (1989). *Drug and alcohol abuse: A clinical guide to diagnosis and treatment* (3rd Ed.). New York: Plenum Medical Book Co.

Seixas, F. A. (1975). Alcohol and its drug interactions. *Annals of Internal Medicine. 83,* 86-92.

Sellers, E. M. (1988). Alcohol, barbiturate and benzodiazepine withdrawal syndromes: Clinical Management. *Canadian Medical Association Journal, 139,* 113-120.

Serdula, M., Williamson, D. F., Kendrick, J. A., Anda, R. F., & Byers, T. (1991). Trends in alcohol consumption by pregnant women. *Journal of the American Medical Association, 265,* 876-879.

Sharp, C. W., Beauvais, F., & Spence, R. (Eds.). (1992). *Inhalent abuse: A volatile research agenda* (NIDA Research Monograph 129). Rockville, MD: National Institute on Drug Abuse.

Sher, K. J. (1991). *Children of alcoholics: A critical appraisal of theory and research.* Chicago: University of Chicago Press.

Siegel, E., & Wason, S. (1992). Sudden sniffing death following inhalation of butane and propane: Changing trends. In C. N. Sharp, F. Beauvais, & R. Spence (Eds.), *Inhalent abuse: A volatile research agenda* (NIDA Research Monograph 129, pp.193-201). Rockville, MD: National Institute on Drug Abuse.

Sommer, R. (1988). Two decades of marijuana attitudes: The more it changes, the more it is the same. *Journal of Psychoactive Drugs, 20,* 67-70.

Synder, S. H. (1986). *Drugs and the brain.* New York: Freeman.

Uddo, M., Malow, R. M., & Sutker, P. B. (1993). Opioid and cocaine abuse and dependence disorders. In P. B. Sutker (Ed.). *Comprehensive handbook of psychopathology* (2nd ed., pp. 477-503). New York: Platinum Press.

van den Bree, M. B. M., Johnson, E. O., Neale, M. C., & Pickens, R. W. (1998). Genetic and environmental influences on drug use and abuse/dependence in male and female twins. *Drug and Alcohol Dependence, 52,* 231-241.

Victor, M. (1976). Treatment of alcohol intoxication and the withdrawal syndrome: A critical analysis of the use of drugs and other forms of therapy. In P. G. Bourne (Ed.), *Acute drug abuse emergencies: A treatment manual* (pp. 197-228). New York: Academic Press.

Weiss, R. D., & Mirin, S. M. (1987). *Cocaine.* Washington DC: American Psychiatric Press.

Wesnes, K. (1988). Nicotine increases mental efficiency: But how? In W. R. Martin (Ed.), *Tobacco smoking and nicotine: A neurobiological approach.* New York: Plenum Press.

Chapter 3

Related Addictive Disorders

Tina Buck & Amos Sales

Introduction

The term "addiction" has taken on a broader meaning in western culture since the founding of Alcoholics Anonymous (AA) in 1935. From that date to present, numerous self-help recovery groups have evolved to assist individuals in dealing with various addictive disorders and issues other than alcohol or drugs. Examples include church-related support groups, Overeaters Anonymous, Bulimorexics Anonymous, Sex Addicts Anonymous, Co-Sex Addicts Anonymous, Sex and Love Addicts Anonymous, Gamblers Anonymous, Gamanon, Workaholics Anonymous, and Debtors Anonymous. Yalom (1995) reports from a 1991 Gallup Poll that 40% of the United States population, age 18 and over, is seeking therapeutic help through these types of self-help groups. Terms from these self-help groups have become common household terms and are regularly used by the media. Treatment centers have expanded to treat these other addictive processes, often referred to as "process addictions" (Donovan, 1988). A legitimate concern is that the term "addiction" has become overused and limits human potential through labeling and deferring responsibility.

Addictions related to substance addictions can be identified when individuals exhibit behaviors typically associated with addiction as follows: (1) preoccupation with the substance or activity; (2) withdrawal symptoms after not engaging with substance or activity; (3) increased tolerance for the substance or activity in order to achieve the same effect; and (4) continued use despite negative consequences. What are often misunderstood and disregarded are the incredible suffering and negative consequences of individuals, their loved ones, and society due to related addictive disorders. Therefore, counselors need to broaden their beliefs and perceptions regarding substance abuse to include behavioral addictions along the same continuum as substance abuse: experimentation to severe addiction. The purpose of this chapter is to provide an overview of the related behavior or process addictions most commonly represented in current literature and addressed in treatment. Diagnostic tools and other resources for counseling clients with behavior addiction issues will be addressed. Characteristics of eating disorders, compulsive gambling, sex addiction, and work addiction will be discussed and related diagnostic and treatment considerations identified.

For most addictions, the *Diagnostic and Statistical Manual, Fourth Addition (DSM-IV)* (APA, 1994) assessment criteria have been included, as it is the best resource for making an accurate assessment. The DSM-IV provides scales and questionnaires to assist in the diagnostic process, and some additional scales and questionnaires are included later in the chapter. It is possible that an individual's relationship or attachment to almost any activity or substance can become an addiction. Simple activity is not an addiction. One must look at the individual situation and make appropriate assessments of the biological, psychological, and sociocultural factors of each client. Assessments need to include ruling out psychiatric disorders such as bipolar disorder, depression, anxiety disorders, obsessive-compulsive disorder, obsessive-compulsive personality disorder, and other personality disorders. It is important to assess and to treat the whole person, or body/mind/spirit/environment/relationship aspects as they relate to the addictive process.

Eating Disorders

The three areas of eating disorders that will be covered in this chapter are anorexia nervosa, bulimia nervosa, and binge eating disorder. Research indicates that cultural expectations about body image, increase of body fat during puberty (Swarr & Richards, 1996), and relationships in early adolescence (Cauffman & Steinberg, 1996) are factors contributing to eating disorders. Studies show that 1% of all adolescent girls develop anorexia nervosa and 2%-3% develop bulimia nervosa (National Institute of Mental Health, 1996). Most individuals begin engaging in disordered eating behavior during adolescence, and the number of persons with anorexia nervosa and bulimia nervosa decreases with age. Self-esteem and self-worth are closely linked to body image, and depression is often present in individuals who are continually dissatisfied with their body image perceptions. Characteristics of persons with eating disorders include denial, control, manipulation, compulsive behaviors, sense of powerlessness, and obsessive thought patterns (National Institute of Mental Health, 1996). Cultural aspects of body image as well as level of acculturation with individuals from different ethnic populations are considerations. Le Grange, Stone, and Brownell (1998) report differences between White, Black, Asian, and Hispanic women: "More Black women were overweight and purged compared to the other groups. Asian women valued the beneficial role of exercise in weight control more, while Black women were more inclined to attribute weight gain to cravings and slow metabolism" (p. 1). History of sexual abuse is associated with eating disorders in one study (Deep et al., 1998): 23% of subjects with anorexia nervosa reported some form of sexual abuse in their history, as compared to 7% of controls. Also reported was that 65% of subjects with bulimia nervosa had substance abuse issues. Other risk factors for development of eating disorders include emotionally distant parental relationships (Swarr & Richards, 1996), excessive focus on body image through sports or modeling, and various forms of abuse and trauma.

Anorexia Nervosa

How thin is too thin? Our cultural expectations of beauty, youth, and "superwoman" traits are factors associated with the onset of anorexia nervosa, the delusional control of body weight and body image. It is estimated that 0.5% to 1% of the U.S. population meet the *DSM-IV* criteria for anorexia and that less than 10% with this disorder are male (APA, 1994). Some of the symptoms associated with anorexia are restrictive eating patterns, preoccupation with body weight and image and distorted body image, use of exercise and stimulant drugs to control body weight, and extreme fear of becoming obese. Clients with anorexia nervosa may engage in an obsession about body parts which they consider "fat", especially buttocks, abdomen, and thighs (APA, 1994). Physical symptoms associated with anorexia nervosa include emaciated physical appearance, electrolyte imbalance, amenorrhea, malnutrition, anemia, cardiac imbalances, physical sensitivity to cold, and general physical weakness.

The following are the *DSM-IV* criteria for Anorexia Nervosa (APA, 1994):

A. Refusal to maintain body weight at or above a minimally normal weight for age and height (e.g., weight loss leading to maintenance of body weight less than 85% of that expected; or failure to make expected weight gain during period of growth, leading to body weight less than 85% of that expected).
B. Intense fear of gaining weight or becoming fat, even though underweight.
C. Disturbance in the way in which one's body weight or shape is experienced, undue influence of body weight or shape on self-evaluation, or denial of the seriousness of the current low body weight.
D. In postmenarcheal females, amenorrhea, i.e., the absence of at least three consecutive menstrual cycles. (A woman is considered to have amenorrhea if her periods occur only following hormone, e.g., estrogen, administration.)

Specify type:

Restricting Type: during the current episode of Anorexia Nervosa, the person has not regularly engaged in binge-eating or purging behavior (i.e., self-induced vomiting or the misuse of laxatives, diuretics, or enemas)

Binge-Eating/Purging Type: during the current episode of Anorexia Nervosa, the person has regularly engaged in binge-eating or purging behavior (i.e., self-induced vomiting or the misuse of laxatives, diuretics, or enemas) (p. 544)

Bulimia Nervosa

Prevalence of bulimia is reported in the *DSM-IV* as 1 to 3% of young adults (APA, 1994). As compared to persons with anorexia, bulimia often presents in a more "normal" body weight range. Clients with bulimia will eat small to very large amounts of food followed by self-induced vomiting. Other forms of purging include use of laxatives, diuretics, enemas, and excessive exercise. A person with bulimia may use one or any combination of these purging techniques, and these may change over time. They can develop financial concerns due to the amount of money they spend on food as well as get into legal trouble by shoplifting or writing bad checks for food. Symptoms of bulimia include lengthy time spent in bathrooms, dental problems, teeth marks on the back of hands, rapid weight gain or loss, chronic sore throat, and depression.

The following are the *DSM-IV* criteria for Bulimia Nervosa (APA,

1994):

A. Recurrent episodes of binge eating. An episode of binge eating is characterized by both of the following:

(1) eating, in a discrete period of time (e.g., within any 2-hour period), an amount of food that is definitely larger than most people would eat during a similar period of time and under similar circumstances

(2) a sense of lack of control over eating during the episode (e.g., a feeling that one cannot stop eating or control what or how much one is eating)

B. Recurrent inappropriate compensatory behavior in order to prevent weight gain, such as self-induced vomiting; misuse of laxatives, diuretics, enemas, or other medications; fasting; or excessive exercise.

C. The binge eating and inappropriate compensatory behaviors both occur, on average, at least twice a week for 3 months.

D. Self-evaluation is unduly influenced by body shape and weight.

E. The disturbance does not occur exclusively during episodes of Anorexia Nervosa.

Specify type:

Purging Type: during the current episode of Bulimia Nervosa, the person has regularly engaged in self-induced vomiting or the misuse of laxatives, diuretics, or enemas

Non-purging Type: during the current episode of Bulimia Nervosa, the person has used other inappropriate compensatory behaviors, such as fasting or excessive exercise, but has not regularly engaged in self-induced vomiting or the misuse of laxatives, diuretics, or enemas. (p. 549)

Binge Eating Disorder

By itself, compulsive overeating is not represented as a psychiatric disorder in the *DSM-IV*. Compulsive overeating can appear to be similar to substance addictions including symptoms such as secretiveness, isolation or both, while engaging in the behavior, inability to control behavior despite negative consequences and repeated attempts to gain control, obsession about the substance (food), social plans arranged around eating behaviors, and medical consequences. Clients with obesity do not necessarily engage in compulsive overeating and may have medical conditions that contribute to, or precede obesity. There are other forms of eating disorders along a continuum from overeating to starvation and counselors are advised to be familiar with different types.

The following are the *DSM-IV* criteria for Eating Disorder Not Otherwise Specified (APA, 1994):

> The Eating Disorder Not Otherwise Specified category is for disorders of eating that do not meet the criteria for any specific Eating Disorder. Examples include:
>
> 1. For females, all of the criteria for Anorexia Nervosa are met except that the individual has regular menses.
> 2. All of the criteria for Anorexia Nervosa are met except that, despite significant weight loss, the individual's current weight is in the normal range.
> 3. All of the criteria for Bulimia Nervosa are met except that the binge eating and inappropriate compensatory mechanisms occur at a frequency of less than twice a week or for a duration of less than 3 months.
> 4. The regular use of inappropriate compensatory behavior by an individual of normal body weight after eating small amounts of food (e.g., self-induced vomiting after the consumption of two cookies).
> 5. Repeatedly chewing and spitting out, but not swallowing, large amounts of food.
> 6. Binge-eating disorder: recurrent episodes of binge eating in the absence of the regular use of inappropriate compensatory behaviors characteristic of Bulimia Nervosa. (p. 550)

Treatment

It is important for counselors to be aware of the physical consequences of active eating disorders that can be significant and often require medical attention. Some physical consequences of anorexia and bulimia nervosa include problems with kidneys, liver, stomach, intestines, and heart; esophageal tears, swelling of parotid glands, dental problems, electrolyte imbalances, low potassium, malnutrition, anemia, dizziness and lightheadedness, thinning of hair, dry skin, sensitivity to cold, growth of fine body hair, amenorrhea, anxiety, depression, and increased risk for suicide. Physical consequences of compulsive overeating include obesity, stress on all major organs, stress on lower extremities, high cholesterol, diabetes, sleep apnea, anxiety, and depression. Surgical procedures such as liposuction, plastic surgery, and stomach staples may be used by persons with any type of eating disorder as a form of self-mutilation as compared to appropriate medical care.

When working with clients who engage in eating disorders, counselors can benefit from collaboration with other health care providers on behalf of the client. A treatment team can include a physician, psychiatrist, and nutritionist, who specialize in eating disorders and who utilize compatible approaches to treatment. Rigidity about meal planning is not necessarily a healthy goal of treatment. An excellent assessment tool for eating disorders is the Eating Disorder Inventory 2 (EDI-2) (Western Psychological Services, 800-648-8857). For information regarding national certification for eating disorders, or other resources related to eating disorders, contact the International Association for Eating Disorders Professionals at 800-800-8126 or www.iaedp.com. Group support is important; however, it is important to recognize that specifically with eating disorders, referral to a 12-step program such as Overeaters Anonymous or Bulimorexics Anonymous is not always a good option because of mixed reactions to control and shame issues related to eating patterns for some individuals. For information on alternative non-12-step based support, a resource is Mirasol which can be contacted at 888-520-1700 or www.edrecovery.com. Another resource for information about eating disorders is *The Eating Disorder Sourcebook* (Costin, 1996).

Gambling

There has been an increase in gambling over the past 20 years with increased availability of casinos, state lotteries, and internet gambling sites. This trend will likely continue as states become reliant on gambling revenue from multiple sources. An estimated 1 to 2% of adults have gambling addictions that range from problematic to pathological (Lesieur, & Blume, 1993), with higher rates in states that have legalized gambling. Estimates of gambling among high school and college students range from 4 to 6% (Lesieur & Blume, 1993).

Pathological gamblers report feeling a "rush" while engaging in the "action" of gambling and may be oblivious to physical needs or social obligations while engaged in "action". This "rush" is associated with an increase of adrenaline and norepinephrine levels (Lesieur & Blume, 1993). Over half of gamblers report withdrawal symptoms (Shaffer, et al., 1989). Consequences of gambling are especially notable in financial loss, incarceration, stress related illness and depressive episodes with suicide ideation and attempts (Lesieur, & Blume, 1993). To get themselves out of trouble, pathological gamblers may turn to family members for "bailout" measures when they have exhausted all resources. Pathological gamblers have distorted thinking and may have superstitions that provide them with confidence for success. They believe that "...money is both the cause of and solution to all their problems" (APA, 1994, p. 616).

Lewis (1994) describes five factors associated with gambling:

(1) external locus of control;
(2) alternating periods of extreme confidence and extreme self-devaluation including polarized mood swings;
(3) underlying personality disorders including Antisocial Personality Disorder and Narcissistic Personality Disorder;
(4) preference for immediate gratification; and
(5) difficulty with intimacy in relationships.

Alcoholism and eating disorders also can be closely linked to pathological gambling (Lesieur, & Blume, 1993) and each of these addictions may interface with a stimulus, or "trigger", to engage in other addictions. Clearly, some of the symptoms of each also overlap, which can create difficulty in assessment and treatment of persons with combined disorders. The South Oaks Gambling Screen (SOGS) is a widely used scale to assist in assessment of gambling addiction (Leisier & Blume, 1988). The Gamblers Anonymous 20 questions are also a useful tool for assessment.

There are different types of gambling such as the following: casino, horse and dog track, stock market, commodities, sports betting, lottery, internet games, private card games, dice games, cockfights, as well as gaming practices in various ethnic groups. Gamblers may be engaged in a sub-culture complete with unique linguistics, rituals, and customs (Ocean & Smith, 1993). Symptoms of active gambling are secretiveness and excessive time with phone calls and internet access, unaccounted time away from work or home, unexplained preoccupation, increased debt and worry over finances, extravagant expenditures, and increased alcohol, drug consumption, or both.

The following are the *DSM-IV* criteria for Pathological Gambling (APA, 1994):

A. Persistent and recurrent maladaptive gambling behavior as indicated by five (or more) of the following:

(1) is preoccupied with gambling (e.g., preoccupied with reliving past gambling experiences, handicapping or

planning the next venture, or thinking of ways to get money with which to gamble)

(2) needs to gamble with increasing amounts of money in order to achieve the desired excitement

(3) has repeated unsuccessful efforts to control, cut back, or stop gambling

(4) is restless or irritable when attempting to cut down or stop gambling

(5) gambles as a way of escaping from problems or of relieving a dysphoric mood (e.g., feelings of helplessness, guilt, anxiety, depression)

(6) after losing money gambling, often returns another day to get even ("chasing" one's losses)

(7) lies to family members, therapist, or others to conceal the extent of involvement with gambling

(8) has committed illegal acts such as forgery, fraud, theft, or embezzlement to finance gambling

(9) has jeopardized or lost a significant relationship, job, or educational or career opportunity because of gambling

(10) relies on others to provide money to relieve a desperate financial situation caused by gambling

B. The gambling behavior is not better accounted for by a Manic Episode (p. 218)

Treatment

Most of the initial treatment issues of compulsive gamblers are related to financial matters. Because the use of money is a daily experience, clients will need to be provided the structure and support to develop a new relationship to money. They will need to develop a financial plan including restitution, if needed. Additionally, providing structure for each day and cognitive restructuring for sensory stimulation that triggers compulsive urges would benefit the client. Gamblers Anonymous and Debtors Anonymous are resources for group support and can be found in most communities. The National Council on Problem Gambling can be contacted for information on state or national certification for counselors wishing to specialize in this area as well as for information on a wide range of gambling issues at 800-522-4700 or www.ncpgambling.org. Another resource for more information about problem gambling is Pathological Gambling: Conceptual, Diagnostic, and Treatment Issues (McGurrin, 1992).

Sexual Addiction

Secretiveness is paramount with any addiction; however, with the puritan cultural views on sexuality in our country, sex addiction carries with it an extreme amount of shame. Thus, the secret of sexual addiction often remains secret unless the counselor is skilled at interviewing and comfortable discussing these issues in order to set the client at ease. Rigid religious beliefs may make disclosure even more difficult. There does not seem to be estimates available for prevalence of sexual addictions, however it is notable that with the privacy of internet access in the home, it appears that sexual addiction is rapidly increasing in the United States. President Bill Clinton's affair with Monica Lewinsky brought national media attention to the idea that sexual addiction is present in our culture (Carnes, 1998); has predictable symptoms, is progressive, and may involve increased risk over time.

There are not yet *DSM-IV* diagnostic criteria available for forms of sexual addiction that do not involve harm to others. Forms of sex addiction that harm others do have *DSM-IV* categories and include exhibitionism, voyeurism, and pedophilia (APA, 1994). Goodman (1989) (as cited in Schneider, 1994) provides a good guide for client assessment regarding addictive processes when diagnostic criteria are not provided for in the *DSM-IV* criteria for diagnosing addictive disorders. At least three of the following criteria must be established in order for a diagnosis to be made:

1. Frequent engaging in the behavior to a greater extent or over a longer period than intended.
2. Persistent desire for the behavior or one or more unsuccessful efforts to reduce or control the behavior.
3. Much time spent in activities necessary for the behavior, engaging in the behavior, or recovering from its effects.
4. Frequent preoccupation with the behavior or preparatory activities.
5. Frequent engaging in the behavior when expected to fulfill occupational, academic, domestic, or social obligations.
6. Giving up or limiting important social, occupational, or recreational activities because of the behavior.
7. Continuation of the behavior despite knowledge of having a persistent or recurrent social, financial, psychological, or physical problem that is caused or exacerbated by the

behavior.

8. Need to increase the intensity or frequency of the behavior to achieve the desired effect, or diminished effect with continued behavior of the same intensity.
9. Restlessness or irritability if unable to engage in the behavior. (Schneider, 1994, p. 28)

It is recommended that counselors become familiar and comfortable with sexual terms to be able to work with clients who have sexual addictions. Indirect or judgmental statements can alienate clients and further add to the sense of shame associated with sexual addiction. Some common terminology is represented in examples of sexual acting out from Carnes (1991) as adapted by Schneider (1994):

1. Fantasy sex: neglecting commitments because of fantasy life, masturbation.
2. Seductive role sex: extramarital affairs (heterosexual or homosexual), flirting and seductive sex.
3. Anonymous sex: engaging in sex with anonymous partners, having one-night stands.
4. Paying for sex: paying prostitutes for sex, paying for sexually explicit phone calls.
5. Trading sex: receiving money or drugs for sex.
6. Voyeuristic sex: patronizing adult bookstores and strip shows, looking through windows of houses, having a collection of pornography at home or at work.
7. Exhibitionist sex: exposing oneself in public places or from the home or car, wearing clothes designed to expose.
8. Intrusive sex: touching others without permission, using position of power (e.g. professional, religious) to sexually exploit another person, rape.
9. Pain exchange: causing or receiving pain to enhance sexual pleasure.
10. Object sex: masturbating with objects, cross-dressing to add to sexual pleasure, using fetishes as part of sexual rituals, having sex with animals.
11. Sex with children: forcing sexual activity on a child, watching child pornography. (p. 29)

Additional forms of sexual acting out referred to as "cybersex" can be accessed by Internet. They include pornographic sites, virtual reality, and sexual chat rooms. One doesn't have to "surf the net" very long to find some of these sites. Electronic access to chat rooms also presents an avenue for love and relationship addiction.

Consequences of sexual addiction can include sexually transmitted disease, including HIV infection, involuntary sexual involvement, unplanned pregnancy, or physical harm from use of foreign objects. Individuals may neglect personal health and social obligations, and engage in a secretive cycle of sexual acting out. Variations on sex addiction can include sex, love, and relationship addiction in which an individual experiences a "high" from initial "falling in love" stages of relationships. Monogamy may or may not be a part of this kind of pattern.

Treatment

Treatment issues for sex addiction include assisting the client in identifying the range of environmental triggers as well as internal triggers. It is important to work with the client on shame reduction and strongly encourage group support for identification with others who have this addiction. The counselor needs to be aware of how to assist clients in developing different goals for clients on the engagement to abstinence continuum. Sex Addicts Anonymous can be contacted in most communities as a diagnostic resource for the *The Sex Addicts Anonymous Questionnaire*, and for client group support. Related support groups include Sexaholics Anonymous, Co-Sex Addicts Anonymous, and Sex and Love Addicts Anonymous. For national credentialing and other related information on sex addiction, contact The National Council on Sexual Addiction and Compulsivity at 770-989-9754 or www.ncsac.org. Another resource for information regarding sex addiction is *Don't Call it Love: Recovery From Sexual Addictions* (Carnes, 1991).

Work Addiction

There do not appear to be statistics indicating the prevalence of workaholism. Seybold & Salomone (1994) provide a summary from a review of the literature describing workaholic characteristics:

...an excessive commitment to work that is manifested by a neglect of other and important aspects of life–workaholism–has been described as the following:

(a) an "addiction" that is uncontrollable or

(b) an escape from personal problems, including the avoidance of intimacy with other persons. In addition, workaholism

may be the result of
(c) a deep and pressing need to control one's life;
(d) an exceedingly competitive nature, often associated with a drive to succeed;
(e) an impaired self-image and limited self-esteem as a result of childhood traumas including poverty; and
(f) workaholic parents or role models. (p. 5)

These traits are similar to Type A or obsessive-compulsive characteristics, but seem to be directly related more to work than to other aspects of daily living. The Work Addiction Risk Test (WART) may be used as a scale to measure workaholism (Robinson, 1989).

It is clear that because of cultural rewards, some aspects of workaholism are promoted within western culture. Entire business structures may be based on work addiction that require executives and other employees to engage in workaholic behavior. This may seem familiar to many a reader as companies downsize/reorganize and reassign responsibilities. Those who produce, survive. So what defines workaholic behavior in comparison to solid, efficient, productive work? Again, the answer is not a simple one and it is the personality traits and negative consequences that seem to guide the definition. It is important to recognize that strong work ethic does not necessarily mean that someone has workaholism. As well as other addictions, there is a continuum from experimentation to dependence. It is important not to make assumptions about a person's relationship to their work without thorough investigation.

Scott, Moore, and Miceli (1997) describe three kinds of workaholism; Compulsive-Dependent Workaholism, Perfectionist Workaholism, and Achievement-Oriented Workaholism. According to their model, Compulsive-Dependent Workaholism seems to manifest as understanding of reasonable expectations; however, obsessive thoughts override healthy thoughts, and work is used as a coping skill to deal with those same obsessive thoughts. Perfectionist Workaholics display an unreasonable need for control and may perceive gain from attempting to control others in the work setting. Last, the Achievement-Oriented Workaholics, in an upwardly mobile style, "...always spend a great deal of discretionary time on work activities, constantly think about work, and work beyond employer and economic requirements" (Scott, Moore, & Miceli, 1997, p. 299). Potential consequences from workaholism may include fatigue, chronic illness, burnout, depression, anxiety, anger, anhedonia, insomnia, poor relations with others, lack of intimacy, low self-esteem, low self-confidence, poor attention, and overall numbing: physical, emotional, mental, spiritual, and interactional.

Treatment

Treatment issues related to workaholism include the need to learn new forms of self-care through body-mind awareness, develop healthy work boundaries with time and energy, and learn how to engage in social outlets. The counselor can support the client in developing a new relationship to self through creative dialogue, experiential assignments, and meditation techniques. Group support can be found in many communities through Workaholics Anonymous and Alanon. In Alanon, clients may be able to identify their needs to control others, to overextend themselves to please others, and to avoid emotions by focusing on others. A resource for more information about work addiction is the book *Work and the Evolving Self: Theoretical and Clinical Considerations* (Axelrod, 1999).

Other Considerations

In comparing assessment of substance addictions with assessment of related addictive disorders, it is clear that there are many similarities. This is also true of the many other process addictions which include addictions to religious, exercise, rage, power, and more. Appropriate interviewing techniques need to be pursued to determine the following factors regarding the relationship a client has to a substance or activity:

(1) intention or motivation;
(2) physical, mental, emotional, social, and spiritual benefits;
(3) how much time and thought is dedicated to the substance or activity;
(4) how long ago the behavior began and under what circumstances; and
(5) whether or not the client has been able to consistently control the use of the substance or activity.

Awareness of clients as individuals, and their individual perceptions of these factors, will assist counselors in understanding unique symptoms of tolerance, withdrawal, dependence, and negative consequences for each without making assumptions that can be damaging.

The "healing" process may peel away "layers of the onion" and clients may have to face many addictions in long-term recovery. Counselors need to be aware that substance addictions may develop last in a chain of addictive processes, and that clients may revert to previous coping strategies such as eating disorders that were present long before the first drink or drug was ingested. Other addictions may be concurrent with the most obvious one, or they may arise during times of stress as older coping strategies surface. Clients might switch addictions as a defense mechanism and it is important for counselors to assist clients in addressing core issues. A trap to avoid is focusing on symptoms and actually enabling clients to rely on addictions as coping skills. Because the core issues relate to events, beliefs, and cognitive patterns, a cognitive/behavioral approach is an effective counseling method when working with clients who have addictive disorders. Clients benefit from cognitive restructuring and relapse prevention planning. Substance abuse relapse prevention plans can be adapted for working with other addictions. As the client increases healthy coping skills, engages in supportive family and community support, and begins to balance the body/mind/spirit/environment/ relationship in daily living, symptoms and relapse compulsions subside.

When treating a client with multiple addictions, it is important to prioritize treatment issues beginning with the most life-threatening first. Psychiatric issues other than addictions must be considered in the process of treatment planning and implementation as well. One of the challenges is sorting out what is most life-threatening when a client presents with multiple forms of self-destructive behavior. In early recovery symptoms of addictions can disguise other mental health issues such as sexual acting out can also be associated with borderline personality disorder, bipolar disorder, or a history of sexual abuse with poor boundaries and current dissociation. Clinicians can develop the ability to distinguish between characteristics of dependent personality disorder, symptoms from being involved in an abusive relationship, and codependency in the role of the enabler/ fixer/controller. In almost every case, clients are faced with challenges in relationships and must address some level of codependency. Ultimately, the challenge of addiction recovery for any individual is reduced to working on issues of relationships to self and others. Melody Beattie's book *Codependent No More and Beyond Codependency* (1997) is a resource for more information on codependency.

When clients are unable to provide an accurate history or current information, and have given permission through appropriate releases, clinicians can enlist family members in completing the assessment process. Family members also suffer consequences of addiction and, if not treated, may contribute to a family member's addiction through enabling behaviors. Additionally, there are usually multiple factors contributing to addictive processes, so obtaining updated and/or previous medical and mental health records on the client may assist in diagnosis. Important information to obtain are records from recent hospitalizations including discharge summary, psychiatric evaluation, history and physical exam notes, and the last two days of chart notes.

A final issue to address is that of treatment and managed care. Managed care companies recognize the need for treatment based on *medical necessity*. It is up to the counselor, health care team members, or another qualified representative to advocate for the client by using medical necessity terms that will be recognized as meeting medical necessity criteria by insurance companies, managed care representatives, and utilization review specialists. This can be challenging because the rules constantly change. It is not likely that insurance will cover treatment for disorders that do not appear to be immediately life-threatening. There are also inconsistencies between what is considered medical and what is considered mental health, therefore insurance will honor the policy according to medical benefits versus mental health benefits. For example, a person with anorexia nervosa may be malnourished and need in-patient medical intervention for re-feeding. The managed care company might list the diagnosis of anorexia nervosa as psychiatric, therefore denying medical benefits, or as medical and deny psychiatric benefits. In another possible scenario with a person who uses substances to deal with the shame of an underlying sex addiction as well as chronic depression with suicidal ideation, the managed care company might recognize the need for a 1- to 5-day in-patient stay for detoxification and/or depression. The same company might not recognize the need for group therapy, in- or out-patient, to address the sexual addiction because it is not classified in the DSM-IV. One of the best ways to advocate for a client can be to refer for a psychiatric evaluation with an addictions medicine specialist who can determine the medical need of the client. Again, the counselor can best serve the client by working with a team of professionals to determine treatment planning and implementation.

Summary

In this chapter, an overview of related addictions has been provided. Basic information, prevalence, diagnostic criteria, assessment tools, and treatment issues have been provided for eating disorders, compulsive gambling, sex addictions, and work addiction. Addictions can be seen on a continuum from experimentation to dependence and it is important for counselors to be aware of the symptoms along this continuum. Many individuals with addictions adopt coping strategies by exchanging one addiction for another or by engaging in multiple addictive processes simultaneously. Individual therapy, group therapy, self-help group support, medications, exercise, nutrition, relaxation, recreation, spirituality, and healthy relationships are all critical factors in addiction recovery. It is important to engage family members in the client's recovery process for relapse prevention purposes.

There are professional counselors, psychiatrists, and treatment centers who specialize in the diagnosis and treatment of these different addictions. Counselors can contact credentialing organizations to locate specialists. A resource for physicians specializing in addictions medicine is the American Society of Addiction Medicine (ASAM), who can be reached at 301-656-3920 or email@asam.org. ASAM members whose backgrounds are extensive in addictions medicine are specialists in substance addictions, not necessarily in other addictions. Another resource is Sierra Tucson, an in-patient dual-diagnosis treatment/psychiatric facility in Arizona treating all addictive disorders. Sierra Tucson has a national data base of specialists and can be contacted at 800-842-4487 for referrals and treatment information. Other information sources are conferences, symposiums, workshops, or on-line conferences that can be located by contacting credentialing organizations, state counselor certification boards, and internet web pages.

References

American Psychiatric Association. (1994). *Diagnostic and statistical manual of mental disorders,* (4th ed.). Washington, DC: Author.

Axelrod, S.D. (1999). *Work and the evolving self: Theoretical and clinical considerations.* Hillsdale, NJ: The Analytic Press, Inc.

Beattie, Melody. (1997). *Codependent no more and beyond codependency.* New York: Communications.

Cauffman, E., & Steinberg, L. (1996). Interactive effects of menarcheal status and dating on dieting and disordered eating among adolescent girls. *Developmental Psychology, 32*(4), 631-635.

Carnes, P. (1991). *Don't call it love: Recovery from sexual addiction.* New York: Bantam Books.

Carnes, P. (1998). Editorial: The presidential diagnosis. *Sexual Addiction & Compulsivity, 15,* 153-158.

Costin, C. (1996). *The eating disorder sourcebook.* Los Angeles, CA: Lowell House.

Deep, A.L., Lilenfeld, L.R., Plotnicov, K.H., Pollice, C., & Kaye, W.H. (1998). Sexual abuse in eating disorder subtypes and control women: The role of comorbid substance dependence in bulimia nervosa. *International Journal of Eating Disorders 25*, 1-10.

Donovan, D.M. (1988). Assessment of addictive behaviors: Implications of an emerging biopsychosocial model. In D.M. Donovan & G.A. Marlatt (Eds). *Assessment of addictive behaviors* (pp. 3-48). New York: Guilford.

Goodman, A. (1989). Addiction defined: Diagnostic criteria for addictive disorder. *American Journal of Preventive Psychiatry and Neurology, 2,* 12-15.

le Grange, D., Stone, A.A., & Brownell, K.D., (1998). Eating disturbances in white and minority female dieters. *International Journal of Eating Disorders, 24*(4), 395-403.

Lesieur, H.R., & Blume, S. (1988). The South Oaks Gambling Screen (SOGS). A new instrument for the identification of pathological gamblers. *American Journal of Psychiatry, 144*, 1184-1188.

Lesieur, H.R., & Blume, S.B. (1993). Pathological gambling, eating disorders, and the psychoactive substance use disorders. *Journal of Addictive Diseases, 12*, 89-102.

Lewis, J. (1994). *Addictions: Concepts and strategies for treatment.* Gaithersburg, MD: Aspen Publishers, Inc.

McGurrin, M.C. (1992). *Pathological gambling: Conceptual, diagnostic, and treatment issues.* Sarasota, FL: Professional Resource Press/Professional Resource Exchange, Inc.

National Institute of Mental Health. (1996). *Eating Disorders.* Washington D.C.: Author.

Ocean, G., & Smith, G.J. (1993). Social reward, conflict, and commitment: A theoretical model of gambling behavior. *Journal of Gambling Studies, 9* (4), 321-339.

Robinson, B.E. (1989). *Work addiction.* Deerfield Beach, FL: Health Communications.

Schneider, J.P. (1994). Sex addiction: Controversy within mainstream addiction medicine, diagnosis based on the DSM-III-R, and physician case histories. *Sexual Addiction & Compulsivity, 1*, 19-44.

Scott, K.S., Moore, K.S., Miceli, M.P. (1997). An exploration of the meaning and consequences of workaholism. *Human Relations, 50*, 287-314.

Seybold, K.C., & Salomone, P.R. (1994). Understanding workaholism: A review of causes and counseling approaches. *Journal of Counseling & Development, 73*, 4-9.

Shaffer, H., Stein, S., Gambino, B., & Cummings, T. (1989). *Compulsive gambling: Theory, research, and practice.* Lexington, MA: Lexington Books.

Swarr, A.E., & Richards, M.H. (1996). Longitudinal effects of adolescent girls' pubertal development, perceptions of pubertal timing, and parental relations on eating disorders. *Developmental Psychology, 32*(4), 636-646.

Yalom, I.D. (1995). *The theory and practice of group psychotherapy* (4th ed.). New York, NY: Basic Books.

Chapter 4

Preventing Addiction

Susan Fordney Moore

Introduction

The purpose of this chapter is to provide the beginning counselor with: an overview of prevention concepts, a discussion of prevention models as they relate to causal theories of addiction, a summary of effective substance abuse prevention approaches, and a description of the various counselor roles in prevention work.

Prevention is a relatively new emphasis in community efforts to stem the rising costs of substance abuse and other high-risk behaviors. According to the former Surgeon General of the United States, C. Everet Koop (1995), preventable illness makes up about 70% of the burden of illness and associated costs. Diseases are of two kinds: those we develop unintentionally, and those we bring upon ourselves with our failure to be active participants in prevention. It is estimated, for example, that alcohol and drug problems cost an estimated $114 billion annually (U.S. DHHS, 1990). The human cost is incalculable as these problems interrelate with other actions such as violence and high-risk sexual behaviors, impacting numerous service systems including education, mental health, and criminal justice. The impact on individuals, families, and communities is significant.

Due to limited success of legal and treatment approaches in lowering the rates of substance abuse, multiple prevention strategies have mushroomed since the 1970's. In spite of the potential of well-designed prevention programs to have greater impact in decreasing substance abuse and increasing healthy behaviors, prevention continues to receive minimal support through state and federal funding. Counselors, irrespective of where they work, need to understand their role in prevention with their students, clients, families, agency, school, and other community partners. It is increasingly clear that the most successful prevention programs involve various partners, are clear of purpose, address multiple risk factors, and have a system of on-going evaluation (see Chapter 12).

Prevention

Prevention is the creating of optimal conditions that nurture and sustain the healthy development of individuals, families, and communities. The goal is to change the conditions under which the undesirable target behaviors occur by promoting the overall wellbeing of people through positive action (Lofquist, 1989). Because addiction has many causes, prevention strategies have multiple objectives and attempt to influence individuals and groups at different stages.

It is obvious, however, that interventions in any of these categories have preventative effects.

Primary prevention focuses on strengthening individuals and communities prior to the instigation of detrimental behaviors that may lead to addiction. Secondary prevention refers to those efforts that attempt to intervene in addictive patterns that are harmful to individuals and communities before these patterns have become entrenched and require treatment. Tertiary prevention includes treatment strategies designed to remediate addictive patterns and prevent a downward trend that may result in death and the dismantling of individuals, families. and communities. An additional stage covers relapse prevention which includes those efforts designed to support individuals, families,

Over thirty years ago, Caplan (1964) suggested that prevention activities could be classed according to three levels: primary, secondary, and tertiary. This has been somewhat confusing as it allows any activity to be described as prevention. and communities who have stopped on their own or who been treated for addiction. All of these stages are important in a comprehensive prevention plan. It is important for counselors and other professionals to recognize at what level they are working and the manner in which their efforts complement interventions in the others.

In the past twenty years, prevention research in addiction has focused almost exclusively on substance abuse. Contemporary researchers and practitioners, however, see many commonalties among addictive disorders (Gold, Johnson, & Stenneil, 1997) and argue for the application of prevention theory to other problematic behaviors such as gambling (Blume, 1997). For the purposes of this chapter, discussion will emphasize primary prevention of substance abuse with the expectation that practitioners will find helpful information applicable to the prevention of other addictions.

Models of Prevention

A model of prevention must reflect a comprehensive understanding of the multiple causes of addiction. Prevention efforts in substance abuse have been based on numerous causal models of addiction which generally reflect trait/genetic determinants, cognitive and attitudinal factors, pharmacological factors, developmental variables, behavioral factors, and socio/cultural influences (Botvin & Botvin, 1997). Most prevention programs address one or more of these factors. The influence of family in relationship to all of these factors is substantial. In efforts to address these numerous causal factors, there has been an interdisciplinary collaboration between behavioral science and the public health field. In public health, an epidemiologic model is used to explain disease as the interplay between the agent of infection, the host, and the environment (Lilienfeld & Lilienfeld, 1994). This model is easily adapted to behavioral science specifically in the area of prevention of addiction. Within this model, the agent is understood as the drug or the behavior (e.g., gambling). Individual characteristics and internal influences (e.g., depression, brain function) comprise the host. The environment consists of those external influences such as media and social norms which have an impact on specific drug use (Vaughn, 1993). Understanding the interaction of these forces is paramount in designing and implementing prevention programs that have a likelihood of being successful in addressing specific risk factors. The epidemiologic model combined with a decision as to whether a prevention approach is primary, secondary, or tertiary provides a structure within which to develop and evaluate any prevention effort. Within the context of the comprehensive epidemiologic model, there are sub-models which are designed specifically to guide prevention interventions at the levels of agent, host, and environment.

Agent prevention models have as their unit of focus the drug or addictive behavior itself. Availability, accessibility, and reactions to the drug or behavior on the part of the user become important considerations in prevention planning (Chen & Kandel, 1995). Programs that disseminate drug information and supply reduction efforts are examples of approaches under this model.

Host prevention models attempt to intervene with addictive potential at the level of the individual. They are based on a number of considerations regarding individuals and their development. First is the assumption that individuals are at risk to develop addictive behaviors because they have certain personality characteristics that increase their vulnerability. Examples include excessive shyness and early anti-social attitudes (Page, 1989; Apgar, 1998). Genetic factors are also believed to be influential in some individuals who develop substance abuse problems. Researchers, Anthenelli and Schuckit (1997), indicate that children of parents with alcohol problems are significantly more likely to develop problems with alcohol than children whose parents are not alcohol abusers. Recent brain research has also demonstrated that vulnerability to addiction may have a genetic component and that addictive behaviors, such as eating and sexual behavior, stimulate the brain reward centers in similar ways as addictive drugs (Dupont, 1997c).

Developmental issues are important to consider in conceptualizing effective prevention. It may be that an individual who is at risk for or who has already developed an addictive behavior pattern has not successfully negotiated developmental tasks across the life span and abuses substances to cope with these deficits. Other concerns relate to what is expected of individuals at certain stages of development relative to substance abuse. For example, experimentation with at least one psychoactive substance occurs during the adolescent years for most young persons in American society (Botvin & Botvin, 1997).

Environmental prevention models take into account the many social and cultural factors which are influential in decisions regarding substance use and other potentially addictive behaviors. These factors may be viewed as contributing to the resiliency or the vulnerability of an individual or a community in relationship to drug use. These are factors characterized by interactions among family, school, peer group, and the broader community. One such factor is the relationship of parental substance use to the onset of use among their children (Wills, Schreibman, Benson, & Vaccaro, 1994). Another environmental variable is the role of media and its substantial power to influence attitudes and behavior.

Purpose

Prevention is important because it offers alternatives to treatment which is costly, available to a select few, and frequently not effective. Prevention strategies can impact large numbers of people or a few depending on the objectives. When prevention efforts fail, it is often because the purpose of these activities is not clear from the outset. Prevention strategies must relate to causal models of addictive behavior if they are to have any likelihood of making an impact. Target populations must be clearly identified. The risk and protective factors being addressed need to be accurately described. Only then can practitioners understand the purpose of their efforts, the appropriateness of their strategies and the degree to which they are successful.

To determine the purpose of a prevention effort, the following questions must be considered:

- Who is the target population., e.g. , adolescents, senior citizens, first generation Mexican-Americans.
- What behaviors, characteristics, factors are to be impacted by the intervention.,e.g., cigarette smoking, inhalant abuse, parenting skills, lack of playground activities.
- Is the intended intervention a primary, secondary, or tertiary prevention approach?
- What strategies targeting which populations have been shown to produce change in the desired direction?
- What other individual or community variables may influence the success of the prevention effort?
- What approaches are necessary and plausible in order to minimize the effects of these additional factors?

The more specific one can be in selecting the population to be impacted and the variables to be modified, the clearer one can be about the purpose of the prevention initiative. Considerations such as age, gender, family, cultural, and social influences should be identified so that the chosen strategy is appropriate for the population and likely to influence the targeted variables.

Developing Effective Prevention Programs

A review of prevention interventions, successes and failures, is an essential first step in the development of new programs. Much has been learned in the last two decades about what works and what does not work! Additionally, although some prevention programs do not accomplish their intended goals, there may be elements of these initiatives that have some unexpected benefits. It is important to note these pluses and replicate them in new programs.

Traditional prevention approaches have used educational intervention strategies to disseminate factual information about drugs and their negative consequences. Scare tactics and real life examples have typically been used in these approaches. Prevention through educational intervention is based on rational theory which contends that once a person is knowledgeable about the consequences of drug use, he or she will choose to abstain. Evaluation studies have shown that these strategies do increase knowledge about drugs and health consequences but they also consistently fail to prevent or reduce drug use among youth (Berberian & Gross, Lovejoy, Parella, 1994; USDHHS, 1994). From today's vantage point, it is easy to see why these approaches were unsuccessful. Focus was on the agent (drug) and there was no consideration of related host and environmental factors. Also, there was no clear connection between information gained and a person's beliefs and attitudes and how these variables influenced drug use in real life situations (Randall & Bruvold, 1988).

Psychosocial prevention approaches are grounded in cognitive development, social learning, and psychological inoculation theories (Jansen, Glynn, & Howard,1996). These strategies focus on the development of health enhancing behaviors and cognitive abilities so that individuals are better able to counter the risk factors which may predispose them toward substance abuse. They build personal competence and include techniques such as problem solving, resisting social influences, and communication skills. Botvin and Botvin (1997) have summarized major strategies which fall under the psychosocial model. They include ther following:

- Affective Education which focuses on increasing interpersonal growth and self-esteem through experiential activities, didactic instruction, and group discussion and problem solving activities
- Personal and Social Skills Training targets individual behavior change in communication, social and assertiveness skills, decision making, and anxiety reduction through discussion and cognitive-behavioral skills training (instruction, demonstration, practice, feedback, and reinforcement). Research results affirm that personal and social skills strategies to prevent drug use and abuse can reduce onset of use and have a positive impact on related

social and cognitive skills among youth (Dielman, 1995).

- Resistance Skills Training focuses on increasing awareness of the social influence to use alcohol, tobacco, and other drugs (ATOD), developing skills to resist these influences, and establishing non-use norms through behavioral rehearsal, extended practice (homework), the use of peer leaders, and group discussion. Prevention practitioners have combined resistance training with training in decision making skills, interpersonal communication skills, and skills to build self control to diminish the power of social influences on the decision to use drugs (Severson, et al. 1991; Susman, et al. 1993).
- Alternatives provide relief from boredom and a sense of alienation while attempting to increase self-esteem and self-reliance through recreational activities, community service projects, vocational training among others.

Environmental prevention approaches focus on those factors outside of the host that influence an individual's choices and actions relative to ATOD use and other addictive behavior. These environmental variables interact and can have synergistic effects in either a positive or negative direction. Examples of prevention approaches that are part of an environmental model include the following:

- Family is perhaps the most significant environmental influence. Young people who feel connected to their families and school are less likely to use cigarettes, alcohol, and marijuana. To a lesser degree, high parental expectations, parental presence in the home at critical times, and shared parent-child activities serve as protective factors from high-risk activities (Resnick, 1997). Three family-based prevention approaches have demonstrated great potential for success. These include parent and family skills training, in-home support services, and family therapy. Parent and family skills are designed to improve poor parent-child communication, child behavior, and family conflict. In-home support services attempt to decrease domestic violence, child abuse, and neglect. Services are also directed toward reducing delinquency and improving social skills, school attendance, anger management, and adherence to curfew laws. The goal of family therapy is to improve family functioning and to reduce antisocial behaviors (SAMHSA, 1998).
- Health communication involves the use of media to convey

well designed messages to remote audiences with the intent of changing health attitudes and behaviors, shaping social norms, and influencing legislative and policy decisions. These strategies are generally a part of the broader context of health promotion, community development, and social change initiatives (Simon-Morton & Donohew, 1997).

Two popular communication-based prevention activities are

- Media Literacy emphasizes the role of the receiver in analyzing media and challenging the assumptions within the messages. The objectives of media literacy training are to improve the target population's knowledge and understanding of how media is developed, what approaches are used, who are the beneficiaries of media messages, and what are the values imbedded in the communications. Medial literacy is a recognized goal of prevention programs and has been integrated into numerous ATOD prevention programs (Hansen, 1992).
- Media Advocacy, in the prevention of ATOD problems, attempts to influence public discussion by changing how health issues are prevented to the public. Media advocates encourage media sources to present information in factual and socially responsible ways. Media advocacy attempts to secure the active support of citizens in order to pressure policy makers to create the desired change in environmental conditions (Simon-Morton, & Donohew, 1997).
- School is a powerful environmental influence in American society. School-based prevention approaches are important in several ways. First, the school is the central and unifying location in many communities. It is in the school setting that many informational, psychosocial, family, and peer prevention programs are provided. Secondly, schools are increasingly called upon to assume more roles in developing resilient youth who will have the personal strength and necessary skills to make healthy choices and avoid addictive patterns.

Community-based prevention strategies allow multiple risk and protective factors to be addressed across domains and developmental levels. They encourage the participation of diverse groups, which enhances the opportunity to reach those at greatest risk. The following checklist (Perry & Williams, 1998) is provided by The National Institute of Drug Abuse to assist in determining whether a specific community-based program includes research-based prevention principles:

- To be comprehensive, does the program have components for the individual, the family, the school, the media, community organizations, and health providers? Are the program components well integrated in theme and content so that they reinforce each other?
- Does the prevention program use media and community education strategies to increase public awareness, attract community support, reinforce the school-based curriculum for students and parents, and keep the public informed of the program's progress?
- Can program components be coordinated with other community efforts to reinforce prevention messages (for instance, can training for all program components address coordinated goals and objectives)?
- Are interventions carefully designed to reach different populations at risk, and are they of sufficient duration to make a difference?
- Does the program follow a structured organizational plan that progresses from needs assessment through planning, implementation, and review to refinement, with feedback to and from the community at all stages?
- Are the objectives and activities specific, time-limited, feasible (given available resources), and integrated so that they work together across program components and can be used to evaluate program progress and outcomes?

Impact

Evaluation of prevention programs indicates that while improvement in knowledge and some attitude changes may occur, there is little evidence demonstrating that these programs result in a reduction or elimination of substance abuse (USDHHS, 1994). This lack of evidence of program effectiveness may be attributed to multiple causes of substance abuse and the difficulty in evaluating prevention programs where risk and protective factors overlap. Most prevention models in recent years have addressed a combination of host and environmental factors. The programs that have gotten the best results are those that are comprehensive, with research-based strategies that address clearly defined multiple components and include the individual, family, peers, and community (Jansen, et al. 1996). The favored paradigm for primary prevention incorporates multiple intervention strategies delivered through a variety of settings tailored toward the target population (Pentz et al., 1996). For example, the "communities that care" approach to drug abuse, which has been adopted in a number of states, targets a wide array of risk factors including economic and social deprivation, low neighborhood attachment, community disorganization, and drug availability among others. This approach also focuses on protective factors which form a solid foundation for behavior change that is lasting (Hawkins & Catalano, 1992).

Pentz (in press) has been successful in reaching the entire community with a comprehensive school program, media efforts, a parents' program, health policy change, and community organization. Research results of this project show positive long-term efforts. Students who began the program in middle school showed significantly less use of marijuana, cigarettes, and alcohol than children who did not receive the program.

The Life Skills Training Program (Botvin & Botvin, 1997) is a classroom-based program designed to address multiple risk and protective factors. The program consists of a three-year prevention curriculum targeting middle school students. It covers drug information and resistance skills, self management skills, and general social skills. Research results demonstrate that this prevention intervention can produce decreases in the use of tobacco, alcohol, and marijuana. Booster sessions can help to sustain program effects.

Strengthening Families (Kumper & Alvarado, 1996) is a multi-component family focused program that targets 6-to-10 year-old children of substance abusers. The program contains a parent training aspect, a children's skills training program, and a family training element. Outcomes include reductions in family conflict, improvement in family organization and communication, and decreases in youth aggressiveness and substance abuse.

One frequent criticism of primary prevention programs has been that while they may impact future occasional users, they may not be effective with youth who are at highest risk for substance abuse. There is a critical need for prevention efforts to focus on subgroups of adolescents who may be at very high risk for certain types of ATOD use (Dent, Sussman, Ellickson, Brown & Richardson, 1996). In addition, prevention programs historically have been designed from a mainstream cultural perspective which has focused on White, in-school populations (Hawkins, et al. 1992). This is changing, however, and there are many current prevention initiatives developed and implemented within a context of respect for cultural differences.

Two significant groups in need of targeted prevention efforts are women and the elderly. Historically, cultural norms have encouraged lower rates of substance use among women. These norms are breaking down as women have become targeted by advertising campaigns to buy and use alcohol and other drugs (Jacobson, Hoeker & Atkins, 1980). Primary prevention efforts with women include educational programs to alert women of their special sensitivity to alcohol, the risks of using substances to cope with feelings, the danger of mixing alcohol with other drugs such as sedatives which are used more frequently among women (Shore, 1994). The risks of substance use during pregnancy constitute an additional prevention focus for women.

Elderly persons are predisposed to higher rates of substance abuse, particularly alcohol and prescription medications (Gambert, 1997). There are many issues to address in prevention of substance abuse with elderly persons. Age and the accompanying physical decline affects how substances will be metabolized by the body. Elderly persons experience considerable loss with the deaths of loved ones, loss of jobs, and often the inability to continue in favored activities due to physical or mental decline. With both groups, prevention workers need to approach the development of prevention service comprehensively. Medical status, the role of family members, the inability to follow one's dreams are factors which place both women and the elderly at increased risk for addiction.

Comprehensive prevention is extremely challenging and requires considerable collaboration. There is much to keep track of when you consider the numbers of people involved, the scheduling of events, the ongoing evaluation demands, and the need for sufficient resources. If prevention is to be successful, it must be planned for and implemented in a detailed and logical manner. All involved need to understand their roles, and continually strive to improve their skills in interpersonal communication, effective collaboration, program planning and evaluation, and community development.

Counselor Role

Counselors play important and varied roles in prevention. They may be working at the primary, secondary, or tertiary levels in prevention programs. Most commonly counselors are involved in intervention and treatment functions. They may intervene with clients or students at the experimentation stage and are involved in referring or treating individuals who develop substance abuse problems.

Emerging roles for the counselor are as advocate and consultant for prevention programming at the primary level. This may include working with teachers in designing classroom strategies that support the development of resiliency in their students. It may be collaborating with community leaders to get a senior citizens center built which would provide activities for elderly persons. It might include collaborating with other professionals to provide parent skill training. School counselors are in an excellent position to work with parents on strategies to support children in achieving success in the classroom. Academic achievement is a significant protective factor in prevention of substance abuse. Counselors, social workers, and mental health professionals must to be aware of the signs of substance abuse problems within their clients so they can receive appropriate services as soon as possible. In prevention work, counselors are challenged to get out of their offices and into the community where their skills in interpersonal communication, problem solving, dispute resolution, and listening can be utilized to promote climates of support and nurturance in order to mitigate risk and reinforce individual and community resiliency.

Summary

Over the past two decades, prevention programs have increased dramatically as an overall national strategy to curb addiction problems in American society. Many of these efforts were not successful; however, recently, some well researched prevention programs are demonstrating positive outcomes including decreases in substance abuse. These approaches share a number of commonalities. They are comprehensive, include multiple components, and address numerous risk and protective factors. They involve key representatives from the entire community in the planning, implementation, and evaluation of programs.

Counselors play a critical role in prevention. They have the skills in interpersonal communication to facilitate problem solving, goal setting, and collaboration. They are in a position to advocate for system change and to model healthy behaviors to their clients, students, and members of the larger community.

Well-constructed programs and competent prevention professionals offer hope that many of the destructive behaviors in contemporary American society can be decreased. It makes sense to prevent or curtail addictive behaviors before they become entrenched. Hopefully, individuals, families, schools, and communities will make prevention an ongoing priority so that there will be fewer persons at substantial risk of developing addiction problems.

References

Anthenelli, R. M., & Schuckit, M. A. (1997). Genetics. In Lowinson, J. H., Ruiz, P. , Millman, R. B., Langrod, J. G. (Eds.). *Substance abuse* (3rd ed.) (pp. 319-330). Baltimore: Williams & Wilkins.

Apgar, Barbara. (1998). Antisocial personality and substance abuse. *American Family Physician, 58*(6), 1418-1420.

Beberian, R. M., Gross, C., Lovejoy, J. & Parella, S. (1976). The effectiveness of drug education program: A critical review. *Health Education Monograph, 4*, 377-398.

Blume, S. B. (1997). Pathological gambling. In Lowinson, J. H., Ruiz, P., Millman, R. B., Langrod, J. G. (Eds.), *Substance abuse* (3rd ed.), (pp. 330-337). Baltimore: Williams & Wilkins.

Botvin, G. J., & Botvin, E. M. (1997). School based programs. In Lowinson, J. H., Ruiz, P., Millman, R. B., Langrod, J. G. (Eds.), *Substance abuse* (3rd ed.) (pp. 764-775). Baltimore: Williams & Wilkins.

Caplan, G. (1964). *Principles of preventive psychiatry.* New York: Basic Books.

Chen, K. & Kandel, D. (1995). The national history of drug use from adolescence to the mid-thirties in a general population sample. *American Journal of Public Health, 85,* 41-47.

Dent, C. W., Sussman, S., Ellickson, P., Brown, P., & Richardson, J. (1996). Is current drug abuse prevention programming generalizable across ethnic groups? *American Behavioral Scientist, 39*(7), 911-918.

Dielman, T. E. (1995). School-based research on prevention of adolescent alcohol use and misuse: Methodological issues and advances. In Boyd, G. M., Howard, J., & Zucker, R. A. (Eds.), *Alcohol problems among adolescents: Current directions in prevention research,* (pp. 125-146). Hillsdale, N.J.: Lawrence Erlbaum.

Dupont, R. L. (1997c). *The selfish brain: Learning from addiction.* Washington, D.C.: American Psychiatric Press.

Gambert, Steven R. (1997). The elderly. In Lowinson, J. H., Ruiz, P., Millman, R. B., Langrod, J. G. (Eds.) *Substance abuse,* (3rd Ed.) (pp. 692-699). Baltimore: Williams & Wilkins.

Gold, M. S., Johnson, C. R., & Stennie, K. (1997). Eating disorders. In Lowinson, J. H., Ruiz, P., Millman, R. B., Langrod, J. G. (Eds.). *Substance abuse* (3rd ed.) (pp. 319-330). Baltimore: Williams & Wilkins.

Hansen, W. B. (1992). School-based substance abuse prevention: A review of the state of the art in curriculum. *Health Education Research: Theory and Practice*, *7*, 403-430.

Hawkins, J. D., & Catalano, R. F., Associates (1992). *Communities that care: action for drug abuse prevention.* San Francisco: Jossey-Bass.

Jacobson, M., Hoeker, C., & Atkins, R. (1983). *The book merchants.* Washington, D.C.: CSPI Books.

Jansen, M. A., Glynn, T., & Howard, S. (1996). Prevention of alcohol, tobacco and other drug abuse: Federal efforts to stimulate prevention research. *American Behavioral Scientist, 39,* 790-807.

Koop, C. E. (1995). A personal role in health care reform. *American Journal of Public Health, 85*(6), 759-760.

Kumper, K. L., & Alvarado, R. (1996). Strengthening families to prevent drug use in multiethnic youth. In Botvin, G. J., Schinke, S., & Orlandi, M. A. (Eds.) *Drug abuse prevention with multiethnic youth,* (pp. 225-294). Thousand Oaks, CA: Sage.

Lilienfeld, A. M., & Lilienfeld, D. E. (1994). *Foundations of epidimiology*. Oxford: University Press.

Lofquist, W. A. (1989). *Discovering the meaning of prevention.* Tucson: AYD Publication.

Okwumaba, J. O., & Duryea, E. J. (1998). A synthesis of etiology and prevention of drug abuse in youth: Application and critique of the epidemiologic model. *American Journal of Health Studies, 14*, Issue 1, 31-41.

Page, R. M. (1998). Shyness as a risk factor for substance use. *Journal of School Health*, *59*(10), 432-435.

Pentz, M. A. (In press). Preventing drug abuse through the community: Multi-component programs make the difference. In David, S. (Ed.) *National conference on drug abuse: Prevention research, presentations, papers, and recommendations*. Bethesda, MD: National Institute on Drug Abuse.

Pentz, M. A., Bonnie, R. J., & Shopland, D. R. (1996). Integrating supply and demand reduction strategies for drug abuse prevention. *American Behavioral Scientist, 39*(7), 897-910.

Perry, C. L., & Williams, C. L. (1998). Project Northland: Outcomes of a community-wide adolescent alcohol use prevention trial. *The Prevention Researcher*, *5*(2), 8-12.

Randall, T. G., & Bruvold, W. H. (1998). A meta-analysis of school-based smoking and alcohol use prevention program. *Health Education Quarterly, 15*, 317-334.

Resnick, M. D. (1997). Protecting adolescents from harm: Findings from the national longitudinal study of adolescent health. *Journal of the American Medical Association*, *78*(10), 823-832.

Severson, H. H., Glasgow, R., Wirt, R., & Brozovsky, P., Zoret, L., & Black, C. (1991). Preventing the use of smokeless tobacco and cigarettes by teens: Results of a classroom intervention. *Health Education Research, 6*, 109-120.

Shore, E. R. (1994). Outcome of a primary prevention project for business and professional women. *Journal of Studies on Alcohol, 55*, 657-659.

Simon-Morton, B. G., & Donohow, L. (1997). Health communication in the prevention of alcohol, tobacco, and drug use. *Health Education & Behavior, 24*(5), 544-554.

Substance Abuse and Mental Health Services Administration (1998). New SAMHSA prevention guidelines focus on family role. *The Brown University Digest of Addiction Theory and Application, 17*(7), 7-8.

Sussman, S., Dent, C. W., Stacy, A. W., Sun, P., Craig, S., & Somon, T. C. (1993). Project towards no tobacco use: 1-year behavior outcomes. *American Journal of Public Health, 83*, 1245-1250.

U.S. Department of Health and Human Services. (1990). *Healthy people 2000: National health promotion and disease prevention objectives.* (DHHS Publication No. (PH5 91-50213). Washington, DC:Author.

U.S. Department of Health and Human Services. (1994). *Preventing tobacco use among young people: A report of the Surgeon General.* (PHS: Centers for Disease Control and Prevention). Atlanta, Georgia.

Vaugn, E. (1993). Chronic exposure to experimental hazard: Risk perception and self-protective behavior. *Health Psychology, 12*, 74-85.

Wills, T. A., Schreibman, D., Benson, G., & Vaccaro, D. (1994). Impact of parental substance use on adolescents: Test of mediational model. *Journal of Pediatric Psychology, 19*, 537-555.

Chapter 5

Assessment, Diagnosis, and Treatment

Thomas Mullis

Introduction

The early diagnosis and intervention in the treatment of individuals with substance abuse is critical. It has long been a given that the earlier the treatment for drug abuse the better the results. The purpose of this chapter is to provide an overview of assessment, diagnosis, and treatment planning for individuals with substance abuse problems. While reference is made consistently to processes related to adolescent development, the intent is to provide information to professional counselors in school, rehabilitation, school psychology, social work, public mental health, and private treatment settings. Consequently, the information provided as applicable to one clinical setting may not apply as fully to others. Counselors will need to select the procedures and approaches that are useful and adaptable to their particular setting.

The information to be obtained in a comprehensive assessment includes

(1) developmental aspects of adolescence,
(2) external influences such as family and peer groups,
(3) diagnostic information relating to etiology and prognosis, and
(4) recommendations and considerations related to a treatment plan.

A structured diagnostic interview is presented as a model for clinicians to use because managed care and other third parties often expect structured interview information and clinical documentation (Appendix A). Accountability in practice is required in most settings. The writer does not take the position that a medical diagnosis is in the best interest of the adolescent. However, since managed care generally requires a medical diagnosis, the information is provided on medical diagnoses because the counselor is often left with limited options.

An important aspect in working with adolescent populations is having an understanding of the maturation process. A knowledge of the developmental processes of adolescence helps in discriminating between normal adolescent behavior and abnormal behavior. Therefore, to aid in assessment, diagnosis and planning, a brief consideration of adolescent cognitive, emotional and peer development is presented. The influence of cognitive development is the first area to be investigated.

New counselors may not know the cognitive developmental stages and need to understand that cognitive functioning in adolescence is central to the understanding of adolescent behavior and related drug use. Cognitive processing is directly related to behavior, especially risk-taking behavior. Adolescents' cognitive processes determine their motivation for drug use, as well as how they evaluate its use and consequences.

It is commonly held that most adolescents enter Piaget's formal operational stage, which involves abstract reasoning, at about age 11 or 12. However, it has been found that this is often not the case (Mullis, 1985). Piaget's stage theory allows for significant variability among individuals of approximately the same age. Chronological guidelines for stage development are only approximate. Kohlberg and Gilligan (1971) found that achieving formal operational thought may be related to socio-economic factors.

Some individuals do not ever attain formal operational thought. In fact, it could be argued that, in the case of early adolescents, many are still in the concrete operational stage. Individuals in the concrete operational stage have limited abilities to understand the consequences of their behavior. They tend to be egocentric which brings about feelings of invincibility. Elkind (1967), a Piagetian theorist, postulates that adolescents believe in "personal fables". He maintains that adolescents believe they are special and different; what happens to others will not happen to them. They do not believe that they will suffer the negative consequences of drug use experienced by other people. Moreover, they may not understand the consequences of their behavior which results in impulsive decisions.

During the comprehensive assessment, the counselor needs to be aware of maturation in relation to diagnostic and treatment decisions. Sometimes, counselors tend to judge the adolescent as having a problem with being self-absorbed when this is often normal behavior among adolescents. Drug use should be examined in the context of cognitive maturity.

Cognitive development and emotional functioning are intricately related, but emotional development and maturity have distinctive separate aspects that need to be addressed in assessment and treatment planning. Erikson's theory (1963) helps in the explanation of emotional behavior in adolescence. According to Erikson, everyone faces predictable developmental crises throughout the lifespan.

Adolescents are in the "identity versus identity confusion stage". The question the adolescent asks is "Who *am I?"* In their search for identity they test limits related to their roles in society. They are vulnerable to social influences and can be very sensitive or insensitive to others feelings. Because they are forming their identity, they are uncertain about issues. This may be reflected in choices made with regard to risk taking behaviors, such as sexual behavior and drug use. The adolescent's identity, or lack of identity, has a dramatic influence on behavior in determining values and behavior. The level of emotional maturation is reflected in the adolescent's ability to understand relationships, and control impulsivity. The counselor needs to understand that a "cocky" exterior often masks a fragile sense of self in the adolescent.

Adolescent development is marked by the emergence of peers who have a dramatic impact on the individual. In attempting to define "who they are", adolescents move from looking to parental influences to validation by peers. Individuation is the process by which the individual develops his or her own sense of identity, and individuation is dramatically influenced by peer group interactions (Mullis, 1997).

Friends are seen as partners in experimentation and their feedback is used to determine what is acceptable and unacceptable behavior. Peer acceptance often determines values and self worth. Consequently, the adolescent is likely to conform to peer norms and expectations. The more cohesive the peer group, the more its influence on behavior. This is manifested in the conformity demonstrated by adolescents who are in gangs. The types of drugs used and frequency of use is often driven by the adolescent peer group control. Early adolescents, adolescents and late adolescents tend to display different drug usage, which is related to the various influences of their different peer groups.

The Comprehensive Assessment Process

There are three important considerations that need to be addressed in conducting an assessment:

(1) the purposes in conducting the assessment,
(2) client and setting issues,
(3) rapport building and informed consent,
(4) and the methods available in assessment (the structured diagnostic interview, drug testing, and psychometric testing) which are used to gather the important information necessary to make diagnosis and referral decisions.

Purposes of Assessment

The three major purposes for a comprehensive assessment are to determine a diagnosis, devise a treatment plan, and to make appropriate referrals. In some instances, the counselor conducting the assessment will be responsible for the treatment and a referral may not be necessary. The assessment should provide a clinical picture of the client's personal level of functioning, history, presenting problems, family, and the social context in which the adolescent lives. It is important to emphasize the assessment process requires the gathering of comprehensive, accurate information, for a valid diagnosis and appropriate treatment.

Diagnosis: The counselor needs to obtain valid, reliable information, which may be vital in drug abuse cases. If the adolescent has had therapy in the past, then a previous assessment can be useful in making modifications in treatment. If not, formal diagnosis, as listed in the *Diagnostic and Statistical Manual of Mental Disorders* (APA, 1994) or an informal diagnosis, which may be more appropriate for public school settings may be done. The writer encourages the counselor to use an informal diagnosis when possible to avoid possible later stigmatization of the adolescent. Managed care and clinical settings tend to require formal diagnoses for reimbursement.

Treatment Plan: A comprehensive assessment is essential in designing a treatment plan. Obviously, the more information provided concerning the etiology, functioning level, and prognosis of the problem, the better the treatment plan. Devising a sound treatment plan is fundamental in helping clients deal with an addiction.

Appropriate Referral: A third reason for conducting an assessment is to provide information in order to make an appropriate referral. Conducting a comprehensive assessment and developing a thorough treatment plan facilitates the referral process. The counselor may decide that he or she solely may provide treatment or provide it in conjunction with some other drug treatment specialists.

In addressing these purposes, counselors need to be aware of some important therapeutic aspects and their approach when conducting an assessment with adolescents. Miller, Zweben, Diclemente, & Rychtarik (1999) emphasize that, during the assessment phase, motivational techniques should be used which will be beneficial in treatment and recovery. They maintain that the assessment should be presented in a motivational fashion, and the counselor should express empathy, avoid argumentation, be flexible with resistance, and help the client with self-efficacy. According to Miller et al., Motivational Enhancement Therapy emphasizes that the counselor should motivate clients to work on their problems. After the assessment, the client should feel positive about the assessment phase and be amenable to enter treatment. It is important to re-emphasize that the assessment process involves the gathering of comprehensive, accurate information, which is required for a valid diagnosis and appropriate treatment. Therefore, the counselor needs to obtain valid, reliable information, which may be vital in drug abuse cases.

There are a number of considerations that should be addressed in the assessment process. Important considerations include the client and setting, rapport building, structured interviewing, types of drugs and use, history of past treatments, psychiatric diagnoses, and co-morbity issues such as family dynamics, school adjustment, and conformity.

Client and Setting Characteristics

In planning an assessment, counselors need to be aware of the circumstances under which the adolescent is being seen. Since adolescent clients may be voluntary or involuntary, counselors should possess counseling skills to work with both types of clients. Many of the adolescent clients involved in the use of drugs are either court referred or school referred. The setting may require drug screening by the counselor or it may restrict confidentiality.

An important concern with involuntary adolescents is facilitating honesty. Strategies that may help in dealing with involuntary clients are

(1) giving them the opportunity to vent their negative feelings and concerns about being assessed, and conveying to them an empathic understanding of their frustrations;

(2) explaining the counselor's role and limitations of the role, legally and ethically; and
(3) attempting to bond with them. Having a truthful account of the drug use is critical in making treatment decisions.

Rapport Building Interview/Informed Consent

While adolescents do not have the same legal rights as adults, the rapport building interview should at the outset provide the adolescent with information related to informed consent. Confidentiality is important, even if the client is a minor and an involuntary referral. The client always has the choice of being non-compliant even in the face of adverse consequences, such as being placed in detention. The adolescent should be provided with an overview of the questions that will be asked, how they will be used, who will have access to the information, how the information provided may impact on him or her personally, what legal options they have, and what kind of legal access they have to their own records.

Adolescents are often resistant to self-disclose to professional counselors, and adolescent clients who are court referred or school referred can be exceedingly resistant. They have serious concerns regarding privacy, violating peer confidentiality, disappointing parents, and incurring legal and other negative consequences of admitting drug use. These concerns are valid because in many instances the counselor cannot guarantee confidentiality. When possible the counselors should not pursue identifying information about peers unless it is essential. It is vital that any concerns that the client has about the process be addressed before the structured diagnostic interview begins. The counselor may need to ask specific questions to determine what anxieties or fears the client has during the interview. Counselors need to be supportive of the client's feelings and thoughts, which can be communicated by being empathic, non-judgmental, and nonconfrontive.

The rapport building interview may be conducted at a separate time or simply precede the structured interview. While the major purpose of this interview is to establish rapport, this is an excellent opportunity to gain a wealth of information. Non-verbal communications such as: eye contact, facial expressions, head movements, tense or relaxed mood, and variations in voice pitch present significant clinical information. Initiating a rapport-building interview prior to a diagnostic structured interview is essential to ensure the validity of the latter.

While it may not be legally necessary, it is helpful to have the adolescent agree to sign a waiver of confidentiality so that the counselor may gain additional information. The adolescent should be informed what a waiver entails, how long it will be in effect, what questions will be asked, who will be contacted, and he or she should be provided with a copy of the signed waiver

The use of an unstructured interview is important in rapport building; however, a structured diagnostic interview is necessary in order to obtain specific details about drug use.

The Structured Diagnostic Interview

A structured clinical interview can be considered an empirically driven instrument if it includes concrete questions and scoring procedures. The structured diagnostic interview needs focus to maximize relevant information gathering. The interview should be direct, concrete, and completed in a logical and timely manner. It should include questions regarding:

(1) the types, combinations, frequency, and duration of substances used;
(2) past history of treatment;
(3) psychiatric/comorbidity issues;
(4) suicide concerns;
(5) family dynamics and family drug use (genetic factors);
(6) school/work performance; and
(7) peer conformity issues.

Counselors should obtain sufficient information to protect the welfare of the client or others. Since adolescent suicide has increased over the years and alcohol is associated with suicide (Rich, Young & Fowler, 1990), counselors need to ascertain in a structured format, suicidal thoughts and drinking behaviors. There are many intake forms used by mental health agencies and other settings to obtain information. However, adolescent compliance is better if the information is taken face-to-face. If written intake forms or psychometric instruments are used, it is recommended that they be used after the diagnostic interview begins.

Type/Combinations/ Frequency/ Amounts/Duration

Accurate information on the kind of drug being used is important for physical and mental health reasons. Inhalants, cannabis, and alcohol are some of illicit drugs more frequently used by adolescents (APA,

1994). Counselors need to develop a substance abuse profile and a history of the progression of the drug use. While this information may be provided in a drug screening or a psychometric profile, there is no substitute for the diagnostic interview. Patterns in drug use at different ages have been found to occur in adolescents. One pattern, proposed by Kandel (1975), is a gateway theory of drug use among adolescents. She contends that adolescent involvement occurs in four stages which progress from beer and cigarettes or liquor, as gateway drugs, to marijuana, and other drugs. Research indicates that 28% of 10th graders and 33% of 12th graders smoke (National Institute on Drug and Alcohol Abuse, 1996).

An analysis of frequency, amount used, and duration issues of substances among this group is complicated because of the different maturational levels of early adolescence, adolescence, and late adolescence. Exposure to various types of drugs, and the number of years that they have to develop drug dependency is quite different among these different age groups. How does the counselor evaluate drug abuse in a 13 year old versus a 17 year old, when both are using the same amounts of drugs? What is abusive drinking for a 13-year-old versus a 17-year-old? Counselors need to be aware of the different norm behaviors for these different groups.

A common mistake of counselors in conducting interviews with adolescents regarding frequency and amounts of drugs used is that the questions are not precise or specific. For example, in response to the interviewer asking how much do you drink, the adolescent responds that he or she drinks "some beer on the weekends". It is important to know the number of cans, bottles, cups, (the size of the container), and over what period of time the drinking occurs. It is not unusual for individuals who are drug dependent to underestimate their consumption. A "couple of drinks" of bourbon might be two 12 ounce glasses without ice. If the counselor is getting contradictory responses to the questions, follow-up questions are required and clinical judgment is needed in accessing the situation. Client background, weight, and age are important variables to consider during the assessment.

Counselors should be aware that "multiple dependence," the simultaneous use of multiple drugs and alcohol, is a major problem and is common (Frances & Miller, 1991).

Past History of Treatment

The past history of treatment is important. If possible, the records from previous providers should be obtained. It is helpful to obtain a waiver of confidentiality from the adolescent, parents, or guardians. Often, the client's memory of previous treatment is faulty. A telephone call to previous therapists is recommended, if confidentiality has been waived.

Psychiatric Diagnoses

The primary problem in diagnosing drug abuse in adolescence is that there is no valid system for diagnosis. Consequently, the diagnoses are at best marginal. The *DSM- IV* (APA, 1994) classifies drug disorders into substance use disorders (substance dependence and substance abuse) and substance-induced disorders (substance intoxication, substance withdrawal, substance-induced delirium, substance induced anxiety, depression, psychosis, mood disorders). The counselor, in using this diagnostic system, should be careful in assigning medical diagnoses to adolescent behavior. The *DSM-IV* (APA, 1994), the most widely-used diagnostic system, defines the term "substance dependency" as:

(1) tolerance (increases in the drug for the desired effects),
(2) withdrawal (distress or impairment when the drug is not available),
(3) increased amounts of use over longer periods of time,
(4) lack of control of use,
(5) high amount of time spent obtaining drugs,
(6) negative influence on social and work activities, and
(7) use continues despite knowledge of health problems.

The client must exhibit three or more of the indicators in a 12-month period to be diagnosed as substance dependent. The diagnostic criteria may be inappropriate for adolescents because adolescents may have developed neither tolerance, nor withdrawal symptoms. They might not meet any three of the criteria, but still have a significant drug problem. The diagnosis becomes particularly problematic for an early adolescent who may be having as much of a problem but may not be involved in the level of drug use that an older adolescent is experiencing. The *DSM-IV* has no developmental norms for the different stages of adolescence (APA, 1994).

The problems of appropriate diagnosis are not resolved by the *DSM-IV*'s second drug category "drug abuse" which is generally defined as a maladaptive pattern of substance use, which brings about adverse consequences. The definition further states that one or more of the following must occur in a 12 month period:

(1) failing to fulfill major role obligations at work, school, and or home (absences from school, suspensions, or expulsions from school);
(2) operating a machine or vehicle in a hazardous manner;
(3) recurring legal problems; and
(4) developing social and interpersonal problems (APA, 1994).

Many adolescents do not drive, do not have legal problems, and in the short run, have minimal conflict with peers because their peers are often using drugs with them. Adolescents who abuse drugs do not develop good interpersonal skills at a critical time of their development.

Inhalant-Related Disorders

According to the *DSM-IV*, children and adolescents are the main users of inhalants, which are low in cost and available. Inhalants use of such substances as gasoline, glue, spray paints, hair spray, and paint thinners usually begins in childhood and ends during adolescence. The *DSM-IV* lists dizziness, in coordination, slurred speech, lethargy, tremor and many other symptoms as relating to this use. Males account for 70%-80% of inhalant emergency room visits (APA, 1994). Research indicates that among 8th 10th and 12th graders, the percentage of adolescents using inhalants is approximately 20%, with use being higher in the 8th and 10th grades (National Institute on Drug and Alcohol Abuse, 1996).

Cannabis-Induced Disorders

Cannabis abuse interferes with performance at work or school and it is hazardous in situations such as driving a car or operating a machine. It is the most commonly used illicit substance and it is not surprising that adolescent usage is high. Marijuana usage for 8th graders was 23%, 10th graders was 40%, 12th graders was 45%, and 5% of seniors reported using marijuana daily (National Institute on Drug and Alcohol Abuse, 1996). It has been found that 81% of juvenile offenders met the *DSM-IV* criteria for substance abuse (Latimer, Winters, & Stinchfield, 1997).

Alcohol-Related Disorders

The first episode of alcohol intoxication is likely to occur in mid-teens. Withdrawal problems are likely to occur in adulthood. It has been found that use of alcohol is 55% in the 8th grade, 72% in the 10th grade, and 79% in the 12th grade. Approximately 4% of the seniors use alcohol daily. Alcohol consumption has increased and has become a major drug problem for adolescents (National Institute on Drug and Alcohol Abuse, 1996).

Comorbidity/Dual Diagnosis

The assessment of drug use of clients presents a major problem because of comorbidity (an additional clinical disorder or disorders occurring at the same time) or dual diagnoses. Latimer, Winters, and Stenchfield (1997) cite research indicating that 80% of adolescents in correctional institutions met the criteria for substance abuse, while 82% of adolescents who were inpatients for drug abuse met the *DSM-IV* for an Axis I disorder. When comorbidity is present, assessment is more difficult because the counselor may have problems determining a differential diagnosis for the presenting two or more diagnoses. Frances and Miller (1991) found that adolescent drug use brings about behaviors which appear similar to various forms of psychopathology since psychiatric symptoms may develop while using drugs. There are a number of dual diagnoses that are specifically associated with drug abuse or drug dependency. These include depression, conduct, anxiety/panic, substance-induced-anxiety, and eating disorders.

Depression

There is no more important situation in which a dual diagnosis must be determined correctly than in the case of depression and drug abuse. It may be a major depression, dysthymia or adjustment disorder with depressed mood (APA, 1994). Depression is often masked in early adolescence. Some of the symptoms to look for are fatigue, poor concentration, and hypochondriasis (Cobb, 1998).

The importance of identifying depression if present cannot be overstated. If the adolescent is depressed, but the drug use covers up the depression so that the counselor does not identify it, a dangerous situation is present. Suicide is the third leading cause of death among 15-to-19 years olds and the rate has tripled over the last three decades

(National Center of Health Statistics, 1991). Many adolescents who attempt suicide either get drunk first or use other drugs prior to the attempt. Individuals who use drugs have two to eight times higher rates of suicide than those who do not use drugs (Cobb, 1998). Counselors should always conduct a suicidal assessment if there is a concern about depression. Suicidal assessments should examine risk factors, prior attempts, family histories of suicide attempts or completions, life stressors, losses, suicide plans, availability of lethal method, and death of family members or friends.

Conduct Disorders

According to the *DSM- IV*, conduct disorders are related to the use of illegal substances and illegal drug use may increase the likelihood that this disorder will persist. Individuals with conduct disorder tend to show little empathy or concern for the feelings of others. They have no real guilt and they tend to have low frustration tolerance. They are reckless and involve themselves in risk-taking behaviors like drug use (APA, 1994). Some other indicators of a conduct disorder are violations of basic rights of others, aggression to people and animals, destruction of property, deceitfulness or theft, and violation of parental rules. The diagnosis is often difficult to reach because many normal adolescents appear self-centered, selfish, and impulsive. The *DSM-IV* indicates that a conduct disorder and repeated antisocial behavior often co-occur with alcohol abuse or with other substance-related disorders (APA, 1994). Grilo, Daniel, Levy, Edell, & McGlashan (1995) found that conduct disorder is predominately diagnosed more often with substance abuse disorder and disruptive behavior is also associated with drug abuse. Milin, Halikas, Meller & Morse (1991) found that approximately 91% of adolescents abusing substance had psychiatric disorders and there was a high rate of conduct disorders in the psychiatric group.

Panic and Anxiety Disorders

Anxiety is characterized by persistent and excessive worry, which includes symptoms of sweating, nausea, dizziness trembling, fear of dying, and palpitations (APA, 1994). Substance-induced anxiety disorder individuals who have panic or anxiety disorders tend to self-medicate most notably with cannabis, alcohol, and cocaine (APA, 1994).

Eating Disorders

While there is limited research on the relationship between eating disorders and drug use, Holderness, Brooks-Gunn, and Warren (1994) did find a relationship between eating disorders and substance abuse. They reported that the concurrence was higher for bulimic anorectics than restrictive anorectics.

Family Dynamics and Drug Behavior

Assessing the family dynamics and drug related behavior in a family is a critical element of the diagnostic interview. Genograms are recommended for family assessments. Gladding (1998) describes a genogram as a visual representation of a family, which is depicted by geometric figures, lines and words. The counselor who would like to conduct a genogram may wish to use a standard marriage and family systems text as a reference on how to do a genogram. The counselor will find that a genogram will provide a wealth of information relating to drug use among family members, suicidal attempts, deaths, illnesses, socio-economic factors, verbal and physical abuse, sexual abuse, family roles, triangulation (the case where two family members develop a coalition against another member), family values, communication patterns, criminal behavior, and family secrets.

While parents who do not use drugs tend to model non-drug behavior in their children, parents who use drugs are more likely to have children who use them (Chassin, Curran, Husson & Colder, 1996). Washton (1995) emphasizes that drug use by parents, grandparents, uncles, aunts, or siblings is related to the client's drug use. If there is a history of chemical dependence in the family of one or both parents, there is a tendency for increased use by children. Washton further maintains that just the history of drug use in the family can provoke the client's continued use. These families often serve as enablers, and financially support the patient's use, help in obtaining the drugs, sabotage the client's recovery, and tolerate the client's dysfunctional behavior.

Counselors should also look for patterns of genetic aspects of addiction, particularly alcoholism. The *DSM- IV* states that alcohol dependence has a familial pattern, and some of the transmission can be genetic (APA, 1994). Alcohol dependence is three to four times higher if the adolescent has family members who have the disease. There is a higher risk with a greater number of affected relatives, and it is higher in monozygotic than dizygotic twins (APA, 1994).

An interview should be completed with the adolescent's family after the structured interview with the adolescent. The counselor should make certain the adolescent knows about the planned interview and what questions will be asked. The counselor may choose to include or not include the adolescent in the family interview.

School Work Performance

The impact of drug abuse can have a dramatic impact on grades, class attendance, completion of work, and involvement in school related activities. Abrupt patterns of dramatic change, grades suddenly falling, truancy, dropping out of athletics or school related activities can be indicative of drug use. Counselors will find it helpful if teachers do a behavioral checklist or give an evaluation of the adolescent's performance.

When adolescents have worked or are working, an assessment by their employer can be helpful. Counselors may ask the adolescent to sign a waiver of confidentiality to contact teachers or supervisors at work. The problems of confidentiality and protecting the privacy of the student may override the opportunities to obtain their input.

According to the *DSM-IV*, school and work problems are often linked to a conduct disorder, wherein teenagers do poorly in school, get into fights, have temper outbursts, have lower than average intelligence, have low academic achievement, get school suspension, get expulsion, or have problems at work (APA, 1994).

Peer Conformity

The major differentiation between children and adolescents is the emergence of the importance of peer groups. Adolescents spend more time with individuals belonging to their age group and persons who share their interests than at any other time in their life. They tend to break away from parents and seek peer group recognition and approval. Conformity is an important aspect of adolescent behavior. It not only impacts on the use of drugs, but influences other behaviors such as sexual activity, music choices, dress preference, and language.

Early and middle adolescents tend to exhibit more conformity behavior than older adolescents (Gavin, Furman & Miller 1989). Urberg (1992) indicates that peer influence impacts on the adolescent in regard to the use of drugs. Conformity research by Kandel (1978) suggests that adolescents seek out friends who engage in the activities they enjoy, and he finds that friendship plays a role in the use of marijuana. Assessment of the adolescent's conformity to peer pressure is essential in determining causation of substance abuse. Cobb (1998) states that gangs have risen in number dramatically in the past generation and believes that gangs have changed their function from protecting certain territories to engaging in criminal enterprises. Violence has increased, and 93% of gangs are involved in drug activities. The gangs no longer are involved just in the streets, but control the schools (Cobb, 1998).

Adolescent Substance Abuse Diagnostic Model Interview.

A diagnostic interview, which has been designed specifically for adolescents, is provided (Appendix A) and addresses the major areas that need to be investigated. Some of the questions are very direct and may be anxiety provoking to the adolescent. The counselor needs to determine based on his/her relationship with the client how the questions are to be asked, how they can be rephrased or whether they should be asked. The purpose in using a structured interview is to provide a means of obtaining sufficient information to make a diagnosis and treatment plan. The questions do not have to follow the sequence that is presented. It may be necessary to complete the interview in two or three sittings. It is recommended that questions concerning depression and suicide should be covered in the first structured interview period. The structured interview includes questions regarding drug usage, previous treatment, psychiatric/diagnostic issues, family influences, school and work information, and peer group influences. Notes should be taken when conducting the interview in order to provide documentation. Some counselors may chose to use mental status examinations to supplement this interview format. The use of a mental status exam is a clinical decision and depends on the severity of the problems. The structured interview that is provided in Appendix A has mental status questions, but the counselor may wish to add additional questions. Mental status exams usually assess appearance, behavior, mood and affect, speech and language, thought processes and content, cognitive functioning, and insight. A full mental status exam should be pursued if the adolescent appears to have severe problems in orientation, thought processes, and mood. Counselors need to determine if the behaviors are due to a drug induced problem or other psychiatric disorders.

Drug Testing

Drug testing is ideally done with the client's permission. However, if the drug screening is involuntary, it is preferable that the counselor not be placed in the role of punishing the client if the results are positive. According to Washton (1995), urine testing is recommended way to confirm whether or not a person is using drugs. He suggests that the testing can occur through a lab that picks up the sample at the counselor's office, or by the counselor requesting that the adolescent go to the screening office. Washton observes that the most common drugs found in urine tests are alcohol, cocaine, amphetamines, benzodiazepines, barbiturates, opioids, cannabinoids and heroin, and LSD.

When counselors request urine testing or blood testing, they need to understand the probabilities of false positives or false negatives. Additionally, it is important to know how long a particular drug stays in the body after use. Interpreting drug tests requires a knowledge about pharmacology. The writer recommends using a consultant for these interpretations.

Psychometric Evaluations

Psychometric tests or inventories have distinct advantages over the structured interviews because they provide norming data. Frances & Miller (1991) suggest that the two best tests for adolescents are the Personal Experience Inventory (PEI) and the Chemical Dependency Assessment Survey. Washton (1995) stresses that structured questionnaires like the Michigan Alcoholism Screening Test (MAST) are not appropriate for adolescents because they were designed for adults. He recommends the PEI because it provides norms for comparisons of client scores with scores of "normal" individuals and also scores with adolescents in drug treatment centers. Latimer, Winters, & Stinchfield (1997) found that the Problem-Oriented Screening Instrument for Teenagers (POSIT) did well in identifying psychoactive substance use disorders in adolescents. Commonly used screening instruments include the *Psychosocial and Substance Use History, Initial Behavioral Assessment and Functional Analysis, Comprehensive Drinker Profile, Michigan Alcoholism Screening Test,* and *Questionnaire on Drinking and Drug Abuse.* Counselors must be aware that managed care or third party payers prefer structured interviews over psychometric testing (Ben-Porath, 1997).

Diagnosis

To arrive at a diagnosis, all the information which has been gathered, including age of the adolescent, frequency of drug use, amount of use, duration, and physical and psychological symptoms, must be organized and analyzed. Washton (1995) makes the following recommendations in determining a diagnosis:

(1) the client's substance use should be placed on a continuum that ranges from normal-to-abuse-to-dependency;
(2) the client's behavior should be assessed in relation to the criteria as found in the *DSM-IV*; and
(3) the counselor needs to be careful in making diagnoses related to illegal drug use because there are societal pressures when dealing with illegal drugs.

The counselor should not be placed into a situation where moral or political considerations are used in making a diagnosis. An informal diagnosis or using a diagnostic procedure other than *DSM-IV* is quite acceptable; however, it generally does not ensure third party payments. Counselors, in their diagnostic statement, need to include considerations regarding etiology, symptoms, and the prognosis of the disorder. At this time, it is necessary to decide if a dual diagnosis is appropriate. This information is essential in devising a treatment plan.

Treatment Planning

Once the diagnosis has been reached, it is important to formulate the treatment plan in conjunction with the client and significant others. The major considerations are:

(1) how severe is the drug disorder;
(2) is it a dual diagnosis situation;
(3) what is the optimal therapy to treat the individual and his or her disorder or disorders (residential vs.outpatient, confrontive vs. supportive, group versus individual);
(4) where should the adolescent reside (in his or her home or at a different location;
(5) what are the referral sources;
(6) what should be the duration of the treatment;
(7) what is the plan for aftercare or relapse;
(8) what role will the family play in treatment (family therapy, couples therapy, etc.);
(9) what are the financial resources that are available;

(10) what will be the arrangements regarding educational needs (should he or she continue to attend the same school, change school or have school provided in a treatment center);
(11) what role will the counselor play in the treatment; and
(12) what role will managed care play in the final decisions.

Most of these considerations interact with each other and need to be assessed in concert with each other. For example, type of drug use and severity impacts on residential or outpatient treatment, cost, possible referral resources, need for specialized treatment, school placement, duration of treatment, relapse issues, type of treatment, family treatment, and the role of the interviewing counselor. The limitation of space prevents examining in detail each of these aspects in treatment planning.

It is essential that the counselor be knowledgeable about the available services in his or her area, as well as outside of the area. Simply having a listing of the agencies and the providers is insufficient. Counselors need to have a good working knowledge of mental health providers who specialize in drug treatment, the population they typically serve (Is it an adolescent program?), the theoretical approach (Is it confrontive or supportive?), the effectiveness of treatment, their credentials, the cost, and the referral procedures to begin treatment. Counselors need to be aware that there are malpractice issues regarding making improper referrals. In the case of residential treatment, it should be with other adolescents not with different age groups.

In some ways, the role that managed care plays in influencing a treatment plan is a most important consideration. Whether the counselor agrees or not, managed care often drives the treatment plan in terms of type and availability of residential treatment, duration of treatment, number or outpatient visits, and type of service provider. The provider often has to be a part of a panel of providers approved by the managed care company.

Summary

In order to conduct a valid, comprehensive assessment, counselors need to be able to:

(1) use developmental norms for the different stages of adolescence (early adolescence, adolescence, and late adolescence) in making any decision regarding normal use or abuse of drugs;
(2) conduct an informal rapport building interview, which

includes providing informed consent information to the client;

(3) conduct a structured diagnostic interview, which includes questions related to drug use, family history, peer relations, psychiatric issues, physical and psychological symptoms, and other relevant information;

(4) devise, if necessary, a drug screening procedure;

(5) select, if necessary, an appropriate psychometric instrument for the assessment;

(6) arrive at a definitive diagnosis (which may require a dual diagnosis);

(7) devise a treatment plan which uses the diagnostic information; and

(8) make an appropriate referral.

References

American Psychiatric Association. (1994). *Diagnostic and statistical manual of mental disorders* (4th ed.). Washington, DC: Author.

Ben-Porath, Y. S. (1977. Use of personality assessment instruments in empirically guided treatment planning. *Psychological Assessment Vol 9,* No. 4.

Chassin, L., Curran, P. J., Hussong, A. M., & Colder, C.R. (1997). The relation of parental alcoholism to adolescent substance use: A longitudinal follow-up study. *Journal of Abnormal Psychology, 105*, 70-80.

Cobb, N. (1998). *Adolescence.* Mountain View, CA: Mayfield Publishing.

Elkind, D. (1967). Egocentrism in adolescence. *Child Development, 38,* 1025-1034.

Erickson, E. H. (1963). *Childhood and Society* (2nd ed.). New York: Norton

Evans, J. P., & Taylor, J. (1995). Understanding violence in contemporary and earlier gangs: An exploratory application of the theory of reasoned action. *Journal of Black Psychology*, 21, 71-81.

Frances, R., & Miller, S. (1991). *Clinical textbook of addictive disorders.* New York: Guilford Press.

Gavin, L. A., Furman, R., & Miller, S. I., (1989). Age differences in adolescents' perceptions of their peer groups. *Developmental Psychology, 25,* 827-824.

Gavin, L. A., Furman., R., & Buhrmester, D. (1992). Age and sex differences in perceptions of networks of personal relationships. *Child Development, 63*, 103-115.

Gladding, S. T. (1998) *Family Therapy History, Theory and Practice.* Upper Saddle River: NJ. Prentice-Hall.

Grilo, C. B., Daniel, W. M., Levy, K., Edell, W., & McGlashan, T. (1995). Psychiatric comorbidity in adolescent inpatients with substance used disorders. *Journal of American Academy of Child and Adolescent Psychiatry, 34*, (8), 1085 (7).

Holderness, C., Brooks-Gunn, J., & Warren, M. (1994). Co-morbidity of eating disorders and substance abuse: Review of the literature. *The International Journal of Eating Disorders,6* (1).

Kandel, D. B. (1975). Stages in adolescent involvement in drug use. *Science,190*, 912-914.

Kandel, D. B. (1978). Similarity in real-life adolescent friendship pairs. *Journal of Personality and Social Psychology, 36*, 306-312.

Kohlberg, L., & Gilligan, C. (1971). The adolescent as philosopher: The discovery of self in a postconventional world. *Daedalus, 100,* 1051-1086.

Latimer, W., Winters, K., & Stinchfield, R. (1997). Screening for drug abuse among adolescents in clinical and correctional settings using the Problem-Oriented Screening Instrumentation for Teenagers. *American Journal of Drug and Alcohol Abuse, 23* (1), 79, (20).

McGlashan, T. (1995). Psychiatric comorbidity in adolescent inpatients with substance used disorders. *Journal of American Academy of Child and Adolescent Psychiatry, 34* (8), 1085, (7).

Milin, R., Halikas, J., Meller, J., and Morse, C. (1991). Psychopathology among substance abusing juvenile offenders. *Journal of the American Academy of Child and Adolescence Psychiatry, 30*, (4).

Miller, W., Zweben, A., Diclemente, C., & Rychtarik, R. (1999). *Motivational enhancement therapy manual: A clinical research guide for therapists treating individuals with alcohol abuse and dependence.* National Institute of Alcohol Abuse and Alcoholism Project MATCH Monograph Services.

Mullis, T. (1985, July). Piagetian formal operational task performance as related to gifted and talented. *Sixth World Conference on the Gifted.* Paper presented at Hamburg, Germany.

Mullis, T. (1997, July). Adult Child Individuation. *Fifth European Congress of Psychology,* Dublin, Ireland.

National Center for Education Statistics. (1968-1991). *Vital statistics of the United States: Vol 2. Mortality-Part A (for 1966-1988).* Washington, DC: Author.

National Institute on Drug and Alcohol Abuse. (1996*), 1996 Monitoring the Future Study.* Washington DC: Author.

Rich, C. L., Young, D., & Fowler, R. C. (1990). San Diego suicide study: The adolescents. *Adolescence, 25*, 855-865.

Urberg, K. A. (1992). Locus of peer influence: Social crowd and best friend. *Journal of Youth and Adolescence, 21,* 439-547.

Washton, A. M. (1995) *Psychotherapy and Substance Abuse*. New York: Guilford Press.

APPENDIX A

ADOLESCENT SUBSTANCE ABUSE DIAGNOSTIC INTERVIEW

A: DRUG, TOBACCO OR ALCOHOL USE

Directions to using the table. (1) Enter the name of the drug used. (2) Enter the number of days that usage occurred in the past week, the number of months the drug was used in the last year, and the number of years the client has been using the drug, (3) Enter the amount of the drug used, and over what period of time, record for the past week the highest usage event (the highest consumption over the shortest period of time). For example, if the client drank 24 beers in 10 hours, which was the highest instance of abuse, circle 10 hours when active continuous drug use occurred, and then write in 24 beers for number, and 12 ounce bottles for volume. For months and years usage, record the high usage behavior reported in the clinical observation column. (4) enter the age at first use. (5) Below the following table indicate the last drugs used how long ago did it occur, and the names of drugs.

Table for Drug Usage

First choice/most used DRUG	Number of days of drug use in past week	Number of months of drug use in Past year	Number of years of Use	Age at first use	Highest usage in the last week, amount used ounces, pills, etc	Clinical observations
____________			____	___	Number	
Maximum usage in relation to hours 1 2 3 4 5 6 7 8 9 10 11 12 13 14 15 16 17 18 19 20 21 22 23 24 (continuing active use)					Type, form container volume amount ________ ________	

Last Drug Used

Approximate last time any drug was used: ___3-10 hours ago, name of drug (s)________________
____________________, ___11-24 hours, drug ________________________
over 24 hours, drugs_______________________________, when______________________

Second choice/most used DRUG ______________ Maximum usage in relation to hours	Number of days of drug use in past week	Number of months of drug use in Past year	Number of years of Use ____	Age at first use __	Highest usage in the last week, amount used ounces, pills, etc Number Type, form container volume	Clinical observations

Last Drug Used

Approximate last time any drug was used: ___3-10 hours ago, name of drug (s)_________________
____________________, ___11-24 hours, drug __________________________
over 24 hours, drugs__________________________________, when________________________

Third choice/most used DRUG ______________ Maximum usage in relation to hours 1 2 3 4 5 6 7 8 9 10 11 12 13 14 15 16 17 18 19 20 21 22 23 24	Number of days of drug use in past week	Number of months of drug use in Past year	Number of years of Use ____	Age at first use __	Highest usage in the last week, amount used ounces, pills, etc Number Type, form container volume amount _______ _______	Clinical observations

Last Drug Used

Approximate last time any drug was used: ___3-10 hours ago, name of drug (s)_________________
____________________, ___11-24 hours, drug __________________________
over 24 hours, drugs__________________________________, when________________________

Fourth choice/most used DRUG ________________ Maximum usage in relation to hours 1 2 3 4 5 6 7 8 9 10 11 12 13 14 15 16 17 18 19 20 21 22 23 24	Number of days of drug use in past week	Number of months of drug use in Past year	Number of years of Use ____	Age at first use __	Highest usage in the last week, amount used ounces, pills, etc Number Type, form container volume amount ________ ________	Clinical observations

Last Drug Used

Approximate last time any drug was used: ___3-10 hours ago, name of drug (s)________________ ___________________, ___11-24 hours, drug ________________________
over 24 hours, drugs______________________________, when______________________

Fifth choice/most used DRUG ________________ Maximum usage in relation to hours 1 2 3 4 5 6 7 8 9 10 11 12 13 14 15 16 17 18 19 20 21 22 23 24	Number of days of drug use in past week	Number of months of drug use in Past year	Number of years of Use ____	Age at first use __	Highest usage in the last week, amount used ounces, pills, etc Number Type, form container volume amount ________ ________	Clinical observations

Last Drug Used

Approximate last time any drug was used: ___3-10 hours ago, name of drug (s)________________ ___________________, ___11-24 hours, drug ________________________
over 24 hours, drugs______________________________, when______________________

Sixth choice/most used DRUG ______________ Maximum usage in relation to hours 1 2 3 4 5 6 7 8 9 10 11 12 13 14 15 16 17 18 19 20 21 22 23 24	Number of days of drug use in past week	Number of months of drug use in Past year	Number of years of Use ____	Age at first use __	Highest usage in the last week, amount used ounces, pills, etc Number Type, form container volume amount ______ ______	Clinical observations

Last Drug Used

Approximate last time any drug was used: ___3-10 hours ago, name of drug (s)______________
__________________, ___11-24 hours, drug __________________
over 24 hours, drugs______________________________, when__________________

1. Are there any other drugs that you have used that you did not mention? Yes No

2. What was the first drug you ever had?
When?
Who did you do it with?

3. What effects have you felt from your drug use?
Physically (list reactions)

Psychologically (list reactions)

4. Do you believe that you can stop using these drugs (be specific)?
Yes No
Have you ever stopped taking a drug? If no, go to questions 4.
Yes No
Which ones and how long?

5. **Have you ever overdosed?** If no, go to question 6. **Yes No**
When and how many times? 1 2 3 4 5 6 What were the drugs used?

6. **Where do you get your drugs?** (this may be a question you may not ask)

7. **Who uses drugs with you?** (the clinician needs to decide if identify information is appropriate)

8. **Do you smoke cigarettes?** If no go to questions 9. **Yes No**

How many per day? 1-5 5-10 15-20 25-30 35+

How many years have you been smoking? Less than 1, 1 2 3 4 5 6 7 8 9 10+

How old were you when you started smoking? 8 9 10 11 12 13 14 15 16 17

9. **Have you ever had a blackout from drinking?** If no, go to question 10. **Yes No**

How many times ? 1 2 3 4 5 6 7 8 9 10+ Tell me about it.

How old were you when you started drinking? 7 8 9 10 11 12 13 14 15 16+

10. **If you have sniffed or used inhalants, would you tell me about it? Yes No**

What have you sniffed? When did you do it?

11. **Did you ever use diet pills? Yes No**

COUNSELOR DRUG SUMMARY

____________________multiple drug use same time _________________single drug use

_____ high drug usage _____moderate _______some_____none

_____ serious health problem ____moderate health ___mild health problem___no problem

_____ self report appears honest ____self report appears guarded ____self report unreliable

_____ problems very serious ______problems somewhat serious______problems not too serious

_____ use disrupts school, social relations, etc______does some disruption___no disruption

Comments:

B. PREVIOUS TREATMENT (Inpatient and Outpatient)

1. Have you ever been treated or seen anyone for a drug problem in the past or for any other personal problem? Yes No (If yes, determine the history of the care, dates, duration, problem treated, and names of providers (obtain a release of information if appropriate)

C. PSYCHOLOGICAL DISORDERS

The counselor asks about the symptoms that the client is experiencing, if any, in order to determine a diagnosis and to determine if there is a coexisting drug use problem.

1. Circle any of these that the client reports having: headaches, vomiting, sadness, unable to sleep, uncontrollable anger, anxiety, fear, panic attacks, no energy, crying, hearing voices, feeling alone, sleeping too much, loss of memory, unable to concentrate, dizziness, speech problems, tremor, blurred vision, sweating, fear of dying, black-outs, shaking, hallucinations, anxiety due past events (sexual abuse, rape, physical abuse), what kinds of problem related to past events?____)
Other problems____
Total number circled or listed_____

2. Do you ever have any these feelings mentioned without drugs?
If no, go to question 3 **Yes No**

Which ones?

How long have you had these feelings or symptoms without the use of drugs?

3. Do you ever feel depressed? Yes No If no, go to question 4
_____very_____somewhat_____a little_____not at all
When and how long?

Can you usually get over it?

How do you get over it?

Do you have trouble getting up in the morning? Yes No

Tell me about your sleeping.

Do you cry a lot? **Yes No** *If yes, what do you cry about?*

Has anyone that is a good friend died recently? **Yes No**
If yes, tell me about it.

4. Have you ever thought of hurting yourself or others? Yes No
If yes, tell me about it. (Look for a plan)

Have had those thoughts today? **Yes No** *If yes, tell me about them?*

How would you do it if you were going to hurt yourself or someone else?

5. Has anyone in your family hurt themselves or someone else?
Yes No

6. Have you ever been in trouble with authorities or your parents? Yes No

If no, go to question 7.

What were some of complaints?

7. Have you ever been arrested when using drugs? Yes No

If no, go to question 8.

What were you charged with?

8. Have you ever destroyed anyone's property? Yes No

If no, go to 9.

9. Have you ever hurt an animal or a person for fun? Yes No

If no, go to 10. Tell me about it.

10. Have you ever hurt a friend with a weapon? Yes No

If yes, tell me about it.

11. Have you ever stayed out all night when your parents did not give you permission?

If yes, how often? Tell me about it.

12. Do you feel upset a lot? Yes No *If yes, tell me about it.*

13. Have you ever been fearful of going to school or going anywhere? Yes No *If yes, tell me about it.*

14. Have you ever felt overcome with fear, sweating, and breathing problems? Yes No

If yes, tell me about it.

15. Do you have mood swings or do you get angry or sad quickly? Yes No

If yes, tell me about it.

16. Do you sometimes seem to stay up all night without any problem? Yes No

If yes, tell me about it.

COMMENTS

Counselor's Psychological Summary

(If necessary)(If necessary)
Tentative Diagnosis (1)__________________ (2) ____________________

______ severely depressed ______somewhat depressed ______not very depressed

______ suicidal ____somewhat suicidal ___does not seem suicidal _____cannot access

______ a lot of anxiety _______some anxiety ________very little anxiety_______

______ very insensitive to others ________somewhat insensitive ________sensitive

______ manic _______somewhat manic________not manic

______ very angry________somewhat angry__________not angry

______ dangerous to self or others__________does not seem dangerous to self or others

______ psychotic features______some psychotic features______no psychotic features

______ Single diagnosis ______dual diagnosis

(If necessary)

Axis I _____. _____ _____ . _____

Axis II ____ . _____ _____ . _____

GAF SCORE:____

Comments:

Code: (3,4,5) depression
(6,7,8,9,19,11) conduct (12,13,14,15) Mood, Anxiety

D. FAMILY DYNAMICS

Complete a genogram on the back of the form. Summarize the finding of the genogram. Include any family psychiatric disorders, dual diagnoses, depression, suicide attempts or completions, overdoses, pay attention to communication patterns in the family, and dysfunctional aspects, note deaths, divorces, blended families, drug use in family.

Genogram Summary:
(check)

Family __intact__divorced.___single parent___parent deceased____blended family

Living situation___both parents_____mother____father____foster parents

____state home_____grandparent_____blended family_____other

History of crime___father____mother___siblings___relatives____stepparents

History of addiction___father___mother______siblings_____relatives____stepparents

History of mental illness__father___mother____siblings_____relatives____stepparents

History of suicide_____father_____mother_____siblings_____relatives____stepparents

Attempts of suicide ____father_____mother______siblings_____relatives_____stepparents

Complete after the interview

1. **Has anyone in your family ever taken drugs?** (if not answered in genogram) **Yes No** *If no, go to question 2*
   What drugs?
   Are they presently doing drugs? (*Check for each if drug use is occurring)*
   Father Stepfather
   Mother Stepmother Siblings

   Who are other members of the family system/boyfriend/ girlfriend/ that use drugs? Look for genetic aspects (particularly alcoholics).

2. **What kinds of problems, if any, have you had with your parents?**

Counselor's Family Summary

_____ family intact _____divorced_______blended_______single parent

_____ family income_____high _____moderate_____low

_____ deaths/parent(s)_____sibling_____other_____none

_____ sexual abuse____parent ____sibling____other____none reported

_____ physical or verbal abuse____parent____sibling____other ____none reported

_____ severe Illness or disability_____none reported

_____ family history drug use ___very involved ____somewhat involved ___none

_______criminal history ______none reported

_______communication_________good______average______poor

_______warmth, coehesion______good______average______poor

_______drug use family high ______moderate_________none

Comments:

E. SCHOOL/WORK ADJUSTMENT

What is the school performance like? Does he or she have a record of poor grades, and other problems at school? The counselor should be looking at any abrupt change in behavior in work or school. Interviews at the school could be helpful.

1. **How are you doing in school? What subjects do you like?** *(be specific)*

2. **What are your grades like?** *(you may not wish to ask if you have the records)*

3. **What grade are you in?**

4. **Do you like school? Yes No** *Why?*

5. **What kinds of things do you do at school other than your studies?** *Are you involved in any clubs, sports or band?*

6. **Do you go to school activities? Yes No** *Which ones?*

7. **Have you had to miss classes lately? Yes No** *If yes, how many times this year?*

8. **Have you had any problems at school? Yes No** *If yes, what?*

9. **Have you ever taken a weapon to school? Yes No** *If yes, tell me about it.*

10. **Have you ever been suspended or expelled from school? Yes No** *If Yes, tell me about it.*

11. **Do you have/had a part time job? Yes No** *How are things going with it?*

Counselor School Adjustment Summary

____ has major school problems __has some problems___has no real problems

_____ has major work problems __ has some problems ____does not apply

_____very involved in school_____some involvement_____little involvement

_______good peer/teacher relations_______poor peer/teacher relations

________good overall school adjustment_____ moderate_______ poor

Comments:

F. PEER RELATIONS

1. **Who are some of your good friends?** *(identifying information is not necessary)*

2. **What do you like to do with your friends?** Do you ever do pranks with friends?

3. **Do you and your friends do drugs?** *If no, go to question 4.* If yes, what drugs?
How long have you been in this group?
Did your friends that you knew before these friends do drugs? Yes No
How do you get drugs? *(you may not wish to ask)*

4. **Are their gangs where you live? Yes No** *If no, go to question 5.*
Do you belong to a gang? **Yes No** *(questions could be asked if this is true)*
How long have you been in this gang?
Who were your friends before? Does the gang you belong to do drugs? Yes No If yes, what drugs? How often?

5. **Have you ever had any problems, fights etc. with individuals your age? Yes No**

6. **Do you have a boyfriend or a girlfriend? Yes No.** How long have you been seeing this person?

Counselor Peer Group Control Summary

____Peer group very controlling ___somewhat controlled_____little control

___is a gang member ___appears to be a gang member___does not appear

___peers support drug use __peers tend to support drugs ___no peer support

Comments:

Chapter 6

Treating Addictive Disorders

Susan Varhely

Introduction

There is ever-increasing attention given to seeking effective treatment for substance abuse. The search for "what works" in treatment has contributed to an explosion of research in the field. In the past two decades, there has been a proliferation of information and perspectives related to the effective treatment of substance abuse. Interestingly, however, is the fact that current treatment practice is reflective of very little of this new knowledge and is still relying on various strategies for which there is no scientific evidence (Miller et al., 1995). It seems that we " know how to do our work far better than we actually do it" (LeShan, 1996).

The purpose of this chapter is to present the "what works" in treating clients with substance abuse based on the current research literature. In order, however, to gain meaningful and thus applicable knowledge from this endeavor, counselors must first take a look at themselves. We must move beyond the "assumptions in which we are drenched" (Rich, 1979, p.35) in order to open ourselves to the variety of alternatives offered to us through the extensive study of research into what seems the most effective way to work with individuals who abuse substances. When it comes right down to it, treatment starts with the person of the counselor!

The Inner World of the Counselor

"What lies behind us and what lies before us are tiny matters compared to what lies within us."
Oliver Wendell Holmes

We, as counselors, have entered the field of counseling to relieve human suffering (Miller, Duncan, et al, 1997). Our ideals are linked to the intention of honoring the full measure and depth of the human experience. We acknowledge that each client is complex, deep, and unique in his or her ability to experience the full gamut of human emotions including hurt, joy, hope, love, and fear. We believe that through listening to clients we teach them to listen to themselves. As we care about our clients, we teach them to care about themselves. We have hopes for the clients and thereby teach them to have hopes for themselves. As we respect the clients, we teach them to respect themselves (LeShan, 1995). Truly, these beliefs are rooted, either consciously or unconsciously, within the hearts of counselors. What is also true, however, is that not infrequently, the idea of counseling someone with a substance abuse problem causes us to question our "skills", to doubt our purpose, to back away. We recall the messages we have heard about people who abuse substances: "they are a tough population to work with" because they are so "resistant" to change. All too often, our own personal experiences with individuals who struggle with substance abuse reinforce our fears and apprehensions. Therefore, before even examining the research pertaining to "what works", we must examine our hearts. We, as counselors, must explore our own inner landscapes, probing and confronting our beliefs, values, myths and fears. We must confront our wounds that have yet to be healed. All this is necessary if we are to let go of our worldview and genuinely be open and present to the worldview of our clients.

This self- confrontation might start with the question: "What do I really believe about people who abuse substances?" Social constructions of substance abuse have included such models of excessive behavior as a moral weakness, a symptom of character pathology, the result of efforts to self-medicate painful feelings, a metabolic deficiency, and a primary progressive disease. The perspectives we hold manufacture our "reality" of substance abuse (Shaffer & Robbins, 1995). We see through the paradigm of our beliefs, filtering out anything that does not fit. These worldviews remain active until new information is allowed in and is assimilated into our belief systems. Under such conditions we, as counselors, can lose the ability to facilitate change in our clients because of this "binding " function of our paradigms. (Shaffer & Gambino, 1979). Through self-awareness we are able to revise and expand "reality", to shift our paradigms, and to develop a position of openness and receptivity to another's reality.

One of the most powerful and positive consequences of the disease concept model of alcoholism is that it removed substance abuse from the realm of morality (Thombs, 1994). All the pejorative beliefs about the intrinsic worth of individuals who abuse substances had to be dismissed in the light of the fact that they had a disease, through no fault of their own. No longer was punishment the appropriate treatment of choice. Those who abused substances could no longer be considered "evil"; they were sick. This opened the door to compassionate care. The tremendous degree of shame and blame that is still associated with substance abuse, however, suggests that in our hearts we may not have let go of this belief as completely as these new conceptualizations suggest. We may actually be experiencing ambivalence in our beliefs about substance abuse. Thus, as counselors, we must honestly struggle with this issue, learning to notice how our beliefs play out in our rationalizations about counseling people who abuse substances, i.e. ,they do not want to change.

Another question that each one of us as counselors should wonder about and ask is, "How ubiquitous do I believe the problem of substance abuse is within the person?" Individuals who attend Alcoholics Anonymous usually introduce themselves to the group by using their first names followed by, "I am an alcoholic." Too often, we as counselors see primarily the label "substance abuser" rather than coming from a holistic perspective of the individual struggling, on one hand, with substance abuse, but also having a wider range of experiences, feelings, and actions. Consider the following situation that a colleague encountered while supervising a practicum student working with her volunteer client. Her client was a young, Hispanic father of two, we'll call him Joe, who worked as a heavy machine operator until a work-related injury caused him to seek vocational re-training. Now, unemployed, his wife had to return to work and he entered college to study to become a teacher. The student-counselor was doing a beautiful job of being with Joe, hearing his frustration with college and his profound grief over losing the ability to engage in work he loved, and his guilt over not being able to provide financially for his family. She was empathic, understanding, and connected. In the course of his sharing, Joe told her that he had a drinking problem in the past. He had not considered it a problem until he showed up at his son's birthday party to overhear his son telling a little friend that he did not know if Dad would be at the party because he was always out drinking. Joe was so moved by his child he decided that alcohol must be a problem for him and that he must stop drinking. Observing the video of this counseling session, the supervisor was struck by the immediate change in the student-counselor. At the sound of the words "drinking problem", all her counseling skills left her. She could no longer hear Joe's concerns nor current behaviors, but rather zeroed in on the drinking and immediately tried to refer him to the local mental health agency to speak with a counselor about substance abuse! During supervision, the student-counselor noticed her shift and realized that it was her own issues with people who abused alcohol. Her fears surrounding abusive drinking and the beliefs that this was such unknown territory, vastly different and more baffling than the experiences previously presented by her client, dominated her vision. These thoughts evoked feelings of helplessness and she shut down, disconnected from the client and focused on the "problem", no longer seeing the struggling human being before her. Robert Heinlein (1985) states: "The hardest part about gaining any new ideas is sweeping out the false ideas occupying that niche. So long as the niche is occupied, evidence, proof, and logical demonstration get nowhere" (p. 230). In this case, the "niche" was filled with personal issues, myths, and stereotypes.

In an old Zen story, a man came to the Zen Master, searching for wisdom. Before the master would teach him about wisdom, he offered the man some tea. The master poured tea into the man's cup until it overflowed onto the floor. The man was puzzled by this and inquired how come the master would do such a thing. To this, the Zen master replied that the man's mind was so filled with his ideas about what was real that he was unable to learn anything new. He must first empty out some of "the cup" by questioning his ideas; then, he could learn something new (LeShan, 1965). As counselors we must challenge our deepest beliefs, making space for new and perhaps larger views of reality to flow through.

Finally, we have come to believe that people who abuse substances feel helpless over their using. They experience a sense of loss of control when it comes to stopping their using. A primary characteristic of the disease model is this loss of control (Thombs, 1994). However, the whole issue of control is central to all of us. From an existential perspective, the fear of not having control is a major source of anxiety (Willis, 1994). It is important, therefore, for counselors to confront their own sense of helplessness in the world and their own struggles with control. Can we, as counselors, let go of control, opening to our own vulnerability, and join our clients in the process of change?

Ultimately, counselors' interior world, their beliefs, values, hopes, and dreams, are mirrored in actions. Our actions reflect who we really are. The process of self-questioning and self-challenge is constant even when the answers may be illusive or unsettling. Are we willing to engage in this process?

Ethical Awareness

> *"Some patients, though their condition is perilous, recover their health simply through their contentment with the goodness of the physician."*
>
> *Hippocrates*

An area of critical concern to counselors is the ethical perspective involved in the work we do. Incumbent upon the counselor is the mandate to do no harm to clients. As Bissell & Royce (1994) have pointed out, "harm" can be in the form of both action and omission. We, as counselors, must have foremost in our awareness the commitment to do what is in the client's best interest. Deciding what is best for the client often feels challenging, confusing and something like walking a razor's edge. The ethical principles of our profession offer us some guidelines and possibilities. Unfortunately, although we seek clarity, a "right-wrong," "black-white" perspective, ethics, by definition, often presents more ambiguity and gives rise to more questions than it does definitive answers. Thus, determining what is or is not ethical behavior often creates a dilemma for the counselor. Not infrequently, the confusion and uncertainty are compounded when the client is dealing with a substance abuse problem. Therefore, before we proceed further with what works in counseling individuals with substance abuse problems, it is important to create a context for ethical inquiry and awareness.

"Ethical principles act as a rudder that guides the behavior of counselors; they are the principles that direct the moral-and-values-based decisions that affect the counseling process"(Miller, 1999, p.211). Ethical principles may be involved with laws, but they are not always interchangeable. Ethical behavior deals with the application of concepts of morality, values, and right and wrong, to the various situations that people encounter in life (Capuzzi & Gross, 1999). The ethical code of the counseling profession offers some very important issues that we, as counselors, must always be cognizant of as we work with our clients. Confidentiality and privileged communication, informed consent, dual relationships, professional responsibility and values are, perhaps, the more frequently encountered areas of ethical concern (For a complete presentation see the American Counseling Association *Code of Ethics and Standards of Practice*, 1995).

Confidentiality and Privileged Communication

A foundation stone of the counseling relationship is trust. A major aspect of this trust is the client's belief that what is shared within the counseling relationship will be kept "in confidence." Thus confidentiality is a crucial aspect of counseling. "Confidentiality is the obligation of professionals to respect the privacy of clients and the information they provide" (Handelsman, 1987, p.33).

Privileged communication is a legal right of clients that rests in state and federal statues. It is this right of clients that prevents the revelation of confidential information in a legal proceeding. In other words, the counselor cannot be made to testify in court about a client if the privilege is protected. Privileged communication is owned by the client, and only the client can waive that privilege thus allowing testimony (Hummel, Talbutt, & Alexander, 1985).

There are, however, limits to both professional and legal confidentiality. One such limit is referred to as the "duty to warn" which requires counselors to warn an endangered party when a client has made a direct threat on the life of that person. The following are additional limits to confidentiality: When child abuse and neglect are suspected or substantiated; if the client has revealed an intent to do harm to society; when the counselor is seeking consultation regarding the client from other professionals (in cases of consultation, when possible, identifying information should be concealed or disguised); and finally, the counselor must reveal information to a parent or legal guardian of a minor child client upon the request of the parent or guardian. A written consent from the client is needed in order to share information under any other circumstances. It is the responsibility of the counselor to inform the client, at the inception of treatment, of the limits of confidentiality. This is part of "informed consent" which will be discussed in more detail later.

The issue of confidentiality when working with individuals who are dealing with substance abuse problems becomes more complicated.

In addition to professional and state legal mandates requiring confidentiality, federal law also limits release of information related to treatment of those individuals with substance abuse problems when treatment providers receive federal funds for their services. Federal confidentiality laws are imposed on any counseling service received: Assessment, diagnosis, individual and group counseling. The protection of client privacy through these laws facilitates individuals seeking help for their substance abuse problems without the fear that in the future such help may have negative consequences for them (Cottone & Robine, 1998).

According to Bissell & Royce (1994), a client's involvement at a facility providing treatment for substance abuse problems cannot be disclosed without the proper consent by the client. Proper consent means that the client is made aware of the need for and extent of the disclosure. In these situations, minors have the same rights as adults. Remley (1985) has indicated that minors, too, must be informed before disclosure occurs. It is not unusual, when working with minor adolescent clients, for issues related to parents and schools to arise. According to Anderson (1996), the welfare of the adolescent client must be the primary motivator for the counselor's actions. The client's age, education, relationship with parents (or legal guardians), and the potential harm of disclosing or not disclosing information must be considered.

Informed Consent

Informed consent is the right of individuals to be fully informed about the nature of the counseling service, alternative treatments available, the qualifications of the professionals involved, the limits of confidentiality, and any other information needed for them to make a knowledgeable decision regarding counseling services (Cottone & Tarvydas, 1998). Clients must give their consent to counseling. Here again, informed consent becomes complicated due to substance abuse issues. Frequently, counseling is initiated while the person is under the direct influence of the substance and thus not in any condition to make an informed consent. After the initial intervention, it is incumbent upon the counselor to recognize and respect the individual's right to refuse counseling

It is not unusual for individuals who abuse substances to engage in substance abuse related behaviors that result in their being mandated to counseling by the judicial system. Compulsory treatment is not an automatic denial of the individual's right to consent. In such cases, it is the responsibility of the counselor to explore with the client alternatives and possible consequences for refusing counseling or terminating early (Cottone & Robine, 1998).

Dual Relationships

Dual relationships are those that contain both professional and person/nonprofessional dimensions (Swenson, 1993). Such relationships hold the potential of damaging the professional objectivity needed in the counseling relationship. The infusion of a personal component threatens the integrity of the therapeutic alliance. Friendships outside the counseling context have the tendency to challenge the needed therapeutic boundaries.

Although not all dual relationships are technically unethical, the primary question that must be foremost for the counselor is, "Does this relationship have the potential to cause physical or emotional harm to the client?" Sexual intimacies between counselor and client have been shown through research to put clients in danger of emotional harm (Bouhoustsos et al., 1983). It is a misuse of power for the counselor to cross the line of sexual intimacy. Sexual intimacies with clients are clearly unethical (Cottone & Tarvydas, 1998).

The issue of dual relationships presents additional challenges when the counselors themselves are recovering from substance abuse and are attending self-help groups such as Alcoholics Anonymous or Narcotics Anonymous. Under such circumstances, if client and counselor attend the same group meetings, the relationships shift from client/counselor to peer. The anonymity of the client within AA or NA is compromised. Recovering counselors must be aware of the potentials for these types of dual relationships to occur and therefore should attempt to seek their treatment in environments that will decrease the likelihood of non-treatment contacts with clients.

Professional Responsibility

Professional responsibility relates to the appropriateness of the counselor's professional actions. The advancement of the client's welfare is paramount for the counselor (Margolin, 1982). This means that counselors do not discriminate against those seeking their services and do not subjugate their obligations to the client to their own personal rewards.

The needs of the client are the primary focus of the counselor. When working with individuals who abuse substances it is not unusual for the counselor to see the family of the client also. The counselor must be mindful not to compromise the client's treatment in the service of the larger family system. If counseling has been undertaken for the purpose of assisting the recovery of the person with a substance abuse problem and with his/her consent, then the individual's welfare is the focus of counselor responsibility (Cottone & Robine, 1998).

Values

As discussed earlier, counselors must strive to be aware of their value system, particularly how it relates to the issues and concerns of their clients. When working with individuals who are struggling with substance abuse, counselors must clearly define for themselves their values regarding the use of substances. Substance abuse can be infused with considerable emotion for counselors depending on their personal experience with substance abuse, their beliefs about people who use substances, and their position within the total abstinence-controlled drinking controversy (Hester & Miller, 1989). It is vital that counselors do not allow their personal issues surrounding substance abuse to influence the work they do with their clients. Self-awareness on the part of the counselor becomes an ethical responsibility.

The Therapeutic Alliance

An important focus of research has been on the nature and quality of the therapeutic alliance and its relationship to treatment outcome (Bachelor & Horvath, 1999). As counselors, we are well aware that Carl Rogers (1951,1957) was a pioneer in exploring the connection between the counseling relationship and the healing process. What may be surprising is that Rogers' core conditions of empathic understanding, positive regard, genuineness, and congruence, and his emphasis upon the therapeutic relationship are supported in research as having a dominant influence on effective intervention in the treatment of people struggling with substance abuse (Miller et al., 1995; Connors, DiClemente, Carroll, Longabaugh, & Donovan, 1997). Briefly, empathic understanding refers to the ability of counselors to feel with their clients. Additionally, it is the ability to understand the feelings, thoughts, ideas, and experiences of the client through the client's eyes. Positive regard refers to the counselor's belief in the innate worth and potential of each client. Finally, genuineness and congruence relate to authenticity within the helping relationship. The counselor's behaviors, words, and actions are real rather than part of a role played (Gross & Capuzzi, 1999).

The therapeutic alliance is a collaborative effort between counselor and client consisting of an emotional bond and a shared presumption regarding the tasks and goals of the treatment process (Bordin, 1979). Research has found that there is a moderate but consistent, positive relationship between the therapeutic alliance and outcome (Horvath & Symonds, 1991). This relationship between alliance and positive outcome is consistent across a variety of therapy modalities (Beutler, Machado, & Allstetter-Neufeldt, 1994; Lambert & Bergin, 1994).

The therapeutic alliance involves the expression of the feelings and attitudes that counselor and client have toward each other (Gelso & Carter, 1985). The critical component of the process is the "working together", the collaboration of counselor and client against a common enemy, that is, the client's suffering (Bordin, 1979). In this alliance, the counselor and the better part of the client feel themselves allied in the search for the best, the thriving, of the whole client. In order to create this environment, there is nothing specific that the counselor does. For too long we have been operating under the assumption that the behaviors associated with this alliance could be standardized and taught (Miller, et al. 1995). However, we have found that the creation of this environment was more complicated than learning techniques (Garduk & Haggard, 1972). Perhaps, the challenge is not about what behaviors should be demonstrated but rather what attitudes need to be held. Research supports that these attitudes must include a real respect for the best of the client, the client's highest self (Miller et al. 1995). The counselor must believe that the healthy parts of the client are already searching for better ways of being, relating, and creating. It is part of the counselor's task to work collaboratively with the client's inner wisdom. If this vision of the client is present, it will naturally influence and help shape the counselor's words, actions, and body language.

We, as counselors, should be motivated, challenged and encouraged by the research findings acknowledging the central role of the counselor-client relationship in the process of client change (Gelso & Carter, 1985; Greenberg & Pinsoll, 1986; Rogers, 1957). Our training as counselors has been rooted in this therapeutic alliance. There is no need to "re-invent the wheel" when working with clients who abuse substances. Perhaps the words of Yalom captures succinctly this message: "It is the relationship that heals...every therapist observes over and over in clinical work that the encounter itself is healing for the patient…" (Yalom, quoted in Willis, 1994, p.109).

Different People, Different Lives, Different Choices

Our own myopia causes us to ignore the diversity of the clients who come to us. In order to be effective with each client, we must loosen the seemingly exclusive hold that our expectations and stereotypes of people with substance abuse problems have on us. Perhaps one of the greatest challenges is to recognize the variability of readiness for change and client motivation that clients who abuse substances present in counseling.

Client motivation is key in recovery. Among those who work with individuals who abuse substance, motivation has been considered a characteristic attributed to the client (Miller et al. 1995). When a client is "resistant" to the counselor's interventions, the client is considered not to be motivated to change. It is the belief that sufficient motivation is acquired by "hitting bottom". This refers to that point when a person experiences enough "world collapse" to admit to having a problem with alcohol or other substances. Within this paradigm, motivation, as a trait of the client, is either present or not. However, more recently, there has been a shift in this black and white type of thinking which can have a tremendous impact upon counseling individuals with substance abuse problems. This shift is influenced by a variety of research findings. Firstly, we have come to realize that extra-therapeutic events have the greatest single impact upon motivation to change (Miller, Duncan, & Berg, 1995). In other words, substance abuse is not just a pathology of one individual, but a complex pattern involving interactions between the individual, those around him or her and the substance (Miller et al. 1995). In addition, despite the many attempts to identify a personality specific to those who abuse substances, longitudinal studies have proven unsuccessful in this regard (Jones, 1968; Vaillant, 1983). Studies have found that substance abusing individuals are as variable in personality characteristics as non-abusers (Loberg & Miller, 1986). Perhaps even more significant, considering the propaganda to the contrary, denial and other defense mechanisms have been found to be no more or less frequent among those who abuse substances than among the general population (Chess, Neuringer, & Goldstein, 1981; Donovan, Rohsenow, Schau, & O'Leary, 1977; Skinner & Allen, 1983). We can no longer hold on to the conviction that people who abuse substances come into counseling with a consistent set of personality traits and defenses. Studies show that although "motivated' vs. "unmotivated" clients do not have predicable characteristics, the counselors who have more motivated clients do have predictable characteristics themselves (Greenwald & Bartmeier, 1963; Rosenberg & Raynes, 1973).

From the above findings, we can conclude that motivation is the result of an interaction between the individual who abuses the substance and those around him or her. Essentially, motivation is not to be viewed as what one has, but rather as something one does. According to Miller et al. (1995), motivation involves recognizing a problem, searching for a way to change it and committing to, and persevering with that change strategy. Counselors' responsibility is to develop ways to increase this movement toward change.

The emphasis on motivation has resulted in the formalization of a stage theory of motivation (Prochaska & DiClemente, 1982, 1986). Recognizing the stage of readiness for change that a client is experiencing and matching counselor intervention to this stage has been found to be the most beneficial approach for positive outcome. The process of change can be viewed as occurring through five stages: precontemplation, contemplation, determination, action, and maintenance (Miller et al., 1995). In the following section, the five stages of change will be addressed, followed by intervention strategies counselors may use to facilitate and encourage increased motivation for change.

Stage I–Precontemplation: Simply, precontemplation describes the situation in which the person, the client, is not even entertaining the possibility of a problem. It is at this stage of change that we frequently first meet our clients who abuse substances. These clients come to counseling because someone else has sent them. This "other" can be a family member, employer, or the judicial system. The "problem" is experienced more as what other people want from them. Therefore, precontemplators are usually in counseling because they are coerced to come. A way to determine this classification is to inquire of the client if he/she is seriously intending to change the "problem behavior" in the near future, the next six months or so. A typical response of the client to such an inquiry might be, "Yea, I know I've got some problems but drinking is not one of them. As soon as I get out of this dead-end job, things are really going to pick up." Or the client may simply say that he/she does not have a problem, the problem belongs to whomever referred him/her for counseling. This lack of recognition of a problem and the belief that no modification of this behavior is needed are hallmarks of the precontemplation stage.

Stage II–Contemplation: In the contemplation stage, the individual is aware that he/she does have a problem with the use of substances and has given some serious thought to overcoming this problem. However, there is no commitment to action. They have the insight, but the resolve to change the behavior has not yet been developed. It is not unusual for people to stay stuck at this stage. Prochaska, DiClemente, and Norcross (1992) have captured the essence of this position quite well: "...knowing where you want to go but not quite ready yet" (p.1103).

Many clients at the contemplation stage experience intense ambivalence (Miller & Rollnick, 1991). On the one hand, they want to move toward change, and on the other hand, they feel a desire to continue with the abusive behavior. Their moods may vacillate between defending the benefits of the abusive behavior and committing to changing it. They struggle with indulgence and restraint. It is this ambivalence conflict that makes these clients so vulnerable to the approach used by counselors. Perhaps, the least effective way to work in this situation is by using confrontation and direct persuasion. Counselors using these strategies usually find themselves faced with a "Yes, but..." response on the part of the client. Empathizing with the client's experience of conflict is found to be a more beneficial way of connecting with the client's experience at this time. In addition, it is important to recognize that the use of the substance, be it drugs or alcohol, felt useful to the client. To the client it was in some way necessary or good. (Rothschild, 1995). The counselor should not be afraid to talk about this with the client and to engage in a discussion that addresses both sides of the ambivalence. To truly experience the worldview of the client, the counselor must be willing to see the role that the substance plays in the client's life. The counselor must see this through the client's eyes!

Caroline Knapp (1996) chronicled her struggles with drinking in her book, *Drinking: A love story,* where she describes her relationship with alcohol: "I fell in love and then, because the love was ruining everything I cared about, I had to fall out" (p. xv). Knapp expressed her relationship with alcohol as being "about passion, sensual pleasure, deep pulls, lust, fears, yearning hungers. It's about needs so strong they're crippling." When she contemplated giving up drinking, she said it was "about saying good-bye to something you can't fathom living without" (p. 5). These words express the depth, power, and intensity of the relationship with a substance. We have, no doubt, experienced love relationships that have enveloped us and then let us down. The need to talk about these types of relationships can be all-consuming. It may be that in order to heal, these feelings of incredible attachment, loss, and betrayal must be expressed. These feelings may be at the heart of the ambivalence.

Stage III – Determination: During this stage, the ambivalence seems to shift towards change. Through interaction with the counselor as well as extra-therapeutic events, there seems to be enough evidence in the "need for change" column to influence the client's conviction that change is in order. We hear this sentiment in the client's words "I just can't go on like this anymore. I must do something!" This is truly a window of opportunity (Miller et al., 1995).

This window may present itself early in counseling or after many years of struggling with substance abuse and many tries at counseling. The latter is the case with "Mark" who was a long-term heroin addict involved in yet another relapse. He has been in and out of both the mental health and judicial systems as a result of his use and abuse of heroin. He has always been a mandated client in counseling. He would come to counseling as a prerequisite for either keeping his job or as a condition included in sentencing by the courts. Each time, Mark would be focused on the reasons others wanted him to give up heroin. Although considering the difficulties his substance use caused in his life, he generally minimized them, preferring instead to see other people or situations as being the real causes of his life problems. He consistently terminated counseling after the required sessions were finished, stayed drug free for various short periods of time, one to two years being the longest, and then gradually resumed his use of heroin. However, the last time he was directed to counseling by the courts, he began to become aware of his world collapsing. He had already lost his job and discovered that no one else was willing to hire him. His family had left him. His health had severely deteriorated and he was incarcerated for a third time for drug-related behaviors. Emotionally, he felt at a point of despair. Confronted with so many losses, the scale of his ambivalence tipped, and Mark was ready for a change. He clearly acknowledged to the counselor that his addiction to heroin had truly caused him to be unable to manage his life. He spoke from his heart: " Heroin was my primary relationship; it was my life. And it betrayed me." He expressed his commitment to find a way to change his continually defeating cycle of abuse.

We might consider this determination to change as a kind of epiphany. This was the case with a female client who came to the realization that her substance abuse was holding her hostage. She drank alcohol to escape from the struggles in her life. Then she would drink to escape the painful consequences that her drinking caused. At one point, she felt a prisoner of this destructive cycle. Although uncertain as to what to do, she believed her only alternative was to do something different!

Perhaps Rollo May (1975) captures the essence of this stage of change when he says that "commitment is healthiest when it is not without doubt but in spite of doubt" (p. 21). The journey of those who abuse substances takes them inexorably into the abyss of darkness and despair. Healing begins when they reach bottom, "let go", and ask for help.

Stage IV–Action: This stage is about doing something different. The client, being presented with a variety of alternative paths to healing, chooses the best fit. The client actively and with intention engages in the process of change. It is the counselor's role to help the client decide on and carry out the plan of action and comply with the strategies for change. What we generally think of as "treatment" comes at this stage (Miller, et al., 1995).

Treatment must be individualized, and the client must have a sense of control over the treatment process. Offering a "menu" of options (see below for a further exploration of treatment options) and discussing the potential consequences of each option, may help to increase the client's commitment to treatment (Miller & Rollnick, 1991). Psychosocial stressors, medical problems, the level of care needed (inpatient, outpatient) and the nature of the abused substance are all considerations in choosing the best approach to treatment.

Goals for change should be negotiated between counselor and client. "Change goals, like the methods to be used to pursue those goals, are better negotiated than prescribed" (Miller et al., 1995, p. 100). Clients present a wide variety of personal goals. A key goal revolves around total abstinence versus controlled drinking. Some clients choose abstinence while others prefer trying to cut down on their drinking before or instead of committing to life-long abstinence. According to research, there is not a strong relationship between clients' prognoses and their beliefs about the necessity of abstinence (Watson, Jacobs, Pucel, Tilleskjor, & Hoodecheck-Schow, 1984). In addition, it is suggested, clients are more highly motivated to change when their own goals regarding abstinence are acknowledge. (Miller, 1987). Miller et al., (1995) believes that an unsuccessful trial at "controlled drinking" can have more of an impact in terms of the need for total abstinence than any type of direct confrontation from the counselor.

Stage V–Maintenance: Maintaining continual motivation to persevere with change can be a tremendous challenge (Marlatt & Gordon, 1985). If deciding to stop abusing substances is difficult, continuing in this conviction can be even harder! Long–term follow-up studies have offered data that suggest that more than 90% of clients will indulge again some time after treatment (Helzer et al., 1985; Polich, Armor, & Braiker, 1981). Stress is frequently associated with relapse among those who are recovering from substance abuse (Hunter & Salmone, 1986; Milkman, Weiner, & Sunderwith, 1984). Those who do relapse experience greater difficulty in coping with unpleasant emotions, frustrating events, and unsatisfactory relationships with others. Counselors, therefore, must help clients learn new coping skills.

If a lapse occurs, the counselor must help the client recover from it as soon as possible. They can reframe relapse as an opportunity for clients to learn about their high-risk situations, and then help clients identify strategies that they can use to prevent relapses in the future. Counselors must help the clients disengage their personal worth from relapsing, thus avoiding the guilt and shame associated with "slips."

Increasing Motivation to Change: Some Intervention Strategies

Clients at the precontemplation and contemplation stages of motivation offer, perhaps, the greatest challenges to the counselor. The counselor is faced with the objective of strengthening these clients' motivation for change. Six elements of effective intervention have emerged as most significant for increasing motivation. Miller and Sanchez (1994) developed an acronym identifying these as FRAMES: Feedback, Responsibility, Advice, Menu, Empathy, and Self-efficacy.

Feedback

Motivation is found to be strongly influenced through the use of feedback directly related to how the individual has been harmed through his/her abusive behavior (Kristenson, Ohlin, Hulten-Voslin, Trell, & Hood, 1983). The objective of the feedback is to create a sense of discrepancy between how the client's life is at the time, and how he/she would like it to be in the future. It must be kept in mind that often the most salient consequences of abuse are positive and thus reinforcing. Feedback, therefore, must focus on those aspects of substance abuse that, although harmful, are experienced by the client with less vividness and remembered less clearly; perhaps, because they are experienced while the individual is intoxicated. For example, nausea and vomiting are experienced when the person has reached a sufficient level of intoxication that distortions in cognition have developed as well. Feedback must be delivered in a neutral, empathic, nonjudgmental fashion in order to lessen the likelihood of resistance (Hester & Bien, 1995). The research emphasizes that this type of feedback should be "personal", not given through the use of lectures or films depicting the harmfulness of substance abuse on the person. According to Bien et al. (1993), personal feedback of impairment is found to be an element in the most effective minimal interventions. One way to utilize this practice of giving feedback regarding personal impairment is through the use of a structured and objective intake evaluation. This intake would include a measure of alcohol or drug consumption, dependence, family history, and problem severity. The client's scores can be compared to norms from the general population as well as to the scores of those in treatment. Serum chemistry profiles and neuropsychological testing can be used to assess the physical effects of excessive substance use. These are all concrete presentations of the problem and offered to the client, empathetically but directly, by the counselor. These results can also be used as a baseline to reinforce movement away from substance abuse.

Responsibility

We, as counselors, have no control over changing the substance abuse behaviors of our clients. Ultimately, change is entirely up to the individual. It has been found to be highly therapeutic to simply and directly acknowledge this to the client. "Only you can decide to change your behavior. The choice is completely yours. It's entirely up to you how you use this feedback." Research studies conclude that individuals are more likely to engage in action directed towards change and to persevere with that action when they believe they have personally chosen to do so (Kessin, Platz, & Su, 1971; Costello, 1975; Parker, Winstead, & Willi, 1979). It is up to the counselor to communicate the message that the client must be the one to make the choice: "No one can make you stop drinking or using if you do not want to."

Advice

This, too, is a simple, straight forward intervention for increasing motivation. Clear and direct advice regarding the need for change and how to change has been found to be an effective strategy in triggering change in drinking problems (Bein et al., 1993). Giving advice in no way assumes responsibility for change in the client, neither does it necessitate an overly-directive approach. Advice is merely a recommendation to change given in an empathic manner. Some authors suggest to wait until advice is requested and then to preface it with something like, "I am not sure what will work for you" followed by an inquiry of what has and has not worked previously for the client. Additional suggestions can then be offered (Hester & Bien, 1995).

Menu/Alternatives

Offering a variety of options for change supports the client's perception that he/she has a choice. A "one-way-fits-all" approach to treatment denies the client's individuality as well as strengthening the client's resistance. Hester & Bien (1995) suggest that the counselor and client work together in developing the client's goals regarding substance use. Proposing alternatives allows the client to find the best fit. Presenting the client with alternative change strategies not only increases motivation, but it also helps to enhance the client's individual responsibility, sense of self-efficacy and the expectation that once the client is motivated to act, these actions toward change will be maintained. Several alternative approaches to treatment will be discussed in the section, "A Smorgasbord of Treatment Options."

Empathy

Rogers' core conditions are found to be one of the strongest predictors of counselor success with regard to motivating and treating clients who abuse substances. Empathy is one of the most powerful of these ingredients. By definition, an empathic counselor is one who maintains a person-centered approach which involves listening to and reflecting the client's messages and inner experiences. The counselor creates a warm and attentive experience for the client. Higher levels of therapist empathy are related to lower levels of client alcohol consumption (Miller & Taylor, 1980). It is important to note here that "empathy" is not synonymous with identifying with the client. Contrary to popular belief, the effectiveness of counselors is not found to be related to the counselors themselves being "in recovery." In fact, Manohar (1973) has found that being in the early stages of one's own recovery interfered with the counselor demonstrating therapeutic empathy.

Self-efficacy

Efficacy expectation is the client's belief that he/she can accomplish the necessary course of action in order to obtain desired outcome (Monte, 1980). Clients must have some hope that change can be achieved, and that their actions have an impact on change. They must believe they can change (Rogers & Mewborn, 1976). In addition to clients' beliefs that change can occur, it is essential that counselors believe change is possible. Research suggests that the expectations of the counselor for a positive prognosis are predictive of favorable outcomes among substance abusing clients (Leake & King, 1977). Optimism is key!

A Smorgasbord of Treatment Options

Outcome research has received tremendous incentive from the strength of the accountability movement. Several promising treatment approaches have risen to the top as a result of this efficacy research (Miller et al., 1995). The following is by no means an exhaustive review but attempts to present those options that seem to be associated with more positive outcomes.

Brief Therapies

Among the modalities explored in the research dealing with substance abuse treatment, briefer and more efficient therapies emerge as having one of the largest literature bases and, at this time, one of the most positive. Cummings, Dorken, Pallack and Henke (1990) studied over 16,000 Medicaid patients with drinking problems and found that only six sessions of counseling resulted in a significant impact on the problem. In general, most of the studies indicate that brief therapy should be an intervention of choice, particularly with less severe substance abusing individuals. This may come as a surprise to many as the more popular perception of treating people with substance abuse problems is that it requires an intensive, extensive intervention process. Research over the past 20 years or more has challenged this belief (Sobell & Sobell, 1993). Heather (1995) suggests that brief interventions may be beneficial for "hazardous drinkers." These individuals are not considered "alcoholics" but do drink excessively and have had their lives affected adversely due to their drinking (Moore & Gerstein, 1981). In addition, brief therapy may be appropriate for low to moderate dependence problem drinkers and high dependence problem drinkers who have not benefited from the more conventional type of treatment. In determining the appropriateness of brief intervention, there are several instruments available that can help assess the level of dependence. Among these are: The *Severity of Alcohol Dependence Questionnaire* (SADQ) (Stockwell, Hodgson, Edwards, Taylor, & Rankin, 1979); the *Alcohol Dependence Scale* (ADS) (Skinner & Allen, 1982); the *Edinburg Alcohol Dependence Scale* (EADS) (Chick, 1980); and the *Short-Form Alcohol Dependence Data Questionnaire* (SADD) (Raistrick, Dunbar, & Davidson, 1983).

Within the variety of brief therapy approaches, **solution-focused brief therapy** has been found to be as effective, if not more so, as the traditional intensive, in-patient treatment (Berg & Miller, 1992). The procedures of the solution-focused approach emerged out of the poststructural and social constructivistic tradition. It requires a paradigm shift from the problem-solving approach to solution building (de Shazer, 1991; Berg & Miller, 1992; Berg, 1994). According to Berg (1995), solution-focused treatment can be either a single contact or a series of brief and intermittent contacts throughout the recovery process. The focus is on the individual goals of each client. Rather than treat substance abuse as a unitary problem, the counselor concentrates on each client's perception and experience of substance abuse. Essentially, solution-focused intervention is atheoretical and client-determined. As such, it allows the counselor to "relinquish the role of expert or teacher in favor of the role of student or apprentice" (Berg & Miller, 1992, p.7). Through attending and listening, the counselor learns about the worldview of the client, discovers what the client wants, and speaks the language of the client. Utilizing the client's strengths and wellspring of resources, client and counselor work together to construct solutions to the client's problem. An underlying assumption of solution-focused brief therapy is the belief that any presenting problem, including substance abuse, has exceptions. Problems are more sporadic than constant. There are periods when the problem does not occur. Therefore, the solution-focused counselor pays attention to these exceptions. This attention offers the client and the counselor clues and ideas for constructing a solution to the client's problem (Berg & Miller, 1992).

Broad-Spectrum Skill Training

Another category of intervention that has been correlated with positive outcome is broad-spectrum skill training which focuses on other life problems rather than just the substance abuse (Miller & Hester, 1980). Underlying this approach is the rationale that the substance abuse problem develops as a result of the individual's lack of important coping skills. In addition, there is the belief that once the individual has stopped using the substance, he/she will be faced with a variety of circumstances that will challenge his/her sobriety due to a lack of effective coping skills.

The **Community Reinforcement Approach** (CRA) is a comprehensive broad- spectrum behavioral treatment approach (Smith & Meyers, 1995). The underlying assumption of CRA is that it takes a variety of supports in one's environment to facilitate the recovery from substance abuse. These supports include social, recreational, familial and vocational. There is an emphasis upon motivational techniques and positive reinforcement. Contingency management is a central theme of CRA, emerging from the belief that environment contingencies have an extremely powerful effect on an individual's behavior. The various reinforcers used in CRA (social, recreational, familial, vocational) are made contingent upon an individual's continuing sobriety. Nathan & Niaura (1985) have noted that for contingency contracting to be effective, the uniqueness of each individual must be taken into consideration. What is rewarding or punishing for one individual is not necessarily rewarding or punishing for another. They also believe that contingencies must be mutually agreed upon, carefully observed and consistently implemented. It is also important to involve people and institutions that are significant to the individual.

Research studies on CRA have consistently shown it to be effective in reducing alcohol use and in improving individuals' over-all adjustment (Institute of Medicine, 1990; Miller & Hester, 1986). For a more extensive description of this approach see Meyers and Smith (1995).

Coping/Social Skills Training (CSST), another broad-spectrum approach, offers general coping skills designed to be used in a variety of problem situations. It has evolved from a social cognitive learning theory orientation. Monti, Rohsenow, Colby, and Abrams (1995) report that research strongly supported the efficacy of CSST, and they believe that it should be "an integral part of any state-of-the-art intervention for...alcohol prevention and treatment" (p. 221). The underlying assumption driving this approach is that substance abuse is a habitual, maladaptive way of dealing with difficult and stressful life situations that can be alleviated through the development of social skills. Accordingly, the focus of this training is upon enhancing relationships through interpersonal skill development, learning cognitive-emotional coping in order to regulate moods, learning to deal with stressful life events, and learning how to cope in the face of substance abuse triggers.

Assertiveness skills training and stress management techniques are two specific strategies that appear often in the literature related to broad-spectrum treatments (Morgan, 1996). The primary purpose of assertiveness skills training is to teach individuals how to be more direct and appropriate in expressing thoughts and feelings. Through learning how to be more assertive, individuals have some tools to resist social pressures to use substances. In addition, they are able to assert their needs in various situations and with a variety of people. There seems to be mixed reviews in the literature regarding the effectiveness of assertiveness skills training for the maintenance of sobriety (Ferrell & Galassi, 1981; Miller, Taylor, & West, 1980). What is suggested, however, is that training in assertiveness skills may be more appropriate for those individuals who have a more severe problem with substance abuse.

Stress management has also been a popular treatment strategy for individuals struggling with substance abuse. The rationale underlying the inclusion of stress management techniques is that stress has been found to be a significant component of substance use as well as relapse. Studies related to stress management training have included relaxation training and systematic desensitization. Research studies offer inconsistent support for the effectiveness of stress management techniques (Miller et al., 1995). Relaxation training has been found to have no positive treatment effects on drinking status (Institute of Medicine, 1990). Rosenberg (1979) did find a relationship between relaxation training and reduced alcohol consumption but only among individuals who were assessed as having high anxiety.

Alcoholics Anonymous

Perhaps the most controversial, least understood and least evaluated approach for treating substance abuse is the 12-step model whose prototype is Alcoholics Anonymous (AA) (Morgenstern, Labouvie, McCrady, Kahler, & Frey, 1997). Developed at a time, 1935, when modern methods of medical therapy, clinical psychology, and professional counseling were nearly non-existent in the field of substance abuse, Alcoholics Anonymous filled a vacuum. In a letter written to Carl Jung in 1961 (cited in the Bill W-Carl Jung Letters, 1987), Bill Wilson, the founder of Alcoholics Anonymous, presents, in abbreviated form, the philosophy upon which Alcoholics Anonymous was built: "...there came a vision of a society of alcoholics, each identifying with and transmitting his (sic) experience to the next – chain-style. If each sufferer were to carry the news of the scientific hopelessness of alcoholism to each new prospect, he (sic) might be able to lay every newcomer wide open to a transforming spiritual experience. This concept proved to be the foundation of such success as Alcoholics Anonymous has since achieved" (p.20). Indeed, it has provided assistance to hundreds of thousands of individuals. For decades after its founding, substance abuse treatment has modeled itself after the same basic philosophy and methodologies as Alcoholics Anonymous (Lemanski, 1997). According to the National Institute of Alcoholism and Alcohol Abuse (1993), approximately one million Americans receive formal treatment for substance abuse each year in 12-step oriented programs (NA, Narcotics Anonymous is a spin-off of AA). Approximately 3.5 million attend Alcoholics Anonymous meetings or similar 12-step self-help groups (Room, 1993).

The prevalence of the Alcoholics Anonymous movement is attested to by the fact that rarely does one come upon a person who does not have familiarity with or an opinion about Alcoholics Anonymous. The media has locked onto Alcoholics Anonymous as the symbol of "recovery" from substance abuse. This is evident in such popular films as "When a Man Loves a Woman" and "Clean and Sober." The "Andy Spiowitz" character in the television series NYPD Blue struggles with his substance abuse and finds recovery in Alcoholics Anonymous which he then "transmits" to another substance abusing character in the series. The population at large has come to view Alcoholics Anonymous, and 12-step treatment, as the primary intervention for someone who abuses substances. AA's supporters believe that the 12- steps and the Alcoholics Anonymous message of powerlessness over alcohol and its accompanying dictum, submission to a higher power, is nothing less than a lifesaving gospel. Critics, on the other hand, are purporting that the 12-steps are outdated, oppressive, and sexist (Judge, 1994).

The professional literature lends itself to ambiguous interpretation when it comes to a precise definition of 12-Step theory, its derivative, 12-step treatment, and outcome (Wallace, 1996; Morgenstern et al.,

1997). Much of the writings focusing on the relationship of Alcoholics Anonymous to outcome are anecdotal. Concern is raised by many regarding the dominance of the 12-step model and the ubiquitous practice of recommending Alcoholics Anonymous affiliation as the prime form of aftercare following treatment, as well as the only source of intervention for those who do not seek formal treatment (Emrick, Tonigan, Montgomery, & Little, 1993; Miller & Hester, 1980).

Two types of theories are proposed to explain the underlying effects of Alcoholics Anonymous affiliation on substance use. The first set of theories, emerging from the proponents of Alcoholics Anonymous, argues that the mechanisms used by AA are unique and are focused on resolving basic characterological problems, such as grandiosity and self-centeredness, that maintain the substance abuse (Brown, 1993). Within the framework of these theories, acceptance of powerlessness, belief in substance abuse as a disease, surrender and conversion experiences are keys in the therapeutic processes facilitated by affiliation with Alcoholics Anonymous (Bateson, 1971).

Another group of researchers propose an alternative approach to understanding the mechanism that is working within AA affiliation. They argue that despite apparent theoretical differences between the Alcoholics Anonymous model and other approaches to treatment, there are a number of common change strategies that are transtheoretical but powerful in terms of effecting change (DiClemente, 1993; McCrady, 1994). Through studies conducted over the past 15 years, DiClemente and Prochaska (1982, 1983, 1985, 1986, 1992) have demonstrated that Alcoholics Anonymous focuses on several levels of change which are found to be common factors related to positive change outcome for substance abusers. These various levels of change are reflected in AA's emphasis on maladaptive thinking and beliefs, interpersonal conflicts, and intrapersonal issues of values and character. It is significant to note that this focus demonstrates AA's concern with a larger transformation of the individual rather than simply drinking behavior modification. DiClemente (1993) also suggested that the action orientation of Alcoholics Anonymous, the lack of personal skills training that is provided and the emphasis upon the intervention of a vague higher power that requires individual interpretation, may make the AA path to change for some difficult to follow. He offers the possibility that some of the drop-out rate from Alcoholics Anonymous may reflect mismatches between some Alcoholics Anonymous principles or practices, and the individual with the substance abuse problem.

There is some research that attempts to explore the question of who are the individuals who partake of what Alcoholics Anonymous has to offer? In other words, what is the relationship between the individual's characteristics and his/her affiliation with Alcoholics Anonymous? The most significant characteristic showing a positive relationship with Alcoholics Anonymous affiliation is related to individuals having a history of using external supports to stop drinking. Also, a modest positive relationship is found between affiliation and being more physically dependent on alcohol (Emrick et al., 1993). Studies attempting to identify personal qualities of individuals who are more likely to affiliate with Alcoholics Anonymous have resulted in only very tentative hypotheses. Consequently, there is a need for additional research in this area. According to McCrady and Irvine (1989) " with increasing interest in matching patients to treatment, it seems that further research to identify the distinguishing characteristics of Alcoholics Anonymous affiliates is important" (p.155).

Summary

"In my end is my beginning."
T.S. Eliot, Four Quartets.

It is apparent that treating people who abuse substances is complex. As the treatment field becomes more professional and is influenced by more and more research, we are developing the awareness that a "one-fits-all" approach to treatment is not effective. We are also learning that there are definitely effective alternatives that recognize the differences among individuals. Although still in its infancy, studies focusing on matching clients with appropriate treatment are becoming increasingly popular (Allen & Kadden, 1995). According to the Institute of Medicine (1990), "There is no single treatment that is effective for all persons with alcohol problems. A number of different treatment methods show promise in particular groups. Reason for optimism in the treatment of substance abuse problems lies in the range of promising alternatives that are available, each of which may be optimal for different types of individuals " (p.147). With the various alternatives that are emerging, counselors are faced, perhaps, with more questions than answers. We, as counselors, must approach our clients with exploring minds, open and compassionate hearts, and a mindfulness of our own struggles. Ultimately, change is not about a particular intervention or treatment model. Change is intimately woven into the fabric of the encounter in which two struggling human beings share the path of discovery and healing.

References

Allen, J.P., & Kadden, R.M. (1995). Matching clients to alcohol treatments. In R.K. Hester & W.R. Miller (Eds.), *Handbook of alcoholism treatment approaches* (pp.278-292). Boston: Allyn and Bacon.

Anderson, B.S. (1996). *The counselor and the law* (4th ed.). Alexandria, VA: American Counseling Association.

Bachelor, A., & Horvath, A. (1999). The therapeutic relationship. In M.A. Hubble, B.L. Duncan, & S.C. Miller (Eds.), *The heart and soul of change* (pp. 133-178). Washington, DC: American Psychological Association.

Bateson, G. (1971). The cybernetics of self: A theory of alcoholism. *Psychiatry, 34,* 1-18.

Berg, I.K. (1994). *Family based services: A solution-focused approach.* New York: W.W. Norton.

Berg, I.K. (1995). Solution-focused brief therapy with substance abusers. In A.M. Washton (Ed.), *Psychotherapy and substance abuse*, pp.204-242. New York: The Guilford Press.

Berg, I.K., & Miller, S.D. (1992). *Working with the problem drinker.* New York: W.W. Norton & Co.

Beutler, L.E., Machado, P. M., & Allstetter-Neufeldt, S.A. (1994). Therapist variables. In B.A. & S.L. Garfield (Eds.), *Handbook of psychotherapy and behavior change* (pp.229-269). New York: Wiley.

Bien, T.H., Miller, W.R., & Tonigan, J.S. (1993). Brief interventions for alcohol problems: A review. *Addictions, 88,* 315-336.

Bill W.-Carl Jung letters (1987). *Revision, 10,* 19-21.

Bissell, L.C., & Royce, J.E. (1994). *Ethics for addiction professionals.* Center City, MN: Hazelden.

Bordin, E.S. (1979). The generalizability of the psychoanalytic concept of the working alliance. *Psychotherapy: Therapy, Research & Practice*, *16*, 252-260.

Bouhoustsos, J., Holroyd, J., Lerman, H., Forer, B.R., & Greenberg, M. (1983). Sexual intimacy between psychotherapists and patients. *Professional Psychology: Research and Practice*, *14,* 185-196.

Brown, S.D. (1993). Therapeutic processes in Alcoholics Anonymous. In B.S. McCrady & W.R. Miller (Eds.), *Research on Alcoholics Anonymous* (pp.137-153). New Brunswick, NJ: Rutgers Center of Alcohol Studies.

Capuzzi, D., & Gross, D.R. (1999). *Counseling psychotherapy* (2nd ed.). Upper Saddle River, NJ: Merrill.

Chess, S.B., Neuringer, C., & Goldstein, G. (1981). Arousal and field dependence in alcoholics. *Journal of General Psychology, 85*, 93-102.

Chick, J. (1980). Alcohol dependence, methodological issues in its measurement; reliability of the criteria. *British Journal of Addiction*, *75*, 175-186.

Connors, G.J., DiClemente, C.C., Carroll, K.M., & Longabaugh, R. (1997). The therapeutic alliance and its relationship to alcoholism treatment participation and outcome. *Journal of Consulting and Clinical Psychology, 65*, 4, 588-598.

Costello, R.M. (1975). Alcoholism treatment and evaluation: In search of methods. *International Journal of Addictions*, *10*, 251-275.

Cottone, R.R., & Robine, S. (1998). Addictions and ex-offender counseling. In R.R. Cottone & V.M. Tarvydas (Eds.), *Ethical and professional issues in counseling* (pp. 383-394). Upper Saddle River, NJ: Merrill.

Cottone, R.R., & Tarvydas, V.M. (Eds.). *Ethical and professional issues in counseling*. Upper Saddle River, NJ: Merrill.

Cummings, N.A., Dorken, H., Pallack, M., & Henke, C. (1990). *The impact of psychological intervention on healthcare utilization and costs*. San Francisco: Biodyne Corporation.

de Shazer, S.D. (1991). *Putting differences to work*. New York: W.W. Norton.

DiClemente, C.C. (1993). Alcoholics Anonymous and the structure of change. In B.S. McCrady & W.R. Miller (Eds.), *Research on alcoholics anonymous* (pp. 79-98). New Brunswick, NJ: Rutgers Center of Alcohol Studies.

DiClemente, C.C., & Prochaska, J.O. (1982). Self-change and therapy change of smoking behavior: A comparison of processes of change in cessation and maintenance. *Addictive Behaviors, 7,* 133-142.

DiClemente, C.C. & Prochaska, J.O. (1985). Processes and stages of change: Coping and competence in smoking behavior change. In S. Shiffman & T.A. Wills (Eds.), *Coping and substance abuse* (pp. 319-344). New York: Academic Press.

Donovan, D.M., Rohsenvow, D.J., Schou, E.J., & O'Leary, M.R. (1977). Defensive style in alcoholics and nonalcoholics. *Journal of Studies on Alcohol, 38*, 465-470.

Emrick, C.D., Tonigan, J.S., Montgomery, H., & Little, L. (1993). Alcoholics Anonymous : What is currently known. In B.S. McCrady & W.R. Miller (Eds.), *Research on Alcoholics Anonymous*. (pp. 41-76). New Brunswick, NJ: Rutgers Center of Alcohol Studies.

Ferrell, W.L., & Galassi, J.P. (1981). Assertion training and human relations training in the treatment of chronic alcoholics. *The International Journal of Addictions, 16*, 959-968.

Garduk, E.L., & Haggard, E.A. (1972). Immediate effects on patients of psychoanalytic interpretations. *Psychological Issues*, *7*, (4).

Gelso, C.J., & Carter, J.A. (1985). The relationship in counseling and psychotherapy: Components, consequences, and theoretical antecedents. *The Counseling Psychologist, 13*, 155-243.

Greenberg, L.S., & Pinsof, W.M. (1986). *The psychotherapeutic process: A research handbook.* New York: Guilford Press.

Greenwald, A.F., & Baitmeier, L.H. (1963). Psychiatric discharges against medical advice. *Archives of General Psychiatry, 8,* 117-119.

Gross, D.R., & Capuzzi, D.(1999). Helping relationships in counseling and psychotherapy. In D. Capuzzi & D.R. Gross (Eds). *Counseling and psychotherapy* (2nd ed.) (pp.3-22). Upper Saddle River, NJ: Merrill.

Handelsman, M.M. (1987). Confidentiality: The ethical baby in the legal bath water. *Journal of Applied Rehabilitation Counseling, 18*(4), 33-34.

Heather, N. (1995). Brief intervention strategies. In R.K. Hester & W. R. Hester (Eds.). *Handbook of alcoholism treatment approaches* (pp. 102-122). Boston: Allyn and Bacon.

Heinlein, R. (1985). *The cat who walks through walls.* New York: Putman.

Helzer, J.E., Robins, L.N., Taylor, J.R., Corey, K., Miller, R. H., Combs-Orne, T., & Tarmer, A., (1985). The extent of long-term moderate drinking among alcoholics discharged from medical and psychiatric treatment facilities. *New England Journal of Medicine, 312,* 1678-1682.

Hester, R.K., & Bien, T.H. (1995). Brief treatment. In A.M. Washton (Ed.), *Psychotherapy and substance abuse*, (pp. 204-222). New York: The Guilford Press.

Hester, R.K., & Miller, W.R. (1989). *Handbook of alcoholism treatment approaches: Effective alternatives.* Boston: Allyn and Bacon.

Hummel, D.L., Talbutt, L., & Alexander, M.D. (1985). *Law and ethics in counseling.* New York: Van Nostrand Reinhold.

Hunter, T.A., & Solmone, P.R. (1986). Dry drunk syndrome and alcoholic relapse. *Journal of Applied Rehabilitation Counseling, 18*, 22-25.

Institute of Medicine. (1990). *Broadening the base of treatment for alcohol problems*. Washington, DC: National Academy Press.

Jones, M.C. (1968). Personality correlates and antecedents of drinking patterns in adult males. *Journal of Consulting and Clinical Psychology, 32*, 2-12.

Judge, M.G. (1994). Recovery's next step. *Common Boundary*, January/ February, 16- 24.

Kessin, B., Platz, A., & Su, WH. (1971). Selective factors in treatment choice and outcome in alcoholics. In N. K. Mello & J. H. Mendelson (Eds.), *Recent advances in studies of alcoholism* (pp. 781-802). Washington, DC: U.S. Government Printing Office.

Knapp, C. (1996). *Drinking: A love story*. New York: Dell Publishing.

Kristenson, H., Ohlin, H., Hulten-Uoslin, M.B., Trell, E., & Hood, B. (1983). Identification and intervention of heavy drinking in middle-aged men: Results and follow-up 24-60 months of long-term study with randomized controls. *Alcoholism: Clinical and Experimental Research*, *7*, 203-209.

Lambert, M. J., & Bergin, A. E. (1994). In B. A. & S. L. Garfield (Eds.), *Handbook of psychotherapy and behavior change*. New York: Wiley.

Leake, G.J., & King, A.S. (1977). Effect of counselor expectations on alcohol recovery. *Alcohol Health & Research World, 1*(3), 16-22.

Lemanski, M.J. (1997, May/June). The tenacity of error in the treatment of addiction. *The Humanist*, 18-23.

LeShan, L. (1996). *Beyond technique*. New Jersey: Jason Aronson Inc.

Loberg, T., & Miller, W.R. (1986). Personality, cognitive and neuropsychological dimensions of harmful alcohol consumption: A cross-national comparison of clinical samples. *Annals of the New York Academy*, 472, 75-97.

Manohar, V. (1973). Training volunteers as alcoholism treatment counselors. *Quarterly Journal of Studies on Alcohol, 34*, 869-877.

Margolin, G. (1982). Ethical and legal considerations in marital and family therapy. *American Psychologist, 37*, 788-801.

Marlatt, G. A., & Gordon, J. R. (1985). *Relapse prevention: Maintenance strategies in the treatment of addictive behaviors.* New York: Guilford Press.

Marmar, C., Horowitz, M. J., Weiss, D., & Marziolie, E. A. (1986). The development of the therapeutic alliance rating system. In L. Greenberg & W. Pinsof (Eds.), *Psychotherapeutic process: A research handbook* (pp.367-390). New York: Guilford Press.

May, R. (1975). *The courage to create.* New York: W.W. Norton & Co.

McCrady, B. S. (1994). Alcoholics Anonymous and behavior therapy: Can habits be treated as diseases? Can diseases be treated as habits? *Journal of Consulting and Clinical Psychology, 62*, 1159-1166.

McCrady, B.S., & Irvine, S. (1989). Self-help groups. In R. K.Hester & W. R. Miller (Eds.), *Handbook of alcoholism treatment approaches: Effective alternatives* (pp.153-169). New York: Pergamon Press.

Meyers, R. J., & Smith, J. E. (1995). *Clinical guide to alcohol treatment: The Community Reinforcement Approach.* New York: The Guilford Press.

Milkman, H., Weiner, S. E., & Sunderwirth, S. (1984). Addiction relapse. *Addictive Behaviors, 3*, 119-134.

Miller, S. D., Duncan, B. L., & Hubble, M.A. (1997). *Escape from Babel.* New York: W.W. Norton & Co.

Miller, G.A.(1999). Needham Heights, MA: Allyn and Bacon.

Miller, W.R. (1987). Motivation and treatment goals. *Drugs and Society*, 1, 133-151.

Miller, W.R., Brown, J.M., Simpson, T.J., Handmaker, N.S., Bien, T.H., Luckie, L.F., Montgomery, H.A., Hester, R.K., & Tonigan, J.S. (1995). What Works? A Methodological Analysis of the Alcohol Treatment Literature." In R.K.Hester & W.R.Miller (Eds.), *Handbook of alcoholism treatment approaches* (pp.12-44). Boston: Allyn and Bacon.

Miller, W. R., & Hester, R. K. (1980). Treating problem drinkers: Modern approaches. In W. R. Miller (Ed.), *The addictive behaviors: Treatment of alcoholism, drug abuse, smoking and obesity* (pp.11-141). Oxford: Pergamon Press.

Miller, W. R., & Hester, R. K. (1986). The effectiveness of alcoholism treatment methods: What research reveals. In W. R. Miller & N. Heather (Eds.), *Treating addictive behaviors: Process of change* (pp. 121-174). New York: Plenum Press

Miller, W.R., & Rollnick, S. (1991). *Motivational interviewing: Preparing people to change addictive behavior.* New York: Guilford Press.

Miller, W.R., & Sanchez, V.C. (1994). Motivating young adults for treatment and lifestyle change. In G. Howard (Ed.), *Issues in alcohol use and misuse by young adults* (pp. 55-82). Notre Dame, IN: University of Notre Dame Press.

Miller, W. R., & Taylor, C. A. (1980). Relative effectiveness of bibliotherapy, individual and group self-control training in the treatment of problem drinkers. *Addictive Behaviors, 5,* 13-24.

Miller, W. R., Taylor, C. A., & West, J.C. (1980). Focused versus broad-spectrum behavior therapy for problem drinkers. *Journal of Consulting & Clinical Psychology, 48*, 590-601.

Monte, C.F. (1980). *Beneath the mask: An introduction to theories of personality*. New York: Holt, Rinehart & Winston.

Monti, P.M., Rohsenow, D. J., Colby, S.M., & Abrams, D. B. (1995). Coping and social skills training. In R. K. Hester & W. R. Miller (Eds.), *Handbook of alcoholism treatment approaches* (pp. 221-241). Boston: Allyn & Bacon.

Moore, M. H., & Gerstein, D. R. (Eds.). (1981). *Alcohol and public policy: Beyond the shadow of prohibition.* Washington, DC: National Academy Press.

Morgan, T. J. (1996). Behavioral treatment techniques for psychoactive substance use disorders. In F. Rotgers, D.S. Keller, J. Morgenstern (Eds.), *Treating substance abuse* (pp.202-240). New York: The Guilford Press.

Morgenstern, J., Labouvie, E., McCrady, B. S., Kahler, C. W., & Frey, R. M. (1997). Affiliation with alcoholics anonymous after treatment: A study of its therapeutic effects and mechanisms of action. *Journal of Consulting and Clinical Psychology, 65,* 768-777.

Nathan, R.E., & Niaura, R.S. (1985). Behavioral assessment and treatment of alcoholism. In J. H. Mendelson & N. K. Mello (Eds.), *The diagnosis and treatment of alcoholism* (pp. 391-445). New York: McGraw-Hill.

National Institute of Alcoholism and Alcohol Abuse. (1993). *National Drug and Alcoholism Treatment Unit Survey.* (DHHS Publication No. SMA 93-200) Washington, DC: Author.

Parker, M W., Winstead, D. K., & Willi, F. J. P. (1979). Patient autonomy in alcohol rehabilitation: I. Literature review. *International Journal of Addictions*, 14, 1015-1022.

Polich, J. M., Armor, D. M., & Bracher, H. B. (1981). *The course of alcoholism: Four years after treatment.* New York: Wiley.

Prochaska, J. O., & DiClemente, C. C. (1982). Transtheoretical therapy: Toward a more integrative model of change. *Psychotherapy: Theory, Research, and Practice, 19,* 276-288.

Prochaska, J.O., & DiClemente, C.C. (1983). Stages and processes of self-change of smoking: Toward an integrative model of change. *Journal of Consulting and Clinical Psychology, 51*, 390-395.

Prochaska, J.O., & DiClemente, C.C. (1986). Toward a comprehensive model of change. In W.R. Miller & N. Heather (Eds.), *Treating addictive behaviors: Process of change* (pp. 3-27). New York: Plenum.

Prochaska, J. O., & DiClemente, C. C. (1992). Stages of change in the modification of problem behaviors. In M. Hersen, R. M. Eisler, & P. M. Miller (Eds.), *Progress in behavior modification 28* (pp. 184-214). Sycamore, IL: Sycamore Publishing.

Prochaska, J. O., DiClemente, C. C., & Norcross, J. C. (1992). In search of how people change: Applications to addictive behaviors. *American Psychologist, 47*,1102-1114.

Raistrick, D., Dunbar, G., & Davidson, R. (1983). Development of a questionnaire to measure alcohol dependence. *British Journal of Addiction, 78*, 89-95.

Remley, T.P., Jr.(1985). The law and ethical practices in elementary and middle schools. *Elementary School Guidance and Counseling, 19*,181-189.

Rich, A. (1979). *On lies, secrets, and silence.* New York: Norton.

Rogers, C. R. (1957). The necessary and sufficient conditions of therapeutic personality change. *Journal of Consulting Psychology, 21*, 95-103.

Rogers, C. R. (1951). *Client-centered therapy.* Boston: Houghton-Mifflin.

Room, R. (1993). Alcoholics Anonymous as a social movement. In B. S. McCrady & W. R. Miller (Eds.), *Research on Alcoholics Anonymous* (pp. 167-189). New Brunswick, NJ: Rutgers Center of Alcohol Studies.

Rosenburg, C. M., & Raynes, A. W. (1973). Dropouts from treatment. *Canadian Psychiatric Association Journal, 18*, 229-233.

Rosenber, S. D. (1979). *Relaxation training and a differential assessment of alcoholism.* Unpublished doctoral dissertation (University Microfilms No. 8004362), California School of Professional Psychology, San Diego.

Rothchild, D. (1995). Working with addicts in private practice: Overcoming initial resistance. In A. M. Washton (Ed.), *Psychotherapy and substance abuse* (pp. 192-203). New York: Guilford Press.

Shaffer, H. J., & Gambina, B. (1990). Epilogue: Integrating treatment choices. In H.B. Milkman & L. Sederer (Eds.), *Treatment choices for alcoholism and substance abuse* (pp. 351-375). Lexington, Ma: Lexington Books.

Shaffer, H. J., & Robbins, M. (1995). Psychotherapy for addictive behavior: A stage-change approach to meaning making. In A.M. Washton (Ed.), *Psychotherapy and substance abuse* (pp.103-123). New York: Guilford Press.

Skinner, H. A., & Allen, B. A. (1982). Alcohol dependence syndrome: Measurement and validation. *Journal of Abnormal Psychology, 91*, 199-209.

Skinner, H. A., & Allen, B. A. (1983). Differential assessment of alcoholism. *Journal of Studies on Alcohol, 44*, 852-862.

Smith, J. E., & Meyers, R. J. (1995). The community reinforcement approach. In R. K. Hester & W. R. Miller (Eds.), *Handbook of alcoholism treatment approaches* (pp. 251-266). Boston: Allyn and Bacon.

Snow, M. G., Prochaska, J. O., & Rossi, J. S. (1994). Processes of change in Alcoholics Anonymous: Maintenance factor in long-term sobriety. *Journal of Studies on Alcohol, 55*, 362-371.

Stockwell, T. R., Hodgson, R. J., Edwards, G., Taylor, C., & Rankin, H. (1979). The development of a questionnaire to measure severity of alcohol dependence. *British Journal of Addiction, 74*, 79-87.

Swenson, L. C. (1993). *Psychology and law for the helping professions.* Pacific Grove, CA: Brooks/Cole.

Thombs, D. L. (1994). *Introduction to addictive behaviors.* New York: Guilford Press.

Vaillant, G. M. (1983). *The natural history of alcoholism: Causes, patterns, and paths to recovery.* Cambridge, MA: Harvard University Press.

Wallace, J. (1996). Theory of 12-step-oriented treatment. In F. Rotgers, D.S. Keller, & J. Morgenstern (Eds.), *Treating substance abuse* (pp. 13-36) New York: The Guilford Press.

Watson, C. G., Jacobe, L., Pucel, J., Tilleskjor, C., & Hoodecheck-Schow, E. A. (1984). The relationship of beliefs about controlled drinking to recidivism in alcoholic men. *Journal of Studies on Alcohol, 45,* 172-175.

Willis, R. (1994). *Transcendence in relationship, existentialism and psychotherapy.* Norwood, NJ: Ablex.

Chapter 7

Change Through Group Work

Les McAllan, Amy Friedman, & Evans Spears

Introduction

In the field of prevention and treatment of addiction, perhaps the most well known treatment modalities have been groups. Group settings serve to bring individuals with addictions together at one time in one place to work on relevant issues together. Groups may serve as a safe environment for learning new social and relationship skills, gaining information about a variety of addiction issues and coping strategies, and learning how to give and accept support. Groups may also provide options for persons struggling with addictive behaviors to find new friends and leave behind older, less supportive social environments. For clients with substance abuse problems, recovery is affected and correlates with success in interpersonal relationships and quality of social skills. Two common goals among most group approaches are the encouragement of taking personal responsibility for one's life and the creation of social environments that support personal empowerment. The purpose of this chapter is to introduce the therapeutic aspects of groups in relationship to empowerment, the nature and history of current group therapy, and some of the research on the efficacy of groups in the addiction field.

Professional and ethical considerations for the beginning counselor also are identified.

Therapeutic Aspects of Groups

Most attempts at defining the concept of empowerment include a social component appropriate to group work. Chamberlin (1997) proposed several qualities of a life-long process identified as empowerment, all of which can be learned in group settings. The quality of not feeling alone as the result of being part of a group emphasizes the social nature of people and the recognition that empowerment does not necessarily occur in isolation. Bolton and Brookings (1996) described twenty facets of empowerment, including cooperating with others to problem solve, engaging in directed interaction with groups of individuals, and acknowledging of one's dependence on and responsibility for others. Both authors agreed that the concept or empowerment rarely is precisely defined in research or common use, but remains an essential goal of most psychotherapeutic interventions.

It is difficult to pinpoint cause and effect in mental health treatment and outcome, especially when it comes to the specific aspects of groups that are considered to have healing qualities. Yalom (1995) observed many groups over time and proposed the following seven therapeutic factors:

(1) instillation of hope,
(2) universality,
(3) imparting information,
(4) altruism,
(5) the corrective recapitulation of the primary family group,
(6) development of socializing techniques, and
(7) imitative behavior.

Although Yalom was writing about psychotherapeutic groups in general, all of these factors can be essential elements in facilitating empowerment and creating effective addiction treatment and prevention programs. Hope, universality, imparting of information, developing social skills, and the modeling of healthy behaviors are important in all types of group intervention and empowerment.

Nature and History of Addiction Treatment Groups

Psychotherapy groups can be classified as self-help, facilitated, facilitated peer, targeted, and psychotherapeutic. In the 1990's self-help groups became one of the most publicized methods of treatment. Yalom (1995) identified self-help groups as groups designed to support individuals with a psychological problem, physical illness, or socially stigmatizing problem that are led by individuals who have the same or similar issues, who are not necessarily trained professionals but rather members of the group. Groups of this type generally meet in churches or other spaces that are available for public use. Group members are generally not screened but are attracted to the groups by flyers or informal referrals from friends or sometimes professionals. The stated purpose of these groups is generally to provide support in overcoming or accepting the behaviors or situations encountered by the group members. These groups can be time limited or ongoing depending upon the nature of the group and the issues the group is addressing. Well-known groups of this type in the addiction field include 12-step programs such as Alcoholics Anonymous, Overeaters Anonymous, and Narcotics Anonymous. Other less familiar groups include Rational Recovery and Women for Sobriety.

Yalom (1995) reported that members of any type of self-help group find the interpersonal interactions within the group to be the most therapeutic and helpful. In a study of church and secular self-help group members, Yalom noted that,

> Members of all groups rated the following as highly important: "members giving you encouragement" (86%), "hearing other members share their views" (85%), "feeling they were no longer alone" (82%), "seeing love and caring in the group" (80%). (p. 482)

Most self-help groups do not have formal professional leaders and may take on a variety of forms.

Inaba, Cohen, and Holstein (1997) described facilitated groups as any group that is led by a therapist who is active in the process of the group. The therapist may propose topics, help analyze information and contribute to the overall growth process of the group. Yalom (1995) indicated that participant screening and preparation are two key elements of successful groups. Therapists must help establish appropriate group norms by addressing issues of confidentiality, shared leadership, and relationships outside of the group at or before the beginning of the group.

Educational groups are one type of facilitated group and are often a part of many addiction prevention and treatment programs. These groups are designed to educate group members about the nature of substances, addiction, and recovery. Educational group leaders may also teach specific skills for recovery and for supporting behavioral changes.

With facilitated peer groups, Inaba et al. (1997) noted that the role of the peer leader is less active. The peer facilitator's primary role is that of group member. The secondary role is resolving problems that arise during the group and facilitating movement forward as a group. Facilitated peer groups place responsibility on the group members and give the members control over group functions and direction. Some 12-step programs are examples of facilitated peer groups.

According to Inaba et al. (1997), all types of groups may also be targeted and/or topic-specific in nature. Examples of targeted groups could include 12-step groups for gays and lesbians or persons with disabilities, facilitated groups for persons with dual diagnosis, and recovery groups for professionals with addiction problems. Topic-specific groups may convene around Acquired Immune Deficiency Syndrome (AIDS), relapse prevention, or social skills development. Yalom (1995) reported that cohesiveness, a critical element in group therapy, might develop more quickly in topic-specific groups.

Psychotherapeutic groups may be part of an overall treatment plan in in-patient, residential and outpatient settings (Hodgins, El-Guebaly, & Addington, 1997). In-patient addiction treatment generally occurs in a hospital, clinic, or residential addiction treatment center that is most often closed or locked. Outpatient therapy is generally hospital or clinic based, but members reside in the community and report for group activities at regularly scheduled intervals. Both types of groups involve goal oriented and time limited therapy using a trained group leader who may or may not be a recovering addict. Washton (1995) described this type of group therapy as an adjunct to individual or family therapy that for the purposes of dealing with addiction is defined as:

> An assembly of chemically dependent patients, usually 5-10 in number, who meet regularly (usually at least once per week) under the guidance of a professional leader (usually a professional therapist or addiction counselor) for the purposes of promoting abstinence from mood altering chemicals and recovery from addiction....The group leader is simultaneously a participant, observer, and manager of the group's activities and assumes responsibility for a variety of 'executive' or management tasks. (p. 44)

Washton concluded that these tasks can include defining and maintaining group rules, screening and selection of group members, formulating treatment goals and guiding the group through the various stages of treatment.

Psychotherapeutic groups often are based on individual counseling theories. Most of the major theoretical approaches to individual counseling also include applications to group work and most have a central theme of acceptance of personal responsibility. A brief review of five major theoretical approaches that involve extensive use of groups follows.

According to Corey (1990), Adlerian groups focus on helping members achieve specific goals. Key to Adlerian groups is the idea that the members are not the victims of their circumstances. Instead, members are encouraged to examine the choices they have made that have led to the current situation and identify new goals. Group members help individual members explore choices, identify goals, and assume personal responsibility for change. Group members teach other members better ways to achieve goals. Prinz (1993) applied Adlerian concepts to group therapy with persons who abuse substances. Central to the process is the instillation of a sense of belonging and the development of social interest. The social nature of the group challenges the isolated and drug-focused life of the individual addict. In relation to the Person-Centered counseling approach, Rogers (cited in Corey, 1990) proposed a therapeutic triad which included unconditional positive regard, empathic understanding, and genuineness. These three factors are considered to be essential elements for facilitating growth in individuals. A major component of Person-Centered group therapy is the opportunity for members to learn and practice ways of promoting these facilitative conditions within the group. As members become better able to create a therapeutic environment, the level of trust and positive regard within the group increases. Toward the end of his career, Rogers was very active in leading groups all over the world with the goal of supporting world peace.

Cognitive-behavioral groups can include a component of measurement and assessment to identify behaviors and develop interventions (Corey, 1990). Behavioral groups operate with more structure and specific techniques than many of the other groups, and a primary goal is the development of group support for sustaining new behaviors. Smokowski and Wodarski (1998) reviewed current strategies for treating cocaine dependency with specific cognitive-behavioral interventions. Their findings support the conclusion that group members learned to reinforce abstinence or confront active drug use behaviors. More experienced members are expected to model abstinence behaviors and provide social reinforcement. Group reward structures, extinction based on social cues, problem-solving activities, and the integration of a buddy system all may support movement toward recovery.

Reality group therapists often search for the internal forces that drive individual members. These forces include fulfilling both psychological and physiological needs, such as the needs for survival, belonging, fun, power and freedom. Corey (1990) noted that self-help is a primary goal of reality groups and members are encouraged to develop new coping strategies and problem solving skills.

Honeyman (1990) studied the degree of perceptual changes in a particular drug free therapeutic community receiving intensive group therapy and educational programming based on the principles of reality therapy. The goal of the therapeutic group environment was to promote changes in thinking, doing and feeling by increasing social responsiveness. The communal nature of the group was expected to minimize distortions of reality and support the use of straight talk, conflict resolution, and confrontation of defense mechanisms and unrealistic self-perceptions as primary interventions. Results of the study offered support for the use of reality therapy in improving self-perceptions that are related to positive treatment outcomes.

In recent years, psychodrama has developed as a legitimate group therapeutic approach based on the belief that, "...spontaneity and creativity are the central forces of human nature" (Corey, 1990, p. 223). Psychodrama proponents argue that members are fully responsible for their actions and that their actions create who they are as a person and who they will become. Group members are taught to support each other as constantly evolving human beings with physical, social, and emotional aspects.The psychological and physical acting out of distressing life situations are considered to be particularly therapeutic in leading to long-term behavioral change, but very little scientific research is available to document this claim.

The history of group work in the area of substance abuse is long and varied. Probably the most familiar and most common groups in the substance abuse recovery arena are the 12-step groups. The first 12-step group was Alcoholics Anonymous, established in the 1930's by Bill Wilson and Dr. Bob Smith (Inaba et al., 1997). The 12 steps are designed for persons with addictive patterns of behavior in breaking down denial and creating a more positive structure for addressing the addiction. Persons who abuse substances attend meetings and share stories about their addiction with abusers participating in the group. When the meetings are facilitated, they are usually facilitated by peers. Essential components of the 12-step process include recognition of a higher power or spiritual center and peer support for movement through the12 steps. In the last 30 years, group work with persons who abuse substances has seen many transformations. In the 1970's, "...the major formulations of social group work method showed a trend toward increased emphasis on evaluating goal accomplishment, a push towards specificity of identified and selected problems as well as specificity of assessment, plan and procedures" (Goldberg & Simpson, 1995, p. 83). In the 1980's, marathon group work showed a re-emergence. With marathon groups, members participate in one group meeting that can last from eight hours to a full weekend. Page, Davis, Berkow, & O'Leary (1989) noted that marathon groups "can provide opportunities for drug addicts to engage in direct and honest relationships, to examine feelings and concerns, and to receive feedback on personal problems" (p. 225). Authors of recent articles on group work in the 1990's have observed that the current emphasis is on short-term interventions and managed care (Weiner, 1987; Rugel & Barry, 1990; Rugel, 1991; and Campbell & Brasher, 1994).

Other types of groups which have appeared throughout the years include art and dance therapy groups, groups targeting family members or significant others of persons who abuse substances, educational/ awareness groups, and culturally specific groups. Virshup (1985) demonstrated the success of a walk-in art therapy group in the lobby of a methadone treatment clinic. Based on experience and a review of the literature regarding art therapy groups, Virshup (1985) compiled the following list of benefits:

1) the focus is on the artwork rather than verbal communication;
2) the public nature of the artwork generates effective group process;
3) the artwork may represent a graphic projection of inner conflicts;
4) clients have reported increased self-esteem;
5) the stereotypic picture of the person who abuses substances is challenged publicly; and
6) the counseling staff found value in the process both personally and professionally.

Milliken (1990) incorporated dance movement therapy into a substance abuse treatment model in an attempt to address the typical lack of body awareness seen in most persons who abuse substances. The author believed that dance movement therapy could be used to deal with resistance, denial, isolation, and low self-esteem. The therapy is seen as a non-verbal form of group therapy with the goals of exploring trust issues, developing tolerance for feelings, identifying loss, and learning new ways in which to cope. The group process aspects of this type of therapeutic intervention allow issues related to dependency and ambivalence to surface, in addition to trust.

Yalom (1995) described the use of structured exercises to facility or speed up group process. Group exercises can be verbal or nonverbal, involve the whole group or individual members, or any combination of participants from the membership. The goal of the activities is to promote appropriate interaction among members and support both group and individual self-awareness. Yalom noted that it is important that group leaders be trained in the effective use of structured exercises and that such exercises be used judiciously. Structured exercises may be used to promote emotional awareness, or to teach specific skills, such as relaxation techniques, cognitive restructuring, alternative coping strategies, or problem solving.

Group work has been used to assist families of persons who abuse substances. Various 12-step programs exist which target family members, such as Adult Children of Alcoholics and Alanon (Inaba et al., 1997). There also have been more structured and facilitated groups which target families and children of substance abusers. Le Pantois (1986) described a study of 25 children of parents with a dependency on alcohol or cocaine in a weekly outpatient therapeutic group. Key to this program was assisting the children in dealing with the feelings and emotions of growing up in a household with substance abuse present. Common issues which surfaced included feelings of abandonment, "...lower self-esteem, embarrassment, loneliness, disillusionment, or anxiety" (p. 50). Clerici, Garini, Capitanio, Zardi, and Gori (1988) showed how involvement of families in groups during treatment resulted in more successful outcomes. Clerici et al. analyzed a study of more than 2000 treatment programs and concluded that "93% involved somehow the family, while 75% considered the engagement of the family absolutely necessary for the successful results for the programme" (p. 213).

Awareness and education programs also have started to gain in popularity. Psychoeducational groups are commonly used in treating individuals with substance abuse problems. Such groups are used with individuals who have been identified as living under the influence of alcohol or other drugs or with individuals who have been diagnosed as having a substance abuse problem (Schilit and Gomberg, 1991). In these groups information is presented in a lecture/discussion format which is supportive and time-limited. In most cases, participation in these groups is court-ordered. For example, Rugel (1990) described different types of alcohol safety action programs that are being formed to work with people who are convicted of driving under the influence. With the rapid spread of Human Immunodeficiency Virus (HIV), commonly through the sharing of needles used in intravenous drug use, many prevention groups of an educational nature have formed. Pugh (1991) reported benefits from an HIV/Drug awareness and prevention group among substance abusing prisoners prior to parole. However, MacNeir, Elliot, and Yoder (1991) cautioned that "...whereas brief psychoeducational prevention groups help members learn pertinent information about AIDS and HIV transmission, participant attitudes regarding risk-reducing behaviors and personal relevance of the information may not be altered" (p. 315).

Dufrene and Coleman (1992) examined the relationship between standard group treatment approaches and traditional Native American healing and spirituality practices. They noted that many Native American cultures have had a long history of conducting healing practices in groups through ceremony and the communal nature of many Native American societies. Specifically, Colmant and Merta (1999) described success in the use of the Sweat Lodge Ceremony for the treatment of Navajo youth. They emphasized that ethical codes mandate that counselors adapt their techniques for use within various cultures and that use of the Sweat Lodge Ceremony is one example of such an adaptation.

Finally, it is important to look at what are the factors that tend to lead to success in groups. Different characteristics of both members and facilitators, as well as the groups as a whole, have been shown to have positive relationship to outcomes with regard to treatment of persons who abuse substances. Some of these factors and characteristics include charisma (Woodward & McGrath, 1988), resiliency (Ingersoll, Lu & Haller, 1995), and involvement of families (Lepantois, 1986; Clerici et al., 1988). Groups that actively assist in helping individual members overcome denial also tend to be more successful (Rugel & Barry, 1990; Campbell & Brasher, 1994).

Campbell and Brasher (1994) listed six guidelines for facilitators of addiction recovery groups:

(1) cooperate with the group by paying attention to the variety of messages individuals give on how to best interact with them;
(2) focus on strengths and help find creative solutions;
(3) look for and analyze the exceptions to problem behaviors

rather than focusing entirely on the problem;
(4) emphasize a future orientation rather than a here and now orientation;
(5) reframe relapses as learning experiences; and
(6) avoid having one-on-one interactions within the group, rather try to involve the whole group in the process.

A strong leader who "gently guides and focuses attention of group members on matters pertaining to group process, group dynamics, and the complicated interpersonal interactions among group members" is desired (Washton, 1995, p. 442).

Group therapy for individuals with substance abuse problems has historically been the most predominant therapeutic intervention strategy (Washton, 1995). However, research has provided inconsistent measures of outcome benefit of groups. Thus, the question of whether this predominant use rests with the efficacy of group therapy or with the fact that group treatment is less expensive has yet to be answered (Galanter, Casteneda, & Franco cited in Frances & Miller, 1991).

Research on the Efficacy of Groups

Alcoholism treatment and recovery are difficult subjects to research and measure with accuracy and reliability. Peele (1990) noted that the addiction treatment system is "founded on a hunch, not evidence, and not on science" (p. 179). Peele concluded that proponents of most standard treatment approaches used in the United States, including Alcoholics Anonymous, have not demonstrated their efficacy. Treatments which have been shown to be effective, but which are not used as frequently, include aversion therapy, social skills training, stress management training, family and marital therapy, community reinforcement, and behavioral self-control.

Breslin, Sobell, Sobell, and Sobell (1997) conducted a review of the methodology of 61 alcohol treatment outcome studies published from 1989-1993. The authors agreed that there is a lack of good studies about therapy and addiction and that the studies that do exist are poor. They pointed out that the most often reported pretreatment variables reported in outcome studies continue to be age and gender and that there is a tendency to overuse self-report data. The authors concluded that very few studies meet the minimum requirements of basic experimental design.

Ethical Considerations for Beginning Counselors

Given the wide variety of options for group counseling for individuals with addictions and the limited scientific research on the efficacy of such groups, there are a number of ethical issues that arise and have been cited in the literature. With regard to psychotherapy groups in general, Gladding (1999) noted that the most important issues are those involving training of group leaders, screening of potential group members, the rights of group members, confidentiality, personal relationships between group members and leaders, dual relationships, personal relationships among group members, uses of group techniques, leader's values, referral, and termination and follow-up. (p. 217)

Moreno (1991) added that a major ethical issue is the difficulty therapists may have in finding a balance between meeting and protecting the needs of the individual and the needs of the group as a whole. The author concluded that group leaders must be highly skilled in making immediate and spontaneous decisions that weigh these two elements and produce a balanced response.

With regard to addiction specific group treatment activities, ethical issues can include the addiction history of the leader and the appropriateness of self-disclosing this history. Stoffelmayr, Mavis and Kasim (1998) studied the effects of professional and paraprofessional treatment staff background on the treatment and recovery of individuals with addictions. They concluded that there was no difference in performance between recovering and non-recovering staff, but that recovering staff had a more positive attitude toward their jobs. Other conclusions drawn from their study included

> Recovering staff members were older, had less education, and worked more often in long term residential programs, rather than in short term outpatient programs. Further, recovering staff had fewer years experience in substance abuse treatment and shorter tenure within the organization, but endorsed 12-step principles more vigorously than either of the two groups. Recovering staff also endorsed a wider range of treatment goals, and reported using more varied treatment practices (p. 143).

Dies (cited in Simcox & Mallinckrodt, 1990) indicated that self-disclosure by leaders of therapy groups may result in increased client perceptions of the therapist as friendly, trustworthy, and facilitating. However, the group leader may also be perceived as less relaxed, strong, and stable when compared to group therapists that use little self-disclosure.

Group therapists working with issues of addiction also will be faced with problems associated with active substance abuse. Many group leaders and addiction treatment facilities expect participants to remain abstinent during the course of therapy. Group norms generally begin to develop which reflect the importance of creating a safe and drug free therapeutic climate. Therapists may be called upon to either enforce the rule of abstinence or encourage the group to respond to the situation as part of the therapeutic process. Yalom (1995) concluded that a norm of direct and honest communication is an essential component of therapeutic group interactions.

Summary

Historically, group activities have been a part of mental health and addiction therapy for centuries. The isolation experienced by many addicts and the social nature of recovery lend themselves well to a variety of group interventions. The use of groups in counseling individuals with substance abuse problems is appropriate and helpful in that it offers, in a supportive environment of peers, opportunities to test perceptions, to receive feedback, and to reduce isolation. When groups are based on empowerment versus confrontation, they can be much more effective.

As with all research on mental health outcomes, results are mixed. There are many anecdotal stories of the value of all types of groups, but there is very little conclusive scientific evidence of actual success directly related to specific group intervention strategies, especially related to facilitating the goals of empowerment and assumption of personal responsibility. Although group interventions will and should continue to be an integral part of the addiction prevention and treatment process, it is important that interventions be more rigorously examined through appropriate research.

References

Bolton, B. & Brookings, J. (1996). Development of a multifaceted definition of empowerment. *Rehabilitation Counseling Bulletin, 39* (4), 256-264.

Breslin, F. C., Sobell, S. L., Sobell, L.D., & Sobell, M.B. (1997). Alcohol treatment outcome methodology: State of the art 1989-1993. *Addictive Behaviors, 22*(2), 145-155.

Campbell, T. C., & Brasher, B. (1994). The pause that refreshes: Opportunities, interventions and predictions in group therapy with cocaine addicts. *Journal of Systemic Therapies, 13*, 65-73.

Chamberlin, J. (1997). A working definition of empowerment. *Psychiatric Rehabilitation Journal, 20* (4), 43-46.

Clerici, M., Garini, R., Capitanio, C., Zardi, L., & Gori, E. (1988). Involvement of families in group therapy of heroin addicts. *Drug and Alcohol Dependence, 21*, 213-216.

Colmant, S. A., & Merta, R. J. (1999). Using the Sweat Lodge Ceremony as group therapy for Navajo youth. *Journal for Specialists in Group Work, 24*(1), 55-73.

Corey, G. (1990). *Theory and Practice of Group Counseling*. Belmont, CA: Brooks/Cole Publishing Co.

Dufrene, P. M. & Coleman, V. D. (1992). Counseling Native Americans: Guidelines for group process. *Journal for Specialists in Group Work, 17*(4), 229-234.

Galanter, M., Casteneda,R., & Franco H. (1991). Group therapy and self-help groups. In Frances, R. J. & Miller, S. D. (Eds.) *Clinical textbook of addictive disorders* (pp. 431-451) . New York: Guilford.

Gladding, S. T. (1999). *Group work: A counseling specialty (3rd ed.)*. Upper Saddle River, NJ: Prentice-Hall, Inc.

Goldberg, E. V. & Simpson, T. (1995). Challenging stereotypes in treatment of the homeless alcoholic and addict: Creating freedom through structure in large groups. *Social Work with Groups, 18*, 79-93.

Hodgins, D. C., El-Guebaly, N. & Addington, J. (1997). Treatment of substance abusers: Single or mixed gender programs. *Addictions, 92* (7), 805-813.

Honeyman, A. (1990). Perceptual changes in addicts as a consequence of reality therapy based group treatment. *Journal of Reality Therapy, 9* (2), 53-59.

Inaba, D. S., Cohen, W. E., & Holstein, M. E. (1997). *Uppers, downers, all arounders: Physical and mental effects of psychoactive drugs.* Ashland, OR: CNS Publications, Inc.

Ingersoll, K. S., Lu, I, & Haller, D. L. (1995). Predictors of in-treatment relapse in perinatal substance abusers and impact of treatment retention: A prospective study. *Journal of Psychoactive Drugs, 27*, 375-387.

Le Pantois, J. (1986). Group therapy for children of substance abusers. *Social Work with Groups, 9*, 39-51.

MacNair, R. R., Elliot, T. R., & Yoder, B. (1991). AIDS prevention groups as persuasive appeals: Effects of attitude about precautionary behaviors among persons in substance abuse treatment. *Small Group Research, 22*, 301-319.

Milliken, R. (1990). Dance/movement therapy with the substance abuser. *The Arts in Psychotherapy, 17*, 309-317.

Moreno, J. D. (1991). Group psychotherapy in bioethical perspective. *Journal of Group Psychotherapy, Psychodrama & Sociometry, 44* (2), 60-71.

Page, R.C., Davis, K. C., Berkow, D. N., & O'Leary, E. (1989). Analysis of group process in marathon group therapy with users of illicit drugs. *Small Group Behavior, 20*, 220-227.

Peele, S. (1990). Research issues in assessing addiction treatment efficacy: How cost effective are Alcoholics Anonymous and private treatment centers? *Drug and Alcohol Dependence, 25*, 179-182.

Prinz, J. (1993). Alcoholics and their treatment: Current Adlerian thinking. *Individual Psychology, 49*, 95-108.

Pugh, J. (1991). Group work with HIV positive misusers in prison. *Irish Journal of Psychological Medicine, 12*, 12-16.

Rugel, R. P. (1991). Addictions treatment in groups: A review of therapeutic factors. *Small Group Research, 22*, 475-491.

Rugel, R. P., & Barry, D. (1990). Overcoming denial through the group: A test of acceptance theory. *Small Group Research, 21*, 45-58.

Schilit, R., & Gomberg, F. S. L. (1991). *Drugs and behavior: A sourcebook for the helping professions.* Newbury Park: Sage.

Simcox, A. M., & Mallincrodt, B. (1990). Effect of workshop presenter self-disclosure on perceptions of the presenter and retention of information. *The Journal for Specialists in Group Work, l5*(3), 171-178.

Smokowski, P. R., & Wodarski, J. S. (1998). Cognitive-behavioral treatment for cocaine addiction: Clinical effectiveness and practice guidelines. *Journal of Applied Social Sciences, 23* (1), 23-32.

Stoffelmayr, B. E., Mavis, B. E., & Kasim, R. M. (1998). Substance abuse treatment staff: Recovery status and approaches to treatment. *Journal of Drug Education, 28* (2), 135-145.

Virshup, E. (1985). Group art therapy in a methadone clinic lobby. *Journal of Substance Abuse Treatment, 2*, 153-158.

Washton, A. M. (1995). *Psychotherapy and substance abuse: A practitioners handbook.* New York, NY: Guilford Press.

Weiner, H. D. (1987). An innovative short-term group therapy model for inpatient addiction treatment. *Employee Assistance Quarterly, 2*, 27-30.

Woodward, B., & McGrath, M. (1988). Charisma in group therapy with recovering substance abusers. *International Journal of Group Psychotherapy, 38*, 223-236.

Yalom, I. D. (1995). *The theory and practice of group psychotherapy (4th ed.)*. New York, NY: Basic Books.

Web Pages

http://www.colstate.edu/coe/asgw/
Association for Specialists in Group Work

http://www.health.org/mhaod/spending.htm
SAMHSA-National expenditures for mental health, alcohol, and drug abuse treatment.

http://www.health.org/txneeds/httoc.htm
DHS report on analysis of substance abuse trends and treament need issues.

Chapter 8

Working with Families Affected by Substance Abuse

R. William English

Introduction

This chapter focuses on assisting families who have been damaged by substance abuse (SA) and on constructive involvement of families to help all members cope. There are four main content sections, or topics:

(1) "Substance Abuse (SA) and Family Systems," including the effects of SA on families and children;
(2) "Theories and Approaches to Family Interventions," including family systems theory, stages in family counseling, main types of family therapies, and other useful approaches;
(3) "Obstacles to Coping," such as codependency and other barriers, which may undermine efforts in prevention and intervention; and
(4) "Best Practices in Assisting and Utilizing Families in Substance Abuse Rehabilitation."

All topical areas reflect a synthesis and integration of published research. Occasionally, I contribute some thoughts from my career in counseling and rehabilitation, and from my life as a family member. The chapter ends with a brief, overview summary and references.

Substance Abuse and Family Systems

Key Definitions: Family and Substance Abuse

Definitions are valuable because they provide guidelines to determine what is normal or standard. Two critical definitions for this chapter are "family" and "substance abuse" (SA).

The *family* is the basic unit in society, responsible for maintaining equilibrium, or social order, and supporting the encouragement of the growth and development of its members across the life span (Freeman, 1993). The family is a united or bonded group of persons who carry out complementary roles (e.g., parent, child, friend) to discharge critical functions such as providing economic security and safety, share a common culture, share labor, create identity, transmit societal values, educate children to become responsible and independent adults, and meet intimacy or affectional needs.

Because American society is complex and rapidly changing, it is impossible to describe a typical family system. Even marriage has become an option to the creation and maintenance of families. Most family structures, however, fit into one of three types: (1) Dual Career Families, where almost 100% of men and 75% of women work (Basow, 1992); (2) Single-parent Families, usually headed by divorced women (Lewin, 1990); and (3) Remarried/Blended Families, created when two previously married partners with children remarry (Hayes & Hayes, 1991). All three types are prevalent and are viable family systems, with leaders and members who enact complementary, functional roles.

Family Systems

Families may be open or closed systems. Open family systems have flexible boundaries and a participatory communication style, where members share information, discuss, and exchange feedback. Closed family systems have rigid boundaries and a controlling communication style, which limits environmental influences to protect the family and maintain the status quo (Brown & Srebalus, 1996). McWhirter, McWhirter, McWhirter, and McWhirter (1993) believe that closed family systems are out of balance, or homeostasis, and typically demonstrate two major problems: "detachment," or exaggerated separateness, and "enmeshment," or exaggerated togetherness.

In a closed family system that is detached, members function separately and very autonomously, with little family interdependence. Family members, however, are like passing ships in the night, who communicate little or not at all, and whose social and emotional needs are often unmet. Also, boundaries in closed, detached families are so rigid that support is rarely offered unless an individual is in serious trouble or crisis (McWhirter et al., 1993).

In a closed family system that has the problem of enmeshment, the system is out of balance by too much togetherness. Interpersonal interactions in such families typically are emotionally intense and the members are overinvolved in and overconcerned with each others' lives. Boundaries in closed/enmeshed families are very weak, easily crossed, and poorly differentiated. This family system usually rushes to rescue a member from a stressful situation, rather than teaching constructive problem solving.

Normative growth, development, and homeostasis generally occurs the most in open-family systems that support and encourage adaptation, individuality, affection, collaboration, flexibility, and togetherness. The open family tends to be the prototype of the functional family in mainstream culture. Children are at the lowest risk of being emotionally damaged in these systems, and have the best chance to live healthy lives as adults.

In contrast, children from closed family systems are at greatest risk of being emotionally damaged and becoming less healthy adults. Children and youth from detached families often form inadequate or dysfunctional relationships outside the family because they have missed good relationships within their families of origin. Individuals most likely to drop out, run away, perhaps become homeless street persons, and develop anti-dependent attitudes are most likely to be products of detached family systems. Children and youth from enmeshed families are shackled by the family's overprotection, prone to be too dependent, and manipulate others to solve their problems. Denial, rationalization, and externalization are common behaviors of such individuals, as is passive-aggressiveness.

Family Life Cycle (Duvall, 1977; Thomas, 1992; L'Abate, Ganahl, & Hansen, 1986) refers to stages or transitions requiring adjustments in attitudes and behaviors that increase family stress and upset family equilibrium. Carter and McGoldrick (1988) reinforce the dynamic nature of each family system where the emotional process of transition and responsibilities shift through six stages:

(1) single adults leave home;
(2) couples marry;
(3) families with young children;
(4) families with adolescents;

(5) launching young adults and moving on; and
(6) families in later life.

It is common sense to recognize the many transitions that families go through and to plan ways to meet the unique challenges of parents and children at all stages of family life.

Substance Abuse is a dysfunctional condition when a person's use of alcohol or other mood-altering drugs interfere with, or have undesirable effects on, the individual's life and the lives of others (Black, 1981; Lewis, Dana, & Blevins, 1994). Clearly, there is a strong interaction between members' abuse of alcohol or drugs and family systems, which often threatens the functioning and wellness of families. Substance abuse exists on a continuum: from substance abstinence, to substance use, to substance abuse, to substance addiction. Substance abuse usually involves psychological dependency while substance addiction typically involves physical and psychological dependence (Lewis, et al., 1994).

Influence of Substance Abuse on Families

Family Effect. The association between substance abuse—especially prolonged and progressive abuse—and the quality of family life is very strong and predominantly negative. In 1983, Ackerman's research reported that more than 10 percent of children in the United States are or have been raised in alcoholic homes, but this figure was 18% in a 1999 study by the National Association or Children of Alcoholics (NACOA). This represents a substantial affected group of children of alcoholics in our society, ranging between 30 million (Ackerman, 1983) and 76 million (National Association for Children of Alcoholics, 1999). Many children of alcoholics will themselves become alcoholic, which Back (1981) estimates to be 50%.

Substance abuse usually has a pervasive effect on almost all aspects of family life, but especially in the psychological and social domains. Families become less stable because of negative emotions (e.g., stress, anger, and depression), inconsistency, neglect, abuse, and dishonesty. Substance abusers become chronic liars and family members often lie as well, as codependents and enablers. Once persons pass being moderate users of alcohol and drugs, and become psychologically and physically dependent, or both, their condition and they themselves change the family system. Problematic substance abuse usually is traumatic to a family system (Hawkins, 1998), which then drives a process of short and long-term adjustment as a defense mechanism by substance abusers and codependent family members, if use progresses to abuse and to addiction (Steinglass, Bennett, Wolin, & Reiss, 1987).

Cecil (1985) says that denial is the chief weapon against any form of surrender to committing to recovery. Denial is a state of self-delusion that persons use to deal with pain and loss. Denial is a temporary state which may, however, continue for years or whenever persons feel safe enough to cope in other ways (Beattie, 1989). Traumatic and very stressful events (e.g., DUI arrests, failing a grade, divorce) especially may trigger a denial response, as persons shut down their awareness and acceptance of reality (Jewett, 1982).

Family responses to a substance abusing parent vary but tend to be divided into four phases, as identified by Robert Ackerman (1983), who co-founded the National Association for Children of Alcoholics. These phases are reactive, active, alternative, and unity. Families in the reactive phase are passive and constantly making adjustments to survive a stressful situation through mechanisms like denial, verbal coping (e.g., "nagging"), behavioral coping (e.g., hiding alcohol), and social, physical, and emotional disengagement/isolation.

Many families do not get out of the reactive phase, which often involves "toxic shame" (Bradshaw, 1988; Hawkins, 1998), where families often keep secrets about emotional, physical, and sexual abuse. Professional help often is needed to advance to the more functional stages of coping. "Functional" is a useful, 10-concept acronym, by Hawkins (1998), for a healthy family that can guide intervention efforts. FUNCTIONAL stands for:

- ***F**reedom* to perceive, think, emote, choose, and be creative;
- *Unfolding* intimacy;
- *Negotiating* differences;
- *Communication*, which is clear and consistent;
- *Trusting*;
- *Individuality*;
- *Open* and flexible roles;
- *Needs* fulfilled for all family members;
- *Accountability*; and
- *Laws* that are open and flexible.

In the second, or "active," phase, Ackerman indicates that non-abusive family members begin to grow in awareness of their own needs and wants, reduce denial, and resume some normal activities. Families in this active phase are emerging from the all-controlling dark shadow of the abuser and demonstrate greater self-efficacy.

Child Impact. Children of alcoholic (or drug-abusing) parents are at greater risk for neglect and abuse, than are so-called normal children, and are more predisposed to become substance abusers or to socialize with and marry substance abusers. Also, children from such families are at high risk for having emotional and social adjustment problems, such as aggression, hyperactivity, relationship conflicts, depression, underachievement or poor school performance, school absenteeism, and school dropout (Parish & Parish, 1983; West & Prinz, 1987).

Social immaturity, lack of self-esteem, low self-efficacy, and deficits in social skills are also common by-products of neglect and abuse. Generally, the negative impact will be greater if it lasts longer and involves multiple forms of traumas (e.g., neglect, various abuses, and divorce).

Pia Mellody (Mellody, Miller, & Miller, 1989), who describes herself as a child of abuse and a codependent, believes that emotional damage is the worst by-product of substance abuse. Feeling emotions like anger, fear, pain, guilt, and shame are framed in an unhealthy and abusive manner in dysfunctional families. While powerful emotions in functional families can be empowering, such as using fear to protect ourselves or guilt to motivate behavior change, the dysfunctional family seems to engineer disempowerment by overreacting in a negative way.

The natural characteristics, with which children are born—to be valuable, vulnerable, imperfect, dependent, immature, highly energetic, and flexible—are thwarted in dysfunctional families affected by substance abuse. Moreover, efforts at positive mentoring often are compromised by parents who overprotect or control, attack, or ignore. Mellody et al.'s (1989) work (p. 77) at a treatment center led to the belief that, when children's natural characteristics are abused, they develop dysfunctional survival traits that become core symptoms of codependence, that can cycle into a chronic illness in adult life. Table 1 shows the specific survival traits that often turn into codependency symptoms when children become adults.

Stress, chaos, and unhappiness act as motivators or triggers for persons to assume roles that will help the family and themselves to survive (Hawkins, 1998). These roles—family hero, lost child, scapegoat, or mascot—are somewhat transparent but frequently shape family interactions. The "Family Hero" is a high achiever, perfectionistic, does what's right, and puts others first. The "Lost Child"

Table 1. **The Effect of Dysfunctional Parenting on the Natural Characteristics of a Child**

Natural Characteristics of a Child . . .	*when abused become . . .* **Dysfunctional Survival Traits . . .**	*that become . . .* **Core Systems of Codependence**
Valuable	Less-than or Better-than	Difficulty experiencing appropriate levels of self-esteem
Vulnerable	Too vulnerable or Too Good/Perfect	Difficulty setting functional boundaries
Imperfect	Bad/Rebellious or Invulnerable	Difficulty owning and expressing one's own reality and imperfection
Dependent: needing, wanting	Too dependent or Antidependent Needless/Wantless	Difficulty taking care of one's adult needs and wants
Immature	Extremely Immature (Chaotic) or Overmature (Controlling)	Difficulty experiencing and expressing one's reality moderately

is withdrawn, joyless, and almost invisible. The "Scapegoat," who is often the substance abuser, appears hostile and defiant but emotionally feels hurt and angry. Scapegoats attract attention through negative behavior, and a child who assumes this role is at highest risk to be a substance abuser as an adult. Finally, there is the "Mascot," a charming, affectionate family clown. This role (Wegschieder-Cruse, 1981) often is adopted by persons who lack self-efficacy and commitment. Malpique, C., Barrias, P., Morais, L., Salgado, M., Da Costa, I., and Rodriguez, M. (1998) report that families who are chemically dependent spend at least part of their lives in a confused and chaotic atmosphere, resulting in role distortion, imbalance, and weak emotional support. There is considerable value, I believe, in assessing family systems which experience trauma in terms of their assumption of major roles. Such understanding can be the basis for making constructive changes as a family unit and as individuals.

The third, or "alternative," phase family response to a substance-abusing parent occurs when everything else seems to have failed. This is characterized by polarization, separation, satisfaction with change, and family reorganization. Since alcoholism contributes to 40% of family court cases, the security of many children is threatened by the double jeopardy of being children of alcoholics and children of divorce (Ackerman, 1983).

Families who reach the fourth, or "family unity" phase, are the most functional and are characterized by substance abstinence and growth. These families want stability, harmony, expansion, and quality—especially in relationships.

Effects on Adult Children. The effects of parental substance abuse are often traumatic and may extend well into adult life, and sometimes through the person's entire life span. In this sense, many adult children of alcoholics and other substance abusers have a post-traumatic stress disorder. Some of the most prevalent feelings and attitudes of adult children of substance abusers include hypermaturity and indecisiveness (Black, 1981); as well as lack of trust; loneliness; emotional denial; feelings of guilt, shame, and rage; sadness; uncertain identity; need for control; lack of assertion; a desperate desire to please others; and overreaction to personal criticism (Seixas & Youcha, 1985). Similarly, in *Adult Children of Alcoholics,* Woititz (1983) discusses 13 characteristics or symptoms that can pose lifelong problems, and which appear to be 20% more prevalent among adult children of alcoholics (Hager, Leerhsen, Monmaney, Namuth, & Springer, 1988). Woititz generalizes that most adult children of alcoholics:

- guess what is normal
- struggle to complete projects
- lie when it would be just as easy to tell the truth
- constantly seek approval and validation
- feel that they are different
- are super-responsible or -irresponsible
- judge themselves very harshly
- have difficulty with close relationships
- overreact to changes beyond their control
- are extremely loyal
- plunge into action without considering consequences

Maintaining balance and being moderate also seems to be a challenge for adult children of substance abusers, who are often too dependent, antidependent, needless, and wantless. Not surprisingly, such persons often have difficulty acknowledging and taking care of their own needs and wants as adults. Mellody, Miller & Miller (1989) write that "too dependent adults" spend considerable energy whining and manipulating to get someone else to meet their needs or wants, but hesitate to or will not ask because of childhood memories of abuse, when they did ask and did not receive. "Needless and wantless" adults basically have no idea that they even have needs or wants, and may even doubt that this is a basic human right (Mellody et al., 1989). Adult children of substance abusers who are too dependent are also likely to come from closed family systems that have the problem of "enmeshment." Usually, however, antidependent, needless, and wantless adult children of substance abusers come from closed families with the problem of detachment.

Cultural Influences on Families and Substance Abuse

Substance abuse is but one of many cultural influences affecting families and individuals. Quite obviously, macro systems like national society, government, ethnic and racial origin, and one's extended family are influences. Gender, genetics, and social support are examples of many more micro factors that influence families and substance abuse. Research by Cork (1969) indicates that, where the mother is alcoholic, children have more behavioral and emotional problems.

Research on genetic or biological determinism is another systemic influence. Although studies report a higher risk for children of substance abusers to be adult abusers themselves, they also fall far short of being able to predict a child's future adjustment on the single factor of parental substance abuse (Hager et al., 1988; Miller & Jang, 1977). The inconclusiveness of consistent or convincing findings in fact underscores the resilience of offspring and supports a transactional model of human development (Werner, 1985).

Increasingly, social support is being realized as a strong influence on mediating the negative effects of substance abuse on families and individuals. Ackerman (1987), for instance, conducted research that children of alcoholics who established close surrogate relationships outside the home were much less likely to grow up to be alcoholics themselves. Millions of substance abusers and their family members also have grown and gained control and balance through peer support groups, in a seemingly ever-expanding nationwide movement.

Comprehensive coverage of cultural influences on families and substance abuse exceeds the scope of this chapter. However, cultural influences are always present and it benefits us to personalize planning and intervention that considers culture. Cultural diversity and its implications for planning and delivering services to persons recently has become a very major research priority in education and the social sciences, with strong potential for shaping more effective efforts at prevention and intervention on social problems (Freeman, 1993). An example of promising cultural aspects research is to assess persons in terms of whether their family background reflects primarily the concept of individualism or collectivism.

Theories and Approaches to Family Interventions

So far, this chapter has emphasized many negative aspects or problems associated with substance abuse, ineffective parenting, and dysfunctional families. Now we'll begin a shift to considering theoretical foundations and strategic approaches for preventing or intervening to solve these problems for families and individuals. Because substance abuse affects families and individuals in every life domain (e.g., physical, mental, social, emotional, vocational, economic, and spiritual), it should be obvious that an overall approach is called for that is comprehensive, systemic, and multidimensional. Many urgent needs and much knowledge are available to draw from, in all disciplines, whether they are broad disciplines (education, applied psychology, medicine, government, and religion, for example) or from more specialized disciplines, such as nutrition and fitness (Larson, 1992) or occupational therapy (Moyers, 1992). Having stated the need for comprehensive solutions, let us give consideration to approaches that are most suited to persons in roles such as counselors, psychologists, social workers, and various rehabilitation specialists.

Systems Theories in General

General systems theory is usually associated with the work of biologist von Bertalanffy (1968) and has led to the more focused family systems model. The main premise of this theory is that humans are living systems composed of subsystems (e.g., parents, siblings, cousins) who are connected together and dependent upon each other. This model of interdependence emphasizes that the whole system is greater than the sum of its parts (Nugent, 1994).

All living things are considered to be dynamic systems, interacting with their environments and each other. General systems theory devotes attention to the transactional process among all persons making up a system, not to specific individuals or units. The main goal in this paradigm is to maintain homeostasis (balance) or a preferred state within the system and by individuals, especially related to "power" and "control" (Brown & Srebalus, 1996).

Each family is unique in its choices of guiding principles and roles that govern its interactions. Every social problem in this scheme is a by-product of the larger family unit and not just individuals. Social units, like the family, are substantially responsible for social problems (e.g., teen violence, teen pregnancy, substance abuse) but are also most able to effectively intervene with contributions to benefit deviant individuals, balance power and control, and increase family functioning (Umbarger, 1983).

The Family Therapy Process

Family systems theory, which has evolved from general systems theory, emphasizes intervention with and by an entire family system. While many families are mostly troubled by a specific individual, the premise of family systems theory is to intervene with everyone (Garrett, Landau, Shea, Stanton, Duncan, Baciewicz, & Brinkman-Sull, 1998). The reasoning is that all members are affected by a troubled member, all can contribute to the problem, and all are part of the problem resolution. Both open and closed family systems contribute to family functioning (Brown & Srebalus, 1996). Substance abuse or dependence acts like any stressor to disturb a family's equilibrium (Kaufman, 1985), and often becomes a primary organizing factor in the structure of the family system (Lewis et al., 1994). Terms such as "the alcoholic family," "codependence," and "enabling" reflect the demands made on families to reorganize roles, rules, and functions caused by substance abuse (Steinglass, P., Bennett, L. A., Wolin, S. J., & Reiss, 1987).

Family counseling is one of the most important intervention strategies used to challenge substance abuse. The process components for family counseling are adapted from individual counseling and consist of assessment, goal setting, treatment plan development, implementation, and termination. The assessment phase of family counseling is used like a window, to see how the family functions, deals with stress, communicates interpersonally, solves problems, and interacts with the outside world.

For instance, the assessment of family function, often through observing them in action, may reveal triangular relationships, where two family members align themselves to oppose another family member (Bowen, 1978). The implementation phase of family counseling is used for change. Counselors model and train effective communication skills, such as active listening. They contribute by guiding conflict resolution and problem solving while being supportive of all family members, but notably persons who are confronting a problem and need extra support (Brown & Srebalus, 1996). Reframing interactional patterns and realities is used as a technique to redefine problems in a more acceptable manner and reduce defensiveness (Watzlawick, Weakland, & Fisch, 1974). The complexity of working with a somewhat dysfunctional family group demands that counselors be managers or coordinators. Sometimes, familial tension, anger, and conflict require counselors to be referees, allies, or advocates.

The termination phase brings family counseling to a close while building bridges to maintaining goal achievement. Since family systems are dynamic, members need to be instructed to have a developmental perspective about the growth challenges to family members of different ages and how the family life cycle calls for numerous transitions over time (Carter & McGoldrick, 1980).

Stages in Family Counseling

Family needs differ at various stages of recovery and healing. Various theorists suggest somewhat different looks at layers in stage composition, but all who write about family counseling believe in a continuum of stages or care from beginning to end of treatment.

The following similar processes, for instance, have been postulated by several family specialists as four predictable stages in family counseling (Brock & Barnard, 1988; Hershenson & Power, 1987; Perez, 1979):

I. *Initial Stage:* Developing a relationship and assessing family problems.

II. *Middle Stage:* Achieving emotional awareness and acceptance of dysfunctional family patterns.

III. *Last Stage:* Helping the family to learn how to change their systems.

IV. *Termination:* Helping the family separate from therapy and continue with other supports.

Several theorists also have postulated somewhat related phases or stages for family coping and family intervention where substance abuse is a critical problem. Ackerman (1983) writes that family response to alcoholism can be divided into reactive, active, alternate, and family unity phases. Ackerman cautions that not all families will progress through phases, and states that many remain in the first phase and do not get beyond family denial and inadequate coping, nor move further into social disengagement.

The model of Bepko and Krestan (1985), for instance, defines three stages in intervention:

(1) attainment of sobriety;
(2) adjustment to sobriety; and
(3) long-term maintenance of sobriety.

Schlesinger and Horberg (1988) believe that the recovery process is a journey through three regions: exasperation, effort, and empowerment. In the beginning region of "exasperation," individuals feel emotionally overwhelmed and out of control; family life reflects chaos, shame, and helplessness. In the middle region of "effort," members of families begin to realize the chance of a better life and perceive a release from chaos. Families who reach and complete the final stage of "empowerment" begin to believe in their own competence, or self-efficacy, and perceive that their dreams may come true. Feelings of safety, respcct, pride, and trust (which are very threatened in region one) increase substantially for families that progress through region three.

Another model for families affected by alcoholism (Usher, 1991) separates recovery into four sequential phases:

(1) "treatment initiation," where the counselor makes clinical assessments and guides the family in treatment;
(2) "learning," where the family acquires new coping skills to use after alcohol is removed from the family system;
(3) "reorganization," where the therapist evaluates the family's ability to maintain abstinence and facilitates the healing process; and
(4) "consolidation," where the alcoholic member is securely abstinent, permitting the family to reorganize in a system featuring intimacy and affirmation.

All of these models of family counseling, where there is trauma from substance abuse, share the common belief that recovery is a process, not a final event. Also, they all embrace the assumption that most family systems have the resources to recover and recognize themselves to be healthy units. All of these models also warn that ability to constructively change systems is strongly associated with the degree of readiness to change.

Lewis (1992) has created yet another model for family counseling that is claimed to reconcile the others. This so-called "overarching" approach emphasizes three stages:

(1) interrupting ongoing patterns,
(2) facing the reality of change, and
(3) deepening and maintaining change.

When treatment starts, the counselor assists family members to interrupt negative patterns, which have previously characterized their dysfunctional family system, through the alternatives of confrontation or disengagement. The desired outcome of confrontation is that the substance abuser takes ownership of having a problem that needs treatment. Disengagement occurs when family members need to initiate the change process without the participation of the substance abuser. Schlesinger and Horberg (1988) believe that the disengagement process can interrupt rigid patterns of interaction, provide stability by redefining boundaries, and help family members to move away from the codependency feature of taking responsibility for others' behavior. In somewhat similar fashion, Ackerman (1983) suggests that disengagement can help family members change or shift from a "reactive" (passive mode) to an "active" (assertive) style.

In the second stage, according to Lewis (1992), family members face another major adjustment related to dealing with problems and each other without the use of substances. While this may not seem to be a major problem, Lewis believes it is actually a crisis situation because families have been living everyday lives based on transactional patterns involving alcohol or drug abuse, and they have not learned adequate problem-solving or conflict resolution skills. Sometimes, families resolve the crisis successfully, but many families react to the crisis pressure by separation or divorce, and some try to re-establish the warped homeostasis of substance abuse that they have so long known (Usher, Jay, & Glass, 1982).

Counselors can be extremely helpful to families by assisting them to understand that the exodus from the chaos of substance abuse may be replaced by a different crisis, calling for different roles and different skills (Lewis, Dana, & Blevins, 1994). During this period of time, the family needs to be helped to weather the new crisis situation by focusing on such short-term goals as keeping the family system calm, reducing conflicts, and encouraging individual members to meet their own needs. Also, the family's concerns about possible substance relapse should be addressed within the context of making minor structural changes to give them time to adjust (Bepko & Krestan, 1985).

In the third and last stage of the overarching model by Lewis (1992), the focus is on deepening and maintaining change. Emphasis is placed on achieving realistic hopes, continual improvement in assertiveness, problem solving and negotiation skills, and on empowerment. The responsibilities of the counselor during the phase of deepening and maintaining change are to be a great parent figure and assist by being a barometer of reality, by educating and modeling effective behaviors (Ackerman, 1983).

Six Main Types of Family Counseling

Like all other counseling approaches, family counseling reflects divergent viewpoints. These views are shown in the writings and teachings of prominent therapists and educators. Six of the most prominent theories are:

(1) Psychodynamic Family Therapy;
(2) Experiential/ Humanistic Counseling;
(3) Bowenial Therapy;
(4) Structural Therapy;
(5) Communication Theory; and
(6) Behavioral Intervention.

Each of these perspectives is built around the idea that individuals who are troubled effect and are affected by their family units. Each approach examines the development of the individual in a social context (Lewis, Dana, & Blevins, 1994).

Family dynamics and development related to general systems theory can be applied to substance abuse treatment through a variety of family approaches. Family therapists, regardless of theoretical orientation, address current problematic family dynamics, explore relationships and conflicts within the family, and consider the effects of these dynamics/conflicts on the whole family, as well as individuals. In general, family therapists tend to be very active in sessions and often act as instructors, coordinators, and guide in reorganizing families to have more constructive patterns of interaction (Nugent, 1994).

One very useful and frequently referenced categorization of family therapy is provided by Goldenberg and Goldenberg (1985), who described six types of family therapy on eight criteria:

1. Major time frame
2. Role of unconscious processes
3. Insight vs. action
4. Role of the therapist
5. Unit of study
6. Major theoretical underpinnings
7. Major theorists and practitioners
8. Goals of treatment

Table 2, which follows, replicates the Goldenbergs' (pp. 152-153) comparison on three of these critical criteria.

Readers of this chapter are encouraged to study these and other major theories and therapies in depth, and to do so through original resources by the leaders of various approaches. Additional reading will go far to increase the very brief comments that follow regarding six of the main family therapy strategies.

Psychodynamic Family Therapy. This approach, which is based on psychoanalytic thought, emphasizes the effects of individual deviance/pathology on the family system. It views the family as a group of interlocking personalities; and indicates that insight is important for change. Nathan Ackerman (1981), one of the early pioneers of family therapy, recommends that therapists develop a close bond with family members and use the power of that relationship, as well as their expertise, to counteract defenses and convert dormant conflicts into open, interpersonal encounters. The therapist in this scheme is a benign authority figure, or "great parent figure."

Experiential/Humanistic Therapy. The career of Virginia Satir (1967, 1972) might be associated with communication theorists, but Goldenberg and Goldenberg identify her as a leader of experiential/humanist therapy. Family counseling, as practiced by Satir, focuses on everyday communications of specific families. Among the dysfunctional communication styles that Satir has identified are those of placator, blamer, and super-reasonable person. Therapy tries to move families away from dysfunctional patterns, toward congruent, flexible, and open transmission.

Bowenian Family Therapy. "Differentiation of self" is the cornerstone concept of the family therapy system developed by Murray Bowen. This concept "defines people according to the degree of fusion or differentiation between emotional and intellectual functioning. This characteristic is so universal that it can be used as a way of categorizing all people on a single continuum." (Bowen, 1982).

People at the lowest end of this continuum are less flexible, less adaptable, and less emotionally dependent. At the other extreme are individuals and families who are more flexible, more adaptable, and more independent of the emotionality of those around them.

Another central concept to Bowen (1982) is "multigenerational" transmission of problems, such as marital conflict, dysfunction in one spouse, or projecting blame onto children. One other key notion is that of "triangulation," where two parts of a family form an adversarial alliance to combat another part (e.g., one parent and children versus

Table 2: A Comparison of Three Theoretical Viewpoints in Family Therapy

Dimension	Psychodynamic	Experiential / Humanistic	Bowenian	Structural	Communication	Behavioral
1. Role of Therapist	Neutral, makes interpretations of individual and family problems.	Active facilitator of potential for growth, provides family with new experiences.	Direct but non-confrontational; detriangulated from family fusion.	Stage Director manipulates family structure in order to change dysfunctional sets.	Active, manipulative problem-focused; prescriptive, paradoxical.	Directive, teacher, trainer or model of desired behavior; contract negotiator.
2. Major theorists and practitioners	Ackerman, Framo Boszormenyi-Nagy, Stierlin, Skinner, Bell	Whitaker, Kempler, Satir	Bowen	Minuchin	Jackson, Erickson, Haley Madanes, Selvini-Palazzoli	Patterson, Stuart, Liberman, Jacobson, Margolin
3. Goals of treatment	Insight, psychosexual maturity, strengthening of ego functioning; reduction in interlocking pathologies; more satisfying object relations.	Growth, more fulfilling interaction patterns; clearer communication; expanded awareness; authenticity.	Maximization of self-differentiation for each family member.	Change in relationship context in order to restructure family organization and change dysfunctional transactional patterns.	Change dysfunctional, redundant behavioral sequences ("games") between family members in order to eliminate presenting problem or symptom.	Change in behavioral consequences between persons leads to elimination of maladaptive or problematic behavior.

Source: From Substance Abuse Counseling, An Individuaized Approach (2nd ed.), by J.A. Lewis, R.Q. Dana, and G. A. Blevins, pp. 152-153. Pacific Grove, CA. Brooks/Cole Publishing Co.

the other parent).

Counselors using Bowenian therapy focus on increasing family balance by recognizing multigenerational patterns of behavior (e.g., punishing others through silence or glares), modifying the central family triangle, and encouraging the process of differentiation. The anticipated outcomes of this therapeutic process is increased individuality and identity of each family member and, therefore, increased health of the whole family (Bowen, 1982).

Structural Family Therapy. Salvador Minuchin (1974, 1979, 1993) is the creator of structural family therapy, which is a well-known, systems-oriented approach. Therapists using this strategy must engage the family in interactive activities, where they can objectively observe and assess "enduring interactional patterns that serve to arrange or organize a family's component subunits into somewhat constant relationships" (Umbarger, 1983, p. 13).

The process of change begins as the counselor gains information to understand family dynamics and family structure. Subsequently, the counselor gradually confronts the family's perceived reality and shifts focus from the individual symptom bearer (e.g., substance abuser) to the whole family system. The main outcome goal of this therapy is to "change the structure of the family system, making it more functional in its own environmental context" (Lewis, Dana, & Blevins, 1994, p. 157).

The Communication Model. Much of the pioneering work on the communication model, which also was created from a systems perspective, was begun in the 1950s by Gregory Bateson and an interdisciplinary team that was to become the Mental Research Institute (Lewis, Dana, & Blevins, 1994).

> Bateson's work was instrumental in shifting the focus of family therapy from the single individual to the exchange of information and the process of evolving relationships between and among family members. It was also Bateson who stressed the limitations of linear thinking in regard to living systems. . . . He called instead for an epistemological shift — to new units of analysis, to a focus on the ongoing process, and to the use of a new descriptive language that emphasizes relationships, feedback information, and circularity" (Goldenberg &

Goldenberg, 1985, p. 6).

Application of the communication model is probably best exemplified by the strategic therapy of Haley (1976) and Madanes (1981), who emphasized active methods for changing repetitive communication patterns between family members, and for negotiating solutions to solvable problems. After agreeing on one or several solvable problems, the therapist uses directives for families to follow throughout treatment. An example is the paradoxical directive "where a therapist actually prescribes that a family member continue in a behavior (e.g., cynicism) that would be expected to be targeted for change" (Lewis, Dana, & Blevins, 1994, p. 158).

Behavioral Family Therapy. Liberman (1981) and other behavioral therapists see the family as a "system of interlocking, reciprocal behavior" (p. 153). Counselors using the behavioral family therapy of approach find ways to reinforce new, positive, adaptive behaviors to substitute for undesirable actions. Drinking water, coffee, or tea might substitute as a social aid for liquor; or use of a worry stone to rub might be reinforced over use of cigarettes. Modeling effective behavior, where learners can carefully observe positive behavior, is an important role for counselors using this approach.

Liberman (1981) and other family counselors using social learning approaches focus on specific measurable behaviors and on the environmental contingencies that tend to develop and maintain them. Concrete goals are established by altering the patterns of reinforcement (e.g., talking versus yelling) with the models provided by the social unit (e.g., time out versus punishing silences).

Teaching and training by a therapist leader also is very important to behaviorists, who believe that the description, demonstration, and guidance/supervision of learners contributes to increased competence and confidence. Examples of such training include high attending skills (e.g., eye contact), techniques for managing stress (e.g., time management or negotiation), and self-controlled methods to change behavior (e.g., relaxation exercises and reframing).

Synthesizing Differing Family Therapies

Various approaches to family therapy represent an A to Z continuum, to which a theoretical orientation emphasizes the individual or the family system. Position A therapists, like Ackerman (1983, 1987), focus on the individual's psychodynamics; and position Z therapists focus entirely on the family system as the unit for both pathology and change. The behaviorally disposed position Z therapists are much more likely to infer that traditional psychiatric problems are societal and interpersonal symptoms of maladaptive family functioning (Kolevzon & Green, 1985). Within this model, the therapist guides reality testing, educates, and models skills and situationally appropriate behavior.

Some valuable integration of somewhat different major therapy approaches comes from Freeman (1993), who states that there are five general implications about family treatment that apply to all family system approaches. One universal implication is that a robust combination of modalities can be applied to individual, couple, family, and group sessions (Watzlawick, Weakland, & Fisch, 1974). A second implication is that, in some instances, it is best to attempt keeping the family unit together but at other times it may be best to help family members separate, complete closure, and adapt to new family relationships (Janzen & Harris, 1986). A third implication that overarches all theoretical and therapy approaches, is to invest further in prevention and pretreatment resources. This particularly makes sense when the problematic family member is not yet into actual substance abuse, or abuse is at an acute stage, and when offspring are children.

A fourth implication is that systems theory helps predict the risk potential when natural developmental transitions occur in families, such as teenagers who need to establish unique identities and have intimate relationships (Erickson, 1985). Finally, a fifth implication is that special adaptations of these approaches often may be needed. This range of choices includes multiply addicted family systems, ethnic and minority families, blending family groups, couples, single-parent families, and same-gender families. With rare exception(s), only a few of these approaches have been put into practice to address ethnic issues in families, which is a weakness to correct (Boyd-Franklin, 1989).

Systems Approaches Especially Applicable to Substance Abuse

Table 3, presents a comparison of four family systems approaches that Freeman (1993, p. 7) thinks are well suited in substance abuse treatment. These strategies—communications, task-centered, structural, and problem-solving—are best described by four focusing dimensions or criteria:

(1) related to problems in general;
(2) substance abuse problems;
(3) treatment goals; and

(4) principal treatment strategies.

These same criteria have been used as well by Freeman to describe family therapy that mainly focuses intergenerationally or strategically.

Common denominators exist for all family systems' theoretical

Table 3. **A Comparison of Family Systems Approaches in Substance Abuse Treaments**

Dimensions of Each Approach	**Intergenerational**	**Strategic**
Focus related to problems in general.	Family-of-origin prescriptions, proscriptions, ghosts, secrets, anniversary dates that affect behavior of current family negatively	Family resistances to changes, belief systems assumptions, and demands that lead to impasses among the members
Focus related to substance abuse problems	Family projection process involving addictions in the previous generations, fears of intimacy, and family secrets that enable substance abuse and codependency	False assumptions of the members about the role/ consequences of substance abuse manifested in denial, utopias, demands that members sould be respon sible for each other's happiness
Goals of treatment	Address/resolve unfinished family business and cutoffs from previous generations that can prevent recovery	Resolve family impasses, change family's basic premises/assumptions that enable the addiction, make covert aspects of the family's process overt.
Principal treatment stratgies	Construction of the family genogram and analysis; reenactment; contacts with family of origin to address unfinished business	Paradoxical directives or second-order change(reframing, symptom prescriptiom, using resistance); circular questions; scaling techniques
Chapter(s) in which approach is described in this book	8 and 9	9

Source: From *Substance Abuse Treatment: A Family Systems Perspective,* by Edith M. Freeman, p. 8. Newbury Park, CA: SAGE Publications.

applications, such as: elimination of substance abuse from the family system and reduction of family stressors that could trigger a relapse, and increase in the system's ability to nurture and support members. In addition, Freeman (1993) believes that all family systems approaches emphasize common treatment strategies such as homework assignments, joining functional groups (e.g., a choral group), and objectifying the family system.

Communication, structural, and problem-solving approaches have been previously described. However, it is worthwhile to explain that the focus of task-centered groups is to model, teach, and train so that consumers have greater self-efficacy and competence to perform skills. An example might be to teach parents to use "I" statements and warm body language when they wish to listen actively and negotiate with their teenage children. Psychosocial educational training (e.g., discipline) and parent education are increasingly conducted as task-centered groups (McWhirter, et al., 1993). Social support groups such as AA and Al-Anon (Williams & Swift, 1992) illustrate task-centered groups that are effective at developing and maintaining change to curb substance abuse and improve family functioning. The Circles of Support or person centered planning approach, which began in special education, seems to have great potential to transfer to mobilizing natural supports, to assist focus persons and families affected by substance abuse (Perske, 1998; Snow, 1989).

Obstacles to Coping with Substance Abuse

Barriers exist for almost every challenging accomplishment in life. Coping with substance abuse certainly represents a large challenge for family systems and individuals. The value to having a real grip on real problems and coping strategies is that it sets the stage for significant personal growth. Codependency by significant others is the biggest barrier to coping and will receive the majority of focus in this chapter. Other obstacles to be briefly described include:

- Irrational fears
- Unresolved interpersonal conflicts
- Closed, linear approaches
- High stress and/or anger
- Shame and guilt
- Poor time and organizational skills
- Low self-efficacy
- Non-mainstreamed cultures

- Poor social skills
- Dual diagnoses
- Weak social support

Codependence

The barrier of codependence is part of the notion of family interdependence, and the idea that one member's problem(s) represent a problem in the total family system (Nugent, 1994). When substance use moves to levels of abuse and addiction, families lose their balance (homeostasis) that increases demands on family members to assume responsibilities for the abusive or addicted family members. In circumstances where family boundaries are unclear, members are enmeshed and authentic communication is infrequent. Instead, members often engage in false intimacy. There is a substantial undertow which can pull healthy family members down and compromise them to assume various compensating roles to regain balance.

One such role is that of an "enabler" (Miller, 1988; Williams & Swift, 1992), which usually occurs when a spouse or adult partner covers up the abuse and assumes many of the user's responsibilities. Quite frequently, the enabler also self-identifies and is considered by others to be a martyr (Hogg & Frank, 1992; Schaef, 1986). Children in highly compromised families, because of alcohol or drug abuse, assume complementary roles to help themselves, as well as the family, survive emotional stress while maintaining secrecy, denial, and "face saving." One child may act as the "hero," who achieves success and redeems the family; another may contribute levity as the family clown/ mascot; another may share the responsible role of "enabler;" one may become an invisible "lost child;" and others may act out family problems in the role of "scapegoat" (Ackerman, 1987).

Codependence is defined by Wegscheider-Cruse (1985) as an addition to a relationship that stifles self-growth and self-expression and which closely resembles a person's addiction to alcohol or drugs. In a codependent family, members have not developed their own independence and, consequently, believe that they cannot express their own needs, wants, and feelings (Nugent, 1994). Wegscheider-Cruse (1985) sees codependence as extreme dependence on a person that ultimately becomes a dysfunctional relationship and impacts upon all other close relationships. Subby (1987) views codependence as caused by prolonged exposure to oppressive, closed-family rules that stifle open expression and straightforward discussion of personal problems and problem solving. Hawkins (1998) states that codepency occurs when persons repress their self-awareness or do not get their needs met.

Cermak (1986) believes that codependence reflects exaggerated self-control and control of others, enacted as a maladaptive way to reduce free-floating anxiety or shame (Fossum & Mason, 1986; Subby, 1987). Shame, in fact, is a major cause of codependency, since codependent individuals usually grow up in shame-based family environments and have gained little sense of self or identity.

A family system characterized by codependence has one or more persons who contribute to substance abuse and family disorganization as an "enabler." Miller (1988), in a book called *The Enabler,* offers a definition: ". . . the person who supports someone who is capable of standing on his or her own is an enabler." Miller believes that enabling is a learned role and that enablers work at being virtuous and righteous. The enabler's many virtues, to Miller, include sacrifice, tolerance, acceptance, working hard, capable, courageous, tough, forgiving, wise, and loving (Miller, 1988).

A number of common behaviors are believed to be typical of codependence and are described in a variety of resources (Beattie, 1989; Cermak, 1986; Freeman, 1993; Hogg & Frank, 1992; Mellody, Miller, & Miller, 1989; Subby, 1987; Wegscheider-Cruse, 1985). Typical codependent behaviors include:

(1) Martyrdom: giving up one's own needs in order to meet the needs of others;
(2) Fusion: losing one's identify in an intimate relationship;
(3) Intrusion: controlling the behavior of intimates through excessive caretaking, guilt, or manipulation;
(4) Perfection: holding unrealistic expectations of oneself and others; and
(5) Addiction: using compulsive behaviors to manage one's emotions.

Entire books have been written on the topic of codependence. Beattie (1987, 1989), who is a professional as well as a codependent, has authored two such insightful books. Mellody, et al. (1989) have written another, *Facing Codependence,* which partially emphasizes the lead author's background as a codependent.

The oppressive rules that Subby (1987) believes undermine families and move them to become dysfunctional are silent messages such as: "Don't feel or talk about feeling," "Don't identify, talk about, or solve problems," "Don't be who you are—be good, right, strong, and perfect," "Don't be selfish—take care of others and neglect yourself," "Don't have fun," "Don't trust other people or yourself," "Don't be vulnerable," "Don't be direct," "Don't get close to other people," and "Don't grow, change, or in any way rock this family's boat." (Beattie, 1989, p. 16).

Beattie, in *Codependent No More* (1987) and *Beyond Codependency* (1989) indicates that, in her own experience, oppressive rules were sometimes stated and sometimes sensed but not stated. She concludes that "co-dependency is about the ways we have been affected by other people and our pasts," which can result in damaging other messages like "I'm not lovable," "I don't deserve good things," and "I'll never succeed." (Cermak, 1986; Beattie, 1987, 1989; and Mellody, 1989).

Various authors (Cermak, 1986; Beattie, 1987, 1989; and Mellody, 1989) write that the trauma affecting many children related to substance abuse carries on and affects them as adults. Beattie and Mellody actually believe that codependence is a disease in its own right, and Cermak (1986) believes it is a form of post-traumatic stress disorder. Cermak indicates that "the symptoms of stress disorder in co-dependency are similar to the symptoms of stress disorder in war veterans." Beattie (1989) states that "codependent feelings and behaviors—fear, anxiety, shame, an overwhelming need for control, neglecting ourselves, and focusing on others—may suddenly emerge when something in our current environment reminds us of something noxious."

Cermak (1986) concluded that the two pervasive symptoms of codependence as a stress disorder are "psychic numbing," where persons freeze their emotions to survive; and "hypervigilance," where persons try to be comfortable by continually monitoring their surroundings. Mellody, Miller, and Miller (1989, p. 4) decided that there are five core symptoms where codependents have difficulty:

1. Experiencing appropriate levels of self-esteem;
2. setting functional boundaries;
3. owning and expressing their own reality;
4. taking care of their own adult needs and wants; and
5. experiencing and expressing their reality moderately (p. 4).

Readers are referred to their book on *Facing Codependence* for an in-depth description.

While codependence is viewed as the biggest barrier to prevention and recovery from substance abuse, it is a treatable condition. Metzger (1988) and Nace (1987) make two helpful suggestions for treatment.

First, they indicate that the goals of treatment of partners and families should be to work through their own problems and attitudes, in order to gain sufficient functional separateness or independence to substitute for dysfunctional roles involving exaggerated control, management, or manipulation. Second, Metzger (1988) and Nace (1987) state that intervention will be more successful if family members can overcome the tendency to blame the recovering substance abuser and curb strong negative emotions, such as rage and resentment.

Other Obstacles to Prevention and Recovery

Brief statements follow about other barriers that deserve consideration as part of the effort to prevent substance abuse and to guide rehabilitation efforts.

Irrational Fears. Persons affected by substance abuse often have fears that are excessive; strong, negative emotions like anxiety, panic attacks, shame, guilt, and blame. Sometimes, irrational fears take on a life of their own and increase damage to lives (Beattie, 1989; Mellody, 1989). Cognitive-behavioral therapies appear to be the best antidote to reducing or eliminating irrational fears.

Closed, Linear Intervention Approaches. Substance abusers and their families have multiple needs and will benefit the most from a variety of complementary interventions (Stocker, 1998). The disease model of alcohol and drug addiction is especially restrictive in its narrow focus, rules, and authoritarian insistence that the Twelve-Step model is "the only way" to recovery (Lewis, Dana, & Blevins, 1994). Increasingly, experts are recommending a blended approach, such as the Transtheoretical Model for behavior change, which encourages counselors to provide the appropriate treatment techniques (process) at the appropriate time (stage) (Lam, Hilburger, Kornbleuth, Jenkins, Brown, & Racenstein, 1996).

Shame and Guilt. Nugent (1994) believes that Fossum and Mason (1986) made a major contribution to the treatment of alcoholics and codependents by focusing on the dynamics of guilt and shame, and the difference between them. Guilt involves admitting an inappropriate or destructive behavior and correcting it, which raises self-esteem. In contrast, shame is far more damaging because it is a feeling that one is basically bad, unworthy, or inadequate (Hawkins, 1998). Shame is created and reinforced in alcoholic families so that children carry these feelings into adult relationships. Such adults especially find it difficult to establish intimate or close interpersonal relationships (Ackerman, 1983; Black 1981; Fossum & Mason, 1986).

Low Self-Efficacy. Trauma from substance abuse, including shame, often has a lasting, negative impact on self-esteem and self-efficacy. Achievement obviously is compromised when persons believe that they are unworthy (Fossum & Mason, 1986) or feel inadequate and lack confidence to perform successfully (Cermak, 1986). Children reared in homes emphasizing negative relationships, such as "I'm OK—you're not OK" (Harris, 1969) and prescriptions to "don't talk, don't trust, and don't feel" (Black, 1981) are likely to carry their doubts and indecisiveness into adult life and periodic post-traumatic stress (Beattie, 1989).

Weak Social Support. Most external validation of one's worth comes from the support and encouragement of significant others and natural supports. However, the traumatic impact of substance abuse on families and children usually leads to a dysfunctional family that is isolated and uncommunicative with each other and with outsiders. Disempowerment replaces empowerment and generally denies or lowers the quality and quantity of support for emotional, mental, leisure, and daily living activities (Beattie, 1989; Rubin, 1993; Bennett, Wolin, & Reiss, 1987; Black, 1981).

Inadequate Social Skills. Listening, providing feedback, being appropriate, self-disclosing, identity and self-awareness, expressing feelings verbally and nonverbally, assertiveness, problem solving, and conflict-management negotiation are social skills that contribute greatly to social support (Johnson, 1996). Persons with strong social skills tend to have a constructive social support system, and persons with weak social skills usually have weaker social support, often full of conflict in relationships.

Lewis, Dana, and Blevins (1994) indicate that interpersonal skills training are very important to treatment of people with substance dependency problems, by providing a means for coping with high-risk situations and obtaining more social support. Assertiveness training, including teaching refusal skills, is especially effective in helping persons effected by substance abuse (Goldstein, Reagles, & Amann, 1990).

Unresolved Interpersonal Conflicts. People are often impeded by their unwillingness or inability to resolve conflicts. Beattie (1989) writes that "difficulty dealing with feelings, especially anger, can limit our negotiating skills. The issue may switch from 'How can I solve this problem?' to 'What can I do to punish you for making me angry?'" (p. 191). Thus, some persons are led into interpersonal conflict by their embarrassing mistakes and inadequate social skills. Negotiating is particularly recommended as a strategy for reducing or resolving conflicts (Beattie, 1989; Johnson, 1996).

High Stress and Anger. Some stress and anger can be motivating and productive, but too much is destructive to individuals and family systems. Various approaches to help reduce stress and anger include relaxation training (Jacobsen, 1968); modeling positive communication skills, such as eye contact, posture, and refusal of substances (Miller, 1988; Upper & Cantela, 1979); contingency contracting (Goldstein, Reagles, & Amann, 1990); systematic desensitization (Lewis, et al., 1994); and social skills training (Johnson, 1996).

Non-mainstream Culture. Ethnic cultures may normalize substance abuse and reinforce resisting intervention. Awareness of verbal and nonverbal communication patterns and taking time to create an informal atmosphere is essential to building trust (McRoy, Sharkey, & Garcia, 1985). Many families may have a strong, cultural paranoia because of dissatisfying previous interaction experiences with professionals (Boyd-Franklin, 1989). Quite clearly, a need exists for selecting and training counselors who are culturally sensitive to the wants and needs of minorities (Brown & Srebalus, 1996, pp. 163-186).

Dual Diagnosis. This term usually refers to the co-occurrence of substance abuse and mental disorders. Penick, Nickel, Cantrell, Powell, Read, and Thomas (1990) reviewed the research literature and concluded that between 30% and 70% of persons with substance abuse problems also had at least one additional mental disorder, such as depression or personality disorder. Persons with substantial physical disabilities and a substance abuse problem also have a dual diagnosis. Two or more diagnostic conditions obviously increase the risk to individuals and families, and represent greater challenge to coping.

Summary and Best Practices in Working with Families

Substance abuse (SA) is a major stressor that has profound and primarily negative effects on family systems as well as on individual abusers. As substance use progresses from use to abuse, and possibly to addiction, families usually change to adjust roles, activities, and relationships. A family's struggle to maintain balance or homeostasis is a huge challenge. Family members and even entire family systems often become codependent and assume roles such as the "enabler."

Strategies to cope with substance abuse must be multifaceted and viewed as lifelong processes to maximize the wellness of individuals and family systems. Many, if not most, individuals and families affected by substance abuse are better off by adopting the attitude that they have a chronic condition, similar to epilepsy or diabetes, which requires paying attention to prevention and intervention throughout life, much like a daily medicine. Many of the logical best practices for prevention and intervention are implied or identified in earlier parts of this chapter. All of the obstacles that were just listed are examples of intervention practices.

Since substance abuse is a complex biocultural condition, with substantial intergenerational connections and high recidivism, it is clear that narrowly focused linear treatment approaches will be insufficient in achieving meaningful coping skills and change (Stocker, 1998). This leads me to recommend two broad treatment, or intervention, strategies:

(1) prevention and intervention with family systems and family members, and

(2) involvement of family systems in intervention with their substance abusing member.

Regarding the broad strategy of prevention and intervention with family members and family systems, there should be a continual focus on homeostasis and wellness. Observational assessment of the family in action and a type of family systems group therapy will go far toward improving balance, functionality, and opening up closed systems. Some focus on intergenerational assessment and intervention also may be very useful. In some instances, as with many codependent enablers, individual counseling may be helpful. Training—involving description, modeling, and practice—can be utilized to build a variety of critical coping skills to improve communications, build relationships, reduce stress, reduce anger, and negotiate conflicts.

Social support has been consistently shown to improve family systems, and efforts will be justified if they strengthen the existing family and enhance external support through the extended family, peer supports within the substance abuse arena (such as Al-Anon), and natural supports that evolve from everyday activities (e.g., bowling team, choir, investment club, etc.). Social support networks, especially natural supports who truly care about dependent individuals and their families, can almost always be strengthened, and old supports can be blended with new persons. One very promising approach to consider is building a Circle of Support for an individual or family to meet periodically and collaborate to help realize desired futures (Mount, 1990; Mount & Zwernik, 1988; Perske, 1998; Snow, 1989; Thomas, Shaw, Honey, & Butterworth, 1998).

The smart strategy of involving family systems in the intervention of substance-abusing members also should be multifaceted. First and foremost, families and members contribute by reducing their codependence and taking good care of themselves, regardless of what happens to their family member who is abusing substances. Some of this work will occur within family therapy, and some will take place through other activities such as meditation or pursuing personal goals for growth or achievement. Support, collaboration, and encouragement among all family members will help everyone. Also, family and individual goals will be met best if people refrain from destructive communications such as angry name calling, shaming, or ridicule. "Safety first" sets the foundation for moving towards actualization.

A lifestyle emphasizing purpose, moderation, cooperation, and wellness will go far to help all family members and the system itself. Perhaps it is trite to say "eat a healthy diet, follow nutritional guidelines, exercise regularly, and sleep eight hours a night," but few of us live everyday lives that reflect optimal wellness. Depression, which is an integral dynamic that significantly reduces the quality of life, also should be addressed for many families and individuals. As Gordon (1985) asserts in *When Living Hurts,* if depression is deep or chronic, people should be encouraged to get professional and peer help to minimize the pain. Finally, I advise persons to emphasize empowerment in their communications and relationships, and to be flexible and patient in a lifelong journey of pursuing healthy lives.

References

Ackerman, R. J. (1987). Adult children of alcoholics. *EAP Digest, 7*, 25-29.

Ackerman, R. J. (1983). *Children of alcoholics: A guidebook for educators, therapists, and parents.* Holmes Beach, FL: Learning Publications.

Ackerman, R. J. (1978). Socio-cultural aspects of substance abuse. *Competency-based training manual for substance abuse counselors.* East Lansing, MI: Michigan Department of Health, Office of Substance Abuse Services.

Ackerman, N. W. (1981). Family psychotherapy—Theory and practice. In G. D. Erickson & T. P. Hogan (Eds.), *Family therapy: An introduction to theory and technique* (pp.165-172). Pacific Grove, CA: Brooks/Cole.

Basow, S. (1992). *Gender stereotypes and roles.* Pacific Grove, CA: Brooks/Cole.

Beattie, M. (1989). *Beyond codependency.* San Francisco: Harper & Row.

Beattie, M. (1987). *Codependent no more.* San Francisco: Harper/Hazelden.

Bepko, C., & Krestan, J. A. (1985). *The responsibility trap: A blueprint for treating the alcoholic family.* New York: The Free Press.

Black, C. (1981). *It will never happen to me.* New York: Ballantine Books.

Bowen, M. (1982). *Family therapy in clinical practice.* New York: Aronson.

Bowen, M. (1978). *Family therapy in clinical practice.* New York: Jason Aronson.

Boyd-Franklin, N. (1989). *Black families in therapy.* New York: Guilford.

Bradshaw, J. (1988). *The family: A revolutionary way of self discovery,* 58-61. Deerfield Beach, FL: Health Communications, Inc.

Brock, G. W., & Barnard, C. P. (1988). *Procedures in family therapy.* Needham Heights, MA: Allyn and Bacon.

Brown, D., & Srebalus, D. J. (1996). Counseling in a multicultural society. In D. Brown & D. J. Srebalus (Eds.) *Introduction to the counseling profession.* Needham Heights, MA: Allyn and Bacon.

Carter, B., & McGoldrick, M. (1988). *The changing family life cycle.* New York: Gardner Press.

Carter, B., & McGoldrick, M. (1980). *The family life cycle: A framework for family therapy.* New York: Gardner Press.

Cecil, C. (1985). *Grandiosity.* Minneapolis: Hazelden Educational Materials.

Cermak, T. L. (1986). Children of alcoholics and the case for a new diagnostic category of codependency. In R. J. Ackerman (Ed.), *Growing in the shadow:Children of alcoholics* (pp.23-31). Pompano Beach, FL: Health Communications.

Cork, M. R. (1969). *The forgotten children.* Toronto, Canada: Addictive Research Foundation.

Duvall, E. M. (1977). *Marriage and family development.* Philadelphia: Lippincott.

Erickson, E. H. (1985). Life cycle. In M. Blom (Ed.), *Life-span development: Bases for preventive and interactive helping* (pp.35-43). New York: Macmillan.

Fossum, M. A., & Mason, M. J. (1986). *Facing shame: Families in recovery.* New York: W. W. Norton.

Freeman, E. (1993). *Substance abuse treatment: A family systems perspective*. London: Sage Publications.

Garrett, J., Landau, J., Shea, R., Stanton, D. M., Baciewicz, G., & Brinkman-Sull (1998). Using family and network links to engage addicted persons in treatment. *Journal of Substance Abuse Treatment, 15(4)*, 333-343.

Goldenberg, I., & Goldenberg, H. (1985). *Family therapy: An overview*. Pacific Grove, CA: Brooks/Cole.

Goldstein, A. P., Reagles, K. W., & Amann, L. L. (1990). *Refusal skills: Preventing drug use in adolescents*. Champaign, IL: Research Press.

Gordon, S. (1985). *When living hurts*. New York: Dell Publishing.

Hager, M., Leerhsen, C., Monmaney, T., Namuth, T., & Springer, K. (1988, Jan. 18). Alcohol and the family. *Newsweek*, 62-68.

Haley, J. (1976). *Problem-solving therapy*. New York: Harper & Row.

Hawkins, C. A. (1998). Family systems and chemical dependency. In A. McNeece & D. DiNitto (Eds.). *Chemical dependency: A systems approach* (pp.230-244). Englewood Cliffs, NJ: Prentice Hall.

Hayes, R. L., & Hayes, B. A. (1991). Counseling remarriage families. In J. Carlson and J. Lewis (Eds.), *Family counseling: Strategies and issues* (pp.175-188). Denver, CO: Love Publishing.

Hershenson, D. B., & Power, P. W. (1987). *Mental health counseling: Theory and practice*. New York: Pergamon.

Hogg, J. A., & Frank, M. L. (1992). Toward an interpersonal model of codependence and contradependence. *Journal of Counseling & Development, 70*, 371-375.

Jacobsen, E. (1968). *Progressive relaxation*. Chicago: University of Chicago Press.

Janzen, C., & Harris, O. (1986). *Family treatment in social work practice*. Itasca, IL: F. E. Peacock.

Jewett, C. (1982). Helping children cope with separation and loss. *The Harvard Common Press*, 23.

Johnson, D. W. (1996). *Reaching out: Interpersonal effectiveness and self-actualization.* Englewood Cliffs, NJ: Prentice-Hall.

Kaufman, E. (1985). *Substance abuse and family therapy.* Orlando, FL: Greene and Stratton.

L'Abate, L., Ganahl, G., & Hansen, J. C. (1986). *Methods of family therapy.* Englewood Cliffs, NJ: Prentice-Hall.

Lam, C. S., Hilburger, J., Kornbleuth, M., Jenkins, J., Brown, D., & Racenstein, M. J. (1996). A treatment matching model for substance abuse rehabilitation clients. *Rehabilitation Counseling Bulletin, 3(3)*, 202-216.

Larson, J. M. (1992). *Seven weeks to sobriety.* New York: Fawcett Columbine.

Lewin, T. (1990, July 15). Rise in single-parent families found continuing. *New York Times*, 24.

Lewis, J. A. (1992). Treating the alcohol-affected family. In L'Abate, J. E. Farrar, & D. A. Serritella (Eds.). *Handbook on differential treatments for addictions*, 61-83. Boston, MA: Allyn and Bacon,

Lewis, J. A., Dana, R. W., & Blevins, G. A. (1994). *Substance abuse counseling: An individualized approach.* Pacific Grove, CA: Brooks/Cole Publishing Company.

Liberman, R. (1981). Behavioral approaches to family and couple therapy. In G. D. Erickson & T. P. Hogan (Eds.), *Family therapy: An introduction to theory and technique*, 152-164. Pacific Grove, CA: Brooks/Cole.

Madanes, C. (1981). *Strategic family therapy.* San Francisco, CA: Jossey-Bass.

Malpique, C., Barrias, P., Morais, L., Salgado, M., Da Costa, I., & Rodrigues, M. (1998). Violence and alcoholism in the family: How are children affected? *Alcohol and alcoholism, 33(1)*, 42-46.

McRoy, R. G., Sharkey, C. T., & Garcia, E. (1985). Alcohol use and abuse among Mexican-Americans. In E. M. Freeman (Ed.), *Social work practice with clients who have alcohol problems* (229-241) Springfield, IL: Charles C. Thomas.

McWhirter, J. J., McWhirter, B. T., McWhirter, A. M., & McWhirter, E. H. (1993). *At risk youth: A comprehensive response.* Pacific Grove, CA: Brooks/Cole.

Mellody, P., Miller, A. W., & Miller, J. K. (1989). *Facing codependency.* San Francisco: Harper & Row.

Metzger, L. (1988). *From denial to recovery.* San Francisco: Jossey-Bass.

Miller, A. (1988). *The enabler: When helping harms the ones you love.* Claremont, CA: Hunter House, Inc.

Miller, D., & Jang, M. (1977). Children of alcoholics: A 20-year longitudinal study. *Social work research, 13(4)*, 23-29.

Minuchin, S., & Nichols, M. P. (1993). *Family healing.* New York: The Free Press.

Minuchin, S. (1979). Constructing a therapeutic reality. In E. Kaufman & P. Kaufman (Eds.), *Family therapy of drug and alcohol abuse* (pp.5-18). New York: Gardner Press.

Minuchin, S. (1974). *Families and family therapy.* Cambridge, MA: Harvard University Press.

Mount, B. (1990). *Making futures happen.* Minneapolis, MN: Governor's Planning Council on Developmental Disabilities.

Mount, B., & Zwernik, K. (1988). *It's never too early, it's never too late.* Minneapolis, MN: Governor's Planning Council on Developmental Disabilities.

Moyers, P. A. (1992). *Substance abuse: A multidimensional assessment and treatment approach.* Thorofare, NJ: Slade, Inc.

Nace, E. P. (1987). *The treatment of alcoholism.* New York: Brunner/Mazel.

National Association for Children of Alcoholics (1999). Facts about coa's. http=//www. org/nacoa/coa3.htm.

Nugent, F. A. (1994). *An introduction to the profession of counseling.* New York: Macmillan.

Parish, J. G., & Parish, T. S. (1983). Children's self-concepts as related to family structure and family concept. *Adolescence, 18(71)*, 649-658.

Penick, E. C., Nickel, E.J., Cantrell, P. F., Powell, B. J., Read, M. R., & Thomas, H. M. (1990). The emerging concept of dual diagnosis: An overview and implications. In D. F. O'Connell (Ed.), *Managing the dually diagnosed patient: Current issues and clinical approaches* (pp.1-54). New York, NY: Haworth.

Perez, J. F. (1979). *Family counseling: Theory and practice.* New York: Van Nostrand Reinhold.

Perske, R. (1998). Friends circle to save a life. *TASH Newsletter, 14*, 11-14.

Rubin, D. H. (1993). *Family addiction: An analytical guide.* New York: Garland Publishing.

Satir, Y. M. (1992). *People making.* Palo Alto, CA: Science and Behavior Books.

Satir, Y. M. (1967). *Conjoint family therapy.* Palo Alto, CA: Science and Behavioral Books.

Schaef, A. W. (1986). *Co-dependence: Misunderstood—mistreated.* San Francisco: Harper & Row.

Schlesinger, S. E., & Horberg, L. K. (1988). *Taking charge: How families can climb out of the chaos of addiction.* New York: Simon & Schuster.

Seixas, J. S., & Youcha, G. (1985). *Children of alcoholism: A survivor's manual.* New York: Harper and Row.

Snow, J. A. (1989). Systems of support: A new vision. In S. Stainback, W. Stainback, & M. Forest (Eds.). *Educating all students in the mainstream of regular education*, (pp. 221-231. Baltimore, MD: Paul H. Brookes.

Steinglass, P., Bennett, L. A., Wolin, S. J., & Reiss, D. (1987). *The alcoholic family.* New York: Basic Books.

Stocker, S. (1998). Drug addiction treatment conference emphasizing combining therapies. *National Institute on Drug Abuse, 13(3)*, 1, 13.

Subby, R. (1987). *Lost in the shuffle: The co-dependent reality.* Pompano Beach, FL: Health Communications.

Thomas, J. W., Shaw, D., Honey, K., & Butterworth, J. (1998). Building a future: A study of student participation in person centered planning. *Journal of the Association for Persons with Severe Handicaps, 23(2)*, 119-133.

Thomas, M. B. (1992). *An introduction to marital and family therapy: Counseling toward healthier family systems across the life span.* New York: Macmillan.

Umbarger, C. C. (1983). *Structural family therapy.* New York: Greene & Stratton.

Upper, D., & Cantela, J. R. (1979). *Covert conditioning.* New York: Pergamon Press.

Usher, M. L. (1991). From identification to consolidation: A treatment model for couples and families complicated by alcoholism. *Family Dynamics of Addiction, 1(2)*, 45-48.

Usher, M. L., Jay, J., & Glass, D. R. (1982). Family therapy as a treatment modality for alcoholism. *Journal of Studies on Alcohol, 49*, 927-938.

von Bertalanffy, L. (1968). *General systems theory.* New York: Braziller.

Watzlawick, P., Weakland, J., & Fisch, R. (1974). *Change: Principles of problem formation and problem resolution.* New York: The Free Press.

Wegscheider-Cruse, S. (1985). *Choice making.* Pompano Beach, FL: Health Communications.

Wegscheider-Cruse, S. (1981). *Another chance: Hope and health for the alcoholic family.* Palo Alto, CA: Science and Behavior Books.

Werner, E. E. (1985). Resilient offspring of alcoholics: A longitudinal study from birth to age 18. *Journal of Studies in Alcohol, 47(1)*, 34-40.

West, M. O., & Prinz, R. J. (1987). Parental alcoholism and childhood psychopathology. *Psychological Bulletin 102*, 204-218.

Williams, T., & Swift, H. A. (1992). *Free to care: Recovery for the whole family.* Minneapolis: Hazelden Educational Materials.

Woititz, J. G. (1983). *Adult children of alcoholics.* Pompano Beach, FL: Health Communications.

Chapter 9

Multicultural Issues

Charrles Reid & Charlene Kampfe

Introduction

This chapter will focus on multicultural issues in addictions. Myths and realities regarding substance abuse and minorities will be briefly discussed followed by a brief history of multicultural counseling. The majority of the chapter will present information regarding prevention of addictions, assessment strategies for identifying people with addictions, measuring instruments for evaluating counselor multicultural competencies, and culturally relevant treatment and theoretical approaches. The remainder of the chapter will describe issues related to addictions in the Gay and Lesbian Culture and in the older Population.

Myths and Realities

There appears to be a number of misconceptions concerning special populations and the use/abuse of illicit chemicals. It is widely believed that most of the cocaine users in America are from minority groups. However, according to the Substance Abuse and Mental Health Services Administration's National Household Survey on Drug Abuse (1997), people who are White are the largest group of cocaine users.Furthermore, they account for the majority of people who use heroin. The survey data indicate that African Americans comprise the lowest percentage of heavy drinkers when compared to Whites and Hispanics.

There is also a misconception that minorities make up the largest percentage of the prison population. According to Federal Bureau of Prisons (1999) statistics, Whites comprise approximately 60% of the federal prison population. Although the above-mentioned data may be new information to some counselors who work with diverse populations with addictions, many counselors may be aware that the number of people incarcerated for drug offenses is increasing. According to Federal Bureau of Prisons (1999), in 1970 only 16% of the federal prison population was reported as having drug offenses. By 1987, over 40% of people incarcerated had committed drug offenses; and by 1997, over 60% of federal inmates had drug offenses, with minorities having the largest percentage of increases.

Myths, stereotypes, and misconceptions have often influenced how society and the treatment community have addressed the issues of minorities who use or abuse substances. These have also influenced treatment models and practitioners. Dispelling myths and misconceptions about minorities would be a worthwhile endeavor because prevention, assessment, and treatment efforts could be grounded in knowledge rather than in erroneous beliefs. Furthermore, culturally sensitive treatment approaches may be developed to provide researchers and practitioners with a variety of options and models to address the needs of an increasingly diverse population.

Brief History of Multicultural Counseling

Before addressing other areas concerning multicultural issues in addiction studies, a brief overview of multiculturalism and multicultural counseling will be presented. Although these concepts are interrelated, they will be discussed separately.

Multiculturism

Banks and McGee Banks (1989) defined "multicultural" as the existence of many cultures within one society (p. 39). Banks (1994) described "multiculturalism" as a society in which all cultures are valid and valued, in which the values of others are respected and discussion is open, and in which the individuals from diverse ethnic, cultural, social-class and identity groups have equal opportunity to function in and be valued by society. For the purpose of this chapter, "diverse groups" include individuals from the gay and lesbian community, individuals who are older, and individuals with addictions.

People with addictions may be viewed as a culture because they perceive the world in a unique way. This population has involvement in a specialized drug use subculture with its own lifestyles, behaviors, rituals and experiences. This subculture has language patterns unique to the group, and has societal norms to which group members adhere (e.g., do not give information to the police). Given this, people with addictions are also a part of the general society, and they continue to live and function in the social fabric. They are family members and community members. In order to have communities that function, the needs and experiences of all community members must be addressed, including people with addictions.

Multiculturalism has been an issue since the first people of different backgrounds and different cultures met centuries ago. In America, multiculturalism has been an issue from the time that Europeans first came to the continent (Jackson, 1995). According to Jackson, different cultural groups have continued to arrive in America. Their race and cultural similarity to the dominate group were two important factors that determined the ease with which and extent to which these groups would assimilate into the dominant, Western European-American, cultural group.

Multicultural Counseling

Aubrey (1977) indicated that the multicultural counseling movement began in earnest in the early 20th century when vocational counselors attempted to address the vocational needs of minorities, particularly Afrinesians (persons of African, Indian and Caucasian, or both, decent). Due to discrimination and prejudice, persons from minority groups were inappropriately counseled regarding their professional choices. Some vocational counselors excluded minorities from the process, while other vocational counselors matched the minority clients to employment that did not match their skills and abilities or to employers who would not hire them.

Laws were passed in the 1950s that made segregation illegal, and these laws influenced the way that counseling services were provided to minorities. Copeland (1983) has suggested that that the goal of counseling and vocational guidance for minorities in the 1950s was assimilation into the mainstream of American society with integration as the goal. Diverse cultural groups continued to maintain their heritages through churches, residential enclaves, social organizations, schools, and languages. As counselors continued to work with theories and techniques that were rooted in the ideas of the mainstream worldview, counseling "services" proved ineffective because counselors did not take the cultural backgrounds of their clients into consideration. During this period, practitioners and researchers began to identify the importance of culture and the impact of ethnocentric attitudes on the abilities of counselors to provide effective services (Davidson, Gibby, McNeil, Segal, & Silverman, 1950; Mussen, 1953; Siegman, 1958; Sperrazzo & Wilkins, 1959). According to Jackson (1995), multiculturalism for researchers and practitioners tended to focus on the administration of standardized tests, not the therapeutic relationship. "A major concern was the comparison of Blacks and Whites on various measures of intelligence" (p.8).

The 1960s saw continued growth and change in the movement toward multicultural counseling as American society began to address the concerns of minorities, with Black professional counselors at the front. Before the 1960s, minorities had little or no input in the decision making process of counseling institutions. Jackson (1995) stressed that the Civil Rights Act of 1964 had an impact on multicultural counseling in that this act lead to open discussions about the impact of race, discrimination, and prejudice and their influence on the counseling relationship. Aubrey (1977) observed that the increased racial and cultural diversity of counselors and counselors-in-training had the effect of making the counseling profession more responsive to the nation's diverse populations. Atkinson, Morton, and Sue (1979) noted that as society became more tolerant of cultural differences, the counseling profession mirrored that tolerance. Previously, counseling with minority clients had been done in segregated settings. When American schools and society were increasingly desegregated, cross-cultural counseling became more common and the inadequacies of cross-cultural counselor training became more obvious. Disenfranchised groups in America insisted that their unique counseling needs be met (Atkinson, Staso, & Hosford, 1978).

In the 1960s, the minority groups that received attention were African, Latino, Asian-Americans, and American Indians. In the 1970s, the concept of minority group expanded to include women, sexual orientation, and people with disabilities. (Jackson, 1995). The terms cross-cultural and multicultural counseling appeared in the literature as terms that described interactions between majority group counselors and minority group clients, minority group counselors and majority group clients, or counselors and clients who belonged to different groups. Davis (1978) stated that:

> The available counseling tools and techniques may be inappropriate for clients from a different culture and that

> multicultural counselors must be creative and flexible in their counseling style. A pluralistic perspective in counseling urges researchers, scholars, students, teachers and helpers to question the validity of current theories, techniques and strategies used in the profession. (p. 464)

Ornstein and Levine (1982) noted that this concept challenged majority group counselors to investigate their own cultural assumptions, how those assumptions affected interactions with clients, and the investigation of the value of assimilation and cultural diversity.

Multicultural counseling theory was refined in the 1980s and 1990s because people from diverse cultures were participants in the development of theory, and were active practitioners. Furthermore, diversity of thought was more acceptable. According to Jackson (1995), in past decades the counseling field was uniform because it was developed from one point of view, that of the Anglo-European. People of color were not present in counseling decision-making bodies or as practitioners. Because minorities were not considered a part of mainstream society, the needs and concerns of this segment of American society were often ignored. The techniques and strategies that were developed from the operational counseling theories reflected the implicit Eurocentric approach to client populations. Speight, Meyers, Cox and Highlen (1991) stated that numerous problems in the counseling arena existed because practitioners continued to address the issues of diverse populations with concepts and treatment models that were not culturally sensitive. Increased participation of professionals from diverse populations in the development of counseling theory and practice has influenced the counseling profession. The counseling profession can continue to incorporate culturally sensitive approaches and concepts in the 1990s and beyond, as exemplified by Sue and Sue (1999).

Multicultural counseling theory and practice have relevance when addressing the issues of people with addictions because this population shares much with other diverse populations. These people comprise a culture that transcends race, ethnicity, gender, age, socio-economic status, disability, and sexual orientation. On the other hand, excluding their drug use behaviors, they are also members of families, communities, and society. Multicultural treatment approaches that have been found to be useful with other diverse groups can be useful in addressing the issues of people with addictions. A discussion of multicultural treatment as it relates to addiction will be included later in this chapter.

Prevention

The major concepts of prevention have been covered in previous chapters. The purpose here is to identify a few prevention modalities that may have particular relevance to diverse populations. The concept of resiliency will be given some attention. It is important to remember that all diverse communities will not have the same prevention goals and there may be some disparity between individuals within communities.

Components of Prevention

A major component of prevention is education. The way education is provided to diverse populations may be a key to success. Three stages of prevention are usually recognized in the area of prevention of addictions (Inaba, Cohen, & Holstein, 1997; Ray & Ksir, 1999). These are primary, secondary, and tertiary. Primary prevention is aimed at young people who have not tried licit or illicit substances or have tried them only a few times. Secondary prevention focuses on people who are usually older and have had some experience with substances but do not need active treatment. Tertiary prevention is aimed at relapse prevention for those who have been in treatment or who have completed treatment.

Some authors have suggested that the development of spiritually may be a helpful prevention tool when working with diverse clients (Frame & Williams, 1996; Longshore, Grills, Annon, & Grady, 1998). Like the general population, diverse groups such as American Indians, African Americans, and Latinos have strong spiritual and religious convictions and values. These convictions and values can work as protective factors for those who have not yet begun using drugs or as a basis for relapse prevention for those who have used drugs. It should be noted that some people do not have religious or spiritual beliefs. For these people, the professional counselor and the person receiving counseling would have to clarify the person's value system and identify any of those values that may be helpful in prevention efforts.

Regardless of the site of prevention efforts (e.g., churches, programs, schools, prisons, or communities), it is important to maintain cultural congruence (Longshore et al., 1998). Counselors should use language that is congruent with the population addressed, maintain awareness of the effects of racism and discrimination on drug use behavior and emphasize the effects of each person's behavior on the wider community as well as the community's effect on each person's behavior. Relevant processes for prevention efforts include raising of consciousness, examination of self and the examination of the environment in which prevention efforts are directed. These processes should be presented in a manner that is congruent with the population addressed.

Cultural minorities often reside in communities that provide social/cultural support and social assistance networks. The minorities may share beliefs, values, and experiences. Prevention efforts will have a better chance of success if people who live in the community are actively involved in all phases of the prevention effort because they add credibility and visibility to these efforts due to their social, professional, and familial standing in the community. Community leaders who seem to have social standing across groups include school teachers, sports personalities, newspaper editors, community health clinic personal, leaders in minority-oriented clubs and professional organizations, members of local health related volunteer organizations and businessmen's clubs members (Office of Substance Abuse Prevention, 1989).

Resiliency

The concept of resiliency may have some value when discussing prevention efforts, in general, and with diverse populations, in particular. This perspective emerged when researchers noted that some children were successful despite apparently overwhelming social and environmental odds (Jessor, 1993; Rutter, 1985). These researchers argued that instead of taking the negative approach of identifying "deficits" in children that lead to the "pathology" of drug use, focus should be placed on the strengths and supports that serve to counterbalance and mitigate the child's risk. Thus, resiliency is the ability to learn from adversity and to overcome risk in adverse situations.

Two categories of resiliency factors are the environment surrounding the child and personality traits within the individual child. By determining the environmental and personal sources of social resiliency, people who are concerned with prevention can better plan interactions that create and build the environmental and personal attributes that serve as a basis for healthy development. The extent to which youth are able to grow into healthy, responsible adults depends on the nurturing conditions provided in the major areas of the youth's life: the family, the school, and the community. The protective factors that support resiliency are similar in each environment. These factors include caring and support, high expectations, and the opportunity and encouragement to participate in and contribute to the meaningful activities of family, school, and community. Protective factors in the child can be reinforced within each of these environments. Children who have a sense of their own identity, who can act independently, and who are competent in social situations are better prepared to navigate the diverse streams of today's world (Reid, 1996; Jessor, 1993; Rutter, 1985). Reid (1996) compiled a list of personal qualities that have been consistently linked to resilient children:

- Social competence
- Good communication, problem solving, and critical thinking skills
- A sense of purpose
- A vision of the future
- A belief in one's ability to succeed, as opposed to an expectation of failure
- Independence and the ability to tap into one's own resources
- Feelings of positive self-esteem and of being able to control events in one's life (internal locus of control)
- Feelings of compassion and empathy for others
- An ability to delay gratification and control impulsive behavior
- An ability to make informed choices regarding the use of legal and illegal substances (p. 239)

According to Reid (1996), there may be as many resiliency factors as there are children. Each child is unique and may be reached in a unique way. The strategies discussed here are a starting point for endowing children with strengths that can assist them in avoiding substance abuse. The most effective approach to reduce children's vulnerability to substance abuse may be to help them develop the skills to meet their needs and to develop ways for them to contribute positively to the larger community.

Many of the above mentioned concepts of prevention can be helpful in reducing substance abuse in communities across America. Special attention can be given to at risk minority communities as they face unique and difficult challenges. Social institutions such as schools, mental health agencies, and social support agencies can provide much needed support in minority communities by providing role models, mentors, respite for parents, and examples of community members who have achieved degrees of success in society.

Assessment of the Client and the Professional

Multicultural assessment focuses on two areas. These areas are assessment of the culturally diverse client and assessment of the multicultural skills of the professional. Multicultural assessment in general will be addressed briefly, with the focus here being on multicultural assessment as it pertains to people with addictions.

Assessment for Addiction

In 1993, the Association for Assessment in Counseling, a division of the American Counseling Association, developed Standards and Guidelines for multicultural counseling. According to Prediger (1994), the Standards refer primarily to African Americans, Asian Americans, American Indians, and Latinos. The Standards are also useful in addressing the cultural issues of other groups, including people with addictions. The assessment-related tasks in the 34 Standards are: Selection of Assessment Instruments: Content Considerations; Selection of Assessment Instruments: Norming, Reliability, and Validity Considerations; Administration and Scoring of Assessment Instruments, and Use/Interpretation of Assessment Results. Prediger stated that if an instrument were inappropriate for multicultural populations, counseling based on interpretations of its results would probably be inappropriate.

There are a number of tools used to assess people with addictions, with the purpose of ascertaining if people are using or abusing various substances. Some, such as blood tests, urine tests, and genetic markers are beyond the scope of this paper. Ray and Ksir (1999) designated the American Psychiatric Association's Diagnostic and Statistical Manual, fourth edition, as the unofficial standard diagnostic tool used today. The National Council on Alcoholism Criteria for Diagnosis of Alcoholism is also commonly used (Inaba, et al., 1997). These diagnostic manuals address specific behaviors of substance users without placing a great deal of emphasis on cultural issues. This lack of cultural consideration seems to be standard for the paper and pencil instruments used to assess people with addictions. However, if used by professionals who are culturally aware and if the client answers with veracity and self awareness, the instruments can provide appropriate results for diverse populations (Harley, Greer, & Hackerman, 1997). Harley, et al., 1997 discussed three pencil and paper instruments: the CAGE, the Michigan Alcohol Screening Test (MAST), and the Substance Abuse Subtle Screening Instrument (SASSI). The CAGE is one of the oldest and shortest of the assessment techniques that is often used by medical doctors. It asks only four questions regarding cutting down, annoyance, guilt, and eye opening experiences. The MAST, a 25-item list of problems caused by alcoholism, is the most commonly used assessment method. Inaba et al., (1997) noted that the questions on the MAST focus on the detrimental life effects of alcohol on the user. There is also a short-form, 13-item MAST. Harley, et al. (1997) state that the SASSI was designed to assess substance abuse in a less obvious manner to ease test-taker resistance. The items on this instrument do not seem to be related to substance abuse. Another instrument that is increasingly being used is the Addiction Severity Index (ASI), developed by McLellan et al. (1992). It represents the most comprehensive assessment instrument for people with substance use issues. It can take over an hour to administer. The ASI assesses the person's level of functioning in seven life style areas: medical condition, employment status, legal and criminal status, drug and alcohol use, family history, family/social relationships, and psychiatric status. The ASI provides information on the respondent's age, gender, race/ ethnicity, religion, and income. It appears to be the most culturally sensitive instrument and it has been used with a number of substance using populations.

Assessment for Cultural Sensitivity

A major concern in the treatment of culturally diverse people with addictions is the training of culturally sensitive professionals and assessing that training. Although it is beyond the scope of this paper to present the totality of information that has been generated in these two areas, some information of interest will be presented. The American Psychological Association cultural counseling competencies, a model for developing culturally sensitive professionals, and two instruments that assess the competency of professionals will be presented.

Since 1993, the American Psychological Association has required multicultural competencies for all counselors (Pope-Davis & Ottavi, 1994). The following is a list of those competencies:

1. Culturally skilled counselors have moved from being culturally unaware to being aware and sensitive to their own cultural issues.
2. Culturally skilled counselors are aware of their own values and biases and how they affect minority clients.
3. Culturally skilled counselors have a good understanding of the sociopolitical system's operation in the United States with

respect to its treatment of minorities.

4. Culturally skilled counselors are comfortable with differences that exist between the counselor and client in terms of race and beliefs.
5. Culturally skilled counselors are sensitive to circumstances that may dictate referral of the minority client to a member of his/her own race or culture.
6. Culturally skilled counselors must possess specific knowledge and information about the particular group they are working with.
7. Culturally skilled counselors must have a clear and explicit knowledge and understanding of the generic characteristics of counseling and therapy.
8. Culturally skilled counselors must be able to generate a wide variety of verbal and nonverbal responses.
9. Culturally skilled counselors must be able to send and receive both verbal and nonverbal messages accurately and "appropriately" (APA Education and Training Committee of Division 17, 1980).

Sue et al. (1982) later added two more competencies to the list:

10. Culturally skilled counselors have an awareness of institutional barriers in mental health services.
11. Culturally skilled counselors make use of appropriate intervention skills (p. 651).

These competencies are similar to the framework suggested by Lopez et al. (1989). These authors use the concept of developmental stages for examining the expertise of counselors. Professionals proceed through stages or levels that build on what they have learned before, representing increasingly more intricate and versatile responses. This social cognitive framework provides a basis on which to determine how the professional processes information as his or her knowledge base and skill level increases. Professionals need to know when to apply specific norms for a particular group and when to apply universal norms. According to Lopez and associates, professionals may assume incorrectly that certain actions have the same significance for all people, when the significance of these actions is different for certain cultural group members. Or professionals may apply special norms to the actions of a specific group member when the special norms may not apply, as when a more universal norm is appropriate. Cultural sensitivity refers to the professional's ability to balance a consideration of universal norms, special group norms, and individual norms... Cultural sensitivity then involves balancing different norms and constantly testing alternative hypotheses" (p. 370).

Cultural sensitivity is an important concept for multicultural counseling. Another important concept is that of worldviews. Lopez et al. (1989) and other researchers (Sue & Sue, 1999; Trevino, 1996) have discussed the concept of worldviews with regard to multicultural theory and counseling. Regarding worldviews, Sue and Sue (1999) stated that:

> While there is a strong relationship between racial/cultural identify development and worldviews, the latter are more global and encompassing. Each and every one of us possesses a worldview that affects how we perceive and evaluate and how we determine appropriate actions based upon our appraisal; the nature of clinical reality is very much linked to worldviews. (p. 165)

The stages that reflect the professional's development of cultural sensitivity are:

(1) unawareness of cultural issues,
(2) heightened awareness of culture,
(3) burden of considering culture and
(4) toward cultural sensitivity (Lopez et al., 1989, p. 371).

In the first stage, unawareness of cultural issues, the therapist does not consider culture hypotheses. The result of this stage is that the professional does not comprehend the importance of the client's worldview and experiences to his functioning. In the second stage, heightened awareness of culture, the professional is aware that cultural factors are important in fully comprehending clients and their actions. This heightened awareness leaves the professional at a loss when working with culturally different clients. Therapeutically, the counselor frequently applies his perception of the client's cultural background and therefore, fails to understand how the client perceives his own background and its cultural importance. At times the professional at this stage is aware of the influence of the client's experiences and worldview on his functioning but, at other times, fails to grasp the importance of the client's worldview. The third stage involves the burden of considering culture. Here, the professional is hypervigilant in identifying cultural factors and at times is confused in determining the cultural significance of the client's actions. The result is that the professional perceives having to consider culture as detracting from the therapeutic process and this perception, in itself, detracts from the therapeutic process. In the final stage, toward cultural sensitivity, the professional entertains cultural hypotheses and tests these hypotheses from multiple sources before accepting cultural explanations. This hypothesis testing leads to increased chances that the professional will accurately comprehend the role of culture in the client's functioning (Lopez et al., 1989). Professionals may go through similar stages when working with diverse populations with addiction issues.

According to Sue et al. (1982), culturally competent professionals are those who have moved from being culturally unaware to being sensitive to and aware of their own cultural issues. They consider and evaluate factors such as the impact of the American sociopolitical system on diverse populations. Culturally competent professionals have a knowledge base about particular cultural groups and they are able to formulate appropriate responses to the needs of their clients. Moreover, they are comfortable with the differences and similarities in beliefs between themselves and diverse groups, and are able to refer clients to members of their own culture when that is appropriate for the client to receive such services. Sue and Sue (1999) assert that the goals for culturally skilled professionals are to become aware of their own assumptions about human behavior, to seek an understanding of clients' assumptions about human behavior and to become active in developing appropriate interventions to assist clients.

Assessing the extent to which professionals have integrated awareness, skills and knowledge has been difficult. Two instruments in use that address the issue of cultural competency in professionals are the Multicultural Counseling Awareness Scale-Revised: Form B (MCAS) and the Multicultural Counseling Inventory (MCI). The MCAS is a 45-item self-assessment inventory developed by Ponterotto, Rieger, Barrett, & Sparks (1994). It uses a Likert-type scale to assess multicultural competencies, yielding subscale scores for knowledge/skills and awareness. The MCI is a 40-item inventory developed by Sodowsky, Taffe, Gutkin, and Wise (1994). This inventory uses a 4-point scale to measure self-reported multicultural counseling competency in four subscale areas: multicultural counseling skills, knowledge, awareness, and relationship. With these instruments and others, such as the Cross-Cultural Counseling Inventory developed by Hernandez and LaFromboise (cited in Pope-Davis & Dings, 1994), counselor education programs and professionals will be able to evaluate preparation programs and themselves. Improved skills on the part of professionals can result in better services for diverse populations with addictions.

Culturally Relevant Treatment and Theoretical Approaches

For a number of years, the disease model of addiction, exemplified by 12-step programs, has been widely used in the treatment of people with addictions (Ray & Ksir, 1999). Treatment models from the field of multicultural counseling may allow researchers and practitioners to better address the needs of their clients. Concepts from the field of multicultural counseling can provide a framework that allows professionals working with people to become more culturally sensitive to diverse populations, provide alternative treatment paradigms, and assist the professional in understanding the behaviors of culturally diverse clients.

Multicultural Oriented Approaches to Addiction Treatment

The most common treatment modality for addictions is the 12-step program with the goal of abstinence from all psychoactive substances (Ray & Ksir, 1999). This model continues to be used with culturally diverse populations and has been modified to be culturally sensitive. Alcoholics Anonymous groups now exist that address the needs of groups such as women, Indians, African Americans and Latinos who use substances .

A number of multicultural counseling models have been developed over the years that may be useful when working with people with addictions; among them are the works of Trevino. This author helps professionals understand the history, lifestyles, experiences, and worldviews of culturally diverse populations (Ponterotto & Casas, 1990; Sue & Sue, 1999). In a broad view of multiculturalism, people with addictions can be viewed as having a unique culture (or culture within a culture) because they share aspects of worldviews, history, lifestyles, and experiences.

Trevino (1996) considers the importance of worldviews in counseling. According to Trevino, worldviews differ in levels of abstraction: broad core dimensions versus more specific dimensions. Aspects of the levels of abstraction may be either congruent or disparate between client and counselor. For Trevino, congruence of worldviews can strengthen the relationship between counselor and client, whereas disparate worldviews of client and counselor are better in encouraging client change. In this model of Multicultural Counseling and Therapy, the counselor could attempt to stay congruent with the client's worldview and at the same time encourage exploration of alternative perspectives that may be disparate. Thus, changes might take place in a specific domain of the client's worldview (i.e., substance abuse) while broader ways of perceiving the world would initially remain the same. The client has the ability to change his broad core worldview dimensions if he chooses, but those changes are not demanded or imposed by the professional.

To facilitate the identification by the client of broad core worldview dimensions, a set of core values mutually held by counselor and client can be explored. Illustrations of Natural Law as postulated by Lewis (1947) could be helpful in that exploration. These Laws include The Law of General Beneficence; The Law of Special Beneficence; Duties to Parents, Elders and Ancestors; Duties to Children and Posterity; The Law of Justice; The Law of Good Faith and Veracity; The Law of Mercy; and The Law of Magnanimity. Adherence to the majority of these Laws by counselor and client may form the basis for a therapeutic relationship between people of diverse cultural groups, generally, and with people with issues of addiction, in particular. Sue & Sue (1999) states that worldviews can be conceptualized as a function of individual, group and universal experiences. In that case people with addictions would share many similar experiences with the counselor.

Addiction Theory Approaches for Working with Diverse Populations

Other culturally relevant approaches to working with people with addictions have been presented by De La Rosa, White, Segal, and Lopez (1999). They suggested that models and methods addressing drug behaviors for minority populations have not been effective because, for the most part, these have been modifications from models that were developed for White populations. These models have been restricted to psychological, sociological, and familial factors affecting drug behavior. This narrow perspective has resulted in models that have focused mainly on risk behaviors, and do not take into account the individual differences within minority populations. Furthermore, some theorists have failed to recognize the complexity of the mechanisms underlying drug use behaviors.

According to De La Rosa et al. (1999), a number of changes can be made to alleviate the above mentioned deficiencies in models that deal with minorities. These may also apply to models addressing addiction issues. First, theoretical models should be expanded to include cultural and community factors, because these factors are important to the experience of minority status in America. The effects of the extended family could be included in addiction treatment models, because the effects of extended families may be important determinants of drug behaviors within some groups. For some groups of people with addictions, community may be an important factor. In some urban areas, according to De La Rosa and associates, community factors such as poverty, poor schools, and inadequate housing may impact minority communities. These variables as well as questionable law enforcement have a greater effect on drug use behaviors in urban communities than in suburban communities. Another community factor that could be explored is the drug use behaviors of the community residents, whose behaviors could affect the behaviors of other residents in various ways. Some community residents are more accepting of drug use while other residents band together to eliminate drug dealers from the community.

When developing culturally relevant approaches to treating people with addiction issues, De La Rosa and associates stressed the need to include factors related to minority status such as the different experiences that they may have had with the majority population, the effects of discrimination, and the stress of acculturation.

The second postulate presented by De La Rosa et al. (1999) is that theoretical models need to be flexible so that they can be easily modified to reflect the between and within group differences in drug use populations. Racial classifications such as African American, Latino, and American Indian are much too broad. There are clear differences within the groups, which limit the generalizations that can be made about individuals in each of the groups. It is nearly impossible to develop theories or treatment models that accurately reflect individual differences within groups. It is, therefore, necessary to develop flexible models that can be modified to adjust to individual differences in people with addictions, regardless of their particular minority status or disability.

The third assertion of De La Rosa and associates (1999) is that treatment and theoretical models should be dynamic and multi-disciplinary. Current models are based on psychology and biology, but there is a growing awareness that there is a need to develop models with constructs from other disciplines when addressing the problems of people with addictions. Models of drug use behaviors can be developed that integrate constructs from the disciplines of biology, economics, organizational behavior, sociology and psychology for minority and addiction populations. Examples of integrated models for non-minority populations can be found in Huba, Wingard, and

Bentler (1980) and Glantz (1992). Disciplines such as government, education, and rehabilitation have constructs that can add to our knowledge and understanding of drug use behaviors in minority and addiction populations. In developing models, it is necessary that drug use behaviors and the factors acting on them are viewed as dynamic, as are the social and economic conditions that may impede or facilitate such behaviors.

Finally, according to De La Rosa et al. (1999), theoretical and treatment models should be based on client assets, not solely on risk behavior orientations. Risk orientations focus on an individual's personality, family or environmental deficits, whereas protective orientations focus on factors that prevent or reduce addictions. Protective factors for minority populations with addictions may be different from majority populations because people in minority communities often have easy access to drugs and are living in poverty conditions.

Rehabilitation Approaches to Working with People with Addictions

The holistic discipline of rehabilitation includes approaches that may be useful in addressing the issues of diverse populations with addictions. Harley, Greer, and Hackerman (1997) capsulized some of the more frequently used rehabilitation approaches. Four models of helping are presented: medical, enlightenment, moral, and compensatory. The medical model is based on the assumption that the individual need not take responsibility for the problem or the solution. The enlightenment model (12-step treatment model) assumes that the client is responsible for the problem, but not for the solution. The moral model puts the responsibility, as well as the solution to the problem, on the client. The compensatory model suggests that the client is not responsible for the problem but is responsible for the solution, thus the professional and the client work as a team, with the client being responsible for changes in his or her life. The goal here is to empower the client. This model is person-centered and promotes adjustment and the internalization of healthy coping skills. The compensatory model is seen as the most therapeutic in working with people in general and particularly with diverse populations (i.e., people with addictions) (Harley et al., 1997). By defining culture broadly, rehabilitationists can examine the way they deliver services and the responses of clients from a nonjudgmental and multidimensional perspective, incorporating cultural diversity as well as cultural compatibility when addressing the needs of the various populations they serve.

Institutional Change

When examining culturally relevant approaches for people with addictions, it may be helpful to briefly explore the goals of treatment for the individual, the role of the established organizational institutions that maintain the status quo and the goals of society regarding people with addictions. According to Ray and Ksir (1999), the predominant view is that addiction is a disease with the only acceptable treatment goal being total abstinence from all psychoactive substances. Other theorists (e.g., Peele, 1985) view addiction as one point in a continuum of many substance use behaviors. People can move back and forth on the continuum depending on a variety of factors. For some theorists, controlled drug use can be a beneficial treatment outcome.

Perhaps it would be useful to have more than one treatment goal, so that goals can be tailored to specific populations and individuals. In a society that has diverse populations and many causal factors for drug use, there could be a number of acceptable treatment goals as opposed to the current view that abstinence is the only viable treatment option. Atkinson, Brown, and Casas (1996) have put forth ideas regarding multicultural organizational development that may be generalized to the area of multicultural counseling with people with addictions. First, the reasons for having multiple treatment goals should be clearly articulated. The barriers to multiple acceptable treatment goals should be understood and ways to overcome the barriers developed. Second, a sincere commitment to address multicultural issues when working with people with addictions must come from the top. Program administrators, journal editors, addiction educators, and established practitioners must be convinced that a "one size fits all" model does not serve the client, the field of addictions treatment, or society. Third, change must be directed by the institutions that influence addiction treatment: its programs, policies, practices and structures. For example, professionals may be versed in the concepts of multiculturalism and have the ability to apply those concepts to diverse populations with addictions. Institutions that are accepting of change will be more amenable to accepting a range of treatment goals for clients and more open to professionals who advocate change. Finally, the field of addiction treatment must continue to be proactive, developing nontraditional strategies for working with nontraditional populations, and continue to change as the population changes.

Des Jarlais (1995) has presented some basic components of a harm-reduction framework that may be useful in a societal debate regarding drug policy in America. He has suggested that drug use can be viewed as a public health issue rather than a criminal justice issue (see Erickson, Riley, Cheung & O'Hare, 1997, for a review). From the premise that non-medical drug use will probably continue, it is the job of government, the treatment community and society to reduce its harmful effects as much as possible while educating the populace.

Perhaps the goal of treatment, for all people with addictions, may not be abstinence but the reduction of harmful effects that drug use has on society. Perhaps the goal is to reduce crime, reduce domestic violence, return people to productive employment, increase the person's level of functioning and educate future generations.

Addiction Issues in the Gay and Lesbian Culture

The Issues

The emergence of a gay and lesbian culture presents unique issues with regard to substance use/abuse. Pressures faced by this population such as stigma, discrimination, social rejection by the heterosexual community, and identity and life style development issues challenge the counseling professional to clarify his or her own values regarding this population and to work within the gay and lesbian worldview (Teague, 1992). Stress, due to gender identification issues and social rejection issues, is a factor in gay and lesbian substance use/abuse (Coleman, 1982; Kus, 1988).

For some youth, substance use can be a way of coping with the turmoil associated with sexual development and orientation (Gibson, 1989). This process may be a particularly difficult adjustment for gay men and lesbians because they may go through identity development stages similar to racial and ethnic groups (see Atkinson, Morton & Sue, 1979). A theoretical model proposed by Cass (1979) suggested that people in the gay or lesbian culture progressed through six stages of identity to reach identity congruence. Although not all individuals experienced all stages and time frames, the theoretical model provides a frame work for understanding identify development in gay men and lesbians. The issue of identity congruence is dramatic for gay men and lesbian women who are also otherwise culturally different. Garnets and Kimmel (1991) suggested that, frequently, the dilemma for racial or ethnic minority lesbians and gay men becomes one of managing conflicting allegiances among different communities. They must participate in divergent social worlds, balancing demands and crossing boundaries of the different groups, including the gay male and lesbian community, one's ethnic culture, the majority culture, and for women, the women's or feminist community. Individuals with double or triple minority status may experience discrimination and prejudice as outsiders in each community. Although the goal may be to identify with, or be a part of, both the ethnic or racial and lesbian and gay male communities, typically the result is greater comfort in the gay male and lesbian community but a stronger identity with the ethnic or racial group. (p. 156) This cultural group, like other groups, has a desire to meet with and share experiences with others, receive positive reinforcement from people with similar values and exhibit their culture in areas where that culture is socially accepted. Bars, nightclubs, and "raves" have been places where gay males and lesbians have met to express and solidify their identity (Stevens-Smith & Smith, 1998).

These venues continue to be, at present, indispensable for this community to maintain and increase solidarity, comradeship, and social interaction (O'Donnell, Leoffler, Pollack, & Saunders, 1980). These venues, while serving a social purpose, can also provide opportunities for the increased likelihood of drug and alcohol use and possibly abuse and possible HIV infection, if the person does not maintain a balanced life style with positive self-regard (Blume, 1985; McAllan & Ditillo, 1994). Counselors and other helping professionals can be influential in assisting gay males and lesbians maintain a balanced lifestyle and develop positive self- regard.

Suggestions for Counselors

Counselors and helping professionals should be nonjudgmental, as much as possible, during the counseling process; but as McAllan and Ditillo (1994) suggest, that does not mean that professionals cannot assist clients in self advocacy, provide information or educate themselves about issues of concern to their clients. These suggestions may be helpful in assisting the gay male or lesbian client in identity development, reducing drug and alcohol abuse and maintaining a balanced lifestyle with positive self-regard.

McAllan and Ditillo (1994) provide some specific suggestions that can help the professional become effective when working with gay males and lesbian women, regardless of the presenting problem. They suggest that counselors:

(1) Get to know your clients as individuals, not as stereotypes;
(2) Do not assume heterosexuality or homosexuality about your clients;
(3) Do not assume that marriage and children exempt a person from being gay or lesbian;
(4) Do not assume disability causes gayness or that poor parenting or overprotection result in dependency and gayness;
(5) Do not try to convince your client that she/he is not lesbian or gay and suggest that her/his sexual orientation is caused by limited social contact; and
(6) Do not assume that sexual orientation is the basis of all the psychological and social problems a client identifies. (p. 29)

The above suggestions may be useful when working with clients who are gay males and lesbian women, who have substance abuse issues because the suggestions: can provide a basis to begin the therapeutic relationship, indicate that the professional is willing to work with the whole person and that the professional is non-judgmental during the therapeutic process, and indicate that the individual is important. The importance of treating gay males and lesbians as individuals was noted by Garnets and Kimmel (1991), who indicated that although gay males and lesbian women have some similar sexual orientation issues, the groups are treated differently by family, friends and society. Also, gender identification can be as influential as sexual orientation. For example, gay males may identify with many of the masculine roles and values that heterosexual males value, while lesbians may face the same types of discrimination faced by heterosexual women.

The counselor working with gay males and lesbians with substance issues, as with any population, should have and understanding and appreciation of her/ his own worldview. One must be cognizant of the perceptions, stereotypes, experiences, and beliefs that she/he brings to the counseling process and have an awareness of how these variables affect the therapeutic process (Garnets & Kimmel, 1991; McAllan & Ditillo, 1994).

Substance Misuse Issues for People Who Are Older

The Issues

Although people who are older do not constitute a specific cultural group, they do share specific issues regarding substance use. The major concerns for this group are the misuses of over-the-counter and prescription drugs (George, 1990; Gurwitz & Avorn, 1991) and the excessive use of alcohol (George; Hazelden Corporation, 1996; Stevens-Smith & Smith, 1998). These problems are exacerbated by physical risk factors associated with an aging body. Older peoples' bodies are less able to metabolize drugs and alcohol than younger peoples' bodies, therefore substance use can have more severe effects on older people (Burger, Fraser, Hunt, & Frank, 1996; Stevens-Smith & Smith; U. S. Office of Technology Assessment, 1985). Misuse of medications and alcohol use are often undetected because the typical signs of their use might also be typical symptoms of physical conditions experienced by older people. Examples of warning signs of substance misuse or addiction are tremors, unsteadiness, constipation, depression, malnutrition, fatigue, drowsiness, memory loss, falling, and anxiety. All of these signs could be misread by the professional as symptoms of a medical problem that is unrelated to drug or alcohol use (Hazelden Corporation, 1996; Stevens-Smith & Smith, 1998).

The misuse of drugs can take many forms. It can involve excessive use, inconsistent use, under-use (Gurwitz & Avorn, 1991), medication sharing, and ingestion of multiple drugs without the proper direction of a physician (Stevens-Smith & Smith, 1998). Furthermore, it can be the result of over-or under-medication by individuals who are administering the drugs (Burger et al., 1996; Butler & Lewis, 1982) or of multiple medications that have been prescribed by physicians (Stevens-Smith & Smith). Because older people typically experience a variety of health problems, it is not uncommon for individuals to receive at least 13 prescriptions per year (Stall, 1996). This polypharmaceutical practice can result in adverse effects or in drug potency alterations (Bressler & Conrad, 1983; Burger et al.). In addition to these prescribed medications, older people may be taking a variety of over-the-counter drugs (George, 1990) that may interact negatively among themselves and with other prescription drugs that are being taken (Stevens-Smith & Smith). Individually, and in combination, these types of misuse may result in adverse consequences (Burger et al., 1996; Gurwitz & Avorn, 1991).

Excessive alcohol use is a potential problem for older people (George, 1990). For example, one study reported that 70% of hospitalized older people have alcohol-related problems and that 20% have been diagnosed with alcoholism (Hazelden Corporation, 1996). Older people are at risk of alcoholism for a variety of reasons. Often they have experienced multiple losses not only of their body systems but also of their friends, families, occupations, income, residence, and autonomy. These losses may leave them with reduced mobility, grief issues, declining social support, time on their hands, and a sense of disempowerment (Kampfe, 1993/1994, 1998; Meyers, 1990; Stevens-Smith & Smith, 1998; Waters & Goodman, 1990). If they turn to alcohol, it may have more severe effects on their bodies and functioning than it would have on younger people's bodies. For example, a lower level of alcohol can cause significant impairment in motor skills and cognition for older people. It can increase the output and rate of the heart, and it can result in alcohol-induced hypoglycemia (Levy, Duga, Girgis, & Gordon, 1973 as cited in Stevens-Smith & Smith).

Suggestions for Counselors

It will be important for counselors to identify the risk factors of substance abuse for each of their clients. As mentioned earlier, older individuals experience multiple losses at a much higher degree than do younger people. As a preventative measure, counselors can assist individuals in dealing with these losses and in finding new, meaningful ways to spend their lives. Helping people work through their losses can involve a variety of skills and attitudes. To begin with, counselors need to respect their clients' unique understanding of the life events that they have experienced. That is, the counselor will want to understand each loss from their clients' worldviews, and help them express thoughts and feelings about the loss. This understanding can be accomplished by using active listening skills that involve empathetic paraphrasing, reflecting, questioning, and summarizing (Kampfe, 1993/1994, 1995; Myers & Schweibert, 1996; Schlossberg, 1984; Waters & Goodman, 1990). The counselor can then help these individuals identify ways that their lives are and can be meaningful, focus on their functional capacities, develop or affirm a sense of control over their circumstances (Brandstadter & Baltes-Gotz, 1990; Crewe, 1992; DeLoach, 1992; Folkman, 1984; Kampfe, 1998; Krause, 1986; Myers, 1990; Waters & Goodman), and establish or maintain social support from those around them (Hansson & Carpenter, 1994).

Counselors can work with the environment to encourage greater opportunities for social interaction (DeLoach, 1992; Stevens-Smith & Smith, 1998). This might be done by providing training to health care workers regarding the importance of social support; by starting peer support groups; by identifying social support agencies, organizations, or programs that already exist in the community; and by involving family members in the client's life. Discussions with other people about the client should not be undertaken without the client's permission (American Counseling Association Code of Ethics, 1997), and it is best to include the client in these interactions.

Counselors can also be aware of the signs of substance misuse or excessive alcohol use, and be vigilant when clients have been diagnosed with medical conditions that might share common symptoms of the abuse. Misdiagnosis can be deleterious to an individual's health, and can supersede any appropriate treatment for substance use.

Counselors need to be aware of the potential misuse of substances, and to ask their client about his or her over-the-counter and prescription drugs (Stevens-Smith & Smith, 1998). It is not always enough to ask the client to list the medications being taken, because there are often so many that it is difficult to remember all of them. One technique that is particularly helpful is to ask about each of the client's conditions and then to ask about the drug that is being taken for that condition. Another technique is to walk through the house and ask the client to show you the medications in each room. For example, one might ask to see the medications in the kitchen drawer or windowsill, the drugs beside a favorite chair, those beside the bed, and those in the bathroom. If counselors can not visit the home, they can simply ask the client about the drugs for each condition or in each room. These prompts can assist the client in generating a complete list of the medications being taking. The client can then confer with his or her pharmacist or physician regarding their interactive effects. Counselors can also provide information about the potential deleterious effects of overuse, under use and inconsistent use of medications.

Summary

This chapter examined issues related to working with diverse populations with addictions. Much of the information may be applicable to other populations. Issues particular to the treatment of people with addictions were examined, as well as prevention and assessment issues. Substance abuse issues among people in the gay male and lesbian culture and the older populations were examined. Multicultural models and concepts that could be applied to addiction populations were presented.

Society has a role in addressing the issues of people with addictions because this population can have negative effects on society in general. With appropriate interventions, the negative effects of addiction can be mitigated and perhaps alleviated entirely. It is hoped that society will continue to explore alternative ways of addressing the issues that this population presents.

References

American Counseling Association. (1997). *Code of ethics and standards of practice.* Alexandria, VA: American Counseling Association.

Atkinson, D. R., Brown, M. T., & Casas, J. M. (1996). Achieving ethnic parity in counseling psychology. *The Counseling Psychologist, 24* (2), 230-258.

Atkinson, D. R., Morton, G., & Sue, D. W. (1979). *Counseling American minorities: A cross-cultural perspective.* Dubuque, IA: William C. Brown.

Atkinson, D. R. Staso, D., & Hosford, R. (1978). Selecting counselor trainees with multi-cultural strengths: A solution to the Bakke decision crisis. *Personnel and Guidance Journal, 56* (1), 546-549.

Aubrey, R. F. (1977). Historical development of guidance and counseling and implications for the future. *Personnel and Guidance Journal, 55*(1), 288-295.

Banks, J. A. (1994). *Multicultural education: Theory and Practice* (3rd ed.). Needham Heights, MA: Allyn & Bacon.

Banks, J. A., & McGee Banks S. A. (1989). *Multicultural education: Issues and perspectives.* Needham Heights, MA: Allyn & Bacon.

Blume, E. S. (1985). Substance abuse (of being queer, magic pills, and social lubricants). In H. Hidalgo, T. L. Peterson, & N. J. Woodman (Eds.), *Lesbian and gay issues: A resource manual for social workers* (pp. 79-87). Silver Spring, MD: National Association of Social Workers.

Brandstadter, J., & Baltes-Gotz, B. (1990). Personal control over development and quality of life perspectives in adulthood. In P. B. Baltes & M. M. Baltes (Eds.), *Successful aging: Perspectives from the behavioral sciences.* Cambridge, England: Cambridge University Press.

Bressler, R., & Conrad, K. A. (1983). Clinical pharmacology. In F. U. Steinberg (Ed.), *Care of the geriatric patient* (pp. 256-274). St. Louis, MO: C. V. Mosby.

Burger, S. G., Fraser, V., Hunt, S., & Frank, B. (1996). *Nursing homes: Getting good care there.* San Luis Obispo, CA: Impact.

Butler, R. N. & Lewis, M. I. (1982). *Aging and mental health* (3rd ed.). St Louis, C. V. Mosby.

Cass, V. C. (1979). Homosexual identity formation: A theoretical model. *Journal of Homosexuality, 4,* 219-235.

Coleman, E. (1982). Chemical dependency and intimacy dysfunction: Inextricably bound. *Journal of Chemical Dependency Treatment, 1,* 13-26.

Copeland, E. J. (1983). Cross-cultural counseling and psychotherapy: A historical perspective. Implications for research and training. *Journal of Counseling and Development, 62,* 10-15.

Crewe, N. M. (1992). Functional assessment and the Americans with Disabilities Act. In J. K. O'Brien (Ed.), *National short-term training program: Americans with Disabilities Act* (4th ed., pp. 96-115). Carbondale: Rehabilitation Continuing Education Program, Southern Illinois University.

Davidson, K. S., Gibby, R. G., McNeil, E. B., Segal, S. J., & Silverman, H. (1950). A Preliminary study of Negro and White differences on Form 1 of the Wechsler-Bellevue Scale. *Journal of Consulting Psychology, 13*(1), 298-300.

Davis, R. V. (1978). A paradigm and model for cross-cultural study of counseling. *Personnel and Guidance Journal, 56* (1), 463-466.

De La Rosa, M.R.,White, M.S., Segal, B., & Lopez, R., (1999) Conducting drug abuse research with minority populations: conclusions and recommendations. *Drugs & Society, 14,* 269-283.

DeLoach, C. (1992). The independent living movement. In J.K. O'Brien (Ed.), *National short-term training program: Americans with Disabilities Act* (4th ed., pp.68-95). Carbondale: Rehabilitation Continuing Education Program, Southern Illinois University.

Des Jarlais, D. C. (1995). Harm reduction: A framework for incorporating science into drug policy. *American Journal of Public Health, 85,* (1), 10-12.

Erickson, P. G., Riley, D. M., Cheung, Y. W., & O'Hare, P. A., (1997). *Harm Reduction: A new direction for drug policies and programs.* Toronto: University of Toronto Press.

Federal Bureau of Prisons Quick Facts: 1999. Available Internet (http://.bop.gov/facto598.html).

Folkman, S. (1984). Personal control and stress and coping processes: A theoretical analysis. *Journal of Personality and Social Psychology, 46,* 839-852.

Frame, M. W., & Williams, C. B. (1996). Counseling African Americans: Integrating spirituality in therapy. *Counseling and Values, 41,* 16-25.

Garnets, L. & Kimmel, D. (1991) Lesbian and gay male dimensions in the psychological study of human diversity. In J. D. Goodchilds (Ed.), *Psychological perspectives on human diversity in America.* Washington, DC: American Psychological Association.

George, R. L. (1990). *Counseling the chemically dependent: Theory and practice.* Upper Saddle River, NJ: Prentice Hall.

Glantz, M. (1992). A developmental psychopathological model of drug abuse vulnerability. In M. D. Glantz & R. Pickens (Eds.), *Vulnerability to drug abuse.* Washington, DC: American Psychological Association.

Gibson, P. (1989). Gay men and lesbian youth suicide. In M. Feinleib (Ed.), *Report of the secretary's taskforce on youth suicide* (pp. 3-11). Washington, DC: US Department of Health and Human Services.

Gurwitz, J. H., & Avorn, J. (1991). The ambiguous relation between aging and adverse drug reactions. *Annals of Internal Medicine, 114,* 952-965.

Hansson, R. O., & Carpenter, B. N. (1994). *Relationships in old age: Coping with the challenge of transition.* New York: Guilford.

Harley, D. A., Greer, B. G., & Hackerman, A. E. (1997). Substance abuse and rehabilitation. *Rehabilitation Education, 11* (4), 353-372.

Hazelden Corporation (1996). Alcoholism and drug abuse: A growing problems among the elderly. On the World Wide Web, 1-2.

Huba, G. J., Wingard, J. A., & Bentler, P. M. (1980). Framework for interactive theory of drug abuse. In D. J. Letterie, M. Sayers, & H. W. Pearson (Eds.), *Theories on drug abuse: Selected contemporary perspective* (NIDA Research Monograph 130, Pub. No. (ADM) 84-967, pp. 95-101). Rockville, MD: U.S. Government Printing Office.

Inaba, D. S., Cohen, W. E., & Holstein, M. E. (1997). *Uppers, downers, all arounders: Physical and mental effects of psychoactive drugs* (3rd ed.). Ashland, OR: CNS.

Jackson, M. L. (1995). Multicultural counseling: Historical perspectives. In J. G. Ponterotto & J. M. Casas (Eds.), *Handbook of multicultural counseling* (pp. 3-16). Thousand Oaks, CA: Sage.

Jessor, R. (1993). Successful adolescent development among youth in high risk settings. *American Psychologist, 48* (2), 117-26.

Kampfe, C. M. (1993/1994). Vocational rehabilitation and the older population. *The Southwest Journal on Aging, 9* (2), 65-69.

Kampfe, C. M. (1995). Empowerment in residential relocation and long-term care settings. In K. V. Chandras. *Handbook on counseling adolescents, adults and older persons.* Alexandria, VA: ACES Adult Development, Aging and Counseling Network, Association for Counselor Education and Supervision.

Kampfe, C. M. (1998). Residential relocation of people who are older: Relationship among life satisfaction, perceptions, coping strategies, and other variables. *Journal of Adult Development and Aging: Theory and Research* (On-line). 1 (1). Available: http://www.uncg.edu/ced/jada.

Krause, N. (1986). Stress and coping: Reconceptualizing the role of locus of control beliefs. *Journal of Gerontology, 41,* 617-622.

Kus, R. (1988). Alcoholism and non-acceptance of gay self: The critical link. *Journal of Homosexuality, 15,* 25-41.

Lewis, C. S. (1947). *The abolition of man: How education develops man's sense of morality.* New York: Macmillan.

Longshore, D., Grills, C., Annon, K., & Grady, R. (1998). Promoting recovery from drug abuse: An Africentric intervention. *Journal of Black Studies 28,* (3), 319-332.

Lopez, S. R., Grover, K. P., Holland, D., Johnson, M. J., Kain, C. D., Kanel, K., Mellins, C. A., & Rhyne, M. C., (1989). Development of Culturally Sensitive Psychotherapists. *Professional Psychology: Research and Practice, 20* (6), 369-376.

McAllan, L. C., & Ditillo, D. (1994). Addressing the needs of lesbian and gay clients with disabilities. *Journal of Applied Rehabilitation Counseling, 25* (1), 26-34.

McLellan, A. T., Kushner, H., Metzger, D., Peters, R., Smith, I., Grissom, G., Pettinati, H., & Argeriou, M. (1992). The fifth edition of the Addiction Severity Index. *The Journal of Substance Abuse Treatment, 9,* 199-213.

Mussen, P. H. (1953). Differences between the TAT responses of Negro and White boys. *Journal of Consulting Psychology, 17* (5), 373-376.

Myers, J. E. (1990). *Empowerment for later life.* Ann Arbor, MI: ERIC Counseling and Personnel Services Clearinghouse.

Myers, J. E., & Schweibert, V. L. (1996). *Competencies for Gerontological Counseling.* Alexandria, VA: American Counseling Association.

O'Donnell, M., Leoffler, V., Pollock, K., & Saunders, Z. (1980). *Lesbian health matters.* Santa Cruz, CA: Women's Health Center.

Office of Substance Abuse Prevention. (1989). *Prevention plus II: Tools for creating and sustaining drug-free communities.* (DHHS Publication No. ADM 89-1649). Rockville, MD: National Clearinghouse for Alcohol and Drug Information.

Ornstein, A. C., & Levine, D. U. (1982). Multicultural education: Trends and issues. *Childhood Education, 58,* 241-245.

Peele, S. (1985). *The meaning of addiction: Compulsive experience and its interpretation.* Lexington, MA: Lexington Books.

Ponterotto, J. G., & Casas, J. M. (1990). *Handbook of racial/ethnic minority counseling research.* Springfield, IL: Charles C Thomas.

Ponterotto, J. G., Rieger, B. P., Barrett, A., & Sparks, R. (1994). Assessing multicultural counseling competence: A review of instrumentation. *Journal of Counseling & Development, 72,* 316-322.

Pope-Davis, D. B., & Dings, J. G., (1994). An empirical comparison of two self-report multicultural counseling competency inventories. *Measurement and Evaluation In Counseling and Development, 27,* 93-101.

Pope-Davis, D. B., & Ottavi, T. M. (1994). Examining the association between self-reported multicultural counseling competencies and demographic variables among counselors. *Journal of Counseling & Development, 72,* 293-297.

Prediger, D. J. (1994). Multicultural assessment standards: A compilation for counselors. *Measurement and Evaluation in Counseling and Development, 27,* 68-73.

Ray, O., & Ksir C. (1999). *Drugs, society, and human behavior* (8th ed.). Boston, MA: McGraw-Hill.

Reid, C. R. (1996). Promoting resiliency: Classroom strategies that foster students' strengths. In S. F. Moore & A. Sales (Eds.), *Preparing tomorrow's teachers in substance abuse prevention: A curriculum for teacher education* (Rev. ed.) (pp. 238-242). Tucson, AZ: University of Arizona.

Rutter, M. (1985). Resilience in the face of adversity: Protective factors and resistance to psychiatric disorder. *British Journal of Psychiatry, 147,* 598-611.

Schlossberg, N. K. (1984). *Counseling adults in transition.* New York: Springer.

Siegman, A. W. (1958). The effects of cultural factors on the relationship between personality, intelligence, and ethnocentric attitudes. *Journal of Consulting Psychology, 22* (5), 375-377.

Sodowsky, G. R., Taffe, R. C., Gutkin, T. B., & Wise, S. L. (1994). Multicultural Counseling Inventory (MCI): A self-report measure of multicultural competencies. *Journal of Counseling Psychology, 41*, 137-148.

Speight, S. L., Meyers, L. J., Cox, C. I., & Highlen, P. S. (1991). A redefinition of counseling. *Journal of Counseling and Development, 70* (1), 29-36.

Sperrazzo, G., & Wilkins, W. L. (1959). Racial differences on progressive matrices. *Journal of Consulting Psychology, 23* (3), 273-274.

Stall, R. S. (1996). Drug abuse in the elderly: Major issues. On the World Wide Web, 1-3.

Stevens-Smith, P. and Smith, R. L. (1998). *Substance abuse counseling: Theory and practice.* Columbus, OH: Merril.

Substance Abuse and Mental Health Services Administration (1997). *National Household Survey on Drug Abuse.* [On-line] Available: Internet http://www.health.org/pubs/97hhs/hhsda984.

Sue, D. W., Bernier, J. E., Durran, A., Feinberg, L., Pedersen, P., Smith, E. J., & Vasquez-Nuttall, E. (1982). Position paper: Cross-cultural counseling competencies. *The Counseling Psychologist, 10*, 45-52.

Sue, D. W., & Sue, D. (1999). *Counseling the culturally different: Theory and practice* (3rd ed.). New York: Wiley.

Teague, J. (1992). Issues relating to the treatment of adolescent lesbians and homosexuals. *Journal of mental health counseling, 14*, 422-439.

Trevino, J. G. (1996). Worldview and change in cross-cultural counseling. *The Counseling Psychologist, 24* (2), 198-215.

U. S. Office of Technology Assessment (1985). Technology and Aging in America (OTA-BA-264). Washington, DC: U.S. Congress.

Waters, E. B., & Goodman, J. (1990). *Empowering older adults.* San Francisco: Jossey-Bass.

Chapter 10

Substance Abuse and Disability

Amos Sales

Substance abuse is widespread and of major impact in our society (SARDI, 1996; Beck, Marr, Taricone, 1994). Estimates are that forty-five million Americans attend one hundred-and-forty different kinds of weekly recovery groups. Another 100 million are trying to help those who are in recovery (Yalom, 1995). Studies, over the past fifteen years, of individuals of various disabilities in the United States (U.S.) show their alcohol and drug abuse is up to three (3) times that of the general population (Connecticut Clearing House, 1998).

Given the above estimates, the expectation of practitioners would be that substance abuse on client's with disability caseloads would be much higher than or at least parallel to what is found in the general population, approximately 1 in 3 clients having a substance abuse problem. However, actual agency service delivery experience with clients known as substance abusers indicates agencies are serving a smaller percentage in their caseloads than in the population. For example, in 1990, over 23,000 (11%) of clients who were successfully closed from the State-Federal Vocational Rehabilitation (VR) program in the U.S. had primary diagnoses of substance abuse or dependence, with an additional 8,000 (4%) having a secondary substance abuse disability (DeNitto and Schwab, 1991). However, in addition to these diagnoses, Ohlmer (1992) and others have found that a very high (35 to 52) percent of VR caseloads have undiagnosed substance abuse problems. One of these studies (DiNitto & Schwab, 1991) found, in using the Addictions Severity Index (ASI) to evaluate 86 Texas rehabilitation clients with no substance abuse diagnosis, that 33 (38%) met the ASI criteria for alcohol or drug problems. Similar results were found with the SASSI, where 35 (25%) of 138 clients with no substance abuse diagnosis were classified as chemically dependent or chemical abusers. The high percentages of undiagnosed substance abuse problems reflect individuals who are not being provided services appropriate to their problems.

Undiagnosed substance abuse exists on VR caseloads because of two reasons. The substance abuse is either hidden by the client or overlooked by counseling staff. Clients often "hide" their substance abuse problem because of a fear that knowledge of it will result in their not receiving services. Counselors overlook the problem by conscious choice and by inability to perceive it. Once suspected, the counselor often consciously decides not to pursue the problem because her/she believes the client is stigmatized enough without adding a diagnosis of substance abuse. Other conscious choices involve the counselor having a misguided view of acceptance or under time pressure and choosing not to pursue the suspicion of substance abuse as a service delivery problem. Counselors often simply overlook the problem by not perceiving the signs of it. Whether hidden by client choice or overlooked by the counselor, the impact of an undiagnosed substance abuse problem puts the client at a disadvantage, appropriate services are not provided, and failure of service delivery becomes a strong potential.

Prevalence of Substance Abuse

Estimates of the number of Americans with disabilities range from 35 million (Pope & Tarlov, 1991) to 49 million (Americans with Disabilities Act, 1990), (Rehabilitation Research & Training Center on Drugs & Disability, 1996). These estimates vary depending on how disability is operationally defined. The words disability and handicapped have been used synonymously, but rehabilitation practitioners and communities distinguish between the two. A disability is a physical or mental condition that can be defined by a medical practitioner. Disabilities include blindness or vision impairment, cleft palate, congenital disabilities, deafness or hearing impairments, spinal cord injuries, paraplegia, or quadriplegia, mental disabilities, head injuries or head trauma, learning disabilities, and mental retardation or cognitive impairment. A handicap is a situational or social barrier or obstacle to the person with a disability in achieving his or her maximum level of functioning. Prendergast, Austin, & Miranda, (1990, p. 2) provide the following distinction between disability and handicap, "a person using a wheelchair is handicapped in traveling throughout the city not because of the wheelchair, but because of the inaccessibility of buses or buildings. The disability cannot be changed, but the handicapping condition can be".

People with disabilities have been identified as one of the nation's largest populations at high risk of alcohol and other drug abuse problems (Prendergast, Austin, & Miranda, 1990). Studies have suggested that substance abuse is problematic and estimated to be as high as 80% among some subgroups within population (Boros, 1989; Heinemann, Donohue, Keen, & Schnoll, 1988; Edgerton, 1986). Between 6 and 13 million Americans are physically or mentally disabled and chemically dependent as well (VSA, 1992, Schwab, 1992). However, there is still limited research on prevalence and effective intervention and prevention strategies.

While Greer, Roberts, May, and Jenkins (1985) have discussed the problems related to identifying a comprehensive estimate of the incidence of substance abuse in the general population, the DSM IV (American Psychiatric Association, 1994) states the prevalence of alcohol abuse to be 13 percent and the prevalence of other psychoactive substance abuse (e.g., marijuana, hallucinogens, cocaine, sedatives, etc.) to be 8 percent. While research is scant on incidence of alcohol and other drug abuse for youth with disabilities, such data for adults with disabilities indicate a prevalence rate two to five times that of the general population (Greer et al., 1985). All disability groups studied indicated a higher incidence of alcohol and other drug abuse than in the general population, but substance abuse was much more prevalent with certain types of psychiatric disabilities than with physical disabilities. Given this, one could conclude that the alcohol/drug abuse rate probably is also higher for school-age youth who have disabilities, particularly considering that the factors contributing to being at risk for substance abuse hold across all disabilities at all ages.

More research on alcohol and drug use (Tyas & Rush, 1993) and on alcohol and drug treatment with populations who have a disability (Glow, 1989) is needed. One of the major issues in diagnosis of substance abuse in people with disabilities is that the abuse is viewed as a secondary diagnosis with the disability being recognized first, if the abuse is recognized at all (Benshoff & Riggar, 1990; Kircus & Brillhart, 1990).

The substance abuse among individuals with disabilities may, in part, have caused the disability, may have an impact on rehabilitation through behavioral or cognitive changes or medical problems, and may affect vocational rehabilitation (Heinemann, Mamott, and Schnoll, 1990).

Risk Factors

McMahon (1994), Beck, Marr, & Taricone (1994), and Helwig and Holicky (1994) state that a greater likelihood of substance abuse among populations with disabilities occurs because they have; easy access to drugs, desires to avoid reality, frustration from social alienation, lack of appropriate prevention and information about their disability in association with substance abuse, little knowledge about their medication management, serious health concerns in conjunction with their disability, chronic pain (for some), family issues and problems, feelings of greater differences than peers, few social supports, high unemployment rates, too much idle time, and enabling families, friends, and professional helpers—who often condone drug abuse to avoid confrontation.

Greer, et al., (1985) also indicate that individuals who have disabilities, both congenitally or through acquired disability, are exposed to a set of factors that place them at high risk for substance abuse. The first of these factors is easy access to prescription drugs for valid medical uses such as relieving pain or muscle spasm. The ability to self-medicate for symptoms, in combination with other physiological, emotional, or environmental factors that increase risk for substance abuse, can facilitate the progression from use to abuse.

A related factor is unnecessary medical intervention leading to addiction of prescription medications. Schaschl and Straw (1989) indicate that the majority of congenitally disabled individuals had been prescribed mood-altering medication since early childhood. According to Hepner, Kirshbaum, and Landes (1980/81), 41 percent of clients with disabilities whom they surveyed at a center for independent living received prescriptions for psychoactive drugs that the clients did not believe were needed. Valium, the most frequently prescribed and abused drug among people with disabilities, is commonly prescribed to be taken once a day or as needed.

Other contributing factors appear to be frustration, oppression, or social isolation that some individuals with disabilities experience and seek to escape through substance abuse. In addition, many individuals with disabilities have found themselves surrounded by family, friends, medical practitioners, and others who, by their attitudes, implicitly condone substance abuse. Examples of this would be the doctor who feels helpless to cure a person's disability but who feels helpful by relieving pain through use of medication, or the family and friends who condone alcohol or substance abuse as an acceptable escape (Greer, 1986).

Some studies (Heinemann, Doll, & Schnoll, 1989; Moore & Polsgrove, 1989) conclude that substance abuse is often a precursor of acquired disability, rather than vice versa. This is true for a majority of persons who experience traumatic brain injury or spinal-cord injuries, which often occur as a result of automobile or motorcycle accidents. Many of these persons continue to abuse alcohol or other drugs following injury. The counselor should be alert to the fact that substance abuse is more prevalent in clients with traumatic brain injury, spinal cord injury, deafness, and mental illness.

Specific Disability Data

The following provides an overview of information related to substance abuse within various disability populations. It is well beyond the scope of this chapter to provide in-depth definitions and discussion of these disabilities. The beginning practitioner is referred to Stolov and Clowers' (1981) text for a comprehensive discussion of all body systems and related disabilities.

In a society too frequently preoccupied with defining a person in terms of his/her disability, quality counseling and treatment offers a client an opportunity to define him/herself in terms of his/her abilities. Physical and program accessibility of treatment facilities is the primary issue for the majority of individuals who have a disability and abuse substances. The following discussion by disability identifies these accessibility issues.

Traumatic Brain Injury

Traumatic brain injury, TBI, occurring when a blow or outside force is applied to the head or as a result of stroke or anoxia caused by a heart attack, is the disability most commonly associated with co-existing substance abuse or dependence. Annually, an estimated 50,000 to 70,000 Americans experience head injuries resulting in neurological impairments, and a total of more than a million Americans suffer ongoing neurological problems or loss (National Institute on Disability and Rehabilitation Research, 1994). Alcohol is linked to at least half of all automotive (the leading cause of head injury) and bicycle accidents and is even more commonly associated with head injuries caused by violence. As might be expected, males in their late adolescent and early adulthood years are at greatest risk for traumatic brain injury (Naugle, Cullum, & Bigler 1990).

The data clearly indicate that drugs and alcohol are closely linked to the etiology of traumatic brain injury. Many individuals suffer injury as a result of acute intoxication or drug use and some individuals have accidents as a result of hangovers or withdrawal. Still others are victims of drunk or drug impaired drivers. Yet, evidence is equally clear that trauma center personnel often fail to evaluate or identify alcohol or drug use or abuse as a precipitating event, and fail to make appropriate referrals for drug and alcohol evaluations and treatment (Shipley, Taylor, & Falvo, 1990).

Some individuals with TBI lose the ability to integrate and analyze information or have great difficulty in comprehending simple concepts. Recognizing this, Peterman (1996) has rewritten the 12-Steps in more concrete language. Others may experience problems related to attention span deficits or concentration skills. They may be unable to focus on a task, or may have difficulty following the sequences required to complete a task, or may be easily distracted. In part, these deficits may be related to long-term memory loss. Because they act and behave differently, individuals with TBI may be wrongly labeled and stigmatized, especially by the lay public, as mentally retarded or mentally ill. This can present problems for their participation in peer self-help recovery groups like AA and NA. Peterman (1996) has rewritten the 12-Steps to be more easily understood by this population.

Deaf and Hard of Hearing

Hearing loss, referred to as hard-of-hearing, is a common impairment affecting 20 million Americans, especially as they age. Another two million Americans have no functional hearing and are considered to be deaf. Research data suggest that the prevalence of drug and alcohol problems among individuals who are deaf or hard of hearing at least approximates if not exceeds the rates of drug and alcohol problems in the general population (Guthman, Lybarger, & Sanderg, 1993; Renwick & Krywonis, 1992). Guthman et al.(1993) report that few individuals who are deaf are seen in drug treatment. One barrier is the obvious communication barrier presented by deafness. Another is that, feeling stigmatized and isolated from the general population by deafness, individuals who are deaf are unwilling to assume the added burden within their culture of the label of alcohol or substance abuser.

Five main barriers to substance abuse treatment and recovery exist for this population. They include a general lack of awareness of the problem and a stigma about having such a problem. A close communication network among individuals who are deaf also influences the degree to which they will, in counseling, discuss their problems with alcohol/drugs. Inaccessible resources providing information and services on alcohol and drug addiction and enabling alcohol and drug use behaviors by family members and friends, who may continually rescue these individuals from the consequences of their behavior, are also problems. High costs to receive treatment, which may require traveling long distances to receive assistance from staff that are specially trained, also exist.

Assessment is similar to that of other populations with addictions. Examination of physical, work, school, social, legal, financial, emotional, and spiritual aspects of the person's life with specific emphasis on his/her possible relationship with alcohol/drug-related problems is appropriate. It is important to remember that approximately 75% of Americans who are deaf use American Sign Language (ASL) as their preferred mode of communication (Vernon & LaFalce, 1990). Completing an assessment interview related to the addiction with this population requires that the counselor be fluent in ASL or utilize a qualified interpreter to ensure accurate communication. It is recommended that assessment include evaluation of communication skills, knowledge of chemical dependency, coping skills, decision-making skills, and the need for occupational and recreational therapy (Guthmann, et al, 1993).

Access to treatment can be enhanced for this population through telecommunication devices (TDD), presence of sign language interpreters and counselors, and outreach contacts (McCrone, 1982). In treatment with this population, it is recommended that time be spent addressing defenses, educating and discussing feelings, attending a special focus group on deaf issues, working with the 12-Steps of Alcoholics Anonymous, addressing self-esteem issues, and involving families (Guthmann, Swan, & Gendreau, 1994).

Finally, aftercare planning is important in working with this population. Rehabilitation counselors or other counseling professionals providing services to people who are deaf or hard of hearing should be able to provide information about support resources in the client's community. They should empower the client to advocate for himself or herself within the community.

Mental Illness

One third of the U.S. population will experience a mental disorder at one time in their lives and approximately 50% of all people with mental disabilities are also experiencing substance abuse problems (VSA, 1992). There is a wide range of mental health disorders which are more common with people who have substance abuse problems. The following ratios are especially telling; a 15.6 times greater rate of antisocial personality disorder, a 5.8 times greater rate of bipolar and depression mood disorders, a 5 times greater rate of anxiety disorders, and a 10.9 times greater rate of other poly substance use disorders (Kelley & Benshoff, 1997).

Many individuals with the dual diagnosis of substance abuse and mental illness formerly were institutionalized in state-operated facilities for the mentally ill, but the development of new psychotropic medications and the continuing movement toward deinstitutionalization has resulted in more community-based care. A substantial number of these people are homeless, or live in marginal housing situations, with little consistent contact with either substance abuse or mental health service providers. As a result, their treatment regimens may be dictated more by economic factors, crisis situations, or legal sanctions than by need.

Both chronic mental illness and substance abuse are conditions with high levels of relapse. Individuals with these as dual disorders are seen as more challenging to treat and as having poorer outcome prognoses than individuals with single disorders (Kelley & Benshoff, 1997). Some individuals may develop mental illness-related functional limitations as a result of long-term psychoactive substance dependency. They may, for example, become depressed as a result of familial, social, or vocational losses experienced as a result of chronic alcohol or drug dependence. Exogenous depression is closely linked to long-term alcohol consumption and chronic marijuana usage (Buelow & Hebert, 1995). Others have a pre-existing mental illness preceding the onset of substance dependence. The substance abuse problem is either a symptom or behavioral pattern of the mental illness, or a mechanism to hide or mask the mental illness, or a self-medication of the mental illness.

Specialized programming, variously referred to as Mental Illness-Chemical Abuse (MICA), Mental Illness-Substance Abuse (MISA),

Substance Abuse-Mental Illness (SAMI) programs, and commonly known as dual diagnosis programs developed as the demand and need for services have grown in recent years. The traditional outcome usually sought for both mental illness and substance abuse is entrance into and maintenance of recovery status. For individuals with substance abuse problems, this has traditionally meant abstinence from substance abuse, and resumption of successful functioning in family, community, and vocational spheres, usually supported by participation in peer self-help groups (i.e., Alcoholics Anonymous). For individuals with mental illness, recovery is usually viewed as successful functioning in the community, participation in pharmacologic treatment, avoidance of in-inpatient hospitalization episodes, and supportive outpatient counseling or case management services. Individuals recovering from dual diagnosis are best treated through an approach that combines the best elements of both recovery strategies. Individual or group counseling or pharmacologic medication alone is significantly less effective than approaches that combine counseling, medication, education, and psychosocial interventions based on a variety of community supports and services (Kelley & Benshoff, 1997). Studies reveal that individuals who receive a variety of substance abuse education and psychosocial community support services do significantly better than individuals who receive little or nothing in the way of education and support (Crump & Milling, 1996; Jerrell, 1996).

Mobility Disabilities

Many disabilities, such as spinal cord injuries, arthritis, muscular dystrophy, and cerebral palsy, cause functional impairments in the realm of mobility. Approximately 25 million people of the United States population have a mobility disability and one million of these individuals use wheelchairs as their principal means of mobility. Over 9 million individuals have orthopedic impairment and/or arthritis (VSA, 1992). Spinal cord injury (SCI) occurs in 25 to 35 Americans per million citizens each year and affects approximately 259,000 Americans, with young males who engage in high risk behaviors such as driving too fast, diving, and rock climbing comprising the greatest prevalence group (Heller, et. al., 1996). While the data vary greatly from study to study, alcohol and drug use are thought to be related to spinal cord injury from 25% to 75% of the time (Helwig & Holicky, 1994). Evidence suggests that higher levels of drug and alcohol use occur post injury among individuals with SCI.

O'Donnell, Cooper, Gressner, Shehan and Ashley (1981-82) found that in 86% of the SCI subjects studied in a vocational rehabilitation facility, alcohol was a factor in their injuries and 60% of these patients resumed alcohol or drug use after leaving the hospital. Studies throughout the years have revealed similar results: Moore and Polsgrove (1989) found that 35% of a sample of college students with physical disabilities, used marijuana monthly; Moore and Li (1994) found that both lifetime cocaine or crack use was 28% for applicants for one state's vocational rehabilitation program; and Wright State University's (1996) SARDI program reported that 50% and more of persons with spinal cord injury became injured after use of alcohol and/or other drugs and 28.5% of those evaluated had a high incidence of alcohol dependence. These are catastrophic percentages, many times higher than the general population. Individuals with spinal cord injury may use drugs to self-medicate their physical pain as well as to cope with their feelings of anxiety and depression. Screening for problems with alcohol and drugs as well as careful assessment and appropriate referral are necessary parts of general treatment for individuals with these conditions (Heinemann, 1993).

One of the greatest concerns among individuals with mobility disabilities may be alcohol-drug and drug-drug interactions. The standard treatment course for many includes analgesic and anti-inflammatory medications, the effects of which may be potentiated by alcohol or illicit drug consumption. Alcohol is used by this population to self-medicate physical pain. This is a dangerous practice since multiple prescriptions for pain relief medications often may be obtained from multiple physicians, a practice referred to as polypharmacy (Falvo, Holland, Brenner, & Benshoff, 1990). Another medication interaction problem for individuals with SCI relates to the use of marijuana by some to control muscle spasticity. Long-term marijuana use presents pulmonary and depressed immune system problems.

Physical access is primarily the major issue to overcome in accessing community treatment services for this population.

Blind and Visually Impaired

About 4.25 Americans have severe visual impairment, defined as the inability to read ordinary newsprint with glasses or contact lenses. The vast majority of them are more than 55 years of age, with 600,000 of them being legally blind (Dickerson, Smith, & Moore, 1992). For practical purposes, blindness is usually thought of as the inability to perceive light, while visual impairment implies a loss of function as a result of visual limitations (Moore, 1992). Very limited data exist about the prevalence of substance abuse as a co-existing disability, but studies suggest that individuals with visual impairments have drug and alcohol problems at significantly higher rates than the general population and that this is an underserved population in drug and alcohol treatment. Nelipovich, Wengin, and Rossick (1998) estimate that between 220,000 and 330,000 individuals with visual impairments "may require treatment for addiction." (p.1). Too much isolation, time "on their hands", and lack of employment are risk factors for substance abuse in this population (Nelipovich et al. 1998).

Glass (1980-81) reported two kinds of drinkers who are blind and visually impaired, the client who drank before acquiring the disability (Type A) and the client who drank after the disability occurred (Type B). Glass states that the Type A client uses drinking as a main coping mechanism and requires substance abuse treatment. The Type-B client may be able to stop abusing alcohol if the underlying stressors are resolved in combination with skill acquisition to assist the person in coping with his or her disability. The Type-A client needs psychological or psychiatric help to assist with life problems that existed prior to the disability. This treatment has a skills training component to assist the individual in copying more effectively with his or her problems. The Type-B client needs to learn skills to be able to be more independent. Either abstinence or controlled drinking may be recommended for this individual (Glass, 1980-81).

Barriers to treatment include the following. As non-drivers, individuals with visual disabilities do not get arrested for driving under the influence, and are not referred to treatment through this process. Many individuals with visual impairments are employed in homebound settings, or in independent businesses set up under the provisions of the Randolph-Shepherd Act, and lack employer recognition and referral for job related drug and alcohol problems. Finally, many drug and alcohol treatments and prevention services market their availability through visual media: newspapers, posters, flyers, and magazines. These marketing efforts are inaccessible to individuals with visual disabilities.

Other treatment barriers include treatment centers often relying heavily on treatment activities such as bibliotherapy requiring visual skills. Clients are expected to read AA or other treatment literature, and are often required to write journals and accounts or both, of their drinking and drugging experiences. While most treatment materials are available in large print or Braille, the ability of individuals to use either format is widely variable. Videos are another popular treatment tool which may have limited utility with this population.

Other problems arise because of the extensive use of group therapy in drug and alcohol treatment. Individuals with visual difficulties may have difficulty tracking the flow of the group dialogue, and they risk missing many of the visual clues that are an important and rich component of group therapy. It is especially important with this population to supplement group therapy.

Attention Deficit/Hyperactivity Disorder

Barreda-Hanson & Kilham (1997) define Attention Deficit Hyperactivity Disorder (ADHD) as a "developmental disorder characterized by developmentally inappropriate degrees of inattention, overactivity, and impulsivity" (pg. 34) with essential features being hyperactivity, impulsivity or both (Katisyannis, Landrum, & Vinton, 1997; D'Alonzo, 1996).

A person with ADHD characteristics is diagnosed in either of the following categories: combined type, inattentive type, or hyperactive-impulsivity type (Porter, 1997). A person categorized as inattentive type presents such characteristics as task incompletion and being easily distracted (D'Alonzo, 1996; Barreda-Hanson & Kilham, 1997). Hyperactive characteristics include being "fidgety," "squirmy," (Looff, 1990) talking excessively, and always being 'on the go' (Barreda-Hanson & Kilham, 1997). Last, the impulsive type is characterized as displaying impatient behavior and constantly interrupting or intruding on others (D'Alonzo, 1996; Katisyannis et al. 1997).

Diagnosing ADHD is difficult because the individual often displays other behaviors such as "conduct disorder, developmental learning disorders, and oppositional defiant disorders" (Barrickman, Noyes, Kuperman, Schumacher, & Verda, 1991, pg. 762) and many individuals, in early childhood, display overactive and distracting behaviors. Thus, the diagnosis to insure accuracy must come from a professional specializing with individuals with ADHD (Barreda-Hanson & Kilham, 1997).

Christian, Kerr, Sutphin, & Poling (1997) found that 80% to 90% of the individuals diagnosed with ADHD received stimulant medication at some point in their life, with the most common and effective stimulant medication being Ritalin. Ritalin is prescribed in an attempt to reduce hyperactivity and distractibility and improve compliance and attention span (Barreda-Hanson, & Kilham, 1997; Coger, Moe, & Serafetinides,

1996; D'Alonzo, 1996. Porter (1997) recommends that the decision to prescribe medication should be based on the severity of the condition, attitudes of the parents and child, and capability for supervised medication regime from parents and teachers.

About 3% to 5% of the general population in the United States have a diagnosis of ADHD (Katisyannis, Landrum, & Vinton, 1997; Barrickman, Noyes, Kuperman, Schumacher, & Verda, 1991; Porter, 1997; D'Alonzo, 1996). The ratio of male to female diagnoses usually varies from 4:1 to as much as 9:1 (Katisyannis et al.1997).

About 40% to 50% of the children with ADHD have coexisting disorders such as conduct disorder, oppositional defiant disorder, learning disorder and emotional difficulties (Schubiner, Tzelepis, Isaacson, Warbasse, Zacharek, & Musial, 1995; D'Alonzo, 1996). Adams & Wallace (1994) identify a strong correlation between adolescents with ADHD and conduct disorder and the abuse of substances. Thus, an early childhood diagnosis of ADHD is recognized as a risk factor for adolescent substance abuse (Jaffe, 1991). In adulthood, alcohol and other drug abuse occurs in over 50% (Hechtman, L. & Weiss, G. 1986).

According to Jaffe (1991), individuals with ADHD that are taking stimulants or antidepressants self-medicate in that they can use the medications to achieve desired effects. Porter (1997) found that approximately 10% of adults with ADHD engage in drug abuse. Individuals with mental disabilities usually use and abuse substances for relief from the disability, in the hopes of gaining social acceptance and escaping the realities of the disability (Coger et al.1996).

Individuals with a diagnosis of ADHD have academic problems, poor socialization skills, and low self-esteem (D'Alonzo, 1996; Porter, 1997). Thus, they have difficulties maintaining relationships with peers and family members. Barreda-Hanson & Kilham (1997) indicate that individuals with ADHD also have low frustration tolerance and have difficulties in attending well to stimuli. Thus, prevention and treatment issues will have to target some of these behaviors.

The goals of treatment programs are to help individuals obtain abstinence and restructure life goals and processes (Inaba, et al.1997). Treatment techniques with individuals with ADHD utilize a multi-modal approach (Barreda-Hanson & Kilham, 1997; Katisyannis et al.1997; D'Alonzo, 1996) consisting of family/individual therapy, full individual assessment, and support from a team composed of medical practitioners, counselors, teachers, and parents.

Mental Retardation

Individuals who have mental retardation experience a range of cognitive impairments related to assimilation, organizing, and expressing their experience in the world. Few studies have studied conclusively the related problem of substance abuse with this population; however, it appears that the number of problems associated with substance abuse for this group does not differ significantly from the substance abuse problems in the general population (DiNitto and Krischef, 1984, Krischef, 1986). Factors affecting substance abuse include age, gender, degree of retardation, and residential arrangement, individual, family, or group home. Specific problems include alienation, isolation, acting out, fighting, stealing, decreased school or work productivity, and drug related arrests, (Schwab, 1992).

Individuals who are mentally retarded tend to misunderstand alcohol or other drug prevention and treatment materials. Such materials must be modified to be understood at an individual's intellectual level such as was done with Peterman's (1996) rewrite of the 12-Steps. Information must be kept simple, presented in a very concrete sequence, and clearly defined.

Learning Disabilities

Individuals with Learning Disabilities (LD) have symptoms of delayed maturation and deficits in attention, psychomotor skills, and memory. Few studies exist providing incidence data on learning disability and substance abuse. However, it is projected that substance abuse rates are as high as in youth with behavior disorders (BD). Youth with LD or BD and educable mental handicap are high-risk populations for developing substance abuse problems.

Learning disabilities impact on individual understanding of prevention or drug education materials as well as treatment information. Fox and Forbing (1991) provide a sequence of activities useful in addressing individuals with a learning disability susceptibility to substance abuse.

1. teach them about the effects of misuse of drugs;
2. assist them with developing effective skills related to their learning disability;
3. help them to develop recreational interests and abilities, and
4. help them enhance their communication skills and social support base.

These suggestions would appear appropriate with individuals with other disabilities.

Counseling Considerations

People with disabilities experience the same social pressures and psychological stressors that contribute to substance abuse as do people who do not have a disability. In addition, they experience stressors related to social stigma and the additional psychological, emotional, and social problems of their disability, which can increase their risk for abuse.

The counseling considerations to be addressed in populations with physical disability, mental disability or both, and concurrent substance abuse relate to areas of counseling already addressed in a general way within this text. These include counselor knowledge of self, counselor knowledge of rates of use and abuse; and counselor skill in assessment, intervention, and use of community support systems and treatment referrals.

Counselor Knowledge of Self: Per Varhely's admonitions in Chapter 5, the effective counselor needs to have great self-understanding and needs to be aware of his/her own biases and stereotyped thinking. This is particularly true in counseling individuals with disabilities and substance abuse problems.

There are many facets to the counseling of each human being. Before the counselor sits down with the client, the counselor must sit down and inventory what biases or stereotypes he or she holds toward persons who have a disability or those who are substance abusers or both. If these biases are unresolved and the counselor is busy dealing with his or her own issues during counseling sessions, he or she can not attend to the client. After confronting self awareness about the substance abuse issue, biases, or both imbedded social stigmas with reference to the disability, the counselor is more able to interact in a therapeutic way with clients and more objectively identify the impact of substance abuse behaviors.

Counselor Knowledge of Incidence Data: Familiarity with information as provided within this chapter on incidence data per disability group is suggested as a minimum requirement for counselors. On-going review of the research literature specific to this area is necessary to continue to stay current in terms of understanding.

Assessment: The initial interview should be conducted in part with individuals with disabilities to identify those clients who have a problem with substance abuse (Page & Bailey, 1995). Any substance abuse problem of clients needs to be identified and addressed early in the counseling process. It is extremely important that counselors working with individuals with disabilities have preservice and inservice education in incidence and problems of substance abuse, and knowledge of basic signs and symptoms of substance abuse. Counselor anti-enabling behavior must be present along with emphasis on the importance of being sensitive and alert to possible substance abuse problems of clients. Counselors must be prepared with skills and strategies for positive confrontation, cutting through denial, and identifying effective, affordable, accessible treatment.

Early identification of substance abuse in counseling individuals with disabilities is imperative (Hepner, Kirshbaum, & Landes, 1980-81). "Unless the abuse-addiction is addressed, dealing with the adjustment to a disability will most likely not occur" (Helwig & Holicky, 1994). Substance abuse behaviors need to be identified as to whether they are a consequence or a response to the individual's disability. Heinemann, Doll, and Schnoll (1989) found that, after certain injuries resulting in a disability, clients who developed substance abuse problems responded better than those who experienced abuse problems before a disabling event.

All too often substance abuse behaviors are viewed as secondary disabilities (Benshoff, 1990) or not recognized at all in medical settings (Shipley, Taylor, & Falvo, 1990). Helwig and Holicky (1994) pointed out that, in many independent living centers, the majority of counselors do not regularly ask their clients about alcohol or drug use and this lack of assessment influences appropriate treatment and hence outcomes. While the etiology of substance abuse among people with disabilities is complex (Schaschl & Straw, 1989), a thorough history of substance abuse needs to be evaluated in relation to a client's development of a disability, and the onset of abuse should be scrutinized as to its function in the daily life of individuals with disabilities. This process will facilitate assessment and the choice of appropriate interventions.

Incidence data alone highlights that assessment is a necessary and critical component of the rehabilitation intake and planning process. Counselors should consider using a substance abuse screening instrument such as the SASSI and a structured short interview instrument such as the MAST. If substance abuse is suspected, the agency may require drug testing. These screening measures are pursued not to exclude consumers from service but to better inform counselor and client about the impact of substance abuse problems on counseling goals.

Individual and group counseling needs to be designed to be sensitive to the particular disability and life circumstance of the individual. Accommodations, such as American Sign Language interpreters or educational audiotapes for the visually impaired, need to be utilized in psychoeducation components of counseling. Prendergast, et al.(1990) have suggested that clients be provided more broadly with information about specific drugs and their contraindications, independent living skills, active alternatives to substance use, parent education and involvement, counter-enabling education, self-esteem, peer pressure, and the development of constructive forms of sensation seeking. The client should be assisted in developing new social support networks in conjunction with the above.

As the counseling process progresses, it is important for the counselor to maintain a strong counselor client relationship to insure client involvement and progress in exploring which issues he or she desires. If the client is in denial about his/her substance abuse problem, then he or she is not ready to seek treatment or even fully explore the treatment options available. If the client recognizes that he or she has a substance abuse problem, exploration will identify whether the substance abuse problem preceded the disability or visa versa. The counselor should ascertain how much the client knows about his/her disability, about his/her substance abuse problem, and what limitations or issues are of the most concern. During this time, the counselor emphasis is on developing an understanding of client and their perceptions related to problems of substance abuse.

Other areas to explore with the client are those of social and coping skills. These skills are important because they are potential trouble areas that can lead to relapse of the client after successful recovery from the substance abuse. If the client "recovers" without adequate social and coping skills, any stressors have the potential for sending that client into relapse. Therefore, it is incumbent on the counselor to help the client prepare for a world without substance abuse by helping him or her develop more effective social and coping skills. Insuring or developing a good support system (friends or family) with the client can help him/her avoid relapse following treatment.

When the process of counseling reaches to the point of counselor-client determining the treatment options, the counselor is responsible for making sure that the client is afforded enough information to make an informed decision about which treatment offers the best chance of success. The counselor should make available, if appropriate, information in an alternative and cognitively appropriate means. The counselor should help the client determine which services are needed to gain as much independence as possible. The support services will vary by disability and by person.

Counselor use of community supports: Tyas and Rush (1993) report that few agencies provide alcohol and drug treatment services designed specifically for individuals with disability. Thus, individuals with drug and alcohol problems have had difficulty accessing the rehabilitation system, and, correspondingly, individuals with traditional disabilities have been under-served by the substance abuse treatment network. Prior to and even subsequent to the passage of the Americans with Disabilities Act (1990), many substance dependence treatment facilities were not accessible to individuals who use wheelchairs. In many, the nature of therapy and the shortage of qualified interpreters was thought to preclude participation by individuals who are deaf and the abstract nature of many substance abuse concepts was perceived to limit participation by individuals who had developmental disabilities. Transportation and access problems and the extensive use of bibliotherapy also ruled out participation in therapy by individuals with visual problems. Few people with "traditional" disabilities sought treatment and fewer still were served.

It is, however, recommended that individuals with disabilities be treated within typical alcohol and drug treatment programs. This approach only required that the treatment program review specific disabilities to determine what individuals with that disability might require (Glow, 1989). Unfortunately, many treatment programs would prefer to not serve the disabled population (Tyas & Rush, 1993).

Even when substance abuse treatment services are available and accessible, persons with traditional disabilities face problems accessing aftercare and peer self-help programs. Many AA and NA meetings are held in church basements or similar settings with architectural barriers because the ADA does not require most nonprofit groups to achieve accessibility standards. Individuals who need interpreter services, in many cases, must provide their own at a cost burden that may be prohibitive. Some meetings are held in places inaccessible even by public transportation, ruling out participation by individuals who do not or cannot drive.

Summary

A review of the literature provides the conclusion that individuals with disability versus those without a disability are more likely to have a substance abuse problem and less likely to get effective treatment. Data suggest 10-40% of all individuals in treatment for substance abuse have a coexisting physical or mental disability and alcohol rates for certain disabilities such as spinal cord or head injury exceed 50%. Risk factors are discussed and substance abuse incidence and impact data are provided for several disability groups. Service barriers related to these individual disability groups are identified. Barriers across all groups include

1. Denial on the part of the client since the stigma associated with substance abuse keeps individuals with disabilities from seeking service;
2. Inaccessible treatment facilities; and
3. Treatment staff who do not want to work with or do not know how to work with individuals with disabilities.

Given these barriers, counselors should work with providers to resolve architectural, attitudinal, and communication barriers, and discriminatory policies and procedures. They should know providers, effectively coordinate referrals to appropriate treatment facilities, and provide follow-up as needed.

References

Adams, L., & Wallace, J. L. (1994). Residential treatment for the ADHD adolescent substance abuser. *Journal of Child and Adolescent Substance Abuse*, *4,* (1), 35-44.

American Psychiatric Association (1997). *Diagnostic and Statistical Manual of Mental Disorders* (4th ed.). Washington, D.C. Author.

Americans with Disabilities Act. (1990, July 26). Public Law 101-336.

Barreda-Hanson, C., & Kilham, C. (1997). Attention-deficit hyperactivity disorder in children under five. *Australian Journal of Early Childhood*, *22,* (4), 34-39.

Barrickman, L., Noyes, R., Kuperman, S., Schumacher, E., & Verda, M. (1991). Treatment of ADHD with fluoxtine: A preliminary trial. *Journal of American Academic Child Adolescent Psychiatry, 30,* (5), 762-676.

Beck, R., Marr, K. & Taricone, P. (1994). Identifying and treating clients with physical disabilities who have substance abuse problems. *Rehabilitation Education, 5,* 131-138.

Benshoff, J. J. (1990). Substance Abuse: Challenges for the rehabilitation counseling profession. Editorial. *Journal of Applied Rehabilitation Counseling, 21* (3), 3.

Benshoff, J. J., & Riggar, T. P. (1990). Cocaine: A primer for rehabilitation counselors. *Journal of Applied Rehabilitation Counseling, 21* (3), 21-24.

Boros, A. (1989). Facing the challenge. *Alcohol Health and Research World, 13* (2), 101-103.

Buelow, G. & Hebert, S. (1995). *Counselor's resource on psychiatric medications: Issues of treatment and referral*, Pacific Grove, CA: Brooks/Cole Publishing Co.

Christian, L., Kerr, C. L., Sutphin, G. E., & Poling, A. (1997). Reporting of medication regimen in applied studies of persons with mental retardation and ADHD. *Research in Developmental Disabilities, 18,* (5), 319-237.

Coger, R. W., Moe, K. L., & Serafetinides, E. A. (1996). Attention deficit disorder in adults and nicotine dependence: Psychobiological factors in resistance to recovery. *Journal of Psychoactive Drugs, 28,* (3), 229-239.

Connecticut Clearinghouse (1998). *Substance abuse prevention and disability.* (Funded by the Department of Mental Health and Addiction Services) Retrieved March 26, 1999 from the World Wide Web, http://www.ctclearinghouse.org/fprevdis.hmt.

Crump, M. T., & Milling, R.N. (1996). The efficacy of substance abuse education among dual-diagnosis patients. *Journal of Substance Abuse Treatment, 13* (2), March-April, 141-144.

D'Alonzo, B. (1996). Identification and education of students with attention deficit and attention deficit hyperactivity disorders. *Preventing School Failure, 40,* (2), 88-94.

DiNitto, D. M. & Krischef, C. H. (1984). Drinking patterns of mentally retarded persons. *Alcohol Health and Research World, 8,* 40-42.

DiNitto, D. M., & Schwab, A. J. (1991). *Substance abuse factors which interfere with entry or reentry into employment.* Austin: University of Texas, School of Social Work.

Edgerton, R. B. (1986). Alcohol and drug use by mentally retarded adults. *American Journal of Mental Deficiency, 90* (6), 602-609.

Falvo, D. R., Holland, B., Brenner, J. & Benshoff, J. (1990). Medication use practices in the ambulatory elderly, *Health Values, 14* (3), May-June, 10-16.

Fox, C. L. & Forbing, S.E., (1991). Overlapping symptoms of substance abuse and learning handicaps. *Journal of Learning Disabilities, 21* (1), 24-31.

Gallup Poll (1989, August 4). pp. 10, 16.

Glass, E. J. (1980-81). Problem drinking among the blind and visually impaired. *Alcohol Health and Research World, 5,* 26-30.

Glow, B. A. (1989). Alcoholism, drugs, and the disabled. In G. W. Lawrence & A. W. Lawson (Eds.), *Alcohlism and substance abuse in special populations* (pp. 65-93). Rockville, MD: Aspen.

Greer, B. (1986). Substance abuse among people with disabilities: A problem of too much accessibility. *Journal of Rehabilitation, 52,* 34-38.

Greer, B. G., Roberts, R., May, G., & Jenkins, W. M. (1985). Identification of substance abuse in a vocational evaluation setting. *Journal of Rehabilitation, 54* (3), 42-45.

Guthmann, D., Lybarger, R., & Sandberg, K. (1993). Providing chemical dependency treatment to the deaf and hard of hearing mentally ill client. *Journal of the American Deafness and Rehabilitation Association, 27* (1), 1-14.

Hechtman, L. & Weiss, G. (1986). Controlled prospective fifteen year follow-up of hyperactives as adults: Non-medical drug and alcohol use and anti-social behavior. *Canadian Journal of Psychiatry, 31* (6), 557-567.

Heinemann, A. W., (Ed.) (1993). *Substance abuse and physical disability*. New York: Haworth Press Inc.

Heinemann, A. W., Doll, M., & Schnoll, S. (1989). Treatment of alcohol abuse in persons with recent spinal cord injuries. *Alcohol, Health and Research World, 13* (2), 110-117.

Heinemann, A. W., Donohue, K., Keen, M. and Schnoll, S. (1988). Alcohol use by persons with recent spinal cord injuries. *Archives of Physical Medicine and Rehabilitation, 69,* 619-624.

Heinemann, A. W., Goranson, N., Ginsburg, K., and Schnolls, S. (1989). Alcohol use and activity patterns following spinal cord injury. *Rehabilitation Psychology, 34* (3), 191-205.

Heinemann, A. W., Mamott, B. D., Schnoll, S. (1990). Substance use by persons with recent spinal cord injuries. *Rehabilitation Psychology, 35* (4), 217-228.

Helwig, A. & Holicky, R. (1994). Substance abuse in persons with disabilities: Treatment considerations. *Journal of Counseling & Development, 72*, 227-233.

Hepner, R., Kirshbaum, H., & Landes, D. (1980-81). Counseling substance abusers with additional disabilities: The center for independent living. *Alcohol Health and Research World, 5,* 11-15.

Inaba, D. S., Cohen, W. E., & Holstein, M.E. (1997). *Uppers, Downers, All Arounders: Physical and Mental, Effects on Psychoactive Drugs* (3rd ed.) Ashland, OR: CNS Publications, Inc.

Jaffe, S. L. (1991). Intranasal abuse of prescribed methylphenidate by an alcohol and drug abusing adolescent with ADHD. *Journal of American Academy in Child Adolescent Psychiatry, 30,* (5), 773-774.

Jerrell, J. M. (1996). Toward cost-effective care for persons with dual diagnosis, *Journal of Mental Health Administration, 23*(3), Summer, 329-337.

Katisyannis, A., Landrum, T. J., & Vinton, L. (1997). Practical guidelines for monitoring treatment of attention-deficit disorder. *Preventing School Failure, 41,* (3), 132-136.

Kelley, S. D. M. & Benshoff, J. J., (1997). Dual diagnosis of mental illness and substance abuse: Contemporary challenges for rehabilitation. *Journal of Applied Rehabilitation Counseling, 28,* 43-49.

Kircus E, & Brillhart, B.A, (1990). Dealing with substance abuse among people with disabilities. *Rehabilitation Nursing, 15* (5), 250-253.

Krischef, C. H. (1986). Do the mentally retarded drink? A study of their alcohol usage. *Journal of Alcohol and Drug Education, 31,* 64-70.

Li, L., & Moore, D. (1998a). Acceptance of disability and its correlates. *The Journal of Social Psychology, 138* (1), 13-25.

Li, L., & Moore, D. (1998b). Prevalence and risk factors of illicit drug use by people with disabilities. *The American Journal of Addictions, 7* (2), 93-102.

Looff, D. H. (1990). Recognizing and treating attention deficit disorders in chemically dependent adolescents. *Journal of Adolescent Chemical Dependency, 1,* (1), 5-30.

McCrone, W. P. (1982). Serving the deaf substance abuser. *Journal of Psychoactive Drugs, 14,* 199-203.

McMahon, B. T. (1994). Preface to the special issue on drugs analcohol. *Rehabilitation Counseling Bulletin, 38* (2), 82-83.

Moore, D. (1992). Substance abuse assessment and diagnosis in medical rehabilitation. *Neurorehabilitation: An Interdisciplinary Journal, 2* (1), 7-15.

Moore, D. & Li, Li (1994). Substance use among rehabilitation consumers for vocational rehabilitation services. *Journal of Rehabilitation, 60* (4), 48-53.

Moore, D. & Li, Li (1998). Prevalence and risk factors of illicit drug use by people with disabilities. *American Journal of Addictions, 7* (2), 93-102).

Moore, D., & Polsgrove, L. (1989). Disabilities, developmental handicaps and substance misuse. A review. *Social Pharmacology, 3*(4), 375-408.

National Institute of Alcohol Abuse and Alcoholism (1994). *Alcohol Health and Research World, 18* (3), 243, 245.

National Institute of Drug Abuse (1991) *An economical approach to addressing the drug problem in america.* Rockville, MD. Author.

Naugle, R. I., Cullum, C. M., & Bigler, E. D. (1990). Evaluation of the intellectual and memory function among dementia patients who were intellectually superior, *Clinical Neurologist,4* (4), 355-374.

Nelipovich, M., Wengin, & Kossick, R., (1998). The MARCO Model: Making substance abuse services accessible to people who are visually impaired. *Journal of Visual Impairment and Blindness, 92*(8), 567-570.

O'Donnell, J., Cooper, J., Gressner, J., Shehan, I. & Ashley, J. (1981-82). *Alcohol Health and Research World, 6* (1), 27-29.

Ohlmer, V. L. (1992). *Undetected substance abuse among vocational rehabilitation clients*, Dissertation, University of Arizona.

Peterman, A. (1996). Effects of supportive and conflictual social interventions on cardiovascular responses to stress: *Dissertation Abstracts International Section B: the Sciences and Engineering*, *56* (9-B),1996, 5225.

Pope, A. M. and Tarlov, A. R. (Eds.) (1991). *Disability in America*. Washington, D.C.: National Academy Press.

Porter, L. (1997). Selected perspectives on ADD and ADHD. *Australian Journal of Early Childhood, 22,* (4), 7-14.

Prendergast, M., Austin, G., and Miranda, J. (1990). *Substance abuse among youth with disabilities*. Wisconsin Clearinghouse: University of Wisconsin, Madison.

Rehabilitation Brief (1990). *Substance abuse and disability*, *12*(12). Washington, D.C.: National Institute on Disability and Rehabilitation Research, Department of Education.

Rehabilitation Research and Training Center on Drugs and Disabilities (RRTC). (1996). *Substance Abuse Disabilities and Vocational Rehabilitation*, Dayton OH: Wright State University Counseling Program New York University.

Renwick, R. M., & Krywonis, M. (1992). Personal and environmental factors related to employment: Implications for substance abuse intervention. *Journal of Rehabilitation, 58* (1), 23-27.

Schaschl, S., and Straw, D. (1989). Results of a model intervention program for physically impaired persons, *Alcohol Health and Research World, 13* (2), 150-153.

Schubiner, H., Tzelepis, A., Isaacson, J. H., Warbasse, L. H., Zacharek, M., & Musial, J. (1995). The dual diagnosis of attention-deficit/ hyperactivity disorder and substance abuse: Case reports and literature review. *Journal of Clinical Psychiatry, 56,* (4), 146-150.

Schwab, W. E. (1992). Substance abuse in patients with physical and cognitive disabilities. In M. F. Flemming, & K. L. Barry (Eds.) *Addictive disorders*. St. Louis, MO: Mosby Yearbook, Inc.

Shipley, R. W., Taylor, S. M., & Falvo, D. R. (1990). Concurrent evaluation and rehabilitation of alcohol abuse and trauma, *Journal of Applied Rehabilitation Counseling, 21*(3), Special Issue, Fall.

Smelter, R. W., Rasch, B. W., Fleming, J., Nazos, P., & Baranoswski, S. (1996). Is attention deficit disorder becoming a desired diagnosis? *Phi Delta Kappan, 77,* (6), 429-432.

Stolov, W. C., & Clowers, M. (1981). *Handbook on severe disability.* U.S. Department of Education, Rehabilitation Services Administration.

Tyas, S. & Rush, B. (1993). The treatment of disabled persons with alcohol and drug problems: Results of a survey of addiction services. *Journal of Studies Alcohol, 54,* 275-282.

Vernon, M. & LaFalce, E. (1990). Epilepsy and deafness: The issue of violence, *Journal of the American Deafness and Rehabilitation Association, 23* (3), Jan., 64-67.

VSA Educational Services, (1992). Resource Center on Substance Abuse Prevention and Disability. Washington, D.C.

Wright State University (1996). *Substance abuse, disability and vocational rehabilitation*, Research and Training Center on Drugs and Disability (SARDI). New York: University Press.

Yalom, I. (1995). *The theory and practice of group psychotherapy* (4th ed.) New York: Basic Books, Inc.

Chapter 11

Preventing Adolescent Relapse: Concepts, Theories and Techniques

Shitala P. Mishra & Robert A. Ressler

Introduction

It is now broadly acknowledged by many that drug and alcohol addiction is a disease and, as in the case with many diseases, there is a likelihood of relapse, the returning to abuse of the substance after treatment. Thus, relapse is a major concern for professionals providing drug abuse treatments to individuals suffering from alcohol and drug dependency. Individuals with substance abuse problems have a pattern of trying to stop using drugs, alcohol, or both several times before receiving treatment and have difficulty doing so. The literature seems to indicate that the highest probability of relapse occurs during the first two years of recovery (Talbott & Martin, 1999), a process of healing that results from abstinence and participation in a treatment program. Since the relapse is a typical occurance in drug dependence, it is important to understand the factors that trigger compulsive tendencies to resume the use of drugs and alcohol.

Relapse Defined

Although there are varied definitions of relapse, it essentially involves the resumption of mood altering drug usage following a period of recovery. It usually occurs early in the recovery process. About two-third of adults show relapse tendencies within 90 days of discharge from treatment facilities. Relapse requiring posttreatment ranges from 35 to 85 % among addicts exposed to treatments (Catalano, Hawkins, Wells, Miller, & Brewer, 1991).

In general, the relapse occurs primarily due to an individual's inability to cope with life in sobriety or without drugs. The literature suggests there are possibly two ways to look at the relapse phenomenon. The relapse can be understood as a discrete event occurring with a single use of a drug (Wesson, Havassy, & Smith, 1986). In a discrete event type relapse, the distinction is made between the first use of the individual's primary drug of abuse and first use of any other psychoactive drug. Return to the primary drug presents the most likelihood of returning to abuse (Hubbard & Marsden, 1986). From a process perspective, an individual's addiction can be viewed as a process developing over time, with relapse conceptualized in a number of ways. Relapse can be defined as daily drug use for a specified period; as a return to the pretreatment baseline level; or as return to drug use levels above specified criterion of quantity and /or duration of drug usage (American Psychiatric Association *DSM-IV*, 1994).

Causes and Etiology of Relapse

The factors contributing to relapse may range from socioeconomic and ethnic status of an individual to chronic history of substance abuse. Individuals who abuse drugs often have been found to come from low socioeconomic status (SES) homes, have a chronic history of drug abuse, exhibit poor symptoms of mental health, possess inadequate skills to cope with social pressure, and often have sporadic patterns of involvement in substance abuse treatment programs. Talbott and Martin (1999) report potential factors that contribute to relapse. These are failure to understand/accept drug dependency, denial of loss of control, emotional concealment, extensive rationalization, dysfunctional family, lack of access to spiritual program, stress, isolation, cross addiction, holiday syndrome, withdrawal, overconfidence, returning to drinking friends, and guilt over the past. Many personality factors such as comorbidity, high stress personality, and low impulse control ability have also been found in relapse prone addicts. The influence of familial environment on possibility of relapse has also been found to be quite strong. Individuals experiencing parental separation, loss of family members, and break up of family relationships have shown stronger tendencies to resume to drug use behaviors after the recovery period (Talbott & Martin, 1999). DeJong and Henrich (1980) in a study utilizing samples of adolescents and young adults found three correlates of posttreatment relapse. First, thoughts and feelings about drugs and drug cravings were found to be related to relapse. In contrast to relapsers, these thoughts and feelings decreased more in nonrelapsers than in relapsers at one year posttreatment follow-up. A second finding is that relapsers are much less involved in productive activities including school work. Relapsers were also found to have fewer and less satisfying leisure activities. Similar findings related to posttreatment factors such as drug craving, low involvement in productive and leisure activities were found to be strong predictors of relapse among adult drug abusers by Catalano, Howard, Hawkins, and Wells (1988). The implications of such findings would seem to suggest the importance of cognitive and behavioral skills training to reduce cravings and increase social skills for reducing relapse.

Drug Abuse, Relapse, and Psychological Development

In the early 1900's, G. Stanley Hall (1904) first promoted the study of the psychology of adolescence. Hall identified adolescence as the period from puberty until full adult status. He characterized it as a period of *Sturm und Drang*, "storm and stress." In general, he considers the emotional plight of the adolescent to be filled with contradiction. Consistent with this thinking, Kurt Lewin's (1939) field theory approach to adolescence characterizes the adolescent as having a "marginal man" status. This assumes that the adolescent no longer belongs to the social group of children and does not want to be considered a child; yet he is not yet accepted into the social group of adults. Consequently, the adolescent's behavior will reflect this marginality. Numerous other approaches describe the developmental period of adolescence in a similar way. Psychodynamic (Blos, 1979; Freud, 1935; Erickson, 1950), humanistic (Adler, 1930; Rogers, 1931), cognitive (Kohlberg & Kramer, 1969; Piaget, 1968; Thornburg, 1977), social/ecological (Bronfenbrenner, 1972; Elkind, 1998; Selman, 1980), or sociopolitical (Bowles & Gintis, 1976) approaches all reflect the view that adolescence is a period of marked stress and crisis.

As the adolescent attempts to establish their identity and independence, he/she will begin to explore a variety of behaviors and attitudes (Thornburg, 1977). This explanation is an important factor in understanding the use of drugs and alcohol by our society's youth. Several researchers (Hawkins, Catalano, & Miller, 1992; Norman, Turner, Zunz, & Stillson, 1997) suggest that the various developmental domains in adolescence, including physical, emotional, psychological, social, and cognitive, lead to potential risk-factors for drug and alcohol use/abuse. Evidently, there is a strong relationship between the specific problems associated with adolescent development and the general potential for drug/alcohol use/abuse.

Jessor (1985), who contends that there are four fundamental explanations for adolescent drug and alcohol use, addresses the relationship between adolescent development and drug/alcohol use. First, it appears that drugs and alcohol provide adolescents with a means to relieve feelings of inadequacy and other psychological pains that naturally occur during adolescence (e.g., boredom and loneliness). Drug and alcohol use also offers an opportunity for the adolescent to express opposition to authority. It affirms solidarity patterns with peers, and makes teens feel "grown up" while marking the transition from the inferiority of childhood to the superiority of adulthood.

There are several societal factors which impact adolescent drug and alcohol use. Our society today is more violent and alienating than in the past. The prevalence of abuse, both physical and sexual, and neglect appear to be at significantly high levels (Winzer, 1993). Other problems associated with gangs and gang violence greatly impact our youth (Branch, 1999), and the number of runaway, thrown-away, and homeless youth is growing and constitutes a major social dilemma (Kryder-Coe, Salamon, & Molnar, 1991). In addition, glamorized images of drug use in our media, political ineffectiveness, and economic inadequacies must not be taken lightly for they impact adolescent behaviors tremendously (see for example, Bowles & Gintis, 1976; Gerbner, 1990; Gitlin, 1990).

Hawkins, Catalano, & Miller (1992) conducted an extensive investigation of specific risk factors for adolescent drug and alcohol abuse. The authors identify two categories of factors, contextual (societal and cultural), and individual and interpersonal (physiological, family, school, classrooms, and peer groups). Contextual factors impacting drug and alcohol use include things such as laws and norms, availability of drugs and alcohol, extreme economic deprivation, and neighborhood disorganization. Individual and interpersonal risk factors include the child's level of alienation from the dominant values of school and community, high tolerance level for deviant behaviors and normlessness, high resistance to traditional authority, sensation seeking, little concern for safety, poor school performance, and association with peers who use drugs.

The interpersonal factor that appears to have a great impact on reducing the risk of drug and alcohol use involves the parent-child relationship. Parents who have a close relationship with their children and are involved in a positive way with their children's activities decrease risk factors for drug and alcohol use and abuse (Hawkins, et al. 1992). Hawkins, et al. (1992) also emphasize that further research is necessary to determine the interaction effects among the contextual and individual and interpersonal risk factors, which of these factors are modifiable, and which are specific to drug abuse rather than generic contributors to adolescent problem behaviors.

A study of drug and alcohol behaviors by Bennett (1983) identifies three main patterns of consumption:

(1) experimentation,
(2) episodic, and
(3) addictive or compulsive.

The prominent variable in this classification approach is frequency of use. In reference to this issue, one study conducted by Shedler & Block (1990) provides a look at the relationship between personality and consumption patterns. The authors suggest that there are similar personality traits between the frequent users and those who abstained until the late teen years. They report that those individuals who were the most anxious and had the poorest social skills and most restricted personalities were those who had abstained from drugs and alcohol through the age of eighteen. Those who were the most maladjusted and alienated and who had poor impulse control and the highest levels of emotional stress were the frequent users. It is interesting to note that those who were the 'best adjusted' were the experimenters (Shedler & Block, 1990). Factors contributing to relapse that have frequently appeared in the literature (Bennet, 1983; Catalano et al. 1991; Gorsky & Miller, 1986; Talbott & Martin, 1999) are summarized in the following table.

Table I: Factors Contributing to Relapse

Personality Factors	Family	Social/Cultural	Personal Skills
Feelings of alienation	Stressful parent-child relationship	Lack of support system	Inadequate coping skills to deal with social pressures
Poor inability for impulse control	Divorced parents	Moving away from friends	Inability to deal with interpersonal conflicts
High stress personality	Substance use in the home	Break up of relationships between girlfriend/wife	Harboring negative emotions
Inability to control anxiety and anger	Dysfunctional family structure	Frequent school change	Recurrent thoughts or physical desire to use drugs or alcohol
Depression	Mental illness in parents	Lack of moral, spiritual support	Lack of skills to cope with high risk situations
Denial of drug dependence	Loss or death of family member	Frequent interactions with substance abusing peers	Desires to test personal control over drugs
Reality distortion and emotional concealment	Frequent exposure to physical and/or sexual abuse during developmental years	Inability to avoid substance use during social events (e.g., Thanksgiving, Christmas, birthdays, weddings, etc.)	Denial of loss of control
Thrill-seeking tendencies	Excessive parental absence	Lack of friendships	Inadequate skills to make lifestyle changes
Isolation or withdrawal to avoid conflict and vulnerability to pain	Location of family in high-risk neighborhood	Extreme economic deprivation	Inadequate skills to replace substance use and identify with positive peers
Cross-addictive behaviors	Unemployment	Neighborhood disorganization	Learning Disability
Feelings of guilt over past use	Domestic violence		
Overconfidence	Child neglect		
Defiance to authority			

While discussing the issue of consumption and frequency, Bennett (1983) also addresses the need to distinguish between the concepts of use and abuse. A point of great debate here is whether or not any use of alcohol, drugs, or both by minors should be defined as abuse. According to Norman et al. (1997), simple experimentation of drugs and alcohol is normal behavior for adolescents; whereas, daily use is abusive, dysfunctional behavior. Based on the underlying legal and moralistic implications, any use of illegal substances may be viewed by some as abuse. However, Bennett (1983) emphasizes that, although the term 'use' may imply some degree of acceptance and normality, it should not be interpreted as an attempt to condone teen drug and alcohol use. Rather, of greater concern is the importance of screening out those youth that may need only education or other less intensive forms of guidance from those who need to be treated in programs for substance abuse.

With regard to the relationship of age and use and its impact on future abuse, Jessor (1985) provides evidence that earlier use is more highly correlated to later abuse. He reports that 50% of the males in his study who initiated drug use before the age of 15 later developed a substance abuse problem. In contrast, 26% of those between 15-17, 17% between 18-24 and 11% of those over the age of 25 later developed substance abuse problems.

Jessor's (1985) findings are of great significance in light of the findings, provided by Norman, et al. (1997), which suggest that the greatest age range of risk of initiation is between 12-15. These authors provide several factors that they believe account for the increase in risk of use. These include the physical changes of puberty, the change from elementary school to middle school, an intense pressure to conform with peers, a growing desire to be independent from parents and authority, the increased availability of substances, and the cognitive awareness that drugs and alcohol can temporarily relieve the psychological pain and turmoil of adolescence. The essential timing of the introduction of prevention programs in the school system prior to the age of twelve would appear pivotal in successfully addressing the relatively higher risk of initiation and the growing presence of a variety of factors leading the young adolescent to drug and alcohol use.

An Overview of Drug Abuse Prevention

A review of the history of drug and alcohol prevention programs in the American school system provides an informative look at the evolution of these program methodologies and the development of a growing empirical knowledge base. Norman et al. (1997) suggest that the late 1960's and early 1970's marked the time when the American high schools were targeted for adolescent prevention efforts. According to the authors, this reflected a response to the liberal drug attitudes of the 1960's and the subsequent high frequency rates of drug and alcohol use among American teens. Some estimates suggest that over 75% of adolescents during this time experimented with some form of drugs or alcohol (Kandel,1978). As the programs were implemented and concurrent prevalence rates were not impacted, the shift from targeting high school age students to middle and elementary school students was observed.

Silverman (1988) (as cited in Norman et al., 1997) indicates that four main program strategies were developed over the years:

(1) Information-Only,
(2) Alternative Activities,
(3) Competency Enhancement, and
(4) Social Environmental.

As the effectiveness of each program methodology was gauged by observing the subsequent prevalence rates of use among adolescents, modifications were adopted to address the inadequacies of each approach.

The Information-Only approach was based on the premise that educating the youth about the properties of drugs, the potential physical reactions to drugs, the methods of use, and the short and long term social and health consequences of use would lead to a reduction in drug and alcohol use. Successes from this approach were extremely limited. Norman et al., (1997) report that numerous studies conducted on the effectiveness of these programs reveal that they are the "most ineffective" drug prevention programs. In fact, some studies indicate that they actually increased drug and alcohol use among teens (Moskowitz, Schaps, Malvin, & Schaeffer, 1984 (as cited in Norman et al., 1997)).

The Alternative Activities approach was based on the assumption that involving youth in satisfying non-drug-related activities would reduce drug and alcohol prevalence rates. Norman et al., (1997) suggest that the effects were negligible due in large part to the fact that non-use of substances was not incorporated as a focus of the activities. In fact, the authors argue that in some cases drug and alcohol use was increased during exposure to these programs. The type of activity and the settings where they were offered impacted drug and alcohol use. For example, sporting events, entertainment, vocational, and extracurricular activities were associated with higher drug and alcohol use, particularly when individuals who abused substances were present. In contrast, hobbies, academic preparation (tutoring/mentoring), and religious activities were all associated with lower rates of drug and alcohol use.

The rise of the Competency Enhancement approach grew out of the shortcomings of the prior two approaches. This approach emphasized the need to develop self-esteem, appropriate values, decision-making, problem-solving, and/or communications skills. The assumption of this approach was that education and activities alone are not sufficient to counteract the gravitation toward drug and alcohol usage. Adolescents need strong skills and values to face the challenges of adolescence that lead to drug and alcohol use (Norman, et al.1997). The ideals of this approach were well founded; however, their implementation focused on general goals and coping skills. Norman et al. (1997) argue that the limited success of these programs was directly linked to the lack in specificity of teaching substance use prevention strategies.

As the knowledge base for effective prevention program methodologies grew, the development of a more comprehensive and highly focused approach became warranted. The Information-Only, Alternative Activities, and Competency Enhancement strategies each had their own effective components. The development of the Social Environment strategy was an attempt to build on the positive aspects of the previous approaches. It was based on aspects of social learning theory (modeling and imitating non-use behaviors), cognitive or social inoculation theory (inhibiting unwanted substance-using behaviors), and biopsychosocial theory (stressing the important roles and interaction between family, school, and community). The assumption of this approach was that youth can be inoculated against social pressures to use drugs and alcohol by reinforcing social norms against the use of substances and by supplying them with the essential skills to resist the social pressures to use (Norman, et al.1977).

Prevalence of Drug Abuse

Data collected over the past 30 years indicate that overall prevalence rates for drug and alcohol use have declined steadily since the 1970's (National Household Survey on Drug Abuse, 1997). This may reflect both prevention program effects as well as effects from societal shifts in attitude. Norman et al. (1997) suggest that prevalence rates have declined as a result of five major factors:

(1) The fad quality of taking drugs has worn off;
(2) The symbolic value drugs have provided as a form of rebellion has decreased;
(3) The general movement in the U.S. toward more healthy lifestyles has effected adolescents;
(4) Political and professional leaders have taken a firm stance against using drugs; and
(5) Parents, schools, communities, and the media have become more sophisticated in their message about and their

programs concerning the non-use of such substances.

Although the overall prevalence rates have dropped, there has been an upward swing in drug use by children between the ages of 12-17 since 1992. In 1979, there was an estimated 16.3% of 12-17 year olds who reported using any illicit drug in the past month. The percentage fell to a low of 5.3% in 1992 and has risen to 11.4% in 1997. A further breakdown of this age group in 1997 reveals that the highest rates were found among young people ages 16-17, where 19.2% report to have used any illicit drug in the past month. Among youth ages 12-13, 3.8% reported use in the past month. Approximately 11.5% of youth ages 14-15 and 17.3% of those between the ages of 18-20 report use in the past month (SAMHSA, 1997).

An analysis of the types of drugs being used reveals that Alcohol (20.5%) and tobacco (19.9%) are the most prevalent for youth between the ages of 12-17. Heavy alcohol use was reported by 3.1% and 'binge' (five or more drinks) alcohol use was reported by 8.3%. Marijuana/Hashish is next with 9.4% reporting use in the past month, followed by inhalants at 2.0%, hallucinogens at 1.9%, and cocaine at 1.0% (SAHMSA, 1997).

The National Institute on Drug Abuse analyzed 8th, 10th, and 12th grade students' daily drug and alcohol use for the years 1991 to 1996 in the Monitoring the Future Study, 1996. In the 1996 sample, daily cigarette smoking was listed as the most prevalent substance of use across all three grade levels. 13.0% of students in 12th grade report daily use followed by 9.4% for 10th graders and 4.3% for 8th graders.

Marijuana/Hashish daily usage rates were the next highest. 4.9%, 3.5%, and 1.5% rates were reported by the 12th, 10th, and 8th graders respectively. Daily alcohol consumption rates followed with 3.7%, 1.6%, and 1.0% of 12th, 10th, and 8th graders. It is interesting to note that when looking at the past 30-day usage rates, alcohol far exceeds all the other substances ranging from a high of 50.8% for 12th graders and a low of 26.2% for the 8th graders. In contrast, 21.9% of 12th graders and 11.3% of 8th graders reported use of marijuana/hashish during the past 30 days. These patterns of consumption behaviors were consistent for all years reported (National Institute on Drug Abuse, Monitoring the Future, 1996).

These data suggest that, when looking at overall usage rates, alcohol is the most widely used substance by teens. Although, when looking at the daily use of drugs, excluding tobacco, marijuana/hashish is slightly more prevalent than alcohol. A steady decline of drug and alcohol use has occurred from the 1970s - 1990. However, a general increase has occurred during the years 1991-1996 for all usage categories reported; lifetime, annual, 30-day, and daily use of alcohol, tobacco, and marijuana/hashish. In contrast, usage rates for Inhalants, Hallucinogens, LSD, Cocaine, Crack, Heroin, Stimulants, Tranquilizers, and Steroids have remained relatively stable over the same time period.

Etiology

Apparently, drug and alcohol use among teens is quite common and considered a "normal" adolescent behavior. As previously discussed, consumption patterns include simple experimentation, episodic, and compulsive or addictive behaviors (Bennett, 1983). Macdonald (1989) suggests that drug use is not considered maladaptive or dysfunctional until one passes over a line into the area called "drug abuse." He suggests that as the user progresses from curiosity and experimentation to drug addiction he or she passes through recognizable stages where typical behaviors are noted. In the progression from use to addiction, Macdonald (1989) suggests that the five stages include,

(1) curiosity,
(2) learning the mood swing,
(3) seeking the mood swing,
(4) preoccupation with the mood swing and,
(5) doing drugs to feel okay.

The first stage, curiosity, reflects the developmental nature of the adolescent. According to Macdonald (1989), adolescents are more willing to take risks, have a strong need to be accepted by peers, and desire to experience new feelings or mood states. These factors increase the risk of experimentation with drugs and alcohol and elicit a rationalization by the adolescent that "it won't hurt to try one."

Learning the mood swing is the stage in which the adolescent begins to explore the excitement and pleasurable feelings associated with use. Use in this stage tends to occur in social settings among friends or acquaintances who desire to share in the exciting and pleasurable feelings. The most significant aspect of this stage is learning how easy it is to feel good. The euphoric feelings provide the impetus for progressive use patterns. It is important to note that during this stage there are typically very few, if any, consequences experienced by the user, except for moderate levels of guilt. Consequently, there is significant reinforcement for continued usage during this stage (Macdonald, 1989).

In the seeking the mood swing stage, the user is no longer content with waiting for others to provide the drugs or alcohol. It is now important for the user to have his or her own supply of substances. This apparently leads to more frequent use and the beginning of a series of isolating behaviors takes place. The teen in this stage may discontinue activities they have done for years. Hobbies, extra curricular activities, school achievement, and family interaction all seem to decline during this stage. Old non-using friends may be eliminated and a group of new drug-using friends are adopted (Macdonald, 1989).

Planning the day's activities around being high on drugs or alcohol becomes the focus of the user preoccupied with the mood swing. This stage reflects the point at which the user demonstrates psychological dependency. The "need" to rely on drugs for feelings of comfort is emphasized by the user. Further isolation occurs as the user usually has alienated their family, their true friends, and their schools. It is not uncommon for the user in this stage to have jobs, failing grades, run-ins with the law, a break down of sexual inhibitions, and a costly weekly substance habit (Macdonald, 1989).

The final stage in this progression is the point at which drug and alcohol use is the only way to feel okay. The fun, excitement, and euphoria of using are no longer present. The user needs larger dosages, stronger drugs, or both just to function. This stage of dependency leads to further isolation, failures, depression, and suicidal ideations (Macdonald, 1989).

Obviously, not all teens who use drugs and/or alcohol progress through all these stages. Why some experimenters and episodic or recreational users progress to more serious levels of substance abuse is a complicated question to answer. Substance abuse is typically viewed as a chronic, progressive, relapsing disorder resulting in physical and psychological dependence on chemical substances (Crowe & Reeves, 1994). How one develops this state of dependency is not quite clear.

There have been a variety of etiological models, ranging from moral to biopsychosocial, espousing the how's and why's of chemical dependency or addiction (Catalano et. al., 1991; Crowe & Reeves, 1994; Marlatt & Gordon,1985). A review of this literature suggests that there is no simple explanation that appears adequate in all cases. As a consequence, an eclectic approach seems most appropriate. Investigating and understanding these factors will provide the basis for developing appropriate treatment strategies.

Earlier attempts to explain chemical dependency were predominantly based on the moral model. This model promotes the belief that chemical dependency is the result of individual weakness. It suggests that the individual may overcome dependency via motivational changes and by strengthening one's moral character (Marlatt & Gordon, 1985). Although more contemporary approaches have supplanted this view within the drug treatment community, it is still widely held among significant segments of the general population (Crowe & Reeves, 1994).

The medical or biological model of chemical dependency, which is promoted by groups such as Alcoholics Anonymous and Narcotics Anonymous, has gained support as scientific studies of genetics and brain chemistry have evolved (Crowe & Reeves, 1994; Marlatt & Gordon, 1985). This view maintains that there is a genetic predisposition for dependency. Crowe & Reeves (1994) state that findings from longitudinal studies have uncovered a genetic link of alcohol dependency across multiple generations of families. This research implies a hereditary etiology and suggests that regardless of moral constitution or social and psychological factors a person with a predisposition to alcoholism will progress to dependency if they begin using alcohol. Although a similar assumption is often made about other drugs of abuse, Crowe & Reeves (1994) note that research evidence is much more difficult to obtain.

Other points of focus in the medical/biological model address the issue of brain chemistry and brain reward mechanisms. It has been argued (Suhl, 1998) that most substances of abuse cause short increases in EEG Alpha activity immediately following intake and absorption. According to Suhl, most people experience this brain state as desirable. He also suggests that following a drug/alcohol use episode the brain is unable to reproduce this desired effect and this predisposes the individual to re-abuse in pursuit of this pleasant state, and this may quickly develop into a chronic cycle (Suhl, 1998).

Additionally, it is argued that habitual substance use alters brain chemistry in such a way that the individual becomes progressively less capable of experiencing positive emotional states (Crowe & Reeves, 1994; Suhl, 1998). Consequently, the individual is driven to seek the short-term gratification of the abused substance and therefore, must maintain his or her drug and alcohol (or both) usage.

Psychological causes of chemical addiction are divided into two categories. On one hand are reinforcement processes that maintain the use of substances. On the other hand are personality trait factors that are associated with addiction (Crowe & Reeves, 1994). Basic behavioral theory suggests that a response, which is followed by a satisfying state of affairs, tends to be repeated (Thorndike, 1911). Crowe & Reeves (1994) argue that the substance abuser experiences this satisfying state in one of two ways. The positive reinforcement experienced by the substance abuser may come about from a drug's pharmacological effects, euphoria, or from other social rewards such as peer acceptance and increased self-esteem. In addition, the avoidance of pain serves as another reinforcing quality of substance use. For example, if using drugs or alcohol helps someone who is suffering from physical or emotional pain, their continued usage will be reinforced (Crowe & Reeves, 1994).

The notion of anticipatory goal responses (Hull, 1932) can be applied to the maintenance of substance abuse when viewing the cues associated with drug use. Drug cues as presented by Crowe & Reeves (1994) are those stimuli that are associated with a drug and its rewards. These include being around specific people, engaging in particular activities, or going to certain places. The presence of these cues will reinforce the terminal behavior, which in this case is the maintenance of substance use.

The psychological explanations of chemical dependency involving personality traits assume that substance abuse is linked to emotional problems and personal inadequacies. Some of the psychological characteristics associated with substance abuse include things such as low self-esteem, low self-confidence, low self-satisfaction, need for social approval, high anxiety, low assertiveness, greater rebelliousness, and self-regulatory deficiencies (Crowe & Reeves, 1994). As a result of the psychological suffering endured by individuals with these characteristics, substance abuse provides an escape and a means for survival.

There are several social causes of substance abuse presented in the literature on chemical dependency as well (Crowe & Reeves, 1994; Fisher & Harrison, 1993). An underlying factor to the social perspective is the influence of socialization. The four main socializing agents for the adolescent appear to be parents, peers, school, and the media (Crowe & Reeves, 1994; Gerbner, 1990; Gitlin, 1990; Zunz, 1997 [as cited in Norman et al.1997]). When adolescents develop values that reinforce substance abuse, they are more likely to seek out other drug-involved individuals and subculture groups. This process of socialization can be viewed as the underlying current that runs through the different social perspective models.

Social learning theory (Bandura, 1977), which emphasizes the role of modeling and imitation in developing and maintaining behaviors, provides one explanation for substance abuse. This position maintains that individuals who are exposed to individuals or groups of people who model drug-related behaviors will learn to use and be rewarded for using substances (Bennett, 1983; Crowe & Reeves, 1994).

The subculture view of chemical dependency posits that there are several drug subcultures impacting on youth. These subcultures are established by a variety of groups. These groups may be based on a combination of variables including such things as ethnicity, age, school, or drug of choice. This view suggests that the current members of a subculture teach the new members how to use their drug, how to acquire it, and provide reinforcement for continued usage (Crowe & Reeves, 1994).

Other social factors that surround the issue of substance abuse reflect more of a sociopolitical stance. Numerous authors (Crowe & Reeves, 1994; Hawkins et al.1992) suggest that substance abuse is related to elements of poverty, racism, sexism, family dissolution, feelings of powerlessness, and alienation. Goode (1972) contends that individuals who are more attached to conventional society are less likely to engage in behaviors that are in opposition to societal norms and values. Apparently, those individuals who are detached from the dominant society are more likely to tolerate and/or engage in behaviors that are in opposition to the norm.

The development of the biopsychosocial model of substance abuse reflects an attempt to integrate and synthesize the previously described models. The premise of this model maintains that these other more narrowly focused views cannot adequately account for substance abuse across all individuals and all circumstances (see for example, Falk, 1994; Heather & Robertson, 1994). As such, the need for a wider more eclectic approach is necessary to comprehend the complex phenomenon associated with substance abuse. The significance in adopting this eclectic model can be found in its utility when matching appropriate treatment and prevention strategies to individual characteristics and needs (Brown, 1985; Hawkins, et al. 1992; Suhl, 1998).

In a national study on drug treatment in the U.S., Gerstein, Foote, & Ghadialy (1997) identify the most prevalent treatment settings in descending order as: drug treatment or rehabilitation facilities, self-help groups, hospital inpatient settings, physicians' offices, mental health centers, and hospital emergency departments. Relative to all the treatment settings reported, the 12-17 age group were most likely to use mental health centers and self-help groups. According to Gerstein et al. (1997), there were approximately 700,000 youth between the ages of 12-17 who were in need of treatment for substance abuse in the year 1992-93. The actual reported number of these youth who received treatment totaled approximately 125,000. This suggests that only about 18% of the estimated number of youth who required treatment for substance abuse during the year 1992-93 received such services. It is very significant to note that of all age groups reported in Gerstein et al.(1997) the age group that is least likely to receive services is the 12-17 year old group. Approximately 6-7% of the number of people in treatment were between the ages of 12-17. In proportion to the total estimated population in need of treatment in the 1992-93 sample, roughly 13.3% of them were 12-17 year olds.

When comparing treatment enrollment rates for type of drug, Gerstein et al. (1997) report that 12-17 year olds are more likely to be in treatment for marijuana than any other substance. These authors estimate that there were approximately 31,000 youth in 1993 who were in treatment for marijuana abuse as compared with approximately 10,500 for alcohol abuse. In addition, they report that approximately 27% of 12-17 year olds who have been in some form of treatment program are using drugs and/or alcohol again. It is important to note that in comparison to all other age groups, this age group had the highest reported relapse rates.

Predisposing Relapse Factors

Many addicts find recovery particularly difficult because the drug/alcohol dependency during developmental years may have delayed normal development, which makes it difficult for the recovering youth to function in an age- appropriate manner. Consequently, return back to substance use might be a way of managing the discomfort in adjusting to social milieu of youth. It has been suggested that there are a number of predisposing factors and precipitating events that are likely to trigger relapse in youth and adults. The predisposing factors in relapse include characteristics such as learning disabilities, dual or multiple diagnosis, high stress personalities, inadequate coping skills, absence of social support systems, dysfunctional families, and lack of impulse control. There are also a number of events in social and familial contexts that may amount to as upsetting situations and may interfere with an individual's attempt to work through the recovery process. Such events are divorce or separation of parents, changing schools, relocation and loss of old friends, death of loved ones, breaking up of intimate relationships, and events such as loss of jobs.

Categories for Identifying Relapse-Prone Individuals

Gorsky and Miller (1986) made an attempt to classify individuals who were addicted to some substance based on their history of recovery and relapse history. According to commonly observed patterns of recovery and relapse, individuals primarily fall into three categories; recovery-prone individuals; briefly prone to relapse; or chronically prone to relapse. The relapse-prone youth and adults generally have been found to have three distinct characteristics. They seem to have difficulty in accepting the fact that they have addiction problems despite experiencing adverse consequences due to addiction. In other cases, the relapse-prone tendencies might be due to the failure of treatment in helping individuals with addictions to develop skills necessary for adhering to abstinence, and life style change. A third group of relapse-prone individuals often develops dysfunctional symptoms during the recovery process that lead them back to drug usage. Estimates are that about 40 to 60 percent of persons recovering from drug dependence exhibit relapse tendencies at least once following their first serious attempt at treatment. Among offenders, relapse has been found to accelerate the level of criminal activity (Peters, 1993). Lack of motivation to recover has often been thought as a potential cause for relapse. However, clinical experiences and research evidence do not provide sufficient documentation to support the strength of relationship between levels of motivation and ability to maintain abstinence (Gorsky et al.1986).

Relapse Prevention Techniques

The primary objective of relapse prevention treatment is to help recovering individuals/patients to develop abilities and skills to recognize relapse warning signs and maintain abstinence on their own. Although there are varied techniques that can be utilized for preventing relapse tendencies, there is a common set of principles that underlie most of the relapse prevention treatments. The following are the core principles that constitute the foundational elements of methods used to systematically teach recovering patients to recognize and manage relapse warning signs.

A. Self-Regulation and Stabilization: It is believed that as a client develops abilities and skills to self-regulate thinking, feeling, memory, judgement, and behaviors, the risk of relapse is likely to decrease

(Gorsky et al.1993). The self-regulation is to be achieved through a systematic treatment plan for relapse-prone individuals to stabilize physically, socially, and psychologically. The objective is to help patients develop skills and abilities to perform basic activities of daily living. Since patients' level of stability may differ under low and high stress environments, the assessment of stability across varied environments is highly desirable. The stabilization process often involves detoxification from alcohol and drugs, managing interpersonal crises and stresses that are likely to threaten sobriety, learning skills to manage and identify addictive preoccupation, and structuring daily activities including exercise, eating habits, and contact with treatment personnel and self-help groups.

B. Self Assessment: It involves reconstruction of problems that may have caused the individual to seek treatment. The critical issues and warning signs triggering relapse are identified. In the self assessment process the focus is on the exploration of the sequence of events preceding relapse in order to recognize the fact that there are specific predictable events leading to relapse.

C. Understanding and Self-Knowledge: In order for an individual who has abused substances to minimize the possibilities of relapse, it is important for him/her to develop an understanding of the general factors that cause relapse. A typical procedure for enhancing understanding is to provide systematic and structured education about recovery, relapses, and relapse prevention planning strategies. The information that is provided to individuals who relapse by counselors and therapists generally includes knowledge of medical, clinical, and social models of addictive disease, common "stuck points" in recovery, warning signs identification, management of relapse warning signs, and effective recovery planning. Specific techniques can involve helping individuals with substance abuse problems develop a personal warning sign list and analyze warning signs by identifying irrational thoughts, unmanageable feelings, and self-defense behaviors.

D. Relapse Education: Relapse prevention education involves helping individuals with addictions who may potentially relapse learn specific strategies and skills such as self monitoring, self assessment, and self awareness of risk factors and warning signs. This is generally achieved by a six-step educational process which includes the following:

1. Self-knowledge and identification of warning signs. The objective of this process is to teach individuals with addiction problems to identify the sequence of events and problems that have contributed to their drug and alcohol abuse in the past and then to develop a list of circumstances that could cause them to relapse.
2. Change and recovery planning: This process teaches relapse-prone individuals to recognize, manage, and cope with warning signs as they occur.
3. Change and recovery planning: This involves the development of a schedule of recovery activities that will help the individuals recognize and manage warning signs when encountered in sobriety.
4. Awareness and inventory training: The training is intended to teach relapse-prone individuals to complete daily inventories designed to monitor compliance with the recovery program and check for the development of relapse warning signs.
5. Significant others and involvement of others: The help and support of others is of paramount importance to relapse-prone individuals during the process of recovery. Treatment programs should actively seek the involvement of family members, supportive peers, and 12-step sponsors in the recovery.
6. Maintenance and relapse prevention plan updating: An effective relapse prevention program requires an ongoing continued reinforcement of some type of therapy or treatment. It has been observed that even highly effective short-term treatment programs are often unable to interrupt long-term relapse cycles without continued delivery of therapeutic services and support to clients. Therefore, it is essential to plan and implement counselor-client update sessions that involve
    (a) assessment of initially developed warning sign lists, management strategies, and recovery plans;
    (b) reviewing issues and problems that are significant to maintain continued progress;
    (c) revising relapse warning sign list and incorporating new warning signs that may have developed after the previous update;
    (d) identifying new management strategies for newly

developed warning signs; and

(e) revising recovery plans to add activities necessary for managing new warning signs and eliminating those that are no longer needed.

Relapse Prevention Strategies

Utilizing the principles mentioned above, Marlatt & Gordon (1985) developed a relapse prevention paradigm that incorporates procedures for utilizing specific and global intervention strategies. The underlying assumption in this paradigm suggests that relapse is a normal part of recovery and as such, should be used as an opportunity for growth and development.

The use of self-regulation or self-monitoring strategies in relapse prevention serves as both an assessment procedure as well as an intervention technique (Lewis, Dana, & Blevins, 1994). In this procedure, the client keeps a written account of when, where, and why they want to use drugs or alcohol. They document both their feelings and the coping skills used to avoid or limit the amount consumed. This provides the client with a higher level of awareness of their urges to use and their level of competency in applying coping skills. According to Marlatt & Gordon (1985), increasing awareness is very effective in dehabitualizing the substance-use response. In addition, this allows the counselor to assess the individual's cues for substance use and the client's efficacy in implementing coping skills.

Another self-assessment technique is known as the direct-observation method (Lewis et. al.1994). Clients are asked to rate themselves in different social scenarios in terms of the degree of temptation to use and their level of confidence in their capacity to avoid a slip or relapse. The Situational Confidence Questionnaire (Annis, 1982) was developed to facilitate the identification of high-risk situations. This questionnaire allows the client to increase awareness about high-risk situations and allows the counselor to determine their client's coping skill level. In addition, it has been demonstrated (Kirisci & Howard, 1997) that this instrument is appropriate without modifications for use with adolescents.

Coping skills and stress management techniques have also been found essential for an effective relapse prevention program. Once high-risk situations have been identified, the client can learn how to manage and deal with specific stress situations in an effective manner. Many relapse prevention programs focus on the technique of avoidance as an effective coping skill. There are situations in which individuals with substance abuse problems may simply have to learn avoidance behaviors. However, there are other situations which necessitate the use of systematic relaxation techniques, assertiveness, and effective communication skills to avoid recurrence of substance abuse.

Lewis, et al.(1994) list several specific stress management techniques that are effective in relapse prevention. These include the following cognitive and behavioral components:

(1) taking one thing at a time;
(2) working tension off physically;
(3) learning not to be a perfectionist;
(4) using humor;
(5) seeking outside help when needed;
(6) allowing time alone;
(7) adopting hobbies and activities that do not involve substance use;
(8) striving for moderation, as opposed to rigidity, in thought and action;
(9) sleeping and eating correctly; and
(10) balancing the costs and benefits of life.

The use of efficacy enhancement tools such as imagery or a decision matrix is another important component that has been employed in relapse prevention programs. Imagery in such approaches is used as relapse rehearsal, where the client imagines the successful use of coping skills in high-risk situations. The decision matrix is a form used to list the immediate and delayed positive and negative consequences of quitting or continuing the substance abuse behaviors. The recording of potential positive and negative consequences in a decision matrix is another type of self-assessment instrument, which has been found useful for both the client and the counselor.

The use of behavioral contracts has also been helpful in preventing a return to pre-intervention levels of substance abuse (Lewis, et al. 1994; Miller, 1999). The behavioral contract is a technique to be applied when the client experiences a slip. In this technique, a contract is agreed upon by the client and counselor for the client to strictly follow a set of instructions in the event that a slip occurs. Such instructions may involve calling a counselor or sponsor, going to a support group meeting, calling friends, discussing relapse occurrences with treatment center authorities or physician, and talking with spouse, family, or significant others (Talbott & Martin, 1999). For example, the client may be instructed to carry a card containing such a list along with outlines of other specific coping skills including thoughts to be engaged in and numbers to be called (Lewis, et al. 1994).

In addition to the specific intervention techniques, Marlatt & Gordon (1985) suggest that there are global intervention strategies that are critical to support specific relapse prevention efforts. Balancing one's lifestyle is an example of a global intervention strategy, which assumes that imbalance in one's lifestyle manifests itself as stress and ultimately as frustration. Learning to balance one's lifestyle involves striking an equilibrium between work and recreation, good and bad times, happiness and sorrow, and pain and pleasure. Lewis et al. (1994) indicate that a client in recovery may sometimes become overwhelmed and obsessed with the numerous details that can present themselves in the recovery process. In order to overcome such feelings, a balance can be obtained by emphasizing the "good things" in life such as encouraging clients to involve themselves in leisure activities and non-stressful hobbies. In addition, therapeutic activities such as jogging, meditation, or art (see for example, O'Connell, 1991) combined with healthy eating and sleeping habits promote the type of balanced lifestyle necessary for preventing stress, frustration, and relapse.

Marlatt & Gordon (1985) acknowledge the fact that frustration in life frequently leads to a desire for indulgence. In addition, it is assumed that all individuals regardless of their level of lifestyle balance will encounter frustration. It is, therefore, necessary for client's to learn more adaptive indulgences which can be substituted for their prior maladaptive indulgence patterns (i.e., substance abuse). These can be developed with a counselor and may include very simple things such as going shopping, getting a massage, reading a book, taking a vacation, seeing a movie, or going for a walk. It is important to emphasize that these indulgences should be developed creatively and prior to a client's increased frustration level. The implementation of these indulgences can be applied as discussed in the section on behavioral contracts, where the client has a specific list of behaviors to follow under certain antecedent conditions.

Summary

Relapse prevention issues are critical to the determination of the success of any substance abuse treatment program. It should be understood that understanding the causes of relapse is not simple because relapse does not occur within a vacuum. There are numerous contributing factors and warning signs which may provide an indication that a client may have a high probability of returning to substance abuse. Development and use of successful relapse prevention strategies require that relapse be understood as not only a single event causing return to the pattern of substance abuse, but also as the process during which high-risk behaviors gradually develop prior to the client's resumption of substance abuse. In the process approach to understanding relapse, a client's frequent exposures to "high-risk situations" are likely the cause of relapse. Other factors such as physical or psychological reminders of past drug or alcohol use, desire to test personal control over drug and alcohol use, or both and frequent thoughts and desires to consume drugs and alcohol are potential causes for the development of relapse-prone tendencies.

Considering the multiplicity of factors (personal, familial, social, and attitudinal) contributing to relapse, successful prevention strategies require coordination and communication between various agencies and systems. The state and community treatment programs must work collaboratively to ensure that relapse prevention efforts are comprehensive and successful. In other words, drug prevention treatment centers alone cannot attain desirable prevention results unless successful systems coordination is implemented. A related issue is the enormity of individual variation in social and psychological characteristics of relapsers. As a consequence, the effectiveness of various relapse prevention treatment programs may not be sufficiently generalizable across different groups of substance abusers. This is an area where further research needs to be carried out for determining the efficacy and generalizability of prevention programs.

It is important to note that most prevention strategies for individuals with substance abuse problems have been developed and used with adult populations. Despite the fact that adolescents are particularly at higher risk for relapse because of their developmental stage, little empirical research has been carried out with this population. The importance of studying the youth group is critical because drug dependency may cause delays in normal development making it difficult for recovering youth to function in an age appropriate manner. Developmental delays may complicate the reintegration of youngsters who abuse substances into the social milieu of youth. Failure to make adequate social adjustment may cause their return to substance use as a mechanism to cope with these inabilities (Bell, 1990).

The aforementioned issues lead to four major conclusions with regard to the efficacy of relapse prevention programs. First, more controlled studies are needed to evaluate the long-term effectiveness of relapse prevention strategies with adolescents in reducing factors such as cravings and increasing their ability for self-assessment, monitoring, self-control, and maintenance of abstinence behaviors. Secondly, studies are also needed to examine the posttreatment predictors of relapse. In order to accomplish this, well-designed comparison groups must be utilized and treatment conditions must be sufficiently clarified so that replications and comparisons across studies can be made. Thirdly, there appears to be some confusion among researchers in defining the concept of relapse as utilized in studying the effectiveness of relapse prevention strategies. Some degree of consensus regarding standard definitions would enhance the comparability of studies. Finally, although there is a heightened awareness of the importance of relapse prevention, there is a substantial lack of coordinated attempts to deal with the problem of relapse among adolescents. Overall success of prevention programs will ultimately depend on a well-orchestrated coordination among families, schools, communities, treatment centers, support groups and social institutions.

References

Adler, A. (1930). *The education of children.* New York: Greenberg.

Annis, N. M. (1982). *Situational Confidence Questionnaire.* Toronto: Addiction Foundation of Ontario.

American Psychiatric Association. (1994). *Diagnostic and statistical manual of mental disorders* (4th ed.). Washington, DC: American Psychiatric Association

Bandura, A. (1977). *Social learning theory.* Englewood Cliffs, N.J.: Prentice-Hall.

Bennett, G. (1983). Youthful substance abuse. In G. Bennett, C. Vourakis, & D.S. Woolf (Eds.), *Substance abuse: Pharmacologic, developmental, and clinical perspectives* (pp.156-174). New York: Wiley & Sons.

Blos, P. (1979). *The adolescent passage: Developmental issues.* New York: International Universities Press.

Bowles, S., & Gintis, H. (1976). *Schooling in capitalist America: Educational reform and the contradictions of economic life.* New York: Basic Books.

Branch, C.W. (1999). *Adolescent gangs: Old issues, new approaches.* Philadelphia, PA: Brunner/Mazel.

Bronfenbrenner, U. (1972). *Influences on human development.* Hinsdale, Ill.: Dryden Press.

Brown, S. (1985). *Treating the alcoholic: A developmental model of recovery.* New York: Wiley & Sons.

Catalano, R.F., Howard, M.O., Hawkins, J.D. & Wells, E.A. (1988). *Relapse in addictions: Rates, determinants, and promising relapse prevention strategies.* Prepared for the 1987 Surgeon General's report, *The health consequences of smoking: Nicotine addiction. Washington, D.C.:* U.S. Government Printing Office.

Catalano, R.F., Hawkings, J.D., Wells, E.A., Miller, J. & Brewer, D. (1991). Evaluation of the effectiveness of adolescent drug abuse treatment, assessment for risk for relapse, and promising approaches for relapse prevention. *International Journal of Addictions, 25,* 1085-1140.

Crowe, A.H. & Reeves, R. (1994). *Treatment for Alcohol and Other Drug Abuse: Opportunities for Coordination.* Technical Assistance Publication Series 11 DHHS Publication No. (SMA) 94-2075. Substance Abuse and Mental Health Services Administration. Center for Substance Abuse Treatment. Rockville, MD 20857

De Jong, R. & Hendrich, G. (1980). Follow-up results of a behavior modification program for juvenile drug addicts. *Addictive Behaviors, 5,* 49-57.

Elkind, D.(1998). *All grown up and no place to go: Teenagers in crisis.* Reading, Mass.: Addison-Wesley.

Erickson, E.H. (1950). *Childhood and society.* New York: Norton

Falk, J. (1994). Drug dependence: Myth or motivation. In R. Coomber (Ed.) *Drugs and drug use in society* (pp.38-43). United Kingdom: Greenwich University Press.

Fisher, G.L., & Harrison, T.C. (1993). The school counselor's role in relapse prevention. *The School Counselor, 41,* 120-125.

Freud, A. (1935) *Psycho-analysis for teachers and parents; Introductory lectures.* New York, Emerson Books.

Gerbner, G. (1990). Stories that hurt: Tobacco, alcohol, and other drugs in the mass media. In H. Resnik, S.E. Gardner, Lorian, R.P., & C.E. Marcus (Eds.), *Youth and drugs: Society's mixed messages* (pp.53-128). Rockville, Maryland: USDHHS.

Gerstein, D.R., Foote, M.L. & Ghadially, R. (1997). *The prevalence and correlates of treatment for drug problems.* Rockville, MD: Substance Abuse Mental Health Services Administration.

Gitlin, T. (1990). On drugs and mass media in America's consumer society. In H. Resnik, S.E. Gardner, Lorian, R.P., & C.E. Marcus (Eds.), *Youth and drugs: Society's mixed messages* (pp.53-128). Rockville, Maryland: USDHHS.

Gorsky, T.T. & Miller, M. (1986). *Staying sober: A guide for relapse prevention.* Independence, MO: Independence Press.

Hall, G.S. (1904). *Adolescence: Its psychology and its relations to physiology, anthropology, sociology, sex, crime, religion and education.* New York: D. Appleton and Company.

Hawkins, J.D., Catalano, R.F., & Miller, J.Y (1992). Risk and protective factors for alcohol and other drug problems in adolescence and early adulthood: Implications for substance abuse prevention. *Psychological Bulletin, 112,* 64-105.

Heather, N., & Robertson, I. (1994). Is alcoholism a disease? In R. Coomber (Ed.) *Drugs and drug use in society* (pp.38-43). United Kingdom: Greenwich University Press.

Hubbard, R.L. & Marsden, M.E. (1986). Relapse to use of heroin, cocaine, and other drugs in the first year after treatment. In *Adolescent drug abuse: Analysis of treatment research.* NIDA Research Monograph (DHHS ADM 88-1523). Rockville, MD: National Institute on Drug Abuse

Hull, C.L. (1932). The goal gradient hypothesis and maze learning. *Psychology Review, 39,* 25-43.

Jessor, R. (1985). Bridging etiology and prevention in drug abuse research. *N.I.D.A. Research Monograph Series, 56,* 257-268.

Kandel, D.B. (1978) *Longitudinal research on drug use: Empirical findings and methodological issues.* Washington: Hemisphere Publishing Corp.

Kirisci, L. & Moss, H.B. (1997). Reliability and validity of the situational confidence questionnaire in an adolescent sample: Confirmatory factor analysis and item responds theory. *Measurement and Evaluation in Counseling and Development, 30,* (3), 146-155.

Kohlberg, L. & Kramer, R. (1969). Continuities and discontinuities in childhood and adult moral development. *Human Development, 12,* 93-120.

Kryder-Coe, J.H., Salamon, L.M., & Molnar, (1991). *Homeless children and youth: A new American dilemma.* New Brunswick, New Jersey: Transaction Publishers.

Lewin, K. (1939). Field theory and experiment in social psychology: Concepts and methods. *American Journal of Sociology, 44,* 868-896.

Lewis, J.A., Dana, R.Q., & Blevins, G.A. (1994). *Substance abuse counseling: An individualized approach.* Pacific Grove, California: Cole Publishing Company.

Macdonald, D.I. (1989). *Drugs, drinking, and adolescents.* Chicago: Year Book Medical Publishers, Inc.

Marlatt, G.A.& Gordon, J.R. (Eds.) (1985). *Relapse Prevention: Maintenance strategies in the treatment of addictive behaviors.* New York: Guilford Press.

Miller, G.A. (1999). *Learning the language of addiction counseling.* Boston: Allyn and Bacon.

Moskowitz, J., Schaps, E., Malvin, J., & Schaeffer, G. (1984). The effects of drug education at follow-up. *Journal of Alcohol and Drug Education, 30,* 45-49.

National Institute on Drug Abuse. (1996) *Monitoring the future study: Trends in prevalence of various drugs for 8th-graders, 10th-graders, and high school seniors.* [WWW document]. URL http// www.nida.nih.gov/NIDACapsules/NCMTF91-95.html (visited 1999, March 31).

Norman, E. (Ed.) (1997). *Drug-free youth: A compendium for prevention specialists.* New York: Garland Publishing, Inc

Norman, E., Turner, S., Zunz, S.J., & Stillson, K. (1997). Prevention programs reviewed: What works? In E. Norman (Ed.), *Drug-free youth: A compendium for prevention specialists* (pp.22-46). New York: Garland Publishing, Inc.

O'Connell, D.F. (1991). The use of transcendental meditation in relapse prevention counseling. *Alcoholism Treatment Quarterly, 8,* (1), 53-68.

Piaget, J. (1968). *On the development of memory and identity.* Worcester, Mass.: Clark University Press.

Peters, R.H. (1993). Relapse prevention approaches in criminal justice system. In *Relapse prevention and the substance-abusing criminal offender (An executive briefing).* Technical Assistance Publication Series, Rockville, MD: Center for Substance Abuse Treatment.

Rogers, C.R. (1931). *Measuring personality adjustment in children nine to thirteen years of age.* New York: Columbia University Press.

Selman, R.L. (1980). *The growth of interpersonal understanding: Developmental and clinical analyses.* New York: Academic Press.

Shedler, J., & Block, J. (1990). Adolescent drug use and psychological health: A longitudinal inquiry. *American Psychologist, 45,* 612-630.

Silverman, M.M. (1988). Prevention research: Impediments, barriers, and inadequacies. In *OSAP Prevention Monograph 3 – Prevention Research Findings,* 24-32.

Substance Abuse Mental Health Services Administration (1997). *Preliminary results from the 1997 national household survey on drug abuse.* Rockville, MD: Office of Applied Studies.

Suhl, T. (1998). *Substance abuse: The science of addiction and options for treatment.* Hearing before the Subcommittee on Labor and Human Resources United States Senate. Washington, DC: U.S. Government Printing Office.

Talbott, G.D. & Martin, C.A. *Relapse & Recovery.* (WWW document). URL http://www.Talbottcampus.com/relapse/html (visited 1999, March 31).

Thornburg, H.D.(1977). *You and your adolescent.* Tucson, Ariz.: H.E.L.P. Books.

Thorndike, E. L. (1911). *Animal intelligence.* New York: Macmillan.

Wesson, D.R., Havassy, B.E. & Smith, D.E. (1986). Theories of relapse and recovery and their implications for drug abuse prevention. In F. Tims & C. Leukefeld (Eds.). *Relapse and Recovery, National Institute on Drug Abuse Research Monograph 72.* U.S. Department of Health and Human Services, Public Health Service, Alcohol, Drug Abuse and Mental Health Administration, National Institute on Drug Abuse, DHHS Publication No. (ADM 86-1473).

Winzer, M. A. (1993). *The history of special education: From isolation to integration.* Washington, DC: Gallaudet University Press.

Zunz, S.J. (1997). School climate and community norm change. In E. Norman (Ed.), *Drug-free youth: A compendium for prevention specialists* (pp.47-72). New York: Garland Publishing, Inc.

Chapter 12

Program Planning and Evaluation

Robert Rapp

Introduction

In substance abuse treatment and prevention programs, success depends as much on competent program planning and evaluation as it does on competent service delivery. Substance abuse programs and the needs that they address are dynamic; there is only one constant. That is *constant change* which dictates that program planning and evaluation be an ongoing process, if the programs which are developed are expected to be effective and remain effective. The initial goal of this process is to determine what is believed to be the *most* effective way to address a need. Then, the more challenging aspect of the process is to implement a system of evaluation which will continuously seek to improve the program through the ongoing discovery of even more effective ways to deliver the needed services.

The Process

The program development process encompasses six steps:

1. Recognizing the Problem and Reviewing the Literature.
2. Completing a Comprehensive Needs Assessment.
3. Formulating Goals and Objectives.
4. Determining the Methodology.
5. Implementing the Program.
6. Evaluating the Program.

Those who are familiar with grant writing can readily see that this process includes the same components which are included in all well developed proposals. In fact, for new programs which require obtaining funding for implementation, this process and the development of a grant proposal are essentially linked together. The written grant proposal is generally the initial product of the program development process.

Step One: Recognizing the Problem and Reviewing the Literature.

Recognition of the severity of a problem such as substance abuse requires becoming as well informed as possible, which usually begins with an in-depth review of the literature. Comprehensive knowledge related to causes, treatment, and the impact of the problem is essential in the program planning and evaluation process. This task helps us to determine the extent of the problem and what is being done programmatically about the problem. It should also help us determine what *not* to do in our own program. In substance abuse, there is a well documented history of ineffective treatment. The rate of recidivism among substance abusers is extremely high. Typically, three out of four substance abusers will relapse or return to using alcohol or drugs after treatment.

Therefore, a careful review of the program literature can reveal as much about ineffective treatment as it does about effective treatment. The challenge is to absorb all this information and to use it in the program planning and evaluation process to develop the most effective program possible.

Step Two: Completing a Comprehensive Needs Assessment.

This step is the key to the entire planning process. The success or failure of a program can be directly attributed to the completeness and accuracy of the needs assessment. To insure that a needs assessment is as accurate as possible, it must be comprehensive. A comprehensive needs assessment includes several procedures: a clear identification of the target population, a thorough review of the social indicators directly pertinent to the target population, a survey of the community of which the target population is a part, a survey of other agencies who are either serving or planning to serve the target population, and extensive communication with key informants who have special knowledge or relationships with the target population.

Identifying the Local Target Population and Reviewing Social Indicators

A clear identification of the local target population and a thorough review of the directly pertinent social indicators go hand in hand. Without careful scrutiny during this procedure, the target population and the actual persons receiving services may not be one and the same.

Related to that, a few years ago, the United Way requested proposals to provide delinquency prevention services to at-risk children and youth in the city of Tucson. Two well funded organizations whose services were geared toward middle-and upper-middle-class children in well-to-do neighborhoods were seeking the limited amount of funds which were available. The other agencies who were competing for the delinquency prevention funds, all provided services in areas of the community which had high poverty rates, high crime rates, high rates of substance abuse, high drop-out rates, and ongoing gang activity.

The two well-funded organizations, who had several supporters among the United Way Allocations Committee, justified their requests by arguing that all children are at-risk of becoming juvenile delinquents. This argument, of course, has some merit, but the degree of risk should be considered. When social indicators pertinent to the target population were studied, the picture became very different. Social indicators are most often presented as statistics related to social need. The statistics representative of the social needs of the children targeted by the other agencies clearly demonstrated where the funding for services should be directed. Fortunately, the information gleaned from the review of the social indicators directly pertinent to the target population was so compelling that the funding was properly directed. Unfortunately, that is not always the case. Without careful attention to this part of the process, funding may be misdirected and the needs of the target population may never actually be addressed.

Surveying the Community

For a comprehensive needs assessment to be valid, the community, of which the target population is a part, should always be surveyed. The survey can include several different procedures. It can include questionnaires which may be distributed to community members through schools, businesses, the media, and other organizations. It can include open forums and meetings where the community is invited to provide input. It could include telephone interviews and personal contacts. The survey should always include substantial participation from members of the target population. At times, it could represent a sample of the target population. At other times, it may include the entire population, such as when a questionnaire is administered to an entire school of students or other representative groups. The key is that the information gathered from the target population itself and its immediate community is usually the most reliable and the most valuable. How often are services offered to a community where there are a limited number of persons who utilize them? When this occurs, how often do program staff complain that the community isn't using the services because "they don't know what's good for them?" That conclusion is especially presumptuous when the target population and its community has been excluded from the planning process.

Surveying Local Agencies

A survey of other organizations which are providing services or are planning to provide services to the target population is also mandatory. Lewis and Lewis (1991) depict the folly of two organizations who have targeted the same population for mental health services. Even though one organization has worked closely with the community, and the other has not, neither is able to effectively address the community's mental health needs and potential funding is lost because they have not collaborated and will duplicate services. (Case 2-1. Community Action and Mental Health, pp 71-72). There certainly is no need to duplicate services when there is a plethora of unmet human services needs. The challenge lies in addressing them collaboratively, comprehensively, and effectively, so that services provided are not just band-aids to temporarily stop the bleeding, but which never lead to permanent changes for the better.

When every agency knows what the other local agencies are doing or are planning to do, then staff are able to network with one another and develop formal linkages with one another which can comprehensively address needs, so that the "usual" gaps in services are eliminated.

Communicating With Key Informants

Key informants are individuals or members of organizations who are directly in touch with the target population and its community. They usually are knowledgeable about community needs and how they should be addressed. They are often recognized as local leaders and are able to exert a considerable amount of influence over the reception of human services which are offered in their communities. They are valuable allies in both the program planning and the program evaluation process.

Key informants can play an important part in conducting a comprehensive needs assessment. They can help organize and participate in the open forums and meetings. They can participate in the design and implementation of the surveys of the target population, the community and local agencies. They can identify other individuals who should be included. In short, they are essential to the program planning process. To ignore their input and participation in the process will likely guarantee that a project will be ineffective in addressing local needs.

In reflecting upon this, I am reminded of a situation in which an organization serving homeless persons wrote a proposal and obtained funds from the City Council to lease a vacant facility on West Congress Street in Tucson, Arizona, through which they intended to provide local services. During the planning process, they ignored the steps necessary to conduct a local comprehensive needs assessment and based all need upon statistics related to the entire homeless population of Tucson. A greater flaw was the exclusion of key informants. In this case, the Tucson West Neighborhood Association members represented the most influential group of key informants in the community. To make a long story short, the Tucson West Neighborhood Association opposed the services, the City Council withdrew the funds and the organization never succeeded in offering any services in that community.

Interestingly, an organization which the author directed, planned and built a human services center in the same community less than two years later which included a 12-unit apartment complex to serve homeless families with children. This time, the Tucson West Neighborhood Association did not oppose the program. Instead, they committed their share of Community Development Block Grant

(CDBG) funds to help build the facilities. The difference was that members of the Tucson West Neighborhood Association were included from the beginning of the planning throughout the process because they were recognized as key informants who were essential to the success of the program.

Step Three: Formulating Goals and Objectives

The most common difficulties of this section are related to a general lack of understanding of the difference between goals and objectives. Often, these two terms are used interchangeably. When this occurs the results are usually unclear or "fuzzy" goals and objectives which are difficult or impossible to measure. Goals are broad "mission" statements which are not measurable without specific objectives. For example, a goal statement related to our mission could be "the rate of substance abuse among teenagers in Silver City, New Mexico will be significantly reduced." This is a perfectly reasonable and worthy goal for a substance abuse prevention and intervention program. The problem is how does one clearly measure a significant reduction in the rate substance abuse so that we know our goal has been achieved?

Specific objectives related to this goal enable us to ascertain that the goal is met. Three specific objectives related to this goal could be:

1. The arrest rate for DWI by teenagers in Silver City, New Mexico between January 1, 1999 and December 31, 1999 will be reduced by 25%.
2. The number of teenagers in Silver City, New Mexico who are referred for detoxification between January 1, 1999 and December 31,1999 will be reduced by 25%.
3. The number of teenagers in Silver City, New Mexico who are referred to Juvenile Probation and Parole Office for substance abuse related offenses will be reduced by 25% during the period January 1, 1999 and December 31, 1999.

All of these specific objectives are easily measurable and a 25% reduction during a one year period would reflect a significant reduction in the rate of substance abuse.

Specific objectives clearly address the target population which is identified in the goal statement. In addition, they are always time oriented and measurable. When specific objectives are met, the extent to which the goal is achieved and its impact are readily understood. Also, it should be emphasized here that as soon as goals and objectives are formulated, the evaluation process should be initiated, in that, it should be simultaneously determined how the objectives will be measured and how their achievement will be documented. In the above examples, data should be collected from the proper authorities at the beginning of the project period and again at the end so that the actual reduction can be measured and documented.

Step Four: Determining the Methodology

This determination actually begins with the review of the literature. However, as was stated in Step One, that review helps us determine what not to do as much as it helps us to determine what to do in our treatment methodology. The key to determining effective methodology is most often related to our creative efforts in addressing the problem. More of the *same old thing* should not be expected to produce better results! Instead, we must focus upon what we can do differently to achieve better results. A guide to stimulate our creativity in order to meet the challenge to find a more effective approach to the problem can be very valuable in this step.

Wubbolding (1988,1991) developed the WDEP model to help remember the procedures of Reality Therapy:

WDEP MODEL

W	=	What do you want?
D	=	What are you doing to get what you want?
E	=	Evaluate it! Is it working? What else could you do?
P	=	Develop a plan to get what you want!

When applied to the program planning and evaluation process, Wubbolding's model can also be very helpful. Used in the plural, i.e., "What do we want? What are we doing to get what we want?", etc., the W.D.E.P. model can be effectively used to stir our collective creative juices to respond to the challenge to find a better way.

Any information that can be useful in effective prevention and intervention programs should be strongly considered for inclusion within the design of the methodology. For example, some information that this author has found to be very valuable related to prevention and intervention programs for children and adolescents includes the following.

Erik Erikson (1963, 1982) taught us the importance of mastering psychosocial challenges during the various stages of growth and development. From the stages of Infancy to Adolescence, Erikson has demonstrated the importance of developing a sense of trust, developing self reliance and initiative, developing a sense of competence and developing a healthy identity. If these core psychosocial challenges are not adequately met, children will move through the various stages of development with feelings of mistrust, self doubt, shame, guilt, inferiority and will be mired in role confusion during adolescence. Not coincidentally, adolescence is the time when children are most vulnerable to substance abuse and other self destructive behaviors.

William Glasser (1992, 1998) teaches us that all behavior is purposeful. It represents an attempt to meet one or more of our basic needs for survival, love and belonging, power (recognition or self-worth), freedom and fun. The foundation of his teaching is that our ability to effectively meet our needs within the structure of our society is determined internally through the choices that we make and not as a behavioral response to environmental stimuli. This approach promotes the development of a strong internal locus of control which empowers individuals to take effective control of their lives.

In *Preparing Tomorrow's Teachers In Substance Abuse Prevention* (1991), Moore states that "without the skills of genuiness and respect, teachers are not likely to be successful in building strong relationships with students . . . .Teachers who are respectful allow their students to develop their own solutions believing that they have the capacity to be self-responsible."

In the same work, Kline (1991) states,

Teachers can support prevention of substance abuse and other health-compromising behaviors by gaining student trust and respect, and helping students to:

- Recognize that they can confront feelings of insecurity, rejection, and failure.
- Overcome obstacles by creative planning that increases their autonomy.
- Channel their energy into more productive and self-actualizing ways to foster self-respect.

Amembal (1991) in the same work, states, In most schools, the peer group provides the primary means for satisfying the affiliation needs of students. Because the norms of peer group affiliation may be in conflict with educational and prevention activities, it is important strategically for educators to learn to rechannel this powerful influence into constructive avenues. . .

Another construct which I believe is essential in every program for children and adolescents, I call "The Breakfast Club Effect." "The Breakfast Club" is a movie which stars Molly Ringwald as a high school "princess", Jud Nelson as a "criminal", Emilio Estevez as an "athlete", Ally Sheedy as a "basket case", and Anthony Michael Hall as a "brain". This very different group of high school students had all violated school rules in some way and had to come to Saturday detention as their punishment. As their day together begins, they spend most of their energy trying to hurt each other, in an apparent attempt to validate their own status and their own particular clique. As the day wears on, they become united against the pompous vice principal in charge of their detention. Through this common purpose they finally begin to honestly communicate with each other and they discover each others' vulnerability and uniqueness. Before the day ends, the criminal and the princess become a couple, the athlete and the basket case become a couple and the brain becomes everyone's best friend.

The vice principal demanded that they write an essay on the topic "Who do you think you are?" Before they could leave detention, the "brain" who completed the assignment on behalf of the entire group wrote:

> Dear Mr. Bernard;
> We accept the fact that we had to sacrifice a whole Saturday in detention for whatever it was we did wrong. What we did was wrong. But we think you're crazy to make us write an essay telling you who we think we are. What do you care? You see us as you want to see us, in the simplest terms, with the most convenient definitions. You see us as a brain, an athlete, a basket case, a princess, and a criminal. Correct? That's the way we saw each other at seven o'clock this morning. We were brainwashed. But what we found out is that each one of us is a brain and an athlete and a basket case, a princess, and a criminal. Does that answer your question?
>
> Sincerely yours,
> The Breakfast Club

Since discovering this movie, this author has embraced "The Breakfast Club Effect" as a valuable programmatic construct to address the needs of children and adolescents. When youngsters who appear to be greatly different from one another are given the same status and are put into positions and situations where they work closely together, communicate with each other, and depend upon one another to accomplish various tasks, they are able to break through the barriers between them. They learn that they are really very much alike with the same needs, fears, and dreams and they often become fast friends. At the very least, they learn to understand and accept each other.

All of the above is very valuable information which is interrelated. It mandates that human services professionals create a warm, supportive, and trusting environment in which students can effectively meet their psychological needs for love and belonging, power (recognition and self worth), freedom and fun in every program. It also mandates that the program emphasize activities in which students can develop self reliance or autonomy, initiative, and competence through which their energy will be rechanneled into "more productive and self actualizing ways to foster self respect." This will enable adolescents to move beyond the characteristic role confusion, toward a positive and healthy identity, with an understanding and acceptance of those who appear to be different.

Information from many other authorities on human behavior can also be very helpful and may enable us to develop more effective programs. What will actually determine program effectiveness is our ability to creatively integrate useful information into the program methodology design, and then put it into practice.

Step Five: Implementing the Program

Diligent completion of the first four steps can enable us to find the support necessary to implement our program. If funding is required, then a budget must be developed. For persons who are not experienced in the development and management of programs, the concept of developing a budget can be intimidating. It should not be. "The budget itself is simply a projection of operational plans, usually for a one-year time span, with the plans stated in terms of the allocation of dollars for varying functions or activities" (Lewis and Lewis, 1991). It is a tool which enables us to translate our goals and objectives into actual practice. Some basic calculation skills are needed to develop an accurate budget, but one need not be an accountant.

Budgeting is clearly tied to the planning and evaluation process. Therefore, the most capable persons to develop the budget are the human services professionals who are most capable of planning, implementing, and evaluating human service programs. Relegating the formulation of a budget to bookkeepers or accountants, who are not human service professionals, will limit the agency's ability to effectively meet its goals and objectives. Feldman (1973) notes that a budget can rigidly control expenditures and limit the discretion of program administrators. Hodges (1982) emphasizes that "Budgets are part of the planning phase. As a result, budgeting incorporates not just the monies to be expended but all of the assumptions related to need, objectives, and ability to deliver services that are found in the planning phase" .

Therefore, human service professionals should not shy away from the budgeting process. Instead, they should embrace it as an integral part of the planning process. Accurate costs simply must be calculated for the personnel and services needed to operationalize your program plans. The most typical cost categories are Personnel, Employee Related Expenses, Professional and Outside Services, Travel, Space, Equipment, Materials and Supplies. Anything else generally is assigned to the category of Other Operating Costs. The ability to project and accurately calculate cost in these line item areas is all that is needed to produce a budget which transforms program goals and objectives into actual practice.

Implementing effective prevention and intervention programs for children and adolescents is not always a costly venture. For example, following the above planning process and using the knowledge gleaned from the works cited in the methodology section enabled this author and a high school counselor to implement a highly effective prevention and intervention program at Cobre High School in Bayard, New Mexico. The annual costs of operating the program compared to its benefits were very small. At most, the costs were $5,000.00 per year.

Initially, the program started with less than 20 adolescents who were primarily honor students. It eventually grew to approximately 80 students who represented a cross section of the Cobre High School student body. This number represented about 12% of the entire student population and was the largest single group of students involved in an extracurricular activity at the school, including the individual athletic teams. The program was designed to include honor students, athletes, cheerleaders, ropers, nerds, and students who had abused drugs and alcohol as well as students who had been gang affiliated. The program originally focused upon substance abuse prevention and intervention, but expanded its focus to include gang prevention and intervention when that became a problem at school and in the community.

The program's success was largely due to the inclusion of diverse groups of students who were representative of the entire student body and the program's creative design which emphasized the concepts discussed in the section on methodology. Trust was developed between the adult sponsors and the diverse participants through specifically designed activities. Program ownership was offered to the students through the opportunity to develop and control the program, in contrast to programs that are generally imposed upon the students by their adult sponsors.

The students created dramatizations which vividly portrayed the real dilemmas which affect and seriously impact children and adolescents today. These dramatizations often realistically portrayed the tragedies which often result from substance abuse and gang violence. They also developed several dramatizations which depicted the influence of parents' behavior upon the behavior of their children. These dramatizations were usually performed before younger student audiences to help prevent them from choosing to use drugs or to join gangs. The presentations were followed by a discussion between the older and younger students on the situations portrayed through the dramatizations.

The high school students developed confidence and competence through their presentations. Their commitment to help younger students also helped the high school students to make better choices related to their own experiences with drugs and gangs. Many of these teens also underwent extensive training to become peer counselors at the High School, the Middle School, and two elementary schools. Eventually, hundreds of students benefitted from this inexpensive, yet creative and effective approach to prevention and intervention.

Ultimately, a group of these students were invited to make a presentation before several hundred persons from 14 different countries at The International Convention of The William Glasser Institute held in Albuquerque, New Mexico, in July, 1996. Subsequently, two professional videos were produced featuring many of these students in their prevention activities (Rapp, 1997).

This program was highly successful because it offered the students opportunities to meet their psychosocial needs for love and belonging, recognition, freedom, and fun; and opportunities to master psychosocial developmental challenges in positive ways. The inclusion of a cross section of the student body and emphasis of need fulfilling activities within the program's design were essential to its success. In addition, the fact that the program was owned and operated by the teens magnified its influence among their peers. Tobler (1986) conducted research which concluded that peer programs are more effective than other program modalities in reducing substance abuse among teens. Tobler found that peer programs were very effective for the average school based adolescent program. However, for at-risk adolescents, including drug abusers and juvenile delinquents, peer programs were shown to be *highly* successful.

Related to that, a recent report of the Carnegie Council on Adolescent Development (1996) concluded that, "all students must find ways to earn respect, establish a sense of belonging in a valued group and build a sense of personal worth based upon the mastery of useful skills, including social skills."

Program implementation can be exciting and rewarding when the program planning process is followed carefully and is valued by the planners. It insures that effective approaches to prevention and treatment will be implemented and validated through the program evaluation process.

Step Six: Evaluating the Program

An appropriate preface to this section is the belief that we should be on a constant quest to find a better way to do things, and as soon as we find it, we should start looking for an even better way. This statement emphasizes the importance of ongoing program evaluation. Program evaluation is not very well understood; many service providers view it negatively. Many see it as just another level of bureaucratic interference that requires more paperwork and less time for direct services to clients. For those who view it that way, evaluation procedures will be imposed upon the program externally from funding sources and other stakeholders, and its value will be diminished.

However, when program evaluation is internalized within the program development process, it is clearly one of the most important components related to program effectiveness .Without it, the effectiveness and impact of a program cannot really be determined. Important decisions related to the program will be based upon external perceptions, rather than facts which can establish program effectiveness.

Glasser (1994), in his book, *The Control Theory Manager,* expounds upon the importance of managers promoting on-going internal self evaluation as a basic condition that will improve quality in the workplace. He points out that external evaluation by the "boss" will never produce the quality work which can be produced through self evaluation and continued improvement. He states that, "the traditional 'an inspector inspects, passes or rejects the work' is static and does not involve the worker. It will lead to passable, even good work, but very little quality. Treated this way, workers will rarely, if ever, do what they are capable of doing."

Externally imposed program evaluation can be viewed similarly. It will probably rarely, if ever, produce quality in the delivery of human services. Instead, program staff who do value evaluation will design internal ongoing (self evaluation) procedures which reflect a commitment to continual improvement. This is what will enable quality programs to rise above those who are content to do the same thing over and over with very little regard for effectiveness.

Tripodi, Fellin, and Epstein (1978) define the three basic objectives of program evaluation as:

1. To provide descriptive information about the type and quantity of program activities (program effort).
2. To provide information about the achievement of the goals (program effectiveness).
3. To provide information about program effectiveness relative to effort (program efficiency).

Gathering and analyzing data about program effort, effectiveness, and efficiency provides information to make important management decisions related to the program. It influences decisions about the ongoing need, modifications affecting the size and scope of the program, its impact upon the problem, and substantiation of its value to the school,community, or both.

Designing an evaluation plan which is clearly tied to the program's goals and objectives should provide adequate measures of effort, effectiveness, and efficiency to satisfy all of the stakeholders in the program. The most common stakeholders in prevention and intervention programs which target children and adolescents are parents, teachers, counselors, school administrators, funding sources, and the community.

As was mentioned in Step Three, the program evaluation process actually begins concurrent with the formulation of goals and objectives. As these are formulated, as part of the evaluation plan, there must be means identified to collect data which enables us to accurately assess effort, effectiveness, and efficiency. This can only be accomplished through a *Process Evaluation and an Outcome Evaluation* which measures and documents the achievement, lack of achievement of goals and objectives, or both.

The procedures used to document effort are often referred to as the *Process Evaluation.* The first concern of the *Process Evaluation* is to determine whether the target population has actually received the services according to the program plan. An example of this aspect of the *Process Evaluation* can be illustrated through the following specific objective:

> Five hundred at-risk children from disadvantaged neighborhoods in Tucson will be enrolled in delinquency

> prevention activities between January 1, 1999 and December 31, 1999.

Apropos to this evaluation concern is the situation cited earlier where a well-heeled organization sought funding from The United Way to provide delinquency prevention services to at-risk children using the reasoning that all children were at-risk. Should that organization have been successful in obtaining the funds, whatever they achieved would have little to no value in addressing the needs of the target population, because at-risk children, to any significant degree, would not have actually received the services.

The other concern of the *Process Evaluation* is to determine the number and types of service activities which are delivered to the target population. This determination is linked to the planned treatment methodology. An example can be related to the following specific objective:

> During the period January 1,1999 through December 31, 1999 each of the program participants will receive at least fifty hours of individual counseling focused upon anger management techniques.

If these services and others which are indicators of the program's effort are not actually accomplished, then the process is flawed. If the target population has not actually been served to the degree planned, then the process is flawed. A flawed process *invalidates* any outcomes which have been achieved.

The procedures used to document effectiveness are often referred to as the *Outcome Evaluation*. The specific objectives related to reducing substance abuse which were used as examples in Step Three are all expected to yield measures of effectiveness and are components of the *Outcome Evaluation.* If data is collected through the evaluation process which documents a 25% reduction in the arrest rate for DWI, in referrals for detoxification, and in substance abused related referrals to the Juvenile Probation and Parole Office in Silver City, New Mexico between January 1, 1999 and December 31,1999, then the program's effectiveness will have been documented through this component of the *Outcome Evaluation*.

Another very important component of the *Outcome Evaluation* is the development and implementation of well-planned follow-up procedures. In order to document program effectiveness over a period of time, follow-up procedures enable us to track clients' progress beyond the immediate analysis pre-treatment/post-treatment data. Caddy (1980) emphasizes the importance of establishing follow-up procedures beginning with the initial intake interview, stressing it throughout treatment, and obtaining the client's commitment to participate in the process subsequent to treatment. This approach improves clients' cooperation and enables them to understand that the program's interest in their welfare extends well beyond the formal treatment process. Frequent contact with clients after formal treatment, strengthens the client/therapist relationship which is need satisfying and serves as a form of ongoing treatment that helps prevent problems from occurring and provides immediate intervention or both.

Effective follow-up procedures can be enhanced through the use of well designed instruments which incorporate core indexes of wellness which should be used in all substance abuse treatment/evaluation studies. Emick and Hansen (1983) suggest that the core indexes should include the following criteria: treatment completion, recidivism, mortality, treatment use, physical health, drinking behavior, other substance use, legal problems, vocational functioning, family/social functioning, and emotional functioning.

The following instruments incorporate useful core indexes which have been reproduced in a handbook by Letteri, Nelson, & Sayers (1985) which was developed for The National Institute on Alcohol Abuse and Alcoholism:

Addiction Severity Index (McLellan, Luborsky, Woody & O'Brien, 1980). The ASI assesses medical status, employment, drug use, alcohol use, legal status, family/social relationships, and psychological status. It is well-tested and has been found useful for ongoing follow-up.

ATC Client Progress and Followup Form (National Institute on Alcohol Abuse and Alcoholism, 1979). This instrument was developed to follow-up clients six months after their treatment at NIAAA programs. It addresses marital status, employment, financial support, drinking behaviors, motor vehicle records, institutionalization, and client self perceptions.

ATC Followup Study Questionnaire (Ruggles, Armor, Polich, Mothershead, & Stephen, 1975). This questionnaire was developed for use in 18 months follow-up interviews with clients who were treated in NIAAA programs. It surveys family status, employment, alcohol consumption, treatment history, legal problems, and perceptions of drinking problems.

Behavior Rating Scale-Social, Employment, Economic, Legal, Drinking (Brandsma, Maultsby, &Welsh, 1980). This instrument is used before treatment and in follow-up. The authors used this 64-item scale as a pre-treatment/post-treatment tool to follow-up problem drinkers who had completed an outpatient treatment program.

Client Follow-up Interview (Kelso & Fillmore, 1984). This instrument is used at intake, discharge, and follow-up. It addresses psychological functioning, alcohol consumption, drug use, physical health, personality, treatment, social relationships, employment, legal issues, life events, attitudes, and coping skills.

Health and Daily Living Form (Moos, Cronkite, Billings, & Finney, 1984). This instrument was developed for a longitudinal follow-up study. It can be self administered or used by an interviewer. The HDL assesses social functioning, health related functioning, resources, family and home environment, children's health and functioning, life-change events, and coping skills.

The data gathered through the *Process Evaluation* and the *Outcome Evaluation* is used to determine program efficiency. *Efficiency Evaluation* procedures are intended to make judgments connecting costs to outcomes. They represent a ratio between effort and effectiveness (process and outcome) which is deemed acceptable to address the needs of the target population. The critical question is, "Can the program achieve the same or better results either by reducing the effort or by providing less costly methodology?" To be very blunt, the programs success must be financially feasible. Therefore, the ratio between successful treatment and cost is a major consideration in documenting the value of a program.

A program designed to prevent or treat substance abuse must be proven to be cost effective. If it is not determined to be cost effective, it either will not be initiated, or it will not be continued after it is evaluated. For example, any program designed to operate on the basis of a one-to-five staff/client ratio would be expected to produce a larger percentage of successful treatment than a program designed to operate on a one-to-twenty-five staff/client ratio. However, even if the first program produced an 80% success rate compared to a 40% success rate for the second, it would not necessarily be judged to be more valuable.

From an effort/effectiveness ratio (cost/outcome), the first program would probably be judged inefficient and its value would be diminished. To clarify that from the standpoint of dollars invested, assume that each staff costs $50,000 in terms of salary, benefits, space, travel, etc. In the first program, the cost of successful treatment would be $12,500 per client, for the second, the cost of successful treatment would be $5,000 per client. Related to that, the second program would succeed with ten clients (40% of 25) per each staff; whereas, the first would succeed with only four clients (80% of 5) per each staff. Therefore, the 80% success rate of the first program would not be highly valued.

On the other hand, a program with a one-to-twenty staff/client ratio which has a 60% success rate should be judged more effective and more efficient than either of the other two, because its cost of successful treatment per client would be $4167. It would succeed with 12 clients (60% of 20) per each staff member. Therefore, of the three programs, the third more satisfactorily responds to the critical question related to program efficiency.

A well designed program evaluation plan which documents effort, effectiveness and efficiency through the achievement of goals and objectives will not only satisfy the demand for accountability, but will also enable a program to broaden its base of support. This is especially critical during the current period of shrinking resources in which programs are required to compete for needed funds. Programs which intimately embrace the evaluation process and understand its value in planning and management will undoubtedly be much more effective than programs which view evaluation as an externally imposed requirement which has little value.

Summary

The program development process is very challenging. Planning and evaluation in substance abuse prevention and treatment is continuously affected by change. It requires extraordinary flexibility, adaptability, and creativity to insure that programs are designed to effectively meet the multiple needs of our clientele. We must not only be committed to staying abreast of the current best practices in the broad field of human services, but we must also critically examine and evaluate those practices in an ongoing quest to find more effective approaches to critical problems. This is especially true in the area of substance abuse where treatment outcomes have been consistently poor.

This author has attempted to encourage the reader to not accept the status quo related to program planning and evaluation. Instead, it is hoped that the students for whom this book is intended will take up the challenge, "to always seek a better way, and as soon as you find it, start looking for an even better way"! To understand the process that will enable the reader to respond to this challenge, a six step approach to planning and evaluation has been emphasized in this chapter.

To facilitate the recall of the six steps, the following model is offered to the reader. It is called the RAPPER Model. It requires that you use each letter in RAPPER to recall the key first words which describe the steps in the process.

RAPPER Model

Review the literature
Assess the need
Plan goals/objectives and strategies to achieve them
Practice those strategies which best address the needs
Evaluate the effectiveness of the chosen strategies
Repeat effective strategies. For those ineffective, repeat the process

Program Development Process

As a model which emphasizes a commitment to continuous improvement based upon ongoing program planning and evaluation, it should be viewed dynamically, like a wheel that is in constant motion.

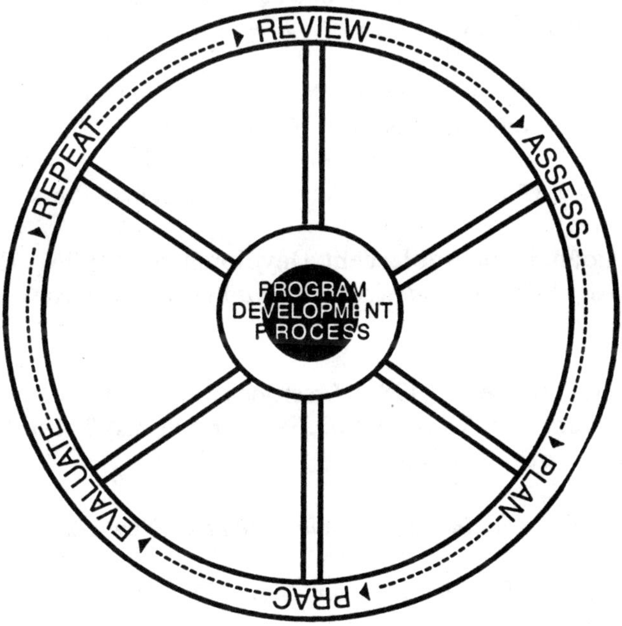

It is hoped that the reader does find this model to be a useful tool to recall and follow this process. Mastery of this challenging process will enable you to become much more competent in planning, implementing, and evaluating programs which specifically address the multiple needs of our target population and offer the best chance for success in the prevention and treatment of substance abuse.

References

Amembal, V. (1991), Peer Leadership: Freeing the Teacher, Building the Student. In S. Moore, A. Sales, & G. Fenstermacher (Eds.). *Preparing tomorrow's teachers in substance abuse prevention*, (pp. 97-106). Tucson, AZ: College of Education, University of Arizona.

Brandsma, J.M., Maultsby, M.C., & Welsh, R. J. (1980). *Outpatient treatment of alcoholism: A review and comparative study*. Baltimore: University Park Press.

Caddy, G. R. (1980). A Review of Problems in Conducting Alcohol Treatment Outcome Studies. In L. C. Sobell, M. B. Sobell, & E. Ward (Eds.), *Evaluating alcohol and drug abuse treatment effectiveness: Recent advances*. New York: Pergamon Press.

Carnegie Council on Adolescent Development. (1996). *Great transitions: Preparing adolescents for a new century*. New York: Carnegie Corporation.

Emrick, C. D., & Hansen, J. (1983). Assertions Regarding Effectiveness of Treatment for Alcoholism: Fact or Fantasy? *American Psychologist, 38,* 1078-1088.

Erikson, E. (1963). *Childhood and society (2nd ed.)*. New York: Norton.

Erikson, E. (1982). *The life cycle completed.* New York: Norton.

Feldman, S. (1973). Budgeting and Behavior. In Feldman, S. (Ed.), *The administration of mental health services*. Springfield, IL: Charles C. Thomas.

Glasser, W. (1992). *The quality school (2nd ed.).* New York: HarperCollins.

Glasser, W. (1994). *The control theory manager.* New York: HarperCollins.

Glasser, W. (1998). *Choice theory: Redefining our personal freedom.* New York: HarperCollins.

Hodges, R.L. (1982). Avoiding Fiscal Management Problems in Human Resource Agencies. *Administration in Social Work, 6,* 61-67.

Hughes, J. (Director). (1984). *The breakfast club* (Film). Universal City Studios.

Kelso, D., & Fillmore, K.M. (1984). *Overview: Alcoholism treatment and client functioning in Alaska.* Anchorage: Center for Alcohol and Addiction Studies, University of Alaska.

Kline, K. (1991). Teachers Count: Making a Difference in Prevention of Drug Use. In S. Moore, A. Sales, & G. Fenstermacher, (Eds.). *Preparing tomorrow's teachers in substance abuse prevention,* (pp.41-45). Tucson, AZ: College of Education, University of Arizona.

Letteri, D. J., Nelson, J. E., & Sayers, M.A. (1985). *NIAAA treatment handbook series 2: Alcoholism treatment assessment research instruments* (DHHS Publication No. ADM 85-1380). Washington, DC: U.S. Government Printing Office.

McLellan, A. T., Luborsky, L., Woody, G. E., & O'Brien, C.P. (1980). An Improved Diagnostic Instrument for Substance Abuse Patients: The Addiction Severity Index. *Journal of Nervous and Mental Disorders, 198,* 26-33.

Moore, S. (1991). Communication Is Not All Talk: The Teacher-Student Relationship. In S. Moore, A. Sales, & G. Fenstermacher, (Eds.). *Preparing tomorrow's teachers in substance abuse prevention.* (pp. 78-86). Tucson, AZ: College of Education, University of Arizona.

Moore, S., Sales, A., & Fenstermacher, G. (Eds.), (1991). *Preparing tomorrow's teachers in substance abuse prevention.* Tucson, AZ: College of Education, University of Arizona.

Moos, R. H., Cronkite, R. C., Billings, A. G., & Finney, J.W. (1984). *Health and daily living form manual.* Palo Alto, CA: Social Ecology Laboratory, Stanford University and Veterans Administration Medical Center.

National Institute on Alcohol Abuse and Alcoholism (1979). *National alcoholism program information system* (NAPIS). Washington, DC: U.S. Government Printing Office.

Rapp, R. (1997). *Reaching the Unreachable Starz* (Video). Columbus, OH: It's A Rapp Productions.

Rapp, R. (1997). *I Remember You Homie* (Video). Columbus, OH: It's A Rapp Productions.

Ruggles, W. L., Armor, D., Polich, J.B., Mothershead, A., & Stephen, M. (1975). *A follow-up study of clients at selected alcoholism treatment centers funded by NIAAA.* Palo Alto, CA.: Stanford Research Institute.

Tobler, N. (1986). Meta-Analysis of 143 Adolescent Drug Prevention Programs: Quantitative Outcome Results of Program Participants Compared to a Control or Comparison Group, *Journal of Drug Issues, 16* (4)537-567.

Tripodi, T., Fellin, P., and Epstein, I. (1978). *Differential social work evaluation.* Itasca, IL: F. E. Peacock.

Wubbolding, R. (1988). *Using reality therapy.* New York: Harper and Row.

Wubbolding, R. (1991). *Understanding reality therapy.* New York: Harper Collins.

Weissbourd, R. (1996). *The vulnerable child.* Reading, MA: Addison-Wesley.

Chapter 13

Substance Abuse and Counseling: An Epilogue

Amos Sales

The focus of this text as outlined in the Preface is on the identification of practical knowledge and skill needed for counseling with individuals with substance abuse problems. The text is written as a resource to assist practitioners, students, and faculty in school counseling, rehabilitation counseling, mental health counseling, or social work in recognizing, preventing, and treating individuals with substance abuse problems. The content is designed to be introductory in nature for counselors in preparation or new to the targeted counseling specialties.

Authors for the text were selected to develop chapters providing in sequence what is believed to be a natural progression of delivery of knowledge about substance abuse and counseling. An early perspective continued throughout the text is that counselors counsel individuals with substance abuse problems. They do not treat substance abuse problems. Information is first provided about substance abuse, defined as including addiction to alcohol, drugs, and process. Models of prevention, diagnosis, and treatment, both individual and group, applicable to various counseling specialty settings are then discussed. Special considerations in working with families and addressing multicultural and disability issues are presented followed by discussions of relapse prevention and program planning and evaluation.

In this content delivery, the authors have met the original intent, to create an overview of the knowledge needed to counsel, within school, rehabilitation, mental health, and social work settings, individuals with substance abuse problems. Information is provided specific to substance abuse and related counseling issues.

Substance abuse as a major social problem and concern for counselors is identified early in the text. It is the most prevalent mind disorder encompassing some 40 percent of the diagnoses in the *DSM-IV* (American Psychiatric Association [APA], 1994) and is estimated to cost the United States billions of dollars yearly (Rice, Kelman, Miller & Dunmeyer, 1990). Substance abuse is also the number one health problem and number one prison problem in the United States (Inaba, Cohen, & Holstein, 1997). Yet, school, rehabilitation, and mental health counselor education programs do not require expertise in this area as a prerequisite to receiving a degree.

As indicated earlier, the text provides an introduction for counselors to the field of substance abuse, an abstract of diagnostic information on drug addictions and related addictive behavior, and an overview of prevention, assessment, and treatment, both individual and group process, issues for counselors. Special considerations in counseling with families, multicultural populations, and individuals with disabilities are identified. Relapse prevention models is discussed as was program planning and evaluation.

The following conclusions regarding counseling with individuals with substance abuse problems are highlighted within different sections of the text.

1. All counselors no matter what work setting or clientele will counsel individuals with presenting or related problems of substance abuse.
2. Counselors must demonstrate the same therapeutic core conditions in counseling individuals with substance abuse problems as they do with other client populations. Their ability to develop an effective relationship is a prerequisite in any counseling setting.
3. Counselors counsel and empower individuals with substance abuse problems versus treat the substance abuse problem.
4. Counselors serve as models of personal awareness and growth for their clients.
5. Counselors need special knowledge and sensitivity to be able to address multicultural, disability, or family issues of clients with substance abuse problems.

6. Counselors working with individuals with substance abuse problems must introspectively assess and resolve their own misbeliefs and stereotypes regarding substance abuse.
7. Counselors must understand that an individual with a substance abuse problem is unique in his/her pattern of use or abuse and treatment needs.
8. Counselors must be able to assess the extent of an individual client's contemporary substance abuse in order to identify, and refer for, appropriate and comprehensive treatment.
9. Counselors must know community resources and procedures for referral to be able to insure access of effective and appropriate support services for clients.

Evaluation of a client's problem with substance abuse can occur in a wide range of counseling settings to include schools, rehabilitation and social service, mental health, and employee assistance programs areas as well as hospital emergency rooms, jails or courtrooms. Depending on the severity of the presenting problem, the client is referred to services appropriate to his/her need. These services can include the short-term, inpatient care lasting three to seven days wherein withdrawal from substance abuse is completed; or intensive outpatient programs lasting eight to twelve weeks wherein clients maintain vocational and family responsibilities while participating in treatment. Another option is the half-way house where moderately structured supportive residential treatment is provided and lasts for three to six months. Here, successful living within the environment becomes part of the treatment plan. Other options, depending on need, include therapeutic communities where clients may remain up to two years in a structured, highly intensive residential treatment program such as Synanon and out-patient alcoholism treatment programs of two kinds, drug-free clinics with services lasting four to six months, and methadone or opiate clinics that a client may attend by medical referral for two to five years.

Within these settings, group treatment is the predominant mode of therapy with individual counseling viewed as adjunct. Counselors should be thoroughly familiar with the facilities and services in his/her community to insure proper referral for clients with substance abuse problems.

Current Issues:

1. The controversy over complete abstinence versus controlled use continues and is the result of lack of conclusive research data. Advantages of abstinence have long been espoused by AA, clinics, hospitals, and supporters of the disease model while others believe that some individuals can learn to control their use and operate at moderate levels of use (Lewis, Dana, and Blevins, 1994). This controversy highlights the issue as to whether or not substance abuse is a disease. Many now view substance abuse on a continuum from problematic to highly problematic. Treatment is related to where the individual is on the continuum and does not assume progression according to the disease model.
2. Coercive versus voluntary treatment continues to be an issue. Voluntary is often a misnomer and "court ordered" treatment is often predominant found in treatment programs. Interestingly, individuals who are court-ordered into treatment do as well or better than those who come to treatment voluntarily (Collins and Allison, 1983). Also, those "coerced" by their employer by the directive of "Either go to treatment or lose your job" do better than voluntary groups (Adelman and Weise, 1989).
3. The professional ownership of career development and its relationship to counseling with individuals with substance abuse problems is receiving much consideration. Career development, all of the psychological, sociological, educational, physical, economic and other factors that are at play in shaping one's career over the life span, is an obvious component of counseling in any setting. School counselors face career development issues with students from pre-school through high school. Agency and mental health counselors have clients who are struggling with life roles, and avocational and vocational issues (Neukrug, 1989). Rehabilitation counselors relate daily with clients whose life choices in terms of work and play have been impacted by recent or long-standing physical or mental disability. Thus, individual problems of substance abuse have singular impact on a client's career development and the career counseling process no matter what counseling setting.

Future Perspectives:

1. The impact of managed care and who and what as third-party payers they would fund continues to have a major impact on substance abuse treatment facilities and counselors. Many programs have gone out of business because of lack of insurance company support of in-patient treatment and have left counselors without employment. Many programs have found new funding but counselors find they no longer meet the requirements these programs must meet to be reimbursed for evaluation and treatment services. There will continue to be a major shift toward credentials and graduate preparation with preparation of counselors requiring the study of multiple disciplines in addition to counseling.
2. Several studies support insurance company trends to not fund in-patient treatment and identify that there is little difference between relatively longer term in-patient treatment and lower cost out-patient therapy (Yung, 1994). This trend will continue as will the even more intrusive "gate keeping" linked to managed care. Managed care gatekeepers, such as pre-authorization specialists, primary care physicians, preferred provider organizations and discharge planners, with more vigor will require counselors and treatment programs to establish precise criteria related to symptoms and behaviors a client must present to be admitted into any level of care. Additionally, they will require counselors to have greater understanding of *DSM-IV* diagnoses to insure employment and receive reimbursement from managed care and insurance companies.
3. National legislation probably will insure more funding through expanded health insurance coverage for counseling of individuals with substance abuse problems. However, as noted earlier, stricter documentation of treatment need and evidence of treatment program effectiveness will be required.
4. New medical breakthroughs will impact the counseling process by eliminating some groups of clients now seeking service by controlling their substance abuse problems through improved psychotropic medications or physical medicine procedures.
5. There will be an increased emphasis on the importance of understanding cultural diversity issues in the counseling process and on the need to recruit underrepresented groups to all the counseling specialties. The concern has been recognized

and emphasized since the 1970's; however, there still exists a relatively smaller representation of minorities in practice than on caseloads in all specialty areas.

6. In the future, there will be an expansion of emphasis on accreditation, credentialing, and standards of practice. One skill-based licensure for all counselors could evolve as a prerequisite for practice. This possibility is influenced in part by managed care and insurance companies. Mental health and school counseling specialties are already seeing themes proposed for their educational preparation which are essentially the same as the content of rehabilitation counselor education programs. These themes include diagnosis and treatment planning, medical issues, crisis intervention, case management, using biopsychosocial assessment data, interpreting assessment data, and systematic case planning.
7. There will be continued innovations in technology and the use of the information highway. This trend will see a parallel increase in the delivery of counseling as well as counselor education degrees on-line.

The above trends will test the limits of our ethical and professional beliefs and practice. Like clients, we, as professional counselors, no matter what counseling setting, must look inward to grow. With exploding change on the horizon, we must empower ourselves. We must take risks, experiment with innovative new strategies and technologies, yet remain grounded in the experience of our past. We, as professional counselors, must be ready to test our personal and professional limits as we move into this new century. I hope this text helps to some degree in that process.

References

Adelman, S. A. & Weiss, R. D. (1989). What is therapeutic about inpatient alcoholism treatment. *Hospital and Community Psychiatry, 40* (5), 515-519.

American Psychiatric Association (1994). *Diagnostic and statistical manual of mental disorders* (4th ed.). Washington, D.C. Author.

Collins, J. J. & Allison, M. (1983). Legal coercion and retention in drug abuse treatment. *Hospital and Community Psychiatry, 34,* 1145-1150.

Inaba, D. S., Cohen, W. E., & Holstein, M. E. (1997). *Uppers, downers and all arounders. Physical and mental effects of drugs and abuse.* Ashland: CNS Publications.

Lewis, J. A., Dana, R. Q., & Blevins, G. A. (1994). *Substance abuse counseling: An individual approach* (2nd ed.). Pacific Grove, CA: Brooks/Cole.

Manfrin, C. (1998). Treatment Settings. In P. Stevens-Smith and R.L. Smith, *Substance abuse counseling theory and practice* (pp. 135-165) Columbus, Ohio: Prentice Hall, Inc.

Neukrug, E. (1989). *The world of the counselor: An introduction to the counseling profession.* Pacific Grove, CA: Brooks/Cole.

Rice, D. P., Kelman, S., Miller, L. S., & Dunmeyer, S. (1990). *The economic costs of alcohol and drug use and mental illness* (U.S. Department of Health and Human Services). San Francisco: University of California, Institute for Health and Aging.

Yung, J. (1994). *Under the influence: Alcohol and human behavior.* Pacific Grove, CA: Brooks/Cole Publishing Co.

Appendices

APPENDIX A

Common Drugs of Abuse

This summary list of common drugs of abuse includes customary methods of administration, general physiological consequences (short-term and long-term), and common slang terms for each.

Several factors determine an individual's response to a drug. These include how the drug is administered, its dosage, whether the drug is taken with another drug, and how quickly it is absorbed and metabolized; individual factors include a person's weight, age, sex, genetic predispositions, physical health, and mental health. Overdose of many of the following drugs can be fatal. All can harm infants of women who use them during pregnancy.

Alcohol

Alcohol is taken orally, and is absorbed into the bloodstream from the entire gastrointestinal tract, affecting the brain, heart, liver, stomach, pancreas, kidneys, and other parts of the body.

Short-term effects: increased heart rate and appetite; dilation of blood vessels; lowered blood pressure; depression of specific areas of the brain, producing lack of coordination, confusion, anesthesia, and coma.

Long-term effects: damage to the brain, heart, liver, pancreas, and nervous system; contributes to certain cancers and various forms of heart disease.

Slang names: booze, liquor, sauce, juice, medicine, moonshine, firewater, cocktails, highballs, nightcaps.

Amphetamines

These substances are taken orally in tablets or capsules, by injection, or smoked or sniffed in powder form. They are absorbed through various parts of the body depending upon the administration mode. These stimulants affect the brain, heart, kidneys, and other organs.

Short-term effects: alertness, mood elevation; increases in heart rate, breathing rate, and blood pressure; dilation of pupils; decreased appetite; dry mouth, sweating; headache, blurred vision, dizziness, and anxiety.

Long-term effects: hallucinations, delusions, and paranoia; weight loss, vitamin deficiencies, and malnutrition; skin disorders; ulcers;

tolerance and dependency.

Slang names: uppers, eye-openers, speed, ups, crystal meth, crystal, hearts, pep pills, ice, jelly beans, black beauties, crank, copilots.

Cocaine

Cocaine is typically sniffed (to inhale fumes), snorted (to inhale the drug in powdered form), smoked (as "crack"), and occasionally injected. Cocaine is absorbed through the mucous membranes in the nose, affecting the brain, lungs and heart.

Short-term effects: muscle relaxation, staggering gait, slow reflexes; sleepiness, slurred speech, disorientation, poor judgment; hangover.

Long-term effects: irritability, agitation, paranoia; nerve damage; impaired liver function; intensification of underlying emotional problems; tolerance and dependency.

Slang names: barbs, blue devils, candy, downers, good balls, reds, red devils, yellows, yellow jacket, pinks, xmas trees, peanuts, ludes, tranks, downs.

Heroin and other opioids

Opioids are a class of drugs that include opium, morphine, codeine, heroin, and methadone. These drugs are absorbed poorly when taken by mouth, so they are usually snorted or injected, although some users inhale fumes off a piece of heated tinfoil. Heroin most easily crosses the blood brain barrier.

Short-term effects: euphoria; pain relief; drowsiness; mood changes; confusion; respiratory depression; dizziness, decreased appetite.

Long-term effects: reduced production of male hormones; vitamin deficiencies, anemia, malnutrition; constipation; indifference to personal hygiene; vulnerability to infection and disease; tolerance and dependence.

Slang names: big H, horse, junk, black tar, brown tar, smack, hard stuff, brown sugar, mud, snow, harry, joy powder, skag, white horse, white stuff, school boy.

Inhalants (solvents, aerosols, and glue)

Inhalants pass without delay through the membranes of the lungs and are quickly absorbed into the bloodstream affecting the brain, lungs, liver, and kidneys.

Short-term effects: euphoria, dizziness, hallucinations; sneezing and coughing; sensitivity to light; nausea; central nervous system (CNS) depression (early stages include blurred vision, headache, skin pallor; medium stages includes drowsiness, incoordination, slurred speech; late stages include seizures, delirium, unconsciousness).

Long-term effects: fatigue; electrolyte (salt) imbalance; nosebleeds; bloodshot eyes; halitosis; facial sores; forgetfulness; tremors; depression, hostility, paranoia; damage to liver, kidneys, and bone marrow.

Slang names: poppers, snappers, glue, laughing gas, locker room, rush, whippets, bullet, bolt.

LSD (lysergic acid diethylamide)

LSD is usually applied in tiny amounts to surfaces that can be licked or ingested such as sugar cubes, small flakes of gelatin, or postage stamps. It is sometimes available in small tablets, capsules, or powder form.

Short-term effects: enlarged pupils; rapid heartbeat, shakiness, rising blood pressure, elevated body temperature, chills and sweats; diminished appetite, nausea; perceptual distortions and hallucinations ranging in nature from pleasurable to terrifying.

Long-term effects: agitation, insomnia, hallucinatory flashbacks after discontinuing use.

Slang names: acid, sugar, fry, window pane, royal blue, heavenly blue, wedding bells, pearly gates.

Marijuana

Marijuana is smoked or taken orally in some foods or beverages and is absorbed by most tissues and organs in the body, finding its way to fat tissues such as those in the brain and reproductive organs. Marijuana predominately affects the brain, lungs, and heart.

Short-term effects: increased heart rate; red eyes; euphoria, reflectiveness, disorientation, sleepiness, lack of coordination; respiratory irritation; memory impairment; increased appetite.

Long-term effects: lung damage; lack of energy and motivation; diminished immune response; accumulation in fatty tissues; impaired learning ability; psychological dependence; paranoia.

Slang names: pot, grass, weed, mary jane, dope, acapulco gold, thai sticks, hemp, reefer, joint, stick, lock weed.

Nicotine

Nicotine is smoked, inhales, or chewed and subsequently is

absorbed through the oral and basal mucous membranes and lungs. It affects the lungs, heart, brain, pancreas, kidneys, bladder, and other organs.

Short-term effects: increased heart rate, blood pressure; stomach acidity; bad breath; reduced sense of taste and smell; decreased skin temperature; stimulation followed by depression of brain and nervous system activity; decreased appetite; diminished physical endurance.

Long-term effects: addiction; chronic bronchitis, emphysema, and other lung diseases; heart disease, stroke; cancers of the lung, larynx, oral cavity, and esophagus; contributes to ulcer disease and cancers of bladder and pancreas; contributes to destruction of gums and discoloration and loss of teeth.

Slang names: smoke, cigs, cancer stick, fag (British term), chew, snuff.

PCP (phencyclidine)

PCP is sold in tablets and capsules, but is more frequently seen in a powder or liquid form that is applied to a leafy material (parsley, mint, oregano, marijuana) and smoked. PCP waned in popularity among young people during most of the 1980s, but beginning in 1989 its use increased again.

Short-term effects: sense of detachment from surrounding environment; numbness; slurred speech; loss of coordination, exaggerated body movements; rapid involuntary eye movements; nausea; elevated blood pressure; auditory hallucinations; sense of strength and invulnerability.

Long-term effects: anxiety; severe depression; violent outbursts; social isolation; schizophrenia-like symptoms; possible irreversible psychosis.

Slang names: angle dust, lovely, hog, killer weed, loveboat.

Reprinted from Moore, S. Sales, A., and Fenstermacher, G. (1991). *Preparing Tomorrow's Teachers in Substance Abuse Prevention.* Tucson, Arizona: University of Arizona Press.

APPENDIX B

Effects of Individual Drugs

Alcohol (depressant)

Alcohol consumption causes a number of marked changes in behavior and impairs judgment and coordination. Signs and symptoms of use include: dilation of blood vessels; lowered blood pressure; lack of coordination; reduced reaction time; and confusion. At the lowest blood levels, the reticular system (a system of numerous large and small neurons and fibers scattered throughout the midbrain, pons, medulla, hypothalamus, and thalamus) begins to malfunction. This disruption interferes with regulation of the cerebral cortex, compromising its integrational and inhibitory ability. Complex, abstract, and poorly learned behaviors are also affected. Moderate to high doses markedly impair higher mental functions, severely altering a person's ability to learn and remember information. At very high doses, alcohol can cause respiratory depression and death.

With continual use, the risk for permanent brain damage increases. In studies comparing brains of rats fed alcohol chronically and in aging rats, findings demonstrate almost identical nervous and cerebrovascular changes, suggesting that chronic alcoholism may accelerate the processes associated with biological aging. Chronic brain injury caused by alcohol is second only to Alzheimer's disease as a known cause of mental deterioration in adults. Many symptoms, such as loss of ability to think abstractly, difficulty with speech, and decreased coordination, are similar in the two types of diseases. Both groups of patients exhibit brain atrophy (shrinkage) and similar abnormalities in brain electrical functioning. One significant difference, however, is that Alzheimer's disease is invariably progressive, whereas alcohol-related mental deterioration can be arrested if alcohol use stops. Lastly, chronic alcohol use has been associated with enlargement of the ventricles and the space between folds in brain tissue.

Amphetamines/methamphetamines (stimulants)

The effects of amphetamines and methamphetamines are in many ways like those of cocaine (to follow in alphabetical order). Amphetamine/methamphetamine effects usually are slower to appear and last longer than cocaine. Both produce euphoria, disappearance of fatigue, and feelings of enhanced physical strength and mental capacity.

In studies with normal volunteers, low doses of amphetamines/

methamphetamines produced elation, increased vigor, arousal, and improved mood; repeated administration, however, adversely affected mood. Conversely, users have reported fright, sensory distortions, hallucinations, chills or sweating, nausea, vomiting, jaw clenching, flushing, increased blood pressure, enlarged pupils, liver problems, impaired balance, and loss of coordination. Other initial physical effects include: increased heat rate, respiratory rate, blurred vision, dizziness, insomnia, anxiety, cardiac irregularities, and loss of weight and appetite. These drugs initially stimulate, then reduce, activity in the brain and central nervous system (CNS). In animals, amphetamines stimulate the medullary respiratory center, reticular activating system (RAS) and cerebral cortex. Such stimulation may lead to lasting symptoms, such as paranoid psychosis in which the user becomes very frightened and out of touch with reality.

Long-term effects of these substances can include hallucinations, delusions, paranoia, depression, and brain damage. Overdose from amphetamines and methamphetamines may cause convulsions, coma, and death.

Caffeine and nicotine (stimulants)

The main pharmacological actions of **caffeine** are exerted on the CNS, heart, kidneys, lungs, and arteries supplying blood to the heart and brain. Caffeine is a powerful stimulant of nerve tissue in the brain. The cortex, being most sensitive, is affected first, followed next by the brain stem. The spinal cord is stimulated last, but only after extremely high doses of caffeine. Heavy consumption (12 or more caffeine-containing beverages a day) can cause more intense effects of agitation, anxiety, tremors, rapid breathing, and cardiac arrhythmias. Excessive doses of caffeine can result in restlessness, depression, increased motor activity, agitation, and hallucinations. Studies raise concern that an association exists between caffeine intake and the incidence of heart attack and increased blood levels of cholesterol.

Like PCP (phencyclidine), **nicotine** acts as both a stimulant and a depressant. It can increase respiration, heart rate, and blood pressure while decreasing appetite. Like caffeine, short-term effects of nicotine lead to increased heart rate and blood pressure, with initial stimulation, then reduction, of brain and central nervous system (CNS) activity. Nicotine intoxication is characterized by euphoria, lightheadedness, dizziness, and elevated heartbeat and respiration. The long-term damage from nicotine use has been widely publicized; regular cigarette smoking is a leading cause of serious diseases of the lungs, heart, and blood vessels. Tobacco use is widely acknowledged as the leading cause of preventable death in the U.S.

Nicotine is a highly addictive drug that may leave some users with a residual nicotine craving, or drug hunger, for life. While use of nicotine among young people generally is not viewed with the same alarm as other drugs, it continues to be a "gateway drug" for many. Adolescents who only smoked cigarettes were significantly more likely to be using other drugs within two years than those who didn't.

Cocaine (stimulants)

Cocaine stimulates at least two sections of the brain, the cerebral cortex (responsible for memory and reasoning), and the hypothalamus (regulates appetite, body temperature, sleep, and certain emotional reactions). Physical signs and symptoms of use include dilated pupils, sweating, constricted blood vessels, increased heart rate and/or palpitations, breathing rate and body temperature, and elevated blood pressure.

The extreme euphoria associated with cocaine use mimics that produced by direct electrical stimulation of the "reward centers" of the brain. Repeated cocaine use upsets the delicate balance of three neurotransmitters (norepinephrine, epinephrine, and dopamine). These chemical messengers function as natural stimulants to the brain. Cocaine causes brain cells to release their supplies of all three, but blocks the brain's normal re-uptake of the neurotransmitters after release, leading to an eventual exhaustion of the natural supply. After constant use, the brain craves this stimulation, progressing to the mental torment associated with cocaine withdrawal.

The first perceptible behavioral change is a loosening of emotional restraint accompanied by a feeling of pleasure. Shortly thereafter, the positive mood intensifies to euphoria and elation. Low doses increase alertness, talkativeness, and feelings of power and energy; they decrease appetite and desire for sleep, sometimes causing anxiety and agitation. Larger doses are associated with impaired judgment, insomnia, irritability, anxiety, and tremors. Long-term or high-dose use leads to seizures, transient psychotic episodes, and paranoia. Acute cocaine poisoning causes profound stimulation of the central nervous system (CNS), progressing to convulsions and respiratory or cardiac arrest. In addition, here are very rare, severe, and unpredictable toxic reactions to cocaine and other local anesthetics in which individuals die rapidly, presumably from cardiac failure.

Depressants (including barbiturates and tranquilizers)

Depressants slow neurochemical activity in the central nervous system (CN). Observable signs of use include: muscle relaxation; calmness, slurred speech; staggering gait; impaired judgment; and slow reflexes. The progression of effects begins with relief from anxiety advancing to suppression of inhibitions and then calmness. Sleep occurs with high doses, and large doses of certain types of barbiturates can produce general anesthesia. Disinhibition (lack of or decreased inhibitions) arises from the suppression of the self-control mechanisms in the cortex and the release of impulses from the lower parts of the brain. This action is also responsible for the drunken euphoria and mood swings characteristic of users. In addition to depression of brain and nerve activity, depressants act similarly on the muscles and heart. They reduce metabolic rate in a variety of tissues and physical systems that use energy as a source of fuel. In normal doses, the sedative-hypnotic compounds appear to be selective in depressing certain CNS pathways affecting wakefulness. The depression of synaptic transmissions with these pathways explains the various stages of behavioral depression caused by these drugs. A depressant overdoes can lower blood pressure and breathing rate, causing coma or respiratory failure and death.

Inhalants (including solvents, aerosols, and glue)

When inhalants are used, vapors pass directly from the lungs into the bloodstream and on to the brain. Short-term effects usually occur in a chain reaction that begins with feelings similar to alcohol intoxication, followed by brief euphoria lasting from a few minutes to an hour, with sensations of excitement and delusions of strength and power. Inhalants such as nitrites trigger a quick drop in blood pressure and a rapid heartbeat that shuts off oxygen to the inner brain. Observable signs include: dizziness, hallucinations, sneezing and coughing, sensitivity to light, nausea, early central nervous system (CNS) depression (disorientation, blurred vision, headache, skin pallor). Medium CNS depression typically follows, including drowsiness, incoordination, and slurred speech, progressing to late CNS depression (seizures, delirium, unconsciousness). Long-term effects produce fatigue, electrolyte (salt) imbalance, forgetfulness, tremors, depression, hostility, paranoia, potential damage to the liver, kidneys, blood, and bone marrow.

Marijuana

Cannabis (the technical name for marijuana) has stimulant, sedative, and hallucinogenic effects on the brain and the body. Absorption of delta-9-tetrahydrocannabinol (commonly known as THC) from the lungs to bloodstream to brain varies, but the average experienced user will absorb into the bloodstream approximately half the ingested dose. Effects are felt almost immediately and reach peak intensity within 30 minutes. The speed of onset is partially determined by the THC concentration. When smoked, the drug increases heart rate and lowers blood pressure, and causes reddening of the eyes.

The effects of low to moderate doses lasts two to six hours and range from relaxation, euphoria, talkativeness, and gaiety to mild fatigue, perceptual changes, lack of coordination, and feelings of heightened sensitivity. High or repeated doses can produce panic reactions in some users, reduced motivation, and distortions of body image. THC becomes concentrated in the body's fatty tissues and further lodges in the liver, lungs, reproductive organs, and brain.

By-products of the chemical breakdown of cannabis remain in the body for several weeks with unknown consequences. It can take three to seven days for the body to rid itself of half the THC in a single joint, and up to 30 days to eliminate completely all traces of the substance. Some THC can remain bound to proteins in the blood.

There is convincing evidence that cannabis produces acute chemical and electrophysiological changes in the brain. Changes in perception, reduced concentration, memory problems, and impaired judgment and coordination can linger up to 24 hours after use. Neurotransmitters, an area in the brain concerned with learning and short-term memory, appear to be the most severely affected.

Some researchers attribute a personality change labeled *amotivational syndrome* to continued marijuana use. This syndrome consists of lack of energy, apathy, absence of ambition, loss of effectiveness, inability to carry out long-term plans, problems with concentration, shortened attention span, impaired memory, impeded communication skills, and a marked decline in school or work performance.

Evidence also suggests that chronic THC exposure damages and destroys nerve cells and causes other pathological changes in the brain. The loss of cells appears to be similar to the loss seen with normal aging, thus long-term marijuana users are at risk for serious or premature memory disorders as they age. These and other effects of cannabis use on memory and thought processing may create long-term problems in learning and social development for adolescent users.

Narcotics (including heroin)

By medical definition, narcotics are opium and opium derivatives or synthetic substitutes. Narcotics act by binding to receptor sites in the brain and digestive tract and stimulating physical reactions. Narcotics act on the central and parasympathetic nervous systems, slowing down body systems, reducing sensitivity to pain, and inducing sleep. Low does produce euphoria, fatigue, analgesia, and impaired concentration, while eliminating the desire for food, sex, and most activity. They also can cause confusion and inability to concentrate. High doses suppress breathing and heart rate, leading to convulsions and death by respiratory failure. Symptoms of use are constriction of pupils, lack of responsiveness to pain, nausea or vomiting, lethargy, slow breathing, and alternating periods of wakefulness and sleep ("nodding off").

PCP and LSD (hallucinogens)

Hallucinogens, including phencyclidine (PCP) and lysergic acid diethylamide (LSD), act primarily on the central nervous system (CSN) by interfering with the production and processing of chemical neurotransmitters in the brain. Effects can last anywhere from four to 12 hours or as long as 24 hours. Hallucinogens produce powerful changes in perception and thinking that are likened to a dream state. Young people who live on the border of reality through frequent drug-induced hallucinations, delusions or false alterations of emotions have little chance of achieving self-fulfillment.

PCP (phencyclidine) interrupts the functions of the neocortex, the area of the brain that controls instincts. Because the drug blocks pain receptors, violent PCP episodes may result in self-inflicted injuries. Time and body movement are slowed down. Muscular coordination worsens and senses are dulled. Speech is blocked and incoherent. A blank stare, rapid and involuntary eye movements, and an exaggerated gait are among the more common observable effects of PCP use. Chronic users of PCP report persistent memory problems, speech difficulties, and emotional and behavior problems, including extreme paranoia and increased aggression. Some of the effects may last six months to a year following prolonged daily use. Some researchers propose that long-term use of PCP is associated with damage to brain tissues, resulting in impaired thinking, memory loss, disorientation, and rapid mood swings, even when the user is not immediately under the influence of the drug.

The question of permanent brain damage resulting from PCP use has not been settled.

Like PCP, LSD can produce mental changes by significantly disrupting normal brain processes due to LSD's close resemblance to the neurotransmitter serotonin. Common physical characteristics of LSD use are dilated pupils, hyperreflexia (exaggerated deep tendon reflexes), nausea, muscular weakness, increased heat rate, and an increase in blood pressure and body temperature. Unpleasant experiences with LSD are relatively frequent and can include confusion, dissociative reactions, acute panic reactions, and reliving of earlier traumatic experiences; in some cases, these reactions have been of an acute psychotic nature necessitating hospitalization.

Reprinted from Moore, S., Sales, A., and Fenstermacher, G. (1991). *Preparing Tomorrow's Teachers in Substance Abuse Prevention.* Tucson, Arizona: University of Arizona Press.

APPENDIX C

Stages of Dependency and Addiction

1. First contact with the substance, person, or activity.

2. Feeling great pleasure with the substance, persons, or activity.

3. Believing that the substance, persons, or activity will improve one's life.

4. Not acknowledging the faults of the substance, person, or activity.

5. Friendships, former interests, work, or health suffer because of one's relationship with the person, activity, or substance.

6. Needing the person, substance, or activity to feel normal.

7. Denying that the substance, activity, or person is hurting one's life when other people point out the problems.

8. Feeling anxious, depressed, angry, or physically ill when the substance, person, or activity is not available.

9. Feeling miserable or uncomfortable when involved with the substance, persons, oractivity but not willing to let it or him/her go.

APPENDIX D

Michigan Alcoholism Screening Test (MAST)*

The Michigan Alcoholism Screening test is probably the most widely used screening instrument to identify someone with an alcohol abuse problem. The MAST is a 25 item true/false tests which asks specific questions about alcohol use and its impact on life situations. The following is a brief version of the MAST.

Brief MAST Questions

- Do you feel that you are a normal drinker?**
- Do friends or relatives think you are a normal drinker?**
- Have you ever attended a meeting of Alcoholics Anonymous?
- Have you ever lost friends or girlfriends/boyfriends because of drinking?
- Have you ever gotten into trouble at work because of drinking?
- Have you ever neglected your obligations, your family, or your work for two or more days in a row because you were drinking?
- Have you ever had delirium tremens (DTs) severe shaking, heard voices, or seen things that weren't there after heavy drinking?
- Have you ever been in a hospital because of drinking?
- Have you ever been arrested for driving drunk?

*Selzer, M. L., Vinokur, A., & Rooijens, L. (1973). A Self-Administered Short Michigan Alcoholism Screening Test (SMAST). *Journal of Studies on Alcohol, 36*(1), 117-126.

**Negative responses are "alcoholic" responses.

APPENDIX E

SARDI Substance Abuse Symptoms Checklist*

Exhibiting one of the symptoms below is not necessarily indicative of substance abuse; however, several or more of these symptoms in combination may suggest that issues related to substance abuse should be explored at greater length.

1. **Frequent intoxication.**
   a. Does the person report or appear to be frequently high or intoxicated?
   b. Do recreational activities center around drinking or other drug use, including getting, using and recovering from use?
2. **Atypical social settings.**
   a. Does the immediate peer group of the individual suggest that substance abuse may be encouraged?
   b. Is the person socially isolated from others and is substance abuse occurring alone?
   c. Is the person reluctant to attend social events where chemicals won't be available?
3. **Intentional heavy use.**
   a. Does the person use "social drugs" with prescribed medications?
   b. Does the person use more than is safe in light of medications or compromised tolerance?
   c. Does the person have an elevated tolerance as evidenced by the use of large quantities of alcohol or other drugs without appearing intoxicated?
4. **Symptomatic drinking.**
   a. Are there predictable patterns of use which are well known to others?
   b. Is there a reliance on chemicals to cope with stress?
   c. Has the person made lifestyle chances yet the drug use has stayed the same or increased? (e.g., changed friends or moved to another area).
5. **Psychological dependence.**
   a. Does the person rely on drugs as a means of coping with negative emotions?
   b. Does the person believe that pain can't be coped with/without medications?

   c. Does the person obviously feel guilty about some aspects of the use of alcohol or other drugs?

6. **Health problems.**
   a. Are there medical conditions which decrease tolerance or increase the risk of substance abuse problems?
   b. Are there recurring bladder infections, chronic infections, bed sores, seizures, or other medical situations which are aggravated by repeated alcohol or other drug use?
   c. Did the disability occur when the individual was under the influence, even if it is denied by the person?
7. **Job problems.**
   a. Is the person underemployed or unemployed?
   b. Has the person missed work or gone to work late due to use of alcohol or other drugs?
   c. Does the person blame the disability for work-related problems?
8. **Problems with significant others.**
   a. Has a family member or friend expressed concern about the person's use?
   b. Have important relationships been lost or impaired due to chemical use?
9. **Problems with law or authority.**
   a. Has the person been in trouble with authorities or arrested for any alcohol or drug-related offenses?
   b. Have there been instances when the person could have been arrested but wasn't?
   c. Does the person seem angry at "the system" and at authority figures in general?
10. **Financial problems.**
    a. Is the person's spending money easily accounted for?
    b. Does the person frequently miss making payments when they are due?
11. **Belligerence.**
    a. Does the person appear angry or defensive but doesn't know why?
    b. Is the person defensive or angry when confronted about chemical use?
12. **Isolation.**
    a. Does increasing isolation suggest heavier substance use?
    b. Is the person giving up or changing social and family activities in order to use?

13. "Handicapism."

a. Does the person focus on disability to the exclusion of other aspects of life?

b. Does the person blame the disability for what goes wrong?

* Ford, J.; Moore, D. (1992). *Substance Abuse Resources and Disability Issues, Training Manual.*

APPENDIX F

Identifying Substance Abuse in Persons with Disabilities

Problem Behaviors	Descriptive Questions
Frequent Intoxication	Does this person report or appear to be frequently high or intoxicated? Do recreational activities center on drinking or other drug use?
Atypical Social Experiences	Does the immediate peer group of the individual suggest that substance abuse may be encouraged? Is the person socially isolated from others and is substance abuse occurring alone?
Intentional Heavy Use	Does the person use "social drugs" with prescribed medications? Does the person use more than is safe in light medications or compromised tolerance?
Symptomatic Drinking	Are there predictable patterns of use that are well known to others? Is there a reliance on chemicals to cope with stress?
Psychological Dependence	Does the person repeatedly rely on drugs as a means of coping with negative emotions? Does the person believe that he or she can't cope with pain without medication?
Health Problems	Are there medical conditions that decrease tolerance or increase the risk of substance abuse problems? Are there recurring bladder infections, chronic infections, bed sores, seizures, or other medical situations that are aggravated by repeated alcohol or other drug use?
Job Problems	Is the person employed or unemployed? Has the person missed work or gone to work late due to abuse of alcohol or other drugs?

Problems with Significant Others	Has a family member or friend expressed concern about the person's alcohol or other drug use?
Problems with Law or Authority	Has the person been in trouble with authorities or arrested for any alcohol or other drug-related offenses?
Financial Problems	Is the person's spending money easily accounted for? Does the person frequently miss making payments when they are due?
Belligerence	Does the person appear angry or defensive but doesn't know why?
Isolation	Does increasing isolation suggest heavier substance abuse? Is the person giving up or changing social and family activities to use alcohol or other drugs?
"Handicapism"	Does the person focus on disability to the exclusion of other aspects of him or herself? Does the person blame his or her disability for what goes wrong?

Note: Reprinted from Journal of Counseling and Development, Vol. 72, Jan./Feb. (1994) with permission.

APPENDIX G

Twelve Steps

Original Twelve Steps

1. We admitted we were powerless over alcohol; that our lives had become unmanageable.

2. Came to believe that a Power greater than ourselves could restore us to sanity.

3. Made a decision to turn our will and our lives over to the care of God *as we understood Him.*

4. Made a searching and fearless moral inventory of ourselves.

5. Admitted to God, to ourselves and to another human being the exact nature of our wrongs.

6. We are entirely ready to have God remove all these defects of character.

7. Humbly asked Him to remove our shortcomings.

8. Made a list of all persons we had harmed and became willing to make amends to them all.

9. Made direct amends to such people wherever possible, except when to do so would injure them or others.

10. Continued to take personal inventory and when we were wrong, promptly admitted it.

11. Sought through prayer and mediation to improve our conscious contact with God *as we understood Him,* praying only for knowledge of His will for us and the power to carry that out.

12. Having had a spiritual awakening as the result of these steps, we tried to carry this message to alcoholics and to practice these principles in all our affairs.

TBI Version by William Peterman

1. Admit that if you drink and/or use drugs your life will be out of control. Admit that the use of substances after having had a traumatic brain injury will make your life unmanageable.

2. You start to believe that someone can help you put your life in order. This someone could be God, an AA group, counselor, sponsor, etc.

3. You decide to get help from others or God. You open yourself up.

4. You will make a complete list of the negative behaviors in your past and current behavior problems. You will also make a list of your positive behaviors.

5. Met with someone you trust and discuss what you wrote in step 4.

6. Become ready to sincerely try to change your negative behaviors.

7. Ask God for the strength to be a responsible person with responsible behaviors.

8. Make a list of people your negative behaviors have affected. Be ready to apologize or make things right with them.

9. Contact these people. Apologize or make things right.

10. Continue to check yourself and your behaviors daily. Correct negative behaviors and improve them. If you hurt another person, apologize and make corrections.

11. Stop and think about how you are behaving several times each day. Are my behaviors positive? Am I being responsible? If not, ask for help. Reward yourself when you are able to behave in a positive and responsible fashion.

12. If you try to work these steps you will start to feel much better about yourself. Now it's your turn to help others do the same.

Helping others will make you feel even better. Continue to work these steps on a daily basis.

b. Stephen Miller House Version of AA 12-Steps (for Individuals who are Deaf)

1. We believe that when we drank, alcohol controlled our lives.

2. We began to believe in a Higher Power that would help us think better.

3. We decided to open our lives to God as we understood Him.

4. With courage, we searched our past to see what was good in us and what should be changed.

5. We admitted to God, to ourselves, and to another person all the wrong things we had done.

6. We became ready for God to take away our defects.

7. We honestly asked God to take away our defects.

8. We made a list of all the people we hurt and wanted to make right the wrongs.

9. We tried to make right the wrong things we did but not when it would hurt another person.

10. We continued to search our lives and when we were wrong admitted it at that time.

11. According to the way we understand God, we prayed and meditated to have better contact with Him and asked that He give us strength and guidance.

12. Having a new understanding of ourselves because of the steps, we tried to help others by sharing what we learned and practice these ideas in all daily activities.

APPENDIX H

Substance Abuse Treatment Approaches

1. Methadone Maintenance

a. For dependence on narcotic analgesics
b. Out-patient
c. Long-term to life
d. Treatment focuses on medication; support services may be provided

2. Therapeutic Community

a. Residential; group centered
b. Long-term: 12-18 months
c. For individuals with negative social adjustments

3. Chemical Dependency Treatment

a. 28 days; Minnesota model; Hazeldon type
b. Intensive, highly structured, 3-6 week regimen
c. Develop and implement recovery plan

4. Out-Patient

a. Short-term to one year
b. Broad range of therapeutic approaches
c. Heterogeneous population

Substance Abuse and Counseling

Facilitator's Manual

Amos Sales, Editor

Preface

This facilitator's resource manual is written to assist in utilizing *Substance Abuse and Counseling*. The text provides several features which makes it a useful tool.

First, this manual is organized on a chapter basis. Each chapter corresponds with the same chapter number and is written by the same author/s as is in *Substance Abuse and Counseling*.

Second, in the beginning of each chapter in this manual, there are brief rationale and overview statements related to the corresponding chapter in *Substance Abuse and Counseling*. These can be utilized as lecture content or reminders to the facilitator of chapter content.

Third, at the end of each chapter are learning objectives with student experiential activities identified for each of the objectives. Authors of each chapter have provided very creative activities to facilitate learning related to their chapters.

Guiding Principles:

The basic purpose of *Substance Abuse and Counseling* is to serve as a resource for developing counseling knowledge and expertise in working with individuals who are substance abusers. It is designed to assist practitioners, students, and faculty in school counseling rehabilitation, counseling, mental health counseling, school psychology, or social work in recognizing, preventing, and treating individual substance abuse problems. The quality of the counseling relationship is viewed as the key factor related to treatment outcome. This is believed to be true across all addictions, populations, and settings, no matter the age of clients or whether treatment is individual or group based.

Text Design:

This text is designed to assist those using *Substance Abuse and Counseling* as a text within a separate course, as a text to integrate or infuse knowledge and expertise into an entire master's sequence of study, or, in relation to suggestions in these areas, as a text for in-service training. It is designed as a practical guide for teaching content through guided experiential experiences. Each chapter is written by the author/s of the corresponding chapter in *Substance Abuse and Counseling*.

The expectation is that students or trainees will have read the chapter content. Then, the facilitator can utilize the chapters herein as classroom or training experiences for students. Each chapter provides a Rationale, Overview, and Objectives statement related to the broader chapter text. Objectives are written for each section within the chapters. Class activities or learning experiences are provided in relation to the objectives. Class activities as provided involve the facilitators and the students in cooperative experiential learning. The experiential class activities are provided for a variety of reasons. They help the instructor move away from the sole delivery of content through the lecture and toward more personalized learning experiences for students. These activities help students explore their own personal values in relation to substance abuse issues. Typically, students run the gamut of substance abuse experience from total abstinence to substance abuse. The majority are students whose own lives have been impacted by their own use of psychoactive substances or by that of family members or friends. They are aware of the negative impact of drugs, and the continuing impact it will have on their personal and professional lives. The exercises provided assist students in clarifying their own beliefs, personal values about, and attitudes toward substance abuse in our society.

Stand-Alone Course:

The chapters in *Substance Abuse and Counseling* and the corresponding chapters in this text are designed to sequentially deliver the knowledge needed to teach an introductory course in substance abuse and counseling. Each chapter in sequence could be utilized as the weekly assigned content for class and the required reading for that class. An abstract of the content covered in the required chapter reading for that week in *Substance Abuse and Counseling* would be presented by the facilitator in class. Alternative means of covering this content could be through films, videos, or guest presentations. Classroom activities then would be utilized from the corresponding chapter in this text to facilitate student experiential learning. More activity options are provided for each chapter than could be utilized in one class period so the facilitator can pick and choose which would more appropriately meet his/her and student needs.

Infused into Curriculum:

Some problems exist for counselor educators in attempting to develop and deliver a stand-alone course. Most counseling sequences of study cannot add another required course without adding another semester or quarter of study to a student's length of study. Even if a course could be added, the decision to integrate or infuse the knowledge related to substance abuse and counseling into current counselor education required courses would be appropriate for several reasons. First, there is some research in the prevention field in public schools that indicates infusion of the knowledge into "regular" offerings has more impact in terms of retention of learning. Second, integration provides for "ownership" of the substance abuse and counseling information by all faculty not just the one teaching the stand-alone course in this area.

If faculty commitment to address infusion into the curriculum exists, a very simple procedure can be utilized for faculty to integrate the knowledge and learning activities in these two texts into a counselor education sequence of study. The procedure is to have one faculty member chair a committee of the faculty as a whole to identify where and how the content and related activities for each chapter fit within current required courses. Individual faculty review both texts to determine which chapter or parts of chapters fit within the courses he/she currently teaches. Obvious examples of how these chapters could be integrated into current counselor education programs relate to the chapters on individual counseling, on group work and relapse prevention, and on assessment. All counselor education programs have required courses in these areas and the content of these chapters could easily be integrated as units to be addressed in these courses. Other chapters such as drug addiction, working with families, multicultural issues, and program planning and evaluation would be linked to coursework wherein these issues or related issues are addressed. Once all faculty have reviewed the texts and identified the content which fits within their courses, they can as a full committee meet to determine if all the content is or can be addressed. The chair of the committee at this time would attempt to insure through negotiation that faculty have accepted all of the content into current required courses. Maintaining a file on how this content has been infused into the curriculum will be beneficial in not having to yearly "reinvent the wheel" but more importantly as documentation of this educational activity for credentialing bodies.

Workshops:

The content of these texts can be utilized by facilitators of workshop and/or training sessions linked to all or part of the knowledge provided in the texts. Much like the strategy discussed under the *Stand-Alone Course* section, the facilitator would first decide the emphasis and length of training and related chapters to cover. The facilitator, as in the *Stand-Alone Course* section, would require that chapter/s be read prior to training, would present an abstract lecture related to the chapter/s, and then involve participants in appropriate experiential learning activities. Versus presenting the brief lecture him or herself, facilitators could utilize films, videos, or guest presenters– professionals and/or clients–to briefly introduce the topic and then move to experiential activities. Use of this content is limited only by creativity.

This manual has been written in a user-friendly manner. It is easy to read and utilize. Readers should find it a crucial supplement to their work as teachers or facilitators in the area of substance abuse and counseling.

Amos Sales

Contributors

Tina Buck, MA, CRC, CPC

Tina Buck has worked in the dual-diagnosis and addictions treatment field since 1991. She has worked in residential treatment settings in Arizona and Hawaii, as well as provided out-patient counseling services in rural Arizona settings with children, adolescents, and adults. Tina earned her bachelor of science and master of arts degrees from the University of Arizona in Tucson, AZ. She is currently a doctoral student and graduate associate in rehabilitation education at the University of Arizona. Her interest is the application of integrated medicine to the field of rehabilitation.

William English, Ph.D.

Dr. R. William (Bill) English received the doctoral degree in Counseling and Behavioral Studies from the University of Wisconsin, Madison. Dr. English's postdoctoral positions have been at Syracuse University, the University of Oregon, and The Florida State University (FSU). Currently, he is a Professor of Rehabilitation Counseling and Counseling Psychology at FSU. Administratively, he is the Coordinator of the FSU Rehabilitation Services undergraduate degree program and Chair of the Department of Human Services and Studies, College of Education.

Dr. English is a recipient of the Research Achievement Award from the American Rehabilitation Counseling Association, for a nationwide, state-of-the-art study of rehabilitation supervision in state vocational rehabilitation agencies. He has produced 65 publications and made over 250 professional presentations on topics concentrated in five content areas: (1) psychological-social aspects of adjustment; (2) supervisory management; (3) leadership development; (4) family involvement in rehabilitation; and (5) service delivery practices in counseling and rehabilitation.

Dr. English has done an extensive amount of continuing education, in addition to teaching over 20 different university courses, and provided research or clinical supervision to numerous students. Bill English is married to a counselor (Norma) and has two grown children (Becca and Robb), both of whom are professionals in human services.

Amy Friedman

Amy Friedman is a graduate of the University of Wisconsin-Madison. She is currently a doctoral student at the University of Arizona in Rehabilitation. She is also the Program Manager for a local vocational rehabilitation agency.

Charlene Kampfe, Ph.D.

Dr. Charlene M. Kampfe has a Ph.D. in rehabilitation counseling from the University of Arizona. She has a CRC, an NCC and an NCGC and is presently an Associate Professor of the Department of Special Education, Rehabilitation, and School Psychology; with a secondary appointment in Gerontological Studies at the University of Arizona, Tucson. Dr. Kampfe has been on the Governing Council of the American Counseling Association (ACA), has served as president of the Association for Adult Development and Aging (AADA), and is presently serving on the Board of the American Rehabilitation Counseling Association (ARCA). She has over 40 publications, has many more than 50 presentations, and has received the Outstanding Research Award from Chi Sigma Iota/ERIC-CASS. She has received the distinguished Service Award and the Mentor Award from AADA. She has received two state awards for outstanding service and teaching. She has received two outstanding faculty awards from the University of Arizona.

Leslie C. McAllan, Ph.D., CRC

Dr. McAllan received his B.S. Degree in Psychology and his MS Degree in Rehabilitation Counseling from the University of Wisconsin-Milwaukee in 1973 and 1975 respectively. Sine that time he has had extensive individual and group clinical experience as a rehabilitation counselor and licensed psychologist in private and public settings. As an Assistant Professor at the University of Arizona for the past eight years, Dr. McAllan has had primary responsibility for coordinating the delivery of undergraduate and graduate degree programs utilizing work-study and distance learning models. He is Past-President of the Arizona Rehabilitation Association and President of the US/Mexico Disability Resource Consortium. Dr. McAllan's research interests include studying the effectiveness of different models of degree delivery, spirituality and disability, and psychosocial responses to disability.

Eva Miller, Ph.D.

Dr. Eva Miller has extensive experience working with adults aged 18 through old age with multiple psychiatric disorders, cognitive impairments, physical and developmental disabilities, and coexisting substance abuse problems. She has taught a number of courses as the University of Arizona at the graduate and undergraduate level, including Rehabilitation Counseling Practicum I and II, Rehabilitation Service Delivery, Strategies of Vocational Development and Supported Employment, Rehabilitation of the Aged, and Interviewing and Client Services. For the past two years, Dr. Miller has been responsible for developing, coordinating, and facilitating ongoing educational opportunities and statewide training for community rehabilitation programs in accordance with a federally funded grant. Prior to obtaining her doctorate degree at the University of Arizona in 1999, Dr. Miller worked for the Arizona Department of Economic Security, Division of Developmental Disabilities for 13 years as a training specialist, case manager, and most recently as the coordinator of residential services.

Shitala Mishra, Ph.D.

Shitala P. Mishra is Professor of School Psychology in the Department of Special Education, Rehabilitation, and School Psychology at the University of Arizona. His research spans a broad array of methodological and substantive concerns related to the delivery of school psychological services to school-age children and youth. He has published widely in the areas of clinical and cognitive assessment, applied psychometrics, and nondiscriminatory assessment. He is currently serving as an Associate Editor of *Journal Adolescent Research.* He also serves as a member on the editorial boards of several journals in education and psychology fields.

Susan Fordney Moore, Ph.D.

Susan Fordney Moore is a faculty member in the Department of Special Education, Rehabilitation, and School Psychology at the University of Arizona. A licensed psychologist and certified rehabilitation counselor, Dr. Moore has extensive experience in prevention, education, and treatment of addiction. As the former Director of the Smith Project for Substance Abuse Prevention/Education, she oversaw the development of a pre-service prevention curriculum for teacher preparation which has been used on a national basis. She teaches coursework in Prevention of Addictions, Problems of Drug Abuse, and Rehabilitation of the Public Offender.

Thomas Mullis, Ph.D.

Dr. Mullis holds a Ph.D. in counseling from the University of Utah. He is a professor of psychology u the counseling center at Radford University in Radford, Virginia. He is a licensed professional counselor in Virginia, He teaches graduate courses in counseling psychology and adolescent psychology. He has worked in private practice for over twenty years. Recently, he published a text on *State Licensure Requirements for Professional Counselors.*

Robert E. Rapp, Ph.D.

Robert E. Rapp, Ph.D. is a Professor of Counseling at Western New Mexico University in Silver City. He is a National Certified Counselor (NCC), a National Certified School Counselor (NCSC), and a Licensed Professional Clinical Mental Health Counselor (LPCC) in New Mexico. He is certified in Reality Therapy and is a Faculty member of The William Glasser Institute. He is also a Professional Associate of The Center For Quality Education. In addition, he currently serves as a consultant and therapist for at-risk students.

During his career, Dr. Rapp has developed and directed numerous innovative human service programs for children, adolescents and adults. He specializes in working with at-risk and delinquent children and adolescents. Most recently, he has concentrated upon developing substance abuse, violence and gang prevention and intervention programs.

Charrles Reid, Ph.D., CRC

Chuck Reid, Ph.D., CRC, is an assistant professor at the University of Texas-Pan American. He earned a doctorate in Special Education and Rehabilitation from The University of Arizona. His research interests include second language acquisition, non-captive cocaine users, cultural compatibility, and mental health issues.

Robert A. Ressler

Robert A. Ressler is a graduate student at the University of Arizona. He is pursuing a graduate degree program in School psychology. He has wide ranging experiences in working with school-age children and youth from Native American and Hispanic cultures.

Amos Sales, Ed.D., CRC

Dr. Sales, Professor, and Director, Rehabilitation Programs, University of Arizona, has devoted his academic, research, and service efforts over the past 34 years to human resource development within education and rehabilitation. Since 1985, Dr. Sales' research, program development, and service have been devoted to the field of prevention of substance abuse and the application of prevention concepts and practices to professional preparation and development. Dr. Sales formulated the original proposal for the University of Arizona Smith Project, which assumed a leadership position nationally in teacher education and substance abuse prevention. His work has resulted in publications and model demonstration programs of national impact.

Dr. Sales, through successful competition, has received yearly funding under grants and contacts to administer research, model service delivery, and personnel preparation programs. He has been awarded over forty grants and/or contracts totaling just over $17,000,000. Dr. Sales has developed and taught coursework in all content and experiential areas in rehabilitation at the undergraduate and graduate levels.

Dr. Sales' significant professional contributions have been recognized at the local, state, and national levels through the receipt of over thirty (30) citations, certificates or awards. He is unique in having received the highest awards provided by the National Rehabilitation Association at the state, regional, and national levels for distinction in professional contributions to the fields of education and rehabilitation. He has served as President of the National Rehabilitation Association and recently received the National Council on Rehabilitation Education's "Distinguished Career Award." Dr. Sales has published over forty (40) refereed articles, chapters, or monographs. Since 1988, he has published eight (8) articles and one (1) book specifically *Preparing Tomorrow's Teachers in Substance Abuse Prevention.* Dr. Sales is an Arizona Licensed Psychologist and a Certified Rehabilitation Counselor.

Mae Smith, Ph.D.

Dr. Mae Smith has been a member of the Rehabilitation Counseling faculty at the University of Arizona for 23 years. She has taught substance abuse courses at the University of Arizona, the University of Wisconsin - La Crosse and the University of Wisconsin - Stout. Dr. Smith has extensive experience working with clients from Junior High School age through old age (mid 90's) who sought assistance for substance abuse problems. Prior to joining the faculty at the University of Arizona, Dr. Smith directed a closed therapeutic community in Florida for female felons who resided in the program 24 hours a day for up to 18 months and whose substance abuse histories and criminal histories were so severe that they qualified for no other available treatment program. In addition Dr. Smith developed a treatment program for persons with narcotics addictions assigned to the Departments of Corrections and Parole in Florida; conducted Ala Teen groups in Wisconsin; has conducted individual, group and couples counseling related to substance abuse issues for young , middle aged and older adults; and provided psychological evaluations related to substance abuse in both hospital and non-hospital settings for persons with a wide-range of disabilities. In addition to publishing in the area of substance abuse, Dr. Smith was the Founding Editor of the Journal of Offender Counseling which has been renamed the Journal of Correctional Counseling and Addictions.

Evans Spears

Evans Spears is a doctoral student at the University of Arizona majoring in Rehabilitation Education and minoring in Special Education. Evans received his BA in Psychology at Coe College in Cedar Rapids, IA and his MA in Rehabilitation Counseling from the University of Iowa. He is a certified Rehabilitation Counselor and has worked in a variety of state, non-profit, and for-profit settings. His major area of expertise is working with persons with HIV/AIDS, especially children with AIDS in educational settings. Evans has done extensive work with groups, again specializing in working with persons with HIV/AIDS.

Susan Varhely, Ph.D.

Dr. Susan Varhely received her doctoral degree in counselor education from the University of North Texas in 1984. Since that time, she has held counselor education positions, maintained a private practice, and provided consultation to a variety of social service agencies, with emphasis in the substance abuse specialty. While an Assistant Professor at Drake University, she created a masters program in Addictive Disorders and worked in close partnership with in-patient treatment facilities in Des Moines. Dr. Varhely is currently an Associate Professor in the Department of Counseling at Adams State College, Alamosa, Colorado and teaches the addictions component of the CACREP program.

TABLE OF CONTENTS

Chapter I

Substance Abuse and Counseling: An Introduction

Amos Sales

Rationale

Substance abuse is a critical problem in the United States across all segments of the population. Given this problem, it is imperative that counseling professionals are educated about substance abuse as a disability. All counselors, no matter what their professional specialty or setting, will encounter clients with presenting or related problems of substance abuse. Thus, it is critical that all counselors in practice or in counselor education programs understand the presenting problems of clients with substance abuse issues and addiction and related prevention and treatment strategies.

Overview

This chapter briefly defines substance abuse and its causation and prevalence. Counseling perspectives related to working with individuals with substance abuse problems are discussed. The types of counselors working with clients with substance abuse problems is identified.

Objectives

1. To identify the definition of substance abuse as utilized within the text.
2. To increase awareness of why the development of a personal position on causation of substance abuse problems is of importance to counselors.
3. To increase awareness of the prevalence of substance abuse in our society.
4. To increase understanding of counseling perspectives and goals important in counseling individuals with substance abuse problems.
5. To increase understanding of who counsels individuals with substance abuse problems in our society.

Activities

Exercise I: Options Linked to Objective I

1. Ask students to discuss the difference between self-medicating with non-prescription drugs for physical pain and discomfort and self-medicating with mind-altering substances for psychic pain and discomfort.

2. Ask students to brainstorm a list of chemical substances that they use to make themselves feel better or relieve pain. Write the list on the board. Ask students to take each example and describe a situation where it is used constructively (if any) or destructively.

   Examples:

   - coffee, tea, or cola
   - over-the-counter drugs such as aspirin, cough and cold remedies, antacids, etc.
   - alcohol
   - cigarettes
   - marijuana or other illegal drugs

3. Have students brainstorm and list expressions and ad slogans that promote alcohol use ("Happy Hour," etc.). Then have students describe the images evoked by these slogans.
4. Have students record the number of messages promoting use of alcohol or other drugs seen in a 24-hour period. Include source of message, name of chemical substance, and brief content description; or have students keep track of messages on TV related to use of alcohol or other drugs during a major sporting event. Discuss any conflicting messages.

Exercise II: Options Linked to Objective 2

1. Brainstorm with the class about reasons why people use drugs. Have several students write down the answers on either the blackboard or flip chart. Remind students that brainstorming does not involve judgments. All comments are accepted "as is" with the exception of asking for clarification to ensure that a student's idea has been accurately captured.

Use the list to begin a discussion that encourages students to examine sociodemographic variables, personality factors, family influences, and the desire for enhanced appearance, recreation, and other major influences that promote substance abuse among youth. The following questions may help students explore these varied reasons:

- What have you become aware of during this brainstorm?
- In what way might it be important or unimportant for counselors to understand these complex reasons?
- Given the many reasons why kids may be using drugs, what role can the school be expected to play in prevention?

Summarize what the class has discussed, emphasizing major risk factors and the need to be sensitive to and respectful of individual differences. Point out stereotypes regarding drug use and reinforce how responding to these generalizations is not helpful in developing and nurturing responsible people.

2. Have students brainstorm reasons for substance use and abuse, and transcribe student responses on large sheets of newsprint or blackboard.
   Examples: boredom, stress, recreation, low self-esteem, peer pressure, rebellion
   List as headings across the board or paper the various prevention approaches that have been employed since the turn of the century:
   - moral objection (1900s)
   - legal sanctions (1920s)
   - scare tactics (1930s and 1940s)
   - drug education (1960s)
   - effective education (1970s)
   - social skills training (1970s and 1980s)
   - health and wellness emphasis (1980s)
   - alternative activities (1980s)

Examine each reason for substance abuse and list it under the prevention approaches that are most likely to be effective in addressing the underlying motivations.

Example:

Wellness	Scare Tactics	Affective Education	Alternative Activities
Recreation	Rebellion	Low self-esteem	Recreation
Boredom		Peer pressure	Boredom
Stress		Stress	Holidays
Low self-esteem			

Finish this activity by facilitating classroom discussion that focuses upon two points:

(1) people use substances for different reasons; and
(2) each of the various approaches to prevention and treatment are associated with some (but not all) of these reasons.

Exercise III: Options Linked to Objective 3

1. Have students break into groups of four to five to have individual members discuss the impact of substance abuse on their lives. Have them identify whether family, friends, or acquaintances have had substance abuse problems. Per personal experience, what do individuals view as the prevalence of substance abuse problems in our society? Leave time for large group discussion of this activity.

Exercise IV: Options Linked to Objective 4

1. Have students work in small groups of four or five to generate ideas for specific counselor behaviors that 1) may help to counteract risk factors among their clients for later substance abuse and 2) may help such clients overcome substance abuse problems.

Leave sufficient time for a designated member from each group to report the group's ideas to the entire class. Summarize input, reinforce appropriate counseling perspectives and goals.

Exercise V: Options Linked to Objective 5

1. Have class break into groups of four or five members. Identify one counseling specialty per group, i.e., school counseling–group one, rehabilitation counseling–group two, etc. Have groups brainstorm and have a recorder list the types of substance abuse problems that their designated counselor might face. Leave time for groups to report to full class. Discuss similarities and differences, if any, across groups.

Chapter 2

Drug Addiction

Mae Smith and Eva Miller

Rationale

Drug addiction has reached epidemic proportions in America over the last decade. The detrimental effects of drugs on the human body and brain are widespread. A number of physiological and psychological characteristics of the user as well as sociocultural environmental factors of the user have been associated with drug addiction. Drug classification systems have been established to organize drugs based on their medicinal properties and their potential for abuse; and the legal system has taken action to reduce and prevent drug addiction. Education on the effects of drugs, characteristics of drug users, and legal measures established to combat drug use can have a major impact on drug addiction.

Overview

The following lesson describes the characteristics of some of the most commonly used drugs in America. The effects of these drugs on functioning are identified. Examination of the physiological, psychological, and sociocultural characteristics of the drug user can assist students in identifying risk factors associated with drug addiction. An understanding of drug classification systems provides valuable information regarding a drug's potential for abuse. Knowledge of the laws that have been enacted to reduce and prevent drug addiction are important to increase students' comprehension of drug addiction.

Objectives

1. To increase awareness of the characteristics of commonly used drugs in America.
2. To increase understanding of acute and chronic effects of drugs on physiological, psychological, and cognitive functioning.
3. To increase understanding of physiological and psychological characteristics of the drug user.
4. To increase understanding of sociocultural environmental characteristics of the drug user.
5. To increase awareness of drug classification systems.
6. To increase awareness of federal laws established to reduce and prevent drug addiction.

Activities

The following exercises will provide students with opportunities to learn about commonly used drugs and the relationship between drug addiction and environmental influences, biological factors, and drug classification systems and laws. Each exercise corresponds with the respective objectives identified above.

Exercise I for Objective 1: Characteristics of Drugs

Divide students into small groups of two to six.

1. Provide each group with written information regarding the characteristics of one or two drugs (e.g., alcohol and/ or marijuana).
2. Inform each group that they will be presenting the information they have received to the other students at a "Drug Fair."
3. Provide examples of the various ways in which students can present the information they have received (e.g., posters, verbal presentations, brochures, overheads).
4. Allow students 20-30 minutes to prepare their presentations.
5. Request half the groups to present their information at the Drug Fair while the other half serve as members attending the fair. Allow 10-12 minutes for students to visit each "drug booth." A bell or switching the lights on/off can be used as the signal for students to move to the next booth.
6. After students have visited each drug booth, request them to provide information on characteristics of the drugs they have been assigned to cover while the other groups visit each drug booth (again 10-12 minutes per booth).

Exercise II for Objective 2: Acute and Chronic Effects of Drugs

A minimum of 11 students are required for this "Hollywood Squares" exercise.

1. Request two students to serve as contestants (contestant "X" and contestant "O").
2. Request nine students to serve as famous celebrities. Provide name tags for students to identify themselves (e.g., Tom Cruise, Nicole Kidman).

3. Request additional students to serve as the TV audience.

4. The instructor serves as the game show host (Whoopi Goldberg).
5. Explain the rules of the Hollywood Squares game ("TIC-TAC-TOE").
   A. Contestants take turns choosing a celebrity who in turns answers a question relating to the effects of drugs on functioning (e.g., "True or False: Chronic use of marijuana does not produce dependence in moderate dosages."). The instructor (Whoopi) reads the questions (questions can also be displayed on overheads).
   B. The contestant has the option of agreeing or disagreeing with the celebrity's response. If the contestant responds correctly (e.g., agrees with the celebrity when the celebrity provides a correct response) the celebrity will hold up an "O" for contestant "O" and an "X" for contestant "X."
   C. The first contestant to get "TIC-TAC-TOE" (three Xs or three Os horizontally, vertically, or diagonally) wins the game.
6. The game takes between 20-30 minutes and can be played several times so students who served as the TV audience can participate as contestants or celebrities.

Exercise III for Objectives 3 and 4: Physiological, Psychological, and Sociocultural Characteristics of the Drug User

Divide students into groups of four to eight.

1. Inform students that they are being given an opportunity to convey information in a creative way by role playing an "infomercial" pertaining to the physiological, psychological, and sociocultural characteristics of drug users.
2. Provide each group with packets of information on the characteristics of drug users.
3. Provide each group with directions informing them of the type of infomercial they are being requested to role play. An example of an "Oprah" infomercial is presented

below:

A. Your group will be acting out a segment from the "Oprah" show.

B. The host (Oprah) and cast in the show will be acting out information provided in your packet (i.e., psychological characteristics of drug users). Everyone is to participate in the Oprah segment (which can include commercial breaks).

C. Your group is to work together to plan the Oprah segment which will be approximately 15 minutes in length. Everyone is expected to play a role in the show (e.g., Oprah, an expert on the psychological characteristics of drug users such as a psychologist or a physician, a drug user and his/her family members).

D. When you convey the information presented in your packet, you are encouraged to be creative. Examples include:

E. Allow approximately 30 minutes for groups to prepare their infomercials.

Exercise IV for Objective 5: Drug Classification Systems

Divide students into five groups.

1. Assign each group member a number from one to five. If there are more than five members in each group, assign two or three students the same number (e.g., if there are 10 students in a group, two students will be assigned as number one, two will be assigned as number two, etcetera.
2. Inform students that they will leave their "home groups" for 15-20 minutes to become experts on the five drug classification categories/schedules. Students in each expert groups will be assigned one drug classification schedule.
3. Students in each expert group are to compile information relating to their assigned drug classification schedule. This information can be obtained from the textbook and additional information (e.g., articles) provided by the instructor.
4. Request students to return to their home groups after 15-20 minutes. Each student will be asked to share information they obtained/compiled in their expert groups. The concept is for each student(s) to provide pieces of information (or parts of a jigsaw puzzle) that will ultimately result in completion of

the entire drug classification system (the five classification schedules or the entire puzzle).

5. Facilitate a debriefing on the five drug classification systems (10-15 minutes) with the entire class to ensure that they have accurate information.

Exercise V for Objective 6: Drugs and the Law

1. Facilitate a discussion on the rationale for laws designed to reduce and prevent drug addiction in the United States. Discuss historical perspectives (e.g., social, economic, and moral implications) that have led to current drug legislation.
2. Facilitate further discussion on federal drug-related laws (state and local if desired) that are currently in existence.
3. Divide students into groups of two to six to discuss their views pertaining to the effectiveness of current drug legislation, reasons why they believe legislation has or has not been effective for reducing or preventing drug addiction, speculation of future trends regarding drug addiction based on current legislation, and recommendations for revising or creating additional drug-related laws.
4. Facilitate a large group (class) debriefing of the small group activity.

Chapter 3

Related Addictive Behavior

Tina Buck & Amos Sales

Rationale

Addictive disorders other than those to alcohol, tobacco, and other drugs are prevalent in our society and it is common for individuals with substance addictions to also struggle with other addictive processes. Counselors need to understand related addictions for the purpose of supporting clients in maximizing their recovery potential.

Overview

This lesson provides criteria established for different process addictions and includes diagnostic and treatment information that are unique to eating disorders, pathological gambling, sexual addictions, and work addiction. Considerations regarding treatment of multiple addictions, issues related to overlapping psychiatric disorders, insurance and managed care, and referrals for more information are provided.

Objectives

1. To increase awareness of the prevalence of addictive disorders other than substances.
2. To increase awareness of the diagnosis and treatment issues that are specific to eating, gambling, sexual, and work addiction disorders.
3. To practice collaboration with other professionals in developing treatment plans for persons challenged with multiple addictive disorders.

Activities

Exercise I for Objective 1: Prevalence of Other Addictive Disorders

1. Request that students work individually to create a family tree for the purpose of bringing awareness of possible process addictions that are present within their own family systems.
2. Request students keep a journal with weekly entries relating to media representations of relationships to food and body image, gambling opportunities, sexual messages, and work related issues. Suggest that they process their own experiences in these areas.
3. Request that students break into groups of eight to ten and develop a list of high profile individuals who have been

identified in the media as having eating, gambling, sex, or work addictions. Have a large class discussion about the stigma attached to each of these people after their addiction became public.

Exercise II for Objective 2: Diagnosis and Treatment

1. Request that students break into four small groups for the purpose of discussing the diagnostic criteria for the four areas covered in this chapter: eating, gambling, sex, and work addictions. Ask each group to discuss the diagnostic criteria for each area, to brainstorm about what substances clients engaging in each area may abuse and why, and then present to the large group their findings.
2. Request students examine the similarities and the differences between substance addictions and related addictive disorders. In a large group discussion, request that they discuss what they imagine the similarities and differences are between treating substance addictions and related addictive disorders.
3. Request that the students break into four small groups, assigning each group one of the related addictive disorders, and have them brainstorm about possible triggers that are unique to each area, and how they would work with clients in a relapse prevention plan to deal with those triggers.

Exercise III for Objective 3: Developing a Treatment Plan

1. Break the class into two groups and have each group assign roles to group members that represent a multi-disciplinary treatment team consisting of a counselor, case manager, psychiatrist, psychologist, family therapist, as well as developing a role that will benefit the team in making treatment decisions specific to their client example. Assign each group one of the following client examples and have them collaborate in developing a treatment plan that is appropriate to the needs of the case.

Client Example

Tania is the youngest in a family of four children. Tania's mother was obese and a chronic dieter. She relied on Tania as her "overeating companion" and placed Tania on her first diet at the age of eight. Tania had mixed messages from her family of origin concerning food and body image. During early adolescence Tania was date raped and became depressed. Shortly after this incident she began reading about nutrition and health in magazines and started refusing to eat foods that had any fat content. Tania stayed busy with sports activities in school and regularly skipped meals. Tania wore baggy clothing and often made negative comments about her body to others. Around the age of 17 she learned how to purge and engaged in this behavior after most meals in addition to using laxatives. Her intake of food began to fluctuate and she went through periods of fasting alternating with other periods during which she ate copious amounts of soft foods such as peanut butter and oatmeal after which she purged. She thought about her body image over 70% of her waking hours. During her freshman year in college, Tania began having posttraumatic stress disorder (PTSD) symptoms from the date rape trauma and began using crystal methamphetamine intravenously. She sought help for her eating disorder when she produced failing grades during her first sophomore year and began experiencing suicidal ideation. During her assessment, she reported daily symptoms including use of one box of laxatives, purging up to three times, and participating in two hours of aerobic exercise, and weekly use of between two to three grams of crystal methamphetamine.

Client Example

At a young age, Jeffrey was repeatedly molested by a babysitter over a two year period. After this, he began masturbating in private and, at times, in the classroom. He was told that the behavior was evil and that he was a bad boy who should know better. To cope with his shame, Jeffrey began overeating and began a lifetime problem with obesity. As Jeffrey got older he began using pornographic material to enhance his sexual experience and, over time, began objectifying women and fantasizing about sexual encounters with women with whom he worked. He began smoking cigarettes in an attempt to control his weight. Jeffrey lost several jobs for repeatedly spending time away from his desk job while masturbating in the company restroom and visiting local peep show during extended lunch breaks. Jeffrey's monthly phone bill amounted to an average of $2300 from calling area code 900 pay-per-minute sex lines. His sexual addiction progressed: when on a new job, he had Internet access and was confronted for masturbating while accessing online pornography at his desk. After losing this well-paying job he began stock market and commodities trading from his home computer, as well as gambling on Internet sites. Jeffrey spent an average of 19 hours per day on the Internet, fluctuating between work related, gambling and pornography sites and chat rooms. He reached a bottom with his addictions after developing a painful case of repetitive strain injury in both arms, wrists, and hands from excessive typing and sought help through a walk-in counseling clinic. During the assessment, he disclosed being 150 pounds overweight, smoking two packs of cigarettes daily, and having approximately $75,000 in gambling debt.

Chapter 4

Preventing Addiction

Susan Moore

Rationale

Substance abuse and other addictive behaviors are harmful to individuals, families, and society. They are expensive to treat and recidivism rates are high. Prevention strategies offer the hope of intervening in this destructive pattern. By becoming knowledgeable about successful elements of prevention programs, students will be prepared to develop, evaluate, and contribute to effective prevention efforts.

Overview

The lesson connects causal models of addictive behavior with prevention strategies. It reviews traditional prevention approaches and examines promising trends in prevention programming.

Objectives

1. To understand the relationship between theories of addiction and prevention program development.
2. To be familiar with traditional and contemporary prevention approaches.
3. To learn the various elements of effective prevention programs.
4. To reflect on one's own risk and protective factors and what is successful prevention on a personal level.

Activities

1. Group students into threes or fours. Ask each group to choose one prevention approach. Answer the following questions: What theory or theories of addiction does it address? What risk and/or resiliency factors does it consider? Who is the target population? What stage of prevention does it represent? Leave enough time for a representative from each group to report to the class.
2. Have each student list their personal risk and protective factors. Have them develop a prevention approach that would work for them. Provide ample time for volunteers to share their work with the entire class.

3. Ask students to bring in an item of media that relates to prevention and/or addiction. Have students pair up and analyze their media examples. Describe the sender, the targeted receiver, the content, and the underlying values of the media message.
4. Have students arrange to visit one prevention program in their community. Ask them to write a description of the program, identifying the stage of prevention (primary, secondary, tertiary), and the risk and resiliency factors addressed.
5. Brainstorm causes of addiction. Ask several students to write them on flipcharts or blackboard. Facilitate class discussion around the most significant risk factors.
6. Ask students to work in small groups of four or five. Develop a description of an "ideal" community. What would it look like? What protective factors would be evident?
7. Have each group share their vision with the entire class.

Chapter 5

Assessment, Diagnosis, and Treatment Planning

Thomas Mullis

Rationale

In order to complete a comprehensive assessment, it is necessary to establish rapport with the client, pursue a structured diagnostic interview, determine a diagnosis (understand dual diagnoses), and develop a treatment plan.

Overview

The chapter content addresses the material identified in the above rationale. During the rapport building interview, the adolescent should be provided with information related to informed consent. Confidentiality is important, even if the client is a minor and an involuntary referral. The client always has the choice of being non-compliant even in the face of adverse consequences, like being placed in detention. The adolescent should be provided with an overview of the questions that will be asked such as: how they will be used; who will have access to the information, and how the information provided may impact on him or her personally, legally, or both, what legal options they have; and what kind of legal access they have to their records. Adolescents are often resistant to self-disclose to professional counselors and many adolescent clients involved in drug use are either court referred or school referred. They have serious concerns regarding their privacy, violating peer confidentiality, disappointing parents, incurring legal and other negative consequences of admitting drug use. These concerns are valid because in most instances, the counselor cannot guarantee confidentiality. The recommendation is that, when possible, the counselor should not pursue obtaining identifying information about peers, unless the information provided is important for legal or personal reasons. Counselors need to be very aware of their feelings and thoughts concerning the situation they find themselves. Counselors should be empathic, non-judgmental, non-confrontive, and use open-end questions to establish rapport in the adolescent and counselor relationship. A sense of trust needs to be developed. The rapport building interview may be conducted at a separate time or simply precede the structured interview. While the major purpose of this interview is to develop rapport with the adolescent, the counselor is provided with significant opportunities to assess a wealth of information. Non-verbal communications such as: eye contact, facial expressions, mood, head movements, tense or relaxed mood, and variations in voice pitch are important to observe in assessment. Initiating a rapport-building interview prior to a diagnostic structured interview is essential to ensuring the validity of the latter. During this interview, while it may not be legally necessary, it could help if the adolescent would agree to sign a waiver of confidentiality so that the counselor may interview significant others. The use of an unstructured interview is important in assessment; however, a structured diagnostic interview is necessary in order to obtain specific detail about drug use.

The purpose in conducting a structured interview is to provide a format that provides the counselor with the essential information needed to conduct a comprehensive assessment. The interview should be direct, concrete and done in a logical and timely manner. It is comprehensive as outlined in chapter 5 and provides a means to identify use and abuse of drugs, alcohol or tobacco, and related social context as well as psychiatric symptoms needed to reach a diagnosis.

Once the diagnosis has been reached, it necessary to formulate the treatment plan in conjunction with the client and significant others. The major considerations that need to be addressed are

(1) How severe is the drug disorder;
(2) Is this a dual diagnosis situation;
(3) What is the optimal therapy to treat the disorder or disorders (residential vs. outpatient, confrontive vs. supportive, group versus individual. Where should the adolescent reside (in his or her home or reside at a different location);
(4) What are the referral sources;
(5) What should be the duration of the treatment;
(6) What is the plan for aftercare or relapse;
(7) What role will the family play in treatment (family therapy, couples therapy, etc);
(8) What are the financial resources that are available;
(9) What will be the arrangements regarding educational needs (should he or she continue to attend the same school, change school or have school provided in a treatment center); and finally
(10) What role will the counselor who does the assessment play in the treatment?

Most of these concerns interact with each other and need to be assessed in concert with other considerations in devising the treatment plan. For example, type of drug use and severity impacts on residential or outpatient treatment, cost, possible referral resources, need for specialized treatment, school placement, duration of treatment, relapse issues, type of treatment, family treatment, and the role of the interviewing counselor.

Objectives

1. To provide an understanding of how to establish rapport with an adolescent drug client.
2. To provide an understanding in how to conduct a structured diagnostic interview, which asks specific personal questions to adolescents.
3. To provide the student an understanding of how to do a diagnosis and how to do dual diagnoses.
4. To provide the student with an understanding of important considerations in how to develop a treatment plan.

Activities

Exercise I: Informal Assessment Interviewing

1. One of the class members is to play the role of a 14-year-old adolescent male who is involved in excessive use of alcohol. He is an involuntary referral who has never been assessed. He is drinking on a regular basis about a six-pack a day. Three member groups will be formed from the class. They will act as counselor, observer, or client. The purpose of the interviewing is to develop rapport, explain the limits of confidentiality, and other issues relating to informed consent. This is a rapport building interview and obtaining specific drug information is not the goal. The primary goal is to develop trust. After the interviewing, the client (student), observer (student), and counselor (student) will discuss the experience in terms of what seems to be effective in working with adolescents. After the small group processing, the entire class will discuss the experience.
2. The client is a 17-year-old female who is an involuntary referral. Students are to complete an assessment, but as in the first, you need to have a rapport building interview. She is reportedly using crack. One member of the class acts as counselor and another member acts as the client. Different members of the class are given the opportunity to interview the client, and the class evaluates the experience.

Exercise II: Interviewing in a Structured Diagnostic Format (Sensitive Areas)

1. Have a number of different counselors (students) take some of the questions from the diagnostic interview as presented in Chapter 5 and role play a situation in which sensitive questions about the history of drug use are asked of a client (student). Questions asked would be what drugs are being using, how often, etc. The instructor will give the client (student) information about his or her drug use. After the interview, the instructor will reveal the drug use, and the class will then evaluate how effective they were in interviewing and determining the drug use.
2. Do the same exercise, however, change it to ask the client (student) about peer use of drugs. Use the diagnostic interview as a format to select questions.
3. This exercise may be modified by age, gender, type of drug use. The client could be interviewed about family.

Exercise III: Diagnoses

1. The instructor provides a group of three students with a dual diagnosis (only for the person playing the client) with background information. The students will not be told that it is a dual diagnosis situation. The counselor (student) will briefly interview the client (student) looking for dual diagnosis issues and the other student will observe. The students should use the questions in the diagnostic intervention proved in chapter 5. The observer may interview the client when the first student finished. The students in each group will make a diagnosis. They will also do a Global Assessment Functioning. When the counselor (student) has finished the interview, members of the class will write down what they did in the small groups.
2. The instructor leads a discussion regarding dual diagnosis and depression and how it relates to suicide.

Exercise IV: Treatment Planning

I. The students are provided with an assessment of a drug client by the instructor. The case is written to reflect the kinds of clients the students in the class will probably encounter, and what treatment options are available in the setting they work. The case needs to be specific in diagnosis and the student needs to be provided with information that is in the structured interview as presented in the text.

2. The students are then divided into groups of three to discuss treatment planning. One of the individuals is designated as spokesperson and reports to the class on a treatment plan.

References

American Psychiatric Association. (1994). *Diagnostic and statistical manual of mental disorders* (4th ed.). Washington, DC: Author.

Cobb, N. (1998). *Adolescence.* Mountain View, California: Mayfield Publishing

Francis. R., & Miller, S. (1991). *Clinical textbook of addictive disorders.* New York: Guilford Press.

Chapter 6

Treating Addictive Behaviors

Susan Moore

Rationale

The field of substance abuse treatment has for many years been dominated by a one-way-fits-all model of treatment. Although relapse rates are consistently high, treatment seemed unchanging. However, more recently, the accountability movement has resulted in a need to re-evaluate and revamp the way counseling addresses substance abuse problems. The strength of this movement has contributed to an explosion of research into more effective and efficient ways of treating substance abuse problems. The purpose of this chapter is to present the most current and promising research in the field of substance abuse counseling.

Overview

This chapter deals with the research exploring the more effective models for counseling individuals with substance abuse problems. The importance of counselor self-awareness and the creation of the therapeutic alliance are examined. Motivation is seen as a key ingredient in changing problem behaviors. The stages of motivation are explored and strategies for increasing and maintaining motivation are described. Finally, various cognitive and behavioral treatment interventions are identified.

Objectives

1. To understand the importance of counselor self-awareness in the effective counseling of individuals with substance abuse problems.
2. To become aware of the significance and importance of the therapeutic alliance.
3. To be able to identify the components of the therapeutic alliance.
4. To be able to engage in a therapeutic relationship in role-play situations.
5. To understand the stages of motivation and the strategies for increasing and maintaining motivation among those individuals with substance abuse problems.
6. To be able to identify the stages of change that clients are experiencing in role-play and simulated situations.

7. To become familiar with the research on effective treatment models.
8. To gain an overview knowledge of various treatment approaches in the field of substance abuse.

Activities

1. The person who is the counselor is key in the counseling process. Counselors must be aware of their inner worlds, their beliefs, biases, and perceptions, in order to be fully present and effective in the counseling relationship. The following three exercises, moving from the cognitive to the experiential, are designed to facilitate self-challenge and to enhance self-awareness within the student-counselor.
   Students, individually, should consider what they believe about substance abuse, in general, and the person who abuses the substance, in particular. After this individual contemplation, students should work in dyads, sharing and discussing with each other their beliefs. This is essentially a cognitive process and thus their thinking should be the focus.
2. Students, again individually, must begin to question where their beliefs came from. How did they develop their perceptions regarding substance abuse? They should each ask themselves questions such as "How did I come to believe this"? "What and e students. Students must focus on what is going on inside of them when they consider and speak about their beliefs regarding substance abuse. In order to get in touch with what they are experiencing, it would be helpful for students to close their eyes and take a few, slow breaths, noticing their inhaling and exhaling. This will help to clear their minds a little and even slow down their thinking. Then, keeping their awareness focused inward, they should ask themselves "What is going on inside of me when I consider what I believe about substance abuse"? The students should be encouraged to just sit with these experiences for a few moments without trying to identify them to themselves. Then, after they have allowed the experience to just "be," they can begin to describe it to themselves. These inner experiences should then be shared in the dyad.

4. The therapeutic alliance creates the environment for healing and growth to occur. Students, working in triads, should role play, one person being the client, another the counselor, and the third person being the observer. The client should present a situation that in some way involves substance use. The counselor's responsibility is to create the therapeutic relationship, communicating to the client a non-judgmental, empathetic interest, encouraging and facilitating the client sharing his or her concerns. After engaging in this process for about 15-20 minutes, the observer should seek feedback from the client and the counselor as well as share his or her observations with the counselor. Each member of the triad should remain mindful of his or her inner experience during the role play and share these with each other. Roles should continually be reversed, until each person has an opportunity to be the counselor and receive feedback.

   Following the role play, the students come together as a group and share their experiences with the whole group.

5. The media has a powerful impact on our perceptions of substance abuse and its treatment. It can contribute to the stereotypes we form as well as offering us opportunities to expand our knowledge. The following activity uses popular films that develop their stories around individuals with substance abuse problems. Some of the films of this genre are "When a Man Loves a Woman," "Clean and Sober," "Less than Zero," and "Days of Wine and Roses." However, other films of this type can be used.

   Although individuals involved in substance abuse may be at varying stages of motivation to change when in counseling, these differences are frequently overlooked or ignored by the counselor. Either during class time or as an out-of-class assignment, the students, considering the stages of motivation, will view the movies "When a Man Loves a Woman" and "Clean and Sober." After viewing the films, they will work in groups of three or four, and will discuss with the main characters in these films, (i.e., the Meg Ryan character in "When a Man Loves a Woman" and the Michael Keaton character in "Clean and Sober," identifying the stages of motivation that each goes through. The students will then discuss how they, should they have been the counselors for these characters, would have used the interventions (FRAMES) to work with them, in order to increase their motivation to change. After discussing this in their small groups, they will return to the larger group and share their ideas.

6. Students will form triads. Using the situations from the films, students will role play a counselor and one of the characters as the client. The counselor will focus on influencing the client's motivation for change through the use of the interventions described in FRAMES. These role plays will last about 15-20 minutes, followed by feedback from the observer and client as well as processing what the experience was like for the counselor. Students will rotate the roles until each one has had the chance to be the counselor and to receive feedback.
7. It is important for students to understand the culture of Alcoholics Anonymous as well as to become aware of the similarities and differences among various AA groups. Students will attend at least one open AA meeting. They will be instructed that they will introduce themselves to the group as students who are learning about AA. During the meeting, they are to stay aware of their inner experiences and record these soon after leaving the meeting. During class, in small groups, they will share what it was like for them during the AA meeting and their reactions to what went on at the meeting. They will then try to identify what they noticed as being key factors within the AA meeting that seem to influence the participant maintaining their commitment to change.

Chapter 7

Empowering Clients Through Groups

Les McAllan, Amy Friedman & Evans Spears

Rationale

Throughout the history of the treatment and prevention of addiction, groups have rapidly become the primary treatment of choice. Over time certain models and approaches have become very popular even though there may not be scientific documentation to support the efficacy of these activities. Many professionals and organizations seem willing to promote a variety of interventions based primarily on tradition or self-report. It is important that students, academicians, and treatment professionals look closely at the values inherent in much of the terminology and practice of addiction prevention and treatment. These values may be at a conscious or subconscious level and can have a powerful influence on public policy and direct treatment. The activities suggested in this section are designed to bring these values to the surface for discussion and understanding.

Overview

These lessons are designed to help students begin to explore the complexity of the language associated with addictive behavior and the concept of empowerment, to gain personal and professional experience with group membership and leadership, and to become familiar with the ethical and legal issues related to group treatment.

Activity 1

Empowerment and the Therapeutic Aspects of Groups:
Small Group Discussion

Goal: To better understand the concepts of "empowerment" and "personal responsibility for behavior," including the values inherent in both.

Objectives: Since these terms/concepts are used frequently in human service settings, but rarely precisely defined, it is helpful for students to explore their meanings and develop greater consciousness of the implied values underlying their use.

Activity: Break into small groups of five to seven students. Generate terms associated with the definitions of empowerment and assuming personal responsibility for one's behaviors. Some groups may be encouraged to explore the definitions; others the organizational, societal cultural and personal values related to these concepts; and others the mechanisms through which helping professionals may support empowerment and encourage responsibility. Small groups can use flip chart paper to summarize their discussions for presentation to the group as a whole.

Activity 2

Nature and History of Addiction Treatment Groups

Activity 2a

Goal: To gain experience with and empathy for the nature of group process from the perspective of the group member in self-help, facilitated, facilitated peer, targeted, and psychotherapeutic groups.

Objectives: Participate in several types of groups to gain self-awareness of the role of group member in short-term and long-term group activities. Students may be able to attend "open" 12-step meetings, sit in on therapy groups led by professional therapists, or become a member of a group which proposes to address an issue with which the student currently is struggling. Groups may also be established within the classroom setting. Yalom (1995) discusses in detail the pros and cons of group experiences related to academic settings.

Activity: Write about your experience in each group. Compare and contrast different formats. Describe the nature of the group, the theoretical perspective if evident, and your personal experience as a member.

Activity 2b

Goal: To gain experience with leading groups.

Objectives: Co-lead a group with an experienced group counselor to gain direct experience with the role of group leader in short-term and long-term group activities.

Activity: Write about your experience in each group. Compare and contrast different formats. Describe the nature of the group, the theoretical perspective if evident, and your personal experience as a leader.

Activity 3

Ethical Considerations for Beginning Counselors

Goal: To encourage students to gain a practical understanding of the ethical codes and laws specific to group work.

Objectives: Allow students to choose an ethical issue specific to treatment of persons in addiction settings. Options could include rights of individuals vs. rights of the group as a whole, dual relationships and/or member relationships outside of the therapy setting, self-disclosure of the leader's addiction history, maintaining confidentiality in groups, or handling problem behaviors (including active addiction) in the group setting.

Activities: After choosing an issue, each student is expected to investigate the appropriate codes and local laws related to the issue and develop a role-play situation to be acted out in class. Class members are asked to participate in active discussions and critique the formal responses provided in the role-play situations.

Chapter 8

Families Affected by Substance Abuse

William English

Rationale

Substance abuse (SA) extracts a very high toll on families. Functional families often lose vitality as they experience crisis, trauma, and post-traumatic stress. Troubled families usually need treatment, especially where there is co-dependency and enabling. Coping families can make many valuable contributions to support and encourage all members, including individuals with substance abuse.

Overview

This lesson defines the family, substance abuse, and the family life cycle. It describes the many influences that SA has on families, impact on children, effects on adult children, and cultural influences. Prevention and Intervention to heal substance abusers and their families emphasize systems theory and various types of family therapy. Explaining major obstacles to coping with SA and best practices in intervention helps students to be prepared to assess, guide, and counsel persons with SA.

Objectives

1. To increase awareness of key definitions—substance abuse, family, and family life cycle—to use in preventing SA and reducing the negative consequences of SA.
2. To increase understanding of the substantial negative influence(s) that SA typically has on families and children.
3. To increase awareness of general systems theory, the family therapy process, and the main types of family therapies, to balance families and cope with SA.
4. To increase understanding of co-dependency and other major obstacles that must be dealt with to empower families to be more functional.
5. To increase understanding of multiple interventions that represent best practices in assisting family systems and relatives of substance abusers.

Activities

The following exercises will personalize learning related to understanding SA and prepare students to intervene to balance SA families and SA individuals. Each exercise connects with one of the four objectives to this lesson.

Exercise I for Objective 1: Key Definitions

Divide students into small groups of two to six.

1. Request students talk about their own family systems in terms of type (dual career, single parent, or blended), style (open or closed), and the family's current place in the family life cycle.
2. Request that students also talk about their extended family systems and conjugal families, in terms of their behavioral patterns on a substance abstinence to substance addiction continuum. Share any efforts to intervene or cope with SA and the outcome.
3. Follow the self-disclosure of family systems and substance use with a guided discussion based on questions like:
   - Is it difficult to share this information with others? Why?
   - Why do we perceive this information as private?
   - What changes do you believe would strengthen your family and its members?
4. Facilitate a large group debriefing of the small-group activities, completed in activities one to three.

Exercise II for Objective 2: Influence of SA on Families

Divide students into smaller groups of eight to ten.

1. Request that students share personal knowledge of the effects of SA on a family system (their own, or some other family) that they know well.
2. Request that students also share perceptions of the impact of SA on children and on adult children of substance abusers. Discuss adults of substance-abusing parents in terms of being too dependent, anti-dependent, needless, and wantless. Discuss the payoffs, dynamics, and consequences of SA for dependent abusers and co-dependent relatives.
3. Conduct a "psychodrama" where students simulate a dysfunctional family group attempting to do problem solving. Decide on the problem (e.g., substance abuse,

communication, or a major event like a move to a new state or town, teen pregnancy, etc.). Assume specific, stilted roles of the scapegoat (i.e., SA), enabler, lost child, hero, and mascot. One group member should be the director and facilitator of the psychodrama. Remaining group members are observers and should facilitate the debriefing of this activity.

4. As a total group, discuss what students learned from the self-disclosure period and psychodrama.

Exercise III for Objective 3: Theories and Approaches to Family Intervention

1. Facilitate a discussion about the rationale for a systems approach, the family process, and stages in family counseling.
2. Facilitate further discussion on the desired outcome goals, which will improve the functioning of family systems and individual family members.
3. Divide learners into groups of eight to ten and have each group choose to simulate a different type of family counseling approach (e.g., psychodynamic, humanistic, Bowenian, structured, communicational, or behavioral). Use specific therapy methods in the simulation.
4. Have each group simulate a specific type of family therapy group, where members enact roles of scapegoat, enabler, hero, lost child, mascot, and therapist/facilitator. Assume the mother is a cocaine abuser with an enmeshed communication style and that the father abuses alcohol and marijuana, and has a detached communication style. Assume that one of the children is "too dependent." Observers should take notes and guide a debriefing period after the therapy enactment.
5. Facilitate a large-group debriefing of the small-group activities, completed in activities one to three.

Exercise IV for Objective 4: Obstacles to Coping with SA

1. Have the entire group discuss the barrier of co-dependence. Consider intra personal and cultural factors that may contribute to co-dependence, especially the enabling. How

have more coping families eliminated or reduced their co-dependency?

2. Divide the students into smaller discussion groups of about six. Have each group self-disclose obstacles that they have observed in families coping with SA: co-dependence, irrational fears, close approaches, low self-efficacy, weak social support, inadequate social skills, unresolved conflicts, stress and anger, non-mainstream culture, and dual diagnosis.
3. Require that each group work on resolving a specific obstacle like a closed family system, low self-efficacy, poor social skills,and weak social support. Identify attitudes, techniques, and activities to cope with this obstacle and specify the measurable outcomes that will connote success.
4. Have each small group prepare an obstacle resolution report (ORR).
5. Have groups present their obstacle resolution reports to the whole group and get feedback and other ideas.
6. Conclude by debriefing the exercise with the whole group.

Exercise V: Best Practices in Working with Families

1. Make a summary overview about working with families affected by SA. Emphasize that SA is a bicultural condition that significantly impacts on abusers, family systems, and individuals. Underscore that effective intervention needs to be multifaceted, intergenerational, and aimed at improving the function or wellness of family systems, family members, and substance abusers.
2. Identify subcultures that are especially at risk in terms of substance abuse (e.g., Native Americans, Mexican Americans, African Americans, Irish, soccer moms, teenagers, persons with disabilities or chronic illnesses). Use a visual aide (e.g., overhead or chalkboard) to record the results of this brainstorm.
3. Divide students into groups of six to discuss the issue of SA in-depth, as it applies to a particularly high-risk group. Let persons volunteer for their preferred problem resolution group. Consider cultural values, roles, and customs that should be respected.

4. Have each group prepare a Family Intervention Plan (FIP) that is tailored to helping families and individuals who are affected by subcultures to better cope with SA. Include specifying measurable outcomes of success.
5. Have groups present the FIP to the whole group, and get feedback and other ideas.
6. Conclude by debriefing the exercise with the whole group.

Chapter 9

Multicultural Issues

Charrles Reid & Charlene Kampf

Rationale

Awareness of multicultural issues has become a dynamic part of the therapeutic process in all counseling disciplines and in American society in general. Professionals who are aware of their own cultural issues and the cultural issues of people with addictions can be more effective in the therapeutic process. Information briefly tracing the history of multicultural counseling with narrow and broad definitions provides a basis for understanding the role of cultural sensitivity when working with diverse populations with addictions. Prevention approaches can be helpful in educating individuals and communities about the dangers of addiction. Assessment of the client with regard to identification of substance abuse will be assistive, however professionals must be aware of any cultural biases of these tests. Counselor education and service programs need appropriate instruments to assess the success of their multicultural instruction and the knowledge base of the professionals associated with these programs. It is also important to have an awareness of how diverse populations with addictions perceive the world. Knowledge about cultural contributions to drug use behavior will help professionals identify therapeutic strategies and interventions that will assist the professional and the client in achieving the agreed upon therapeutic goals. Various multicultural counseling concepts and theories have applications to diverse populations with addictions and the use of a variety of outcome goals can increase treatment success.

Overview

This chapter addresses the myths associated with special populations and their use of chemicals, the history of multiculturalism and multicultural counseling, assessment strategies, various culturally relevant concepts and approaches, and treatment strategies that pertain to working with people with addictions.

Objectives

1. To become sensitive to and aware of society's and one's own myths about special populations and the use or abuse of drugs.
2. To develop awareness of the role of culture for the professional and the person with addictions.
3. To review the history of multiculturalism.
4. To examine the development of multicultural counseling and

its relevance to people with addictions.

5. To become aware of various theories and strategies that can be effective in prevention when working with people with addictions.
6. To experience the assessment process for substance use, and to evaluate various tests for cultural biases.
7. To evaluate one's own cultural competencies using assessment instruments.
8. To be aware of culturally relevant treatment approaches with people with additions.

Activities

These activities will personalize learning related to multiculturalism, prevention strategies, assessment concepts and treatment approaches as they relate to people with addictions.

Exercise I for Objectives 1 & 2: Myths, Realities, and Role of Culture

1. Ask two students to stand in front of the class about 15 to 20 feet apart facing each other. After they have faced each other, tell each of them that they will represent a person from a particular cultural group. (e.g., one could be White and another could be Native American or one could be young and another could be old). Then identify one of these individuals as a counselor and the other as a client.
2. Invite members of the class to identify biases/myths surrounding the culture of the individual who represents the client (e.g., Native American client). Focus can be on myths associated with drug and alcohol use in this culture. As each class member identifies a myth about the client's culture, ask the class member to stand between the two individuals facing the counselor. Continue asking for myths and biases about the client's culture until you have a row of people standing in a line that obscures the view that the counselor has of the client.
3. Discuss the meaning of this experience. If it is not obvious to the class, ask them to consider the following:
   a. like this concrete/objective line, each of the biases or myths might obscure the counselor's perception of the client's worldview,

b. even one of these myths/biases obscures the counselor's ability to see the client, therefore a combination of them might result in dramatic effects,

c. invite them to consider how they, themselves actually perceive people from the particular culture discussed in this exercise.

4. Ask the class members to sit down, the two individuals to remain standing, and to maintain the roles they represented in the first exercise. In a similar manner as before, ask the class members to identify the cultural myths or biases associated with the cultural group represented by the counselor (i.e, White counselor). Again ask them to stand between the client and counselor, but this time facing the client. Students can now see how myths and biases can act as barriers between the counselor and client in yet another way. Follow this with discussions of the meaning of this aspect of the exercise.
5. Ask the class members to sit down again, but ask the two individuals to remain standing one more time. Ask them to reverse the counselor/client roles they represent. For example, if the Native American was the client during the first part of this exercise, he or she can be the counselor during this exercise. In the same manner as before, ask the class to identify myths and biases associated with the culture represented by the new counselor; forming a barrier between counselor and client. Discuss the meaning of this experience. In this instance, students can become aware that myths and biases can work both ways (that is all cultures may have some biases about all others), and that we all must work to maintain a clear view of the other person's unique worldview.

Exercise II for Objective 2 & 3: Culture of Professional and Multiculturalism

1. Request that students express their ideas about the definition of multiculturalism during a discussion based on questions such as these:
   a. What changes have you seen in your family, school, community and society since the advent of multiculturalism?

b. What is your culture and what are the values and beliefs of that culture?
c. How do you feel about other cultures influencing your culture?

2. Divide students into groups of three to five. Ask them to recall and discuss their first encounters with a person with an addiction. What were their personal reactions and the reasons for those reactions? If there were negative attitudes about people with addictions, where did the negative attitudes originate? Ask the groups to share in class discussion.

Exercise III for Objective 4: Multicultural Counseling

1. Divide the class into small groups and give each group a flip-chart. Ask the groups to list important multicultural counseling strategies that they have studied. Following each of these strategies, ask them to indicate how these might be applied to people with addictions. At the end of the class, ask students to report their results back to the entire group. Help them to see common themes and potential ways to expand their ideas.

Exercise IV for Objective 5: Prevention

1. Divide the students into small groups. Have them discuss and evaluate the risk that substance abuse education programs can have on ubstance abuse. Ask students about the effects on them of drug education they received at school, at home and in this course. Facilitate a classroom discussion regarding prevention education and prevention programs that would be useful with diverse populations of substance abusers and in diverse population communities.

Exercise V for Objective 6: Assessment for Substance Abuse

1. Invite students to take each of the following assessment instruments: the screening tool that focuses on cutting down, annoyance, guilt, and needing an eye-opener (CAGE); the Michigan Alcohol Screen Test (MAST); the Substance Abuse Subtle Screen Instrument (SASSI); and the Additions Severity Index (ASI).
2. As a follow-up, ask the class to compare the results of the four tests, focusing on the following questions:

a. Did any of the instruments have obvious cultural biases?
b. Were the results similar/different for each test?
c. What did each test focus on?

3. Invite students to take the same tests again, but as if they were a person from a particular culture and who has a substance abuse issue.
4. Ask the class to discuss the differences between the two different results of each test-taking (i.e., as him or herself and as a person from diverse culture). Focus on questions such as the following:
   a. Did being from a minority culture influence the results of the test?
   b. Did some tests have more biases than others?
   c. What would a culturally sensitive counselor need to do when administering,scoring, and interpreting these tests?

Exercise VI for Objective 7: Assessment for Multicultural Counselor Competency

1. Require the students to take the Multicultural Counseling Awareness Scale-Revised: Form B (MCAS) or the Multicultural Counseling Inventory (MCI).
2. Ask them to write a brief report regarding the results focusing on their level of cultural awareness of diverse populations with addictions. Ask them to include a possible rationale for their personal assessment, and a prescriptive plan for improvement of their cultural awareness.

Exercise VII for Objective 8: Cultural Concepts, Theories, and Treatment Approaches for People with Addictions

1. Divide the class into small groups. Have each group discuss the role of society in the treatment of people with addictions. Is society's role different or the same for people with addictions from diverse populations? Discuss these issues with the class.
2. Divide the students into small groups. Invite them to discuss the benefits and limitations of abstinence as a treatment goal for diverse populations with addictions. Ask them to brainstorm alternative treatment goals for this population followed with a classroom discussion.

Chapter 10

Substance Abuse and Disability

Amos Sales

Rationale

Data about individuals with disabilities indicate they are as likely or more likely to abuse alcohol and drugs as others, and are less likely to access treatment for their substance abuse problems. Knowledge about the factors contributing to these situations will help prospective counselors identify prevention, diagnosis, and treatment approaches that offer the most promise for success.

Overview

This chapter defines disability in a counseling context, identifies incidence of substance abuse among persons with disabilities, and examines possible factors that may contribute to higher risk for substance abuse in this population than among the U.S. population in general. It provides background and rationale needed to implement prevention, diagnosis, and treatment approaches considered appropriate for persons with disabilities who also have problems of substance abuse.

Objectives

1. To become aware that persons with mental or physical disabilities face equal or greater risks for substance abuse as individuals in the general population, and to review possible reasons for the increased risk.
2. To develop a personal awareness of and means of identifying effective prevention and treatment strategies for individuals with disabilities who have substance abuse problems.

Activities

These activities will personalize learning related to definitions of disability, factors related to increase abuse of substances in this population, and treatment needs of individuals with disabilities.

Exercise I: Definitions

1. Have students share whether or not they have disabilities using the definition provided. Approximately half of the class should have a disability. Follow with a discussion based on questions such as these:

- Why is it difficult to share this information with others?
- Why do we perceive this information as private?
- To what degree does each person consider his or her disability to be a handicap?

2. Have students brainstorm examples of communication shortcuts that constitute negative labels and incorrect use of definitions (i.e., "The retarded" instead of "individuals who are mentally retarded"). Discuss personal reactions to these examples.

Exercise II: Myths

1. Divide students into small groups of twos or threes. Ask them to reflect back on their first encounters with individuals who had disabilities in order to recall their personal reactions and the reasons behind them. Ask students to share their experiences with the class for discussion. An important point to be made in the discussion is that negative attitudes toward individuals with disabilities are overcome through positive personal contact.
2. Divide class into four groups to discuss myths related to each disability. Have students brainstorm and list on newsprint myths and behaviors linked to the myths. Have the groups share their lists for class discussion.
3. Divide students in small groups and have them brainstorm examples of stereotypes about disabilities that are still evident in the news and entertainment media. Follow with classroom discussion about ways stereotypes have improved or worsened and what can be done to eliminate stereotypes.

Exercise III: Prevention Programming

1. Group students by twos or threes. Have each group list the types of information and activities related to substance abuse prevention they either remember from their school days or believe might work.
2. Have each group reflect on why these prevention efforts were expected to work, or project how their own suggestions might impact drug-using behavior.
3. Facilitate classroom discussion on what prevention programming worked and what did not. Identify individual

differences in response to prevention. Conclude with a discussion about what might work for individuals with disabilities. An important point to be made is that effectiveness depends on the individual, not the disability.

Exercise IV: Treatment Programming

(Follow same three activities above but exchange reference to prevention with treatment.)

Chapter 11

Preventing Adolescent Relapse: Concepts, Theories, and Techniques

Shitala P. Mishra & Robert A. Ressler

Rationale

Relapse is a process through which an addict develops inability to cope with life in sobriety. Maintaining posttreatment sobriety is a serious problem. The rates of relapse among drug and alcohol dependent adults and youth are very high. The estimates are that relapse rates range from 35% to 85%. The posttreatment abstinence or avoiding relapse is a challenging issue for the success of many drug intervention programs. Despite the fact that a number of drug and alcohol treatment programs have produced promising results in reducing drug usage, the maintenance of posttreatment gains, however, has been more difficult.

Overview

This lesson is intended to acquaint the reader with the concepts, theoretical background, and principles that can be applied in preventing relapse of drug and alcohol dependency. The information gained through the lessons and exercises develop a clear understanding of the fact that relapse is a process that starts slowly and builds in intensity. Relapse is to be understood as a typical occurrence in drug and alcohol dependency unless contributing factors, often called "trigger mechanisms" are understood and addressed by families, friends, and treatment providers. The knowledge and understanding of the relapsing nature of drug and alcohol dependency should be to help students and interested professionals develop, evaluate, and implement intervention programs for maintaining posttreatment success and uninterrupted recovery.

Objectives

1. To enhance the knowledge and awareness of the concept of relapse and relapse prevention.
2. To increase understanding of potential relapse triggers.
3. To gain an understanding of fundamental principles underlying relapse prevention treatment.
4. To gain knowledge and understanding of psychological development as it explains addiction, recovery, and relapse tendencies.
5. To develop skills essential for identifying and managing warning signs.
6. To develop skills in planning and implementing successful relapse prevention programs.

Activities

The following exercises are intended to help students enhance their learning about relapse prevention by focussed discussion of key concepts and salient issues in small group situations. The exercises are also to help students develop skills to identify factors contributing to relapse and develop skills in devising tasks and activities to deal with relapse prevention's issues. Individual exercises are linked to the objectives of the lesson.

Exercise 1 for Objective 1: Definitions and Concepts

1. Divide students in two groups and have each group define the concepts of drug dependency/addiction, treatment, recovery, and relapse. Then have one group consider the concept of relapse as a single event. Have the other group consider relapse as process of development over time. Both groups are to provide arguments in support of each view. Have both groups report the results of their discussion to the entire class.
2. Have two students role play in front of the entire class. One student plays the role of a client with an addiction problem who is at the recovery stage and the other of a relapse prevention counselor. The goal is to have the counselor conduct a counseling session to determine where the client is in the recovery process, how motivated the client is to abstain from drug and alcohol use, and the thoughts and feelings that the client has about his/her tendency to return to using drugs and alcohol.
3. Have the class discuss and develop a list of possible reasons as to why clients might find it difficult to stay sober and clean after treatment.

Exercise II for Objective 2: Relapse Triggers

1. Ask a small group to identify, list, and discuss kind of things recovering patients are likely to do and not do in their attempt to abstain from drug or alcohol use. Ask another small group of students to identify the patterns that repeat themselves

during periods of abstinence. The discussion in a small group is initiated regarding the causes of relapse. Ask the group to identify what suggestions for learning they would have for relapsing clients in order to focus their thinking on what they can do to change.

2. Ask students to identify problems that are likely to appear to cause clients to return to using drugs and alcohol after treatment. Ask them to think of situations like: problems with
   a) people,
   b) situations,
   c) thoughts and feelings,
   d) health and sickness.

Exercise III for Objective 3: Principles Underlying Prevention Treatment

1. Ask students to have small group discussion on principles (such as self-assessment, self-knowledge, coping skills, understanding and awareness, and the involvement of significant others in recovery) underlying relapse prevention strategies.
2. Ask students to develop a relapse education program using principles listed in number 1 such as self-knowledge and self-assessment, etc.
3. Ask students to develop an instrument to be used as pre-and post-test to measure the effectiveness of relapse prevention education sessions. The purpose of this test will be to test clients their understanding and retention of content used in relapse education program.
4. Select a commercially available film on a relapse prevention program for the class to observe. After watching the film, student should be asked to discuss the content of the film and to critically evaluate the overall effectiveness of the procedures used in the film for education and treatment of relapse.

Exercise IV for Objective 4: Developmental Theories

1. Ask students to select a theory of adolescent development and critically examine the aspects of development that can

help identify relapse-prone personality traits.

2. Have small group discussion on the salient features of cognitive and vehavioral approaches that are used in relapse prevention therapies.
3. Have stydrebts develop a set of tasks and activitis that can be used in eduction of youth to avoid relapse. Ask students to link these activities to pertinent theoretical approached.

Exercise V for Objective 5: Identifying and Managing Warning Signs

1. Assign students tasks of developing warning sign identification process involving the education of clients for developing and reviewing personal relapse warning lists.
2. Have students develop a warning sign checklist that possibly can be used to predict relapse. This check or rating scale may contain items indicating things such as trouble remembering things, difficulty managing emotions, feeling of loneliness, denial of concerns, loneliness, daydreaming, etc.
3. Have students develop some procedures such as sentence completion measures to be used with clients to analyze and develop treatment procedures. Examples of such techniques will contain items such as "I know my recovery is in big trouble because...................., My thoughts are.................., and My feelings are................, etc."

Exercise VI for Objective 6: Prevention Program Planning

1. Assign students the task of preparing recovery plan sheets for the clients to use in avoiding relapse. This will consist of making a list of activities such as seeing counselor and talking to sponsor that the clients will carry out each day.
2. Have students prepare the content and procedures that will be used for giving a one day seminar to relapse prevention counselors.
3. Ask students to prepare a list of questions to be used for evaluating the implementation of the relapse prevention plan for a client. Following are examples of questions to ask the client:
    a) What risk situations did you encounter today?

b) How do you think or feel about your encounter with the situation?
c) How did you handle the risk situation?
d) What warning signs did you have today?
e) What is the most important thing in the plan that helped you cope with the stresses of the day?

Chapter 12

Program Planning and Evaluation

Robert E. Rapp

I. Conducting a Comprehensive Needs Assessment

Rationale

A comprehensive needs assessment provides the foundation for the program planning process. Knowledge about the essential components of comprehensive needs assessments, their importance, how they are developed and utilized will enable prospective human services professionals to plan and implement programs that will effectively address the multiple needs of their clientele.

Overview

This lesson identifies and describes the essential components of a comprehensive needs assessment. It emphasizes the importance of each and how they are interrelated. It provides the rationale for using the assessment as the foundation for developing program goals, objectives, and methodology.

Objectives

- To examine the importance of utilizing social indicators (statistics) to clearly identify the target population and to validate their needs for services.
- To understand the importance of involving the community, including the target population, in the assessment process to ensure that the program will be utilized.
- To become more aware of how agencies often compete for services and/or duplicate services, even though significant gaps in services exist, because they fail to collaborate in planning.
- To understand the importance of including key informants in the assessment so they will have a significant role in promoting the need for the program.
- To understand the importance of offering opportunities for the general public to provide input into the assessment and planning process.

Activities

Exercise I: Social Indicators

1. Divide the students into groups of three or four. Have each group elect a reporter to convey the respective group's ideas to the class as a whole.
2. Ask each group to determine the best sources to obtain social indicators related to substance abuse. Those sources could be national, state, county, city, or even local neighborhoods.
3. Ask each group to decide whether all sources should be included to present the best picture of need. Ask them to determine how social indicators from all sources can be integrated in relation to the others, e.g., if you compare the neighborhood's incidence of substance abuse to the city, county, state, and U.S., will the picture of local need become clearer?
4. Have the groups share their conclusions with the class as a whole. After each group has reported their conclusions, summarize and synthesize the information.
5. Ask the class members to identify situations in which funds or services may be directed to recipients who are not members of the target population.

Exercise II: Community Surveys, Agency Surveys, Open Forums/ Meetings and Key Informants.

1. Divide the students into four groups. Identify a target community or neighborhood in which they will conduct a mock needs assessment.
2. Have group one outline the process of conducting a community survey which will include members of the target population. After they have completed that, ask them to develop a rationale to support this activity as the most important part of the assessment process.
3. Have group two outline the process of conducting an agency survey. After they complete that task, ask them to develop a rationale to substantiate this activity as the most important part of the assessment process.
4. Have group three outline the process for scheduling and advertising open forums/ meetings to solicit input. Have them identify appropriate locations within the given target area. Ask them to develop a rationale that substantiates this activity as

the most important part of the assessment process.

5. Have group four outline a process to identify key informants from the given target area. Ask them to develop a rationale to substantiate the activity as the most important part of the assessment process.
6. Have a vocal member of each group debate the importance of their needs assessment activity.
7. After the debate,have the groups reconvene to carefully consider all the information to determine the importance of each activity. Have them rank order the activities in terms of their importance and provide a rationale.
8. Ask each group to report their conclusions.

II. Formulating Goals and Objectives in Conjunction with a Program Evaluation Plan

Rationale

Effective programs have clear goals with measurable specific objectives which are designed to address the needs of the target population. As goals and objectives are determined, an evaluation plan should be established to document their level of achievement, in order to determine the programs success and to make decisions related to improving the program. Successful programs can use their evaluation results to build increased support from the community and funding sources.

Overview

This lesson differentiates goals from specific objectives. It emphasizes the importance of each and how they are interdependent. It provides the rationale to develop an evaluation plan which documents the achievement/lack of achievement of the goals and objectives.

Objectives

- To examine the mutuality of goals and objectives, but to promote an understanding that objectives are very specific (may identify who, what, when, where) and must be measurable.
- To be able to easily distinguish goals from objectives.
- To become more aware that for every goal, there are generally

several specific objectives.

- To understand that some goals and objectives are related to effort (process) while others are related to effectiveness (outcome).
- To be able to easily distinguish effort from effectiveness.
- To understand that the purpose of program evaluation is to determine the level of achievement of goals and objectives by documenting effort, effectiveness, and efficiency.
- To understand that formulating goals and objectives without developing anevaluation plan invalidates the program planning process.

Activities

Exercise I: Formulating Goals and Objectives.

1. Provide an example of a goal, e.g. "Reduce substance abuse among teenagers."
2. Provide an example of a specific objective, e.g. "Reduce the rate of DWI among teenagers by 25% during the period January 1, 1999 and December 31, 1999."
3. Ask each student to write down one goal and three specific objectives related to the goal.
4. Ask students to share their examples.
5. Emphasize that the first example of a goal is related to effectiveness or outcome, and provide an example of a goal related to effort or process; e.g. "All students will receive both group and individual counseling."
6. Provide an example of a specific objective related to effort or process, e.g. "One hundred students will each receive two hours of individual counseling and two hours of group counseling each month during the period January 1, 1999 through December 31, 1999."
7. Ask each student to identify whether their goal and objectives are related to effort or effectiveness. Ask them to write down one new goal and three specific objectives related to the opposite of their first example.
8. Have each student share both examples and solicit agreement from the other class members that they are correctly differentiating between effort and effectiveness.

Exercise II: Determining an Evaluation Plan.

1. Assign the class into pairs.
2. Have each person trade their two sets of goals and objectives. Ask each person to develop a plan to collect data that will document the achievement/lack of achievement of his partner's goals and objectives.
3. Have them share their plans with their partners, discuss them, and if necessary, help the other with an evaluation plan.
4. Have the partners share their examples with the class.
5. Introduce the concept of efficiency as a concern of program evaluation. Emphasize that it represents an acceptable ratio of success between effort and effectiveness as it relates to cost.
6. Ask students to review the example in the text. Break the class into groups of four or five and ask them to think of an example whereby a program's efficiency would not be acceptable, even though it may have achieved its goals and objectives related to effort and effectiveness.
7. Have each group share their examples with the class and discuss how their example would not satisfy the critical question of program efficiency.

III. Internalizing the Program Development Process

(Robert Rapp and Jeff Davis)

Rationale

The program development process is dynamic. It requires the internalization of an ongoing system of planning, practice, and evaluation. Effective systems are flexible, adaptable, and promote creativity in response to change.

Overview

This lesson is designed to promote better understanding of program development as an ongoing process. It is based upon the use of the RAPPER model which emphasizes the interdependence of the six steps of the process.

Objectives

- To facilitate the recall of the six steps in the process.
- To understand how each step individually contributes to the process, and how they are all interdependent.
- To understand that the process is continuous, in that once the planning, practice, and evaluation cycle is completed, it is repeated.
- To understand the purpose of an ongoing system of planning, practice and evaluation is tied to a constant and a quest for quality.

Activities

1. Divide the students into six groups, one group for each step in the RAPPER model. Instruct each group to elect a reporter to convey the respective group's ideas to the class.
2. Hand out a sample written scenario to each group. The scenario should include all of the *objective parameters* of a human services program. An example could be:

    A local community mental health agency has recently acquired a contract for a high school prevention program to address the substance abuse of its students. The school's records from the previous year indicate that 25% of its student population is actively abusing substances of some kind. The agency has 25 hours-per-week for it's program.

- Scenario should be modified or created to fit the demographics of the students' community.

3. Randomly assign each group one of the six steps of the RAPPER model of the Program Development Process; i.e., one group would have "Assess the need," another "Evaluate the effectiveness. . .", etc.
4. Instruct each group to brainstorm strategies, information, or resources that they might need to implement their step as it relates to the scenario. Emphasize to the individual groups the importance of not censoring their ideas at this point, but to allow consideration of *all* ideas from each student. Emphasize further that there is to be no exchange of ideas between groups at this point.

5. Instruct each group to come to a consensus as to which seem to be the most *useful* ideas/information sources/plans for their group's step, and to record them on one sheet of paper.
6. Come together as a class. Instruct each reporter to present the group's step to the class.
7. Lead a process discussion after the presentations. Topics for discussion may include:
   - Ways in which many of the steps are similar/ways in which they differ.
   - Interdependence of steps, i.e. sources of information that are useful or may be useful for more than one step.
   - Topics that arise that are unique to the *particular* area and do *not* necessarily generalize to other areas with this particular program.
   - How many different useful perspectives can come from one scenario.

Chapter 13

Substance Abuse and Counseling: An Epilogue

Amos Sales

Rationale

The overall purpose of this chapter is to provide a summary of the content as presented in the text, to discuss current issues, and future perspectives related to substance abuse and counseling. Substance abuse as a major problem and concern for counselors is identified early in the text with models of prevention, diagnosis and treatment applicable across various counseling specialties provided. The information creates an overview of the knowledge needed to counsel individuals with substance abuse problems, within school, rehabilitation, mental health, and social work settings.

Overview

This chapter provides a summary of the text content related to prevention, diagnosis, and treatment considerations of substance abuse and counseling. Conclusions regarding counseling with individuals with substance abuse problems are highlighted and current issues are addressed. Future perspectives are provided and identified as challenges that will test ethical and professional beliefs and practices.

Objectives

1. To review in summary the content of the textbook.
2. To review conclusions regarding counseling individuals with substance abuse problems.
3. To highlight current issues related to counseling and substance abuse.
4. To identify future perspectives regarding substance abuse and counseling.

Activity I for Objectives 1-4

1. Ask males to raise hands; have them count out in sequence; 1-2-3-4; then have females follow the same sequence to identify four groups.
2. Convene the four groups in the four corners of the room.
3. Instruct the group members to brainstorm the content listed in either one of Objectives 1-4, with one member serving as recorder.

4. After ten minutes, ask that they a) individually identify what they view as the top five identified and then b) have the group reach consensus on the top five, with recorder again keeping the list.
5. After ten minutes, have recorders from each group report to the full group their top five. After each group reports, discuss consensus and agreement or variance and disagreement.

Activity II for Objective 2

Facilitator's note:

The following exercises provide opportunity for students to practice basic skills in counseling and communication. It should be stressed that communication is a process that occurs constantly, so these skills can be reinforced consistently throughout any training or classroom experience regardless of the content. Trainees can be encouraged to reflect on their communication patterns and make conscious decisions to use these skills to enhance their relationships with others. Facilitators need to remind themselves to model the skills they are asking students to practice.

Exercise A: Observation/Inference

1. Ask students to pair up, preferably with someone they do not know (or with whom they are least familiar).
2. Instruct them to *silently* make three observations and three inferences about their partners based on the observations. This is to be done without talking.
3. After several minutes, instruct them to share their observations with their partners and check out the accuracy of their inferences.

Example of an observation/inference:

(Observation) I notice that you are wearing bright colors.

(Inference) My guess is that you enjoy getting attention from others.

Facilitator's note:

You may choose not to give an example at the beginning. Frequently, individuals confuse inferences with observations. This point can be made after the exercise with examples of how easily our inferences become what we believe to be true about others.

4. Process the activity through discussion in the large group. Possible questions for discussion.
   - What did you notice about your observations and inferences?
   - What situations can you think of where failure to check out impressions would present obstacles to the counselor-student?
   - What did you learn about yourself and others during this exercise?

Exercise B: Listening

1. Ask students to work in groups of threes: a speaker, a listener, and an observer.
2. The first student (speaker) talks about whatever he chooses.
3. The listener, using the skills of paraphrasing, clarifying, and summarizing, reflects the thoughts and feelings of the speaker.
4. The speaker shares with the listener whatever he felt, heard, and understood.
5. The observer gives feedback to each person regarding their use of listening and empathy skills.
6. Repeat this exercise three times so that each student has an opportunity to play each role.
7. Process the exercise in the larger group. Suggested questions.
   - What did you learn about listening, giving, and receiving feedback?
   - How do you see these skills impacting counseling interactions?
   - How do these skills relate to prevention of substance abuse?
   - How do these skills relate to treatment of substance abuse?

Exercise C: Group Facilitation

Facilitator's note:

This exercise allows students to increase their awareness of group process and practice communication skills that facilitate group interaction. It requires an integration of skills and a sense of which skill is most useful to use at any given time.

1. With student input, review the communication skills that have been discussed, including: observation/inference/checking impressions; empathy (paraphrasing, clarifying, summarizing); self-disclosure; "I" statements; feedback, genuineness; and respect.
2. Ask for eight to ten volunteers to form a circle within a circle of observers. Ask those in the inner circle to interact, while those in the outer circle observe and keep track of skills they notice.
3. At the end of the discussion, ask observers to provide feedback to volunteers in the inner circle regarding their demonstration of specific communication skills.
4. After the feedback, process the activity as a group. It is important to keep the discussion focused on skills. This may be difficult, as participants often will want to rehash the content instead.

Suggested questions for discussion:

- What is my role in the group process?
- What is my role in prevention of substance abuse?
- How might these skills help me in working with clients?